I0138950

HOW THE COURT BECAME SUPREME

LOUISIANA STATE UNIVERSITY PRESS
BATON ROUGE

PAUL D. MORENO

HOW THE
COURT BECAME
SUPREME

THE ORIGINS OF AMERICAN JURISTOCRACY

Published by Louisiana State University Press
lsupress.org

Copyright © 2022 by Louisiana State University Press
All rights reserved. Except in the case of brief quotations used in
articles or reviews, no part of this publication may be reproduced or
transmitted in any format or by any means without written permission of Louisiana State University Press.

Manufactured in the United States of America
First printing

DESIGNER: Mandy McDonald Scallan
TYPEFACE: Minion Pro

Library of Congress Cataloging-in-Publication Data are available at
the Library of Congress.

ISBN 978-0-8071-7786-0 (cloth) | ISBN 978-0-8071-7840-9 (pdf)
|ISBN 978-0-8071-7841-6 | (epub)

for Diane and Susan, with brotherly love

CONTENTS

ACKNOWLEDGMENTS

I would like to acknowledge and thank above all my colleagues and students at Hillsdale College, where I have been blessed to be able to teach constitutional history for over twenty years. I am very fortunate to have had the help of Alice Arnn on the graphic art work, and I thank Dan Coupland for grammatical help and the Article III sentence diagram. My lovely wife and fellow historian, Lisa, read the manuscript carefully.

HOW THE COURT BECAME SUPREME

INTRODUCTION

This history explains how the United States Supreme Court turned itself into the most powerful court the world had ever seen, and supreme not only *within* the judicial branch but over the legislative and executive branches. Every June, as the Court nears the end of its term and delivers anticipated decisions, political junkies zoom in on the marble temple on Capitol Hill. Will abortion remain legal? Will we have "marriage equality"? What about my right to bear arms? Will Obamacare survive?

Hardly anybody knew or cared about the Court's opening or closing a generation ago. Every time a vacancy occurs today, an epic political bloodbath can ensue, something virtually unknown before 1987. The Court's importance brought millions of voters who would otherwise never have considered it to vote for Donald Trump in 2016. Trump took the extraordinary step of providing a list of potential nominees because, as he said, voters consider the appointing of justices among the president's most important functions. (How remarkable that a "populist" leader took the power of the least popularly accountable Court's power for granted.) Liberals would remember that the Court has acquired the power to choose presidents, as it effectively did in *Bush v. Gore.*

At least since that election, both parties have complained about judicial supremacy. A hundred years ago, progressives griped about a Court that had taken the side of capital on the "social question"; a half century ago, conservatives bemoaned a Court that had taken the progressive side in the "culture wars." How did we get here?

We cannot blame the Constitution itself. Nothing would surprise the Founders more than the imperial judiciary. A few—a *very* few—Anti-Federalists anticipated the abuse of judicial power.[1] The Founders did establish a judiciary more distinct and *potentially* powerful than in any previous constitutional system. The experience of the previous two centuries made them expect the courts to abet popular liberty. They also assumed that judges could distinguish between law and politics and would stay on their side of the line. Their Constitution contained a multitude of safeguards to prevent judicial supremacy. Those safeguards remain, though they have fallen into desuetude.

Our imperial judiciary did not come from the great Chief Justice John Marshall or any of his nineteenth-century successors. And it most emphatically did not result from *Marbury v. Madison,* the case most often fingered as its father. Marshall made the Court all that the Founders intended, but no more. Among the last of the Founders when he died in 1835, Marshall would have shared his generation's dismay at his twentieth-century successors' transformation of judicial power. Chief Justice Taney and the *Dred Scott* decision perhaps most presaged today's version of judicial power, but Lincoln and the Republicans quickly and completely put down that decision.

Many scholars see an "intermediate period," from the 1890s until the New Deal, when the Court began more boldly to cross the line between law and politics, or judicial and legislative power.[2] During this period of "laissez-faire jurisprudence," the myth of *Marbury v. Madison* establishing judicial supremacy arose. Progressives accused the Court of taking sides in the economic and class conflict of the era, on the side of big business and against farmers and workers. Historians have exaggerated the extent of judicial power in this period as well as the opposition to it. *Lochner v. New York,* one of the best-known cases of this era, became a mythological "great case," alongside *Marbury.* One scholar aptly describes opposition to the Court by populists and progressives in this period as a "*muted* fury."[3] Others see this Court as too lax rather than too active, opining that it did not do enough to protect Black civil rights that almost everyone today would agree on. Those of a libertarian bent would say that it should have struck down more economic regulations. The Court's popular esteem seems to have *increased* in this period, allowing it to build up sufficient political capital to withstand the crucial face-off with Franklin Roosevelt in 1937. Above all, the old Court was not assertive and self-conscious about establishing a new kind of judicial review.

The Court's record in this intermediate period more resembles that of the first period, moderate in both procedural and substantive terms. We cannot conflate judicial supremacy with "judicial activism." Mere numbers cannot determine whether the Court is doing more or less than it should, for the Court has a *duty* to strike down unconstitutional acts.[4] The other branches have a similar duty to execute their constitutional executive and legislative powers and to keep the judiciary in its allotted sphere—a duty they have often shirked.

As we shall see, scholars recently have called attention to the political sources of judicial supremacy: legislators and executives often happily invite the courts to take difficult political questions out of their hands.[5] Abraham Lincoln noted this in his first inaugural address, one of the greatest statements against judicial supremacy, in which he said, "Nor is there [in the repudiation of *Dred Scott*] any assault upon the Court, or the judges. It is a duty, from which they may not shrink, to decide cases properly brought before them; and it is no fault of theirs, if others seek to turn their decisions to political purposes."[6] We should ask, Did the justices exercise the judicial power that the Constitution gave them to maintain that Constitution?

Ironically, the Court began to assert *modern* judicial supremacy when it appeared weakest. In 1938, just after the Court had capitulated to the New Deal, following FDR's proposal to "pack" it, the Court announced its modern agenda. In the *United States v. Carolene Products* case, buried in a footnote, the Court explained that some groups and some rights would enjoy more judicial protection than others—non-economic rights and the rights of minority groups, especially. The 1930s also saw the coming-of-age of jurisprudential theories like legal realism, whose devotees did not blink at judicial activism and its potentially antidemocratic character. Older, late nineteenth-century Populist critics of the Court attacked judicial *power*. Their successors in the progressive movement recognized the potential value of judicial power and concentrated on getting the right judges, with the right ideas—the ideas that they nurtured in the modern law school—onto the bench. After a brief "Roosevelt Court" rehearsal in the 1940s, modern judicial supremacy finally arrived under Chief Justice Earl Warren in 1953.

Brown v. Board of Education, Warren's first great case, launched today's omnipotent Court. It gave the Court the reputation for wisdom and courage, and above all "empathy," as it cut through the constitutional obstacles to racial justice. The justices caught the cresting wave of racial egalitarianism and exercised just the right amount of "leadership." They moved ahead, but not too far ahead, of public opinion. Above all, they kept in sync with *elite* opinion. Antiracism trumps all other values in modern America. Its rise heralded the beginning of the "rights revolution" that spread to other groups and causes. The Court and its defenders recognized this and made the most of it.

In 1958, the Court declared that its interpretations of the Constitution *equaled* the Constitution, the "supreme law of the land." In 1992, when the

Court had to explain its refusal to overturn the less than unanimously popular abortion right, it reminded the public of its *Brown* heroism. It made the claim that constitutional government requires judicial supremacy. It became normal for scholars to equate the term "constitutionalism" with judicial supremacy. Out of this came a new term, coined by political scientist Ran Hirschl, "juristocracy." By the twenty-first century, that model, born in mid-twentieth-century America, had extended to countries all over the world.

Several generations of critics have wrung their hands about the "counter-majoritarian difficulty" of judicial review, arguing that it has no legitimate place in a democracy.[7] But judicial review cannot avoid this difficulty if the people want the Court to protect constitutional limits against the usurpations of the elected branches. It only becomes—and *has* become—a problem, a threat rather than an aid to constitutional democracy, when the Court itself exercises legislative or executive power under the guise of judicial review. What follows will tell the story of the origin and development of that problem.

1

BEFORE THE CONSTITUTION

J udicial supremacy arose only in the last half century. The idea of a separate but equal, or even inferior, judicial branch dates back only to the England of the seventeenth and eighteenth centuries. Before then, political theorists considered judges (or magistrates, as they were often called) part of the legislative or, more often, the executive branch of government. Before Montesquieu in the eighteenth century, Western political science identified two governmental powers—the legislative, declaring the law, and the executive, applying the law to particular cases. Sometimes they divided executive power into domestic and foreign realms—John Locke called the latter the "federative" power. But even so the same person almost always exercised both the federative as well as the domestic executive power. Aristotle did refer to legislative, executive, and judicial powers in his *Politics,* but with little sense of a separate judicial officer corps, and the twofold rather than a threefold classification prevailed for centuries.

HEBREW "JUDGES"

The judicial office stands out in ancient Hebrew political life. God initially ruled his chosen people directly, in a theocracy. God gave the Hebrews the law, and Scripture mentions "commandments," "statutes," "judgments," "ordinances," and "decrees" in a rather undifferentiated way. Judaism (like Islam) entailed legalism; "righteousness" consisted in following the rules. Yahweh made covenants with the patriarchs from Abraham to Joseph. We can call these "constitutions" of a kind—voluntary self-limitations by the sovereign God. Those patriarchs personified such earthly government as the children of Israel recognized. Tribal chieftains, "elders," and priests probably performed most judicial functions, criminal and civil.[1]

The Hebrews regarded God alone as sovereign, as the founding Federalists would declare the American people sovereign in the US Constitution. A sovereign God chose to limit Himself by covenants, as the American people did by the Constitution. In antiquity, the question "Who interprets the covenant?" never arose, as God by His nature cannot violate it—only man can. But how could He make men *see* that they had violated it? Through prophet-judges. In the view of Saint Paul, humans could not help but violate the covenant—the Old Testament intended to show people the futility of the old covenant of works and to prepare us for the new covenant of grace. This made the Old Testament "the education of the human race." It opened the door to juristocracy—rule by judges who claimed to speak for God.

When it came time to rescue the Israelites from bondage in Egypt, God acted through Moses, the great prophet. "Prophet" and "judge" served as equivalents under his successors. At first, the Hebrews brought their legal disputes to Moses, who referred them to God and delivered judgment. Later, Moses appointed assistants to help him (Exodus 18:13–26), but the Old Testament provides only a faint outline of the judicial office.[2] In the third century, the church father Tertullian likened them to censors, the highest Roman magistrates.[3] Spartan ephors and Roman tribunes also resembled judicial protectors of constitutional norms.

"The Lord thy God will raise up unto thee a Prophet from the midst of thee, of thy brethren, like unto me," Moses told God's people, "unto him ye shall hearken" (Deuteronomy 18:15). As the Hebrews entered the Promised Land, God inspired more of these prophet-judges as necessary, usually to battle their Canaanite enemies. The historical books of the Old Testament tell a story of the repeated cycles of rebellion and restoration. God makes a covenant with the Hebrews, He punishes them for doing "evil in the sight of the Lord," then He rescues them and they enjoy a time when "the land had rest." The book of Judges relates the political fortunes of the Hebrews—rising when the people adhere to, and falling when they traduce, the covenant. It begins:

> The Lord raised up judges, which delivered them out of the hand of those that spoiled them. And yet they would not hearken unto their judges, but went a whoring after other gods. . . . And when the Lord raised them up judges, then the Lord was with the judge, and delivered them out of the hand of their enemies all the days of the judge: for it repented the Lord because of their groanings by reason of them that oppressed and vexed them. And it came to pass, when the judge was dead, that they returned, and corrupted themselves more than their fathers, following other gods. (Judges 2:16–19)

Scripture presents about a dozen major and minor judges. Judges did not hold permanent office; they arose as God occasionally inspired them—though Deborah, identified first as a "prophetess," does not seem to have risen to a particular occasion (4:4).

The refrain of Judges, that "there was no king in Israel, and every man did what was right in his own eyes," sounds less than ideal, and perhaps reflects a later, monarchical judgment on the first juristocracy. Later interpreters, such as John Wyclif in the late fourteenth century, continued to regard judicial rule as an ideal.[4] The Hebrews' eleventh-century BCE demand for a monarchy sinfully repudiated the theocratic norm. After Gideon saved them, the people proposed to make him king. But Gideon replied (8:22), "I will not rule over you, neither shall my son rule over you: the Lord shall rule over you." Nonetheless, his son Abimelech did make himself king, killing his seventy brothers in the process. His tyranny lasted three years, until an upper millstone brained him. God finally relented and gave the Hebrews a king. But He told the last of the judges, Samuel, that He took their desire for a king as a personal rejection. Prophet-judges like Samuel and Nathan continued to hold the Hebrew kings accountable to God. Deuteronomy (16:18) suggests that the people and elders, not the king, chose these officers.

The king did not "make" law—only God did that.[5] The king would proclaim or express written and customary law.[6] He administered the law, sometimes personally. David's failure to provide justice to the people (in addition to his failure to do justice in the particular case of the rape of his daughter by his son) provoked his son Absalom to rebel (2 Samuel 15). His son Solomon, however, exemplified the wise king-judge. In the end, the monarchy absorbed the budding juristocracy. And while the details of the ancient Hebrew judicial system remain profoundly obscure, some sources suggest the revival of an independent judiciary in the postexilic Second Temple period.[7]

GRECO-ROMAN LAW

The ancient Greeks laid the foundation of almost all the intellectual disciplines of Western civilization, but they did not offer much in jurisprudence. In this field, they had little to teach the Romans, providing theory about law but little practical help.[8] The ancient *polis* centered on religion, but the Greeks had no "church" or priestly class. Likewise, though religious norms defined law and justice, the Greeks developed no legal class and few discernible legal institutions. Some hints of Greek legal procedure appear in drama: divine justice administered by Athena in Aeschylus's *Eumenides*, royal justice in Sophocles's *Antigone,* and the abuses of democratic justice in *Wasps by* Aristophanes.[9]

Aristotle described the constitutions of many Greek city-states, but only that of Athens remains extant. In book 4 of his great work *Politics,* he described the functions of government as belonging to a deliberative body, to magistracies, and to judges. He went on to classify law courts by their judges, their mode of selection, and their subject matter. Aristotle principally analyzed courts in terms of "political cases which, when mismanaged, create division and disturbances in states," but he never fleshed out the details of such controversies, focusing instead on whether the courts reflected the oligarchic and democratic options that characterize most of the work.[10]

We know the most about the extreme democracy of Athens. Citizen jurors decided cases—no judicial offices existed—just as the citizens made the law themselves without representative legislators to do it for them. (However, a committee of the assembly, the *boule,* set the agenda and acted as a kind of representative body.) The Athenians similarly assigned magistracies by lot, though they elected the chief military officers, the generals (*strategoi),* on the basis of merit. In Thucydides's account, the repeated election of the great general Pericles made Athenian democracy manageable—one could call the democracy a "Periclocracy." Athens had no judges as a distinct class, only mass juries of the kind that condemned Socrates.

In the Anglo-American court system that we know, juries used to compose the popular part of the judicial branch, a kind of democratic lower house to check and balance the aristocratic judges. In Athens, nothing checked or balanced the jury. Any citizen could challenge the constitutionality of a law, calling the author of an unconstitutional law to account before a citizen jury, but this resembled bicameralism more than it did judicial review. The popular courts exercised political functions (holding public officials to account), and the popular assembly exercised judicial functions; they appeared to be equal in power.[11] The rule of the people left no room for the rule of law, let alone the rule of lawyers and judges. Juristocracy, as a kind of aristocracy, had no place in Athens. After its defeat in the Peloponnesian War and the scapegoating of Socrates, the Athenians moderated their democracy by introducing the *nomothetai,* composed of the *boule* plus 1,001 citizens, to consider the acts of the assembly in light of traditional laws (*nomoi).* This vaguely resembled the late colonial American state "councils of revision" and judicial review.[12]

Above all, the Greeks gave us the idea of the law of nature, evident in Plato and Aristotle and developed by generations of Stoics. For the Hebrews,

God gave the law; He revealed it to his chosen people. For the Greeks and Romans nature provided the law; they apprehended it by reason. (Jefferson would nicely fuse these as "the laws of Nature and of Nature's God" in the Declaration of Independence.) In Western political theory, men did not *make* law but declared or discovered the law that God or nature had made. Humans could only do their best to conform actual, existing, historical law to the eternal, unchanging natural law.

The crucial question immediately presents itself: *Who* got to declare or discover? The American judiciary became established in the late eighteenth century, during the heyday of the declaratory/discovery theory, but almost nobody believed that the judges had a privileged—or even an equal—power to consult the natural law, or that they could refer to it to limit the other branches of government. As the nineteenth century unfolded and the Western view of law shifted to positivism or human-made law, judges enhanced their power by reviving the older natural law tradition, trumping legislation with adjudication, largely through the due process clauses of the Fifth and Fourteenth Amendments.[13]

We have more of a sense of the structure of the Roman legal system, given the longer duration of their regimes and their genius for practical administration, but we still have little understanding of their judicial institutions.[14] Early sources do not distinguish judicial from legislative and executive bodies. Roman judges (*praetors*) multiplied as Rome expanded, serving as assistants to the chief executive officers, the consuls. The chief democratic body, the plebian assembly, acted as a court in overseeing capital criminal cases. Romans probably arbitrated much everyday conflict through the extensive, informal system of patronage and clientage controlled by local potentates. Don Corleone administering justice in the opening scene of *The Godfather* shows the persistence of this ancient practice. And much injustice surely prevailed because of the vastly unequal economic resources of various parties.[15]

The New Testament provides some glimpses into Roman law in the empire.[16] The Romans allowed the Jews to maintain their system of priestly law enforcement, but Jesus suffered under Pontius Pilate, the Roman procurator of Judea. (In one account, Pilate tried to punt the case to Herod, the part-Jewish tetrarch of Galilee, Jesus's native land. Roman officers dispensed justice more informally abroad than at home.)[17]

Saint Paul endured several trials by Roman governors Felix and Festus as well as by Herod's successor, Agrippa. Paul, a Roman citizen, claimed the privilege of having his case heard in Rome. Agrippa said to Festus, "This man might have been set at liberty, if he had not appealed unto Caesar" (Acts 26:32). Unfortunately, the narrative breaks off there, and we do not know the result of this particular appeal.[18]

The early Christian church added nothing to its Judaic predecessor or to Greco-Roman jurisprudence. Christians regarded Jesus as the ultimate judge-king, but He would come to judge all only at the end of time. Scripture does not detail the legal-judicial element of his ministry. Christians await the last judgment as His only judgment. He emphasized that "my kingdom is not of this world," and declined jurisdiction in the one (recorded) suit brought to him on earth (Luke 12:14). He issued a pardon in the case of the woman taken in adultery, but moderns usually consider pardons executive acts (John 8:11). He told the Pharisees, "Ye judge after the flesh; I judge no man" (8:15). Early Christianity eschewed legalism, as Jesus repeatedly rebuked the ultralegalistic Pharisees. This would change dramatically as the church went from persecuted to tolerated to established in the fourth century. In the second millennium, the church would generate an elaborate legal system and provide the model for, and rival, the most powerful kingdoms.

Roman law shaped law and legal education all over continental Europe, but not in England, and therefore not in England's American colonies. Roman law had evolved over centuries in an unsystematic way. As one scholar puts it, Western Europe had a legal *order* but no legal *system*, and law still derived from custom and religion.[19] The great lawyer orators like Cicero did more to shape Roman law than did the judicial officers—bar mattered more than bench, as Sir Henry Maine put it.[20] This changed dramatically in the sixth century, when the Emperor Justinian commissioned the great *Institutes*. Teachers and students now possessed a codified, organized body of law, treatable in a scientific or philosophical, or at least an academic, way. But the *Institutes* disappeared in the ensuing "dark age" centuries, rediscovered only in the eleventh century.

Historians have exaggerated the distinction between English customary or common law and continental Roman law. Medieval English jurists defending their system claimed that the common law made England free and constitutional, while absolute despotism prevailed across the Channel. English jurists knew some Roman (or "civil") law. Some of the earliest commentaries on English law, in fact, smuggled in great swaths of Roman law.[21] But they confined it to ecclesiastical courts, where it had shaped the canon law of the church. Roman law also influenced a variety of other, specialized English courts, such as admiralty and mercantile courts, and it also applied in Scotland. But certainly the English common law had distinctive features, such as pleading through the complex "writ system," and especially in the use of juries. Early modern British judicial history saw the expansion of the common law at the expense of Roman-tinged courts, a project largely led by Sir Edward Coke.

The survival of common law in England and America shaped legal education. Nobody studied the common law in English universities until Sir William Blackstone took the first chair of English jurisprudence at Oxford in 1758. Continental universities had taught Roman law since its recovery in the eleventh century, with study centered on the University of Bologna. But scholars disdained the common law as unfit for university study. They viewed the common law as a haphazard and historical product, not a rational, organized science. Englishmen learned the law the way they learned a trade, at the "inns of court." Americans also adopted formal legal education late in the day. As late as 1941, a Supreme Court justice (Robert Jackson) had not attended law school.

We should note that American judicial power rose in tandem with formal legal education, whereas it had not arisen in countries that had earlier developed systems of legal education. The late blooming of American legal education coincided with the rise of radically new legal theories such as positivism in the nineteenth and twentieth centuries.

THE ENGLISH CONSTITUTIONAL CRISIS

While the American Founders possessed an idea of the (rather scanty) history of adjudication in classical and biblical sources, they better knew the role of the judiciary in the more recent and well-documented English constitutional struggle of the seventeenth century. This conflict, centered on the English Civil War of the 1640s–50s and the Glorious Revolution of 1688–89, pitted divine right or absolute monarchy and the established church ("throne and altar") against Parliament and dissenting Protestantism. In general, the common-law courts took the right (Parliamentary and Protestant) side, especially as Sir Edward Coke deployed them against the royal or proprietary courts. The courts came out of the conflict as esteemed guardians of constitutional government.[22] As a "constitutionalist revolution," this century let the judiciary present itself as necessary for constitutional government.[23]

In the second millennium, England developed a judicial system that today's British and Americans can recognize. (Continental states did the same along Roman law lines.) After the eleventh-century Norman Conquest, English kings began to construct a set of royal courts to provide a uniform ("common") system of justice and displace that of the local feudal magnates. Like Parliament, common-law courts became a monarchical arm that raised itself against the monarchy in the seventeenth century. They ended up the arm of a sovereign Parliament.

The creation of the common law took centuries. Eventually, it centered on three common-law courts: King's Bench (for crimes), Common Pleas (for private lawsuits), and Exchequer (for fiscal affairs). From time to time the king established special "prerogative" courts to amend or augment the common-law courts. Above all of them stood Parliament, which itself began as a court, "the high court of Parliament." Even after it became primarily a legislative or statute-making body, the House of Lords remained the highest court in the kingdom. (Similarly, what we would call the legislature in the Massachusetts Bay Colony called itself the "general court," as distinguished from the "judicial courts," headed by the "supreme judicial court." The medieval French *parlements* and Spanish *cortes* also look to us like legislative–judicial hybrids.) This reflected the theory that all parts of the government made or discovered law. England's lord chancellor, for example, simultaneously headed the Chancery courts, served as an adviser to the king and as a member of his cabinet, and was the president of the House of Lords.

The Tudor dynasty had brought England a semblance of peace and unity after the Hundred Years' War of the fourteenth to fifteenth centuries and the Wars of the Roses in the fifteenth. Henry VIII's desire to maintain that order through a male heir precipitated the religious conflict of the sixteenth century, the English Reformation. Ironically, the long reign of his prudent daughter Elizabeth I (1558–1603) secured the regime. Even more ironically, Parliament, which Henry had used to enact the law declaring him the head of the church in England, eventually attained the sovereign power that the Tudors sought.

The Tudor family line ran out with Elizabeth, and the crown passed to the Scottish Stuarts, who tried to bring to England the continental (and Scottish) model of absolutism. This involved a preference for the numerous royal or prerogative courts over the English common-law courts. These courts followed continental, Roman law procedures (no juries, presumption of guilt, no oral testimony), though the common-law courts used "adversarial procedures," whereas Roman law courts used "inquisitorial" ones, including torture.[24] English writers had long boasted of the superiority of their common law to continental Roman law,[25] arguing that common law made Englishmen free, while Roman law made Frenchmen slaves. Constitutionalists excoriated the most notorious of the prerogative courts, the Star Chamber, which became a synonym for arbitrary and abusive judicial proceedings. The Court of High Commission, established in 1559 to enforce religious orthodoxy, drew even greater obloquy.

The learned King James I, who took the English throne in 1603, did not wear his learning lightly (he was "the wisest fool in Christendom," to his detractors), and he propounded a well-developed theory of absolutism. He published this in his *True Law of Free Monarchies* ("free" here meaning "absolute") as King James VI of Scotland, five years before he became king of England. He accepted the declaratory or natural law theory. "Not that I deny the old definition of a king, and of a law," he said, "which makes the king to be a speaking law, and the law a dumb king." But he insisted that nobody could challenge the king's declaration of the law; the king stood above the law. Nevertheless, "a good king will not only delight to rule his subjects by the law, but will even conform himself in his own actions thereunto."[26] A prudent king would maintain the rule of law, though he need not. Though James would have dramatic confrontations with the parliamentarians and common lawyers, he avoided provoking the rebellion and civil war that would erupt under his son Charles.

Sir Edward Coke wrangled with James as well as with James's son. He provided the first sustained argument for an independent and powerful judiciary, making him arguably the most ancient ancestor of judicial supremacy. He transformed politics while always denying that he did so, claiming that he did nothing more than restore the ancient constitution. He began to weave the "myth of Magna Carta," depicting English history as the story of the constant recurrence to that great charter of individual rights.

English historian Herbert Butterfield noted that Coke constructed an anachronistic, tendentious story of the antiquity of English liberty—the "whig interpretation of history," which Coke carried "to the wildest extremes." But his historiographical "sins became service to the cause of liberty."[27] The great English legal historian William Holdsworth wrote, "What Shakespeare has been to literature, what Bacon has been to philosophy, what the translators of the authorized version of the Bible have been to religion, Coke has been to the public and private law of England."[28] The American Founders lauded Coke. Jefferson said that "a sounder Whig never wrote," despite Jefferson's suspicion of the common law and later battles with the federal courts.

We call common law "judge-made law," though "judge-declared" or "judge-discovered" would better capture the traditional idea that man did not "make" law. Coke distinguished common from statute and customary law. We can say that ordinary people made customary law in an everyday, largely unconscious fashion, as people went about their business and settled disputes without formal adjudication. Sir Henry Maine called this "ancient law," and Harold Berman more recently dubbed it "archaic law," characteristic of all Indo-European peoples. If disputes arose about custom, a judge could declare or clarify it. Though they might in fact alter custom, judges bent over backwards to pretend that they merely gave latter-day expression to ancient norms. Similarly, while Parliament "made" statutes, for ages jurists maintained the claim that these acts merely declared or, especially, restored the common or customary law. For a long time, judges adhered to the maxim that "statutes made in derogation of the common law are to be strictly construed."

Coke equated the common law and supreme law. (Coke called himself the Chief Justice of *England,* not of its highest court.)[29] He equated common law with reason itself. "Reason is the life of the law," he wrote. "Nay, the common law itself is nothing else but reason." But Coke emphasized the law's *artificial reason,* the work of generations of men who had studied it. "No man (out of his own private reason)," he wrote, "ought to be wiser than the law, which is the perfection of reason." This belief led to his famous clash with King James, who, considering himself as wise as the judges, claimed the power to decide cases personally.

"The King said that he thought the law was founded upon reason, and that he and others had reason as well as the judges." Coke replied, "that true it was, that God had endowed his Majesty with excellent science, and great endowments of nature; but his Majesty was not learned in the laws of his realm of England, and causes . . . are not to be decided by natural reason but by the artificial reason and judgement of the law, which law is an art which requires long study and experience." The king took offense at this reply, which implied "that he should be under the law, which was treason to affirm." Coke replied with a phrase of Bracton: "The King ought not to be under any man, but under God and the law."[30]

This view of law as "artificial reason" tended to make the common law "lawyers' law." It fed the suspicion that lawyers tried to maintain the law as a mysterious, occult science, accessible only through their exclusive guild. James had legitimate concerns about the confusion of seventeenth-century English law. Coke also recognized that legal incoherence led to abuses by the wily and well-connected. This led him to write his great works on English law, the thirteen-volume *Reports* and the four-volume *Institutes,* to show the order and certainty in English jurisprudence, making him a kind of Justinian of the common law. But James did not trust the common law courts to reform themselves, as Coke did.[31] And James conceded that the law might "be a mystery and skill best known" to lawyers. But as for judgments unreasonable to nonlawyers who "have logic and common sense . . . I will never trust such an interpretation."[32]

Many historians see Coke's decision in *Dr. Bonham's Case* (1610) as the original source of what we now call "judicial review."[33] The case concerned an act of Parliament that allowed the London College of Physicians to license the practice of medicine in the city. Dr. Thomas Bonham had a university degree but no license, and the college fined him (keeping half the fine for itself, as the statute allowed) and then had him imprisoned. Coke held that the statute did not give the college the power to imprison except for malpractice and, more important, that it could not let the college impose a fine because that would make the college a judge in its own case, which violated reason and natural justice. Members of the college "cannot be judges, ministers, and parties; judges, to give sentence or judgment; ministers, to make summons; parties, to have the moiety of forfeiture." He claimed that "it appears in our books, that in many cases, the common law does control acts of Parliament, and sometimes shall adjudge them to be void. For when an act of Parliament is against common right and reason, or repugnant, or impossible to be performed, the common law will control it, and adjudge such an act to be void."[34]

Judges and scholars have disputed *Bonham's* significance for centuries. As an assertion of judicial supremacy over Parliament, it contradicts Coke's statement, "Of the power and jurisdiction of the Parliament for making of laws and proceeding by bill, it is so transcendent and absolute, as it cannot be confined either for causes or persons within any bounds."[35] And Parliament sat atop the courts. Perhaps Coke did nothing more than read the statute as inapplicable in this particular case because one should never assume Parliament to have meant to enact an unreasonable statute. Coke may have regarded the London College as a rival court, like those of the High Commission and Star Chamber, what the twentieth century would call an "administrative tribunal." He had exercised judicial control of similar local administrative bodies and evinced an abiding concern with the reckless delegation of power.[36]

On the other hand, *Bonham* did strike contemporaries as a bold assertion of judicial power. Lord Chancellor Ellesmere said that it "derogates much from the wisdom and power of the Parliament. . . . Three judges on the bench destroy and frustrate all their points because the act agrees not in their particular sense with common right and reason, whereby [they] advance the reason of a particular court above the judgment of all the realm."[37] Though Coke only cited *Bonham* once himself, he did so in saying that the common law "corrects, allows, disallows both statute law and custom."[38] Three years later, he asserted that "authority belongs to the King's Bench [the chief common-law court] not only to correct errors in judicial proceedings, but other errors and misdemeanors extra-judicial, tending to breach of peace, or oppression of the subjects, or to the raising of faction, controversy, debate, or to any manner of misgovernment; so that no wrong or injury, either public or private, can be done but that the same shall be reformed and punished by the due course of law."[39] Ellsmere said that this amounted to a claim of power "sufficient in itself to manage the state."[40]

A few years later, Lord Hobart said, "Even an act of Parliament made against natural equity, as to make a man a judge in his own case, is void in itself."[41] In 1702, Lord Holt added, "What my Lord Coke says in Dr. Bonham's case is far from any extravagancy, for it is a very reasonable and true saying, that if an act of Parliament should ordain that the same person be party and judge . . . it would be a void act." But, like Coke, Holt seemed to say that nobody could overturn acts of Parliament, unlike acts of lower courts or corporations.[42]

Moreover, the principle that "no man should be a judge in his own case" had wide implications. The London physicians' power to control entry into the medical profession, even absent the power to fine or imprison, amounted to judging their own case—power to limit competition. Coke had a strong aversion to monopolies as the use of public power to serve private ends.[43] In nineteenth-century America, judges displayed a similar hostility to what they called "class legislation." This animus became a fertile source of judicial activism, but it lay fallow for two hundred years.

Coke also helped transmit English constitutionalism to the American colonies. He probably contributed to the 1606 charter of the Virginia Company.[44] In it, the king declared that all subjects who went to Virginia, and those born there, "shall have and enjoy all liberties, franchises and immunities within any of our other dominions to all intents and purposes as if they had been abiding and born within this our realm of England." In 1776, Americans would declare independence on exactly these grounds, claiming that they had all the "rights of Englishmen" in England. These rights included the common law, which derived from the "laws of Nature and of Nature's God" that they claimed in the preamble of the Declaration of Independence.[45]

One can see poetic justice if later constitutionalists distorted Coke as Coke had distorted Magna Carta. If Coke actually believed in parliamentary supremacy, his successors nevertheless enlisted him in the cause of judicial supremacism. Those today who equate constitutionalism with juristocracy still begin with Coke.[46]

Coke had irritated James enough for the king to "promote" Coke from the Court of Common Pleas to the Court of King's Bench in 1613, hoping both to reduce his income and to flatter him into submission. Coke continued to assert the common-law courts' supremacy over the prerogative courts, especially Chancery, and in 1616 James removed him entirely. He returned to the King's Council in 1617, became lord commissioner of the Treasury in 1620, and went into Parliament. He continued his opposition, and James arrested him and other parliamentarians in 1621.

Coke had more impact as a member of Parliament than as a judge.[47] The weakness of judges who could be removed by the king showed itself in the courts' submission to the royal abuses of Charles I in the *Five Knights* (1627) and *Ship-Money* (1637) cases, involving forced loans and extraordinary taxes.[48] Coke helped draft the Petition of Right in 1628, in which Parliament reiterated the guarantees of Magna Carta and complained about Charles's violations of them. To those who objected that the petition limited the king's sovereignty, Coke replied that "Magna Carta is such a fellow as will have no sovereign."[49]

In the eighteenth century, the question would arise whether Coke's mythical Magna Carta would limit parliamentary as it had monarchical sovereignty. Parliament's truculence so annoyed Charles that in addition to prohibiting the publication of Coke's commentary on Magna Carta, he tried to govern without Parliament, which precipitated a parliamentary rebellion and a civil war when it convened again in 1641. Parliament impeached and attainted many of the king's judges and officers, but this indicated suspicion of particular judges rather than of the judiciary per se.[50] Notably, Parliament proposed to the king that he appoint judges "always . . . with the approbation of both Houses of Parliament," that they take an oath to support the Petition of Right, and that they "hold their places *quam diu bene se gesserint*" ("during good behavior") rather than at his pleasure.[51]

The rebels abolished the monarchy and the House of Lords, and beheaded Charles, in 1649. They also abolished the prerogative courts that Coke had battled, the High Commission and Star Chamber. Chancery, or equity, remained, but the chancellors learned to be more restrained. Thus the US Constitution would define the judicial power as extending to "all cases, in law or equity." (See appendix A.)

Parliament did establish good-behavior tenure and fixed salaries for judges, but the emerging "lord protector," Oliver Cromwell, could easily remove difficult judges by "writs of ease," a sort of early retirement.[52] Political thinkers began to articulate theories of modern separation of powers, including an independent judiciary with power to curb legislative or executive excesses.[53]

By the end of the 1650s, this unprecedented British "commonwealth" had turned into a military dictatorship, and Parliament ultimately invited back Charles's son, Charles II, to restore the monarchy in 1660. But the new king had to accept the constitutional limits of the Declaration of Breda. Charles did return to at-pleasure judicial appointments, and he removed about a dozen judges. He could not, however, browbeat his judges, who responded to the competing pressure of Parliament, until near the end of his reign.[54]

The common-law courts emerged as heroic defenders of English liberty in the seventeenth-century constitutional crisis.[55] Thus they aroused the ire of anticonstitutionalists, or absolutists.[56] Thomas Hobbes wrote his classic argument for despotic government, *Leviathan,* in response to what he regarded as the anarchy of the civil war. Popular defiance of authority returned the English people to the original "state of nature," the war of every man against every man, which made life "solitary, poor, nasty, brutish, and short." *Leviathan* resounded the refrain of the book of Judges, lamenting a period in which "every man did what was right in his own eyes" because "there was no king in Israel."

In *Leviathan* and other works, Hobbes developed his legal theory, called positivism, the principal rival to the natural law or discovery theory (to be joined by the theory of historicism in the nineteenth century). Hobbes defined law as the command of the sovereign, "the word of him that by right has command over others."[57] That "right" would belong to whomever the people had given their power when they formed the social contract to escape the state of nature. This sounded much like the Roman law idea of *lex regia,* in which the people had given all their power to the emperor. The distinction between natural law (made by nature or God) and positive law (made by humans) arose in antiquity.[58] But before Hobbes, philosophers asked whether or how much human-made law conformed to the natural "norm." For the modern positivists, no norm existed. The sophists who argued against Socrates that might makes right at least believed that nature *intended* might to make right.

Hobbes took on Coke more directly and extensively in a little-known and posthumously published "Dialogue Between a Philosopher and a Student of the Common Laws." He could not understand why law would derive from the "artificial" reason of lawyers rather than from "natural" reason, but in any case, law really did not depend on reason. "It is not wisdom," the philosopher said, "but authority that makes a law. . . . None can make a law but he that has the legislative power. That the law has been *found* by grave and learned men . . . is manifestly untrue, for all the laws of England have been *made* by the King," in consultation with Parliament (emphasis mine).[59] Judges and courts merely served the king. Hobbes probably preferred a one-man sovereign, but his theory allowed for a body of men to exercise ultimate power. In Britain, the Parliament took that role. But if in their social contract a people decided to live under the rule of judges, Hobbes's theory allowed for that as well.

Charles's successor, his brother James II, reopened the constitutional conflict and produced the Glorious Revolution of 1688, which effectively established the sovereignty of Parliament insofar as Parliament controlled the succession to the throne. It defused the religious conflict by providing for toleration of dissenting Protestants. The Glorious Revolution involved two other steps toward the American constitutional system: John Locke's political theory of constitutionalism and the Act of Settlement, which gave English judges life tenure during good behavior, though they were removable by a majority of both houses of Parliament in a "bill of address." The parliamentarians sought make the judges independent of the king, not of themselves, and members did exert influence on the bench in the eighteenth century.[60]

Locke had little to say about judicial institutions, though his theory stressed "judgment." In the pre-political state of nature, every man must enforce the law of nature himself. And as Coke observed in Bonham, men make poor judges in their own cases, for their self-interest inclines them to exact more than justice when wronged—not an eye for an eye, but a life for an eye. This will produce a similar desire for disproportionate revenge among the victim's survivors, who will kill the one-eyed man's entire family, producing endless vendetta and feud, making the state of nature a state of war. Thus, the key to escaping the state of nature lies in giving the government the power to enforce our natural rights.

Locke continued the traditional view that only two governmental powers exist: the legislative and the executive. He added to the executive a third, the "federative power," concerning the execution of the law of nature with regard to other sovereign powers—war, peace, treaties, trade, and the like. This meant that the state of nature obtained in foreign affairs, since each sovereign state had to enforce the natural law (the law of nations, or *jus gentium*) itself. Thus, the executive's power abroad included the "prerogative"—the power to act in the absence of, or even in violation of, domestic law. Having largely eradicated the prerogative power domestically, Locke and his Whig fellows kept it alive abroad.[61]

In keeping with the Glorious Revolution's establishment of parliamentary primacy, Locke maintained that "the legislature is not only the supreme power in the commonwealth, but sacred and unalterable in the hands where the community have once placed it." But Locke did not assert legislative *sovereignty*. Even the supreme legislature cannot act arbitrarily, can only enact laws for the public good, and must conform to the law of nature. Nor could it act by "extemporary arbitrary decrees, but is bound to dispense justice, and decide the rights of the subject by *promulgated standing laws, and known, authorized judges.*"[62]

But Locke had little to say about these judges. He noted that all "inferior magistrates" derived their power from the chief executive. But "of other ministerial and subordinate powers in a commonwealth we need not speak, they being so multiplied with infinite variety, in the different customs and constitutions of distinct commonwealths, that it is impossible to give a particular account of them all."[63] This certainly described England, with its dozens of disparate and overlapping courts.[64] They would certainly not determine the constitutional limits of the legislative and executive powers. In disputes about that, "there can be no judge on earth," because this reached the point of the people's "appeal to heaven" or the right to revolution.[65] Judicial supremacy could not arise out of the courts' umpiring legislative–executive contests.

THE EIGHTEENTH-CENTURY BRITISH CONSTITUTION

French nobleman and judge Charles-Louis Secondat, Baron de la Brède et de Montesquieu, made a major contribution to the modern theory of judicial power. Montesquieu provided a tripartite division of the powers of government and argued that the separation of those powers alone could preserve liberty.[66] His great admiration for the British constitution rested in this. Older constitutional analysts saw in Britain three "estates" or social orders—king, lords, and commons (or "lords spiritual and temporal," and commons). These personified or represented the one, the few, and the many, in monarchy, aristocracy, or democracy. Montesquieu instead saw the institutions of British government embodying not social orders but governmental functions—legislative (Parliament), executive (king), and judicial. But Montesquieu's treatment of the separation of these powers in the eighteenth-century British constitution lacks clarity and detail. He calls the three powers "legislative power, executive power over the things depending on the rights of nations, and executive power over the things depending on civil right." The second equates to Locke's "federative" power. The third would become the judicial, which he next terms "the power of judging." In his famous statement on the separation of powers Montesquieu wrote:

> When legislative power is united with executive power in a single person or in a single body of the magistracy, there is no liberty, because

one can fear that the same monarch or senate that makes tyrannical laws will execute them tyrannically. Nor is there liberty if the power of judging is not separate from legislative power and from executive power. If it were joined to legislative power, the power over the life and liberty of the citizens would be arbitrary, for the judge would be the legislator. If it were joined to the executive power, the judge could have the force of an oppressor. All would be lost if the same man or the same body of principal men, either of nobles, or of the people, exercised these three powers: that of making the laws, that of executing public resolutions, and that of judging the crimes or disputes of individuals.[67]

Like Locke, Montesquieu's statements on judicial offices lack depth or precision. He went on to say that "the power of judging should not be given to a permanent senate but should be exercised by persons drawn from the body of the people at certain times of the year in the manner prescribed by law to form a tribunal which lasts only as long as necessity requires." These look more like jurors, not judges, as in ancient Athens, and Montesquieu tries to minimize their role. "In this fashion the power of judging, so terrible among men, being attached to neither a certain estate nor a certain profession, becomes, so to speak, invisible and null. Judges are not continually in view; one fears the magistracy, not the magistrates." Montesquieu envisioned a judicial machine. "Judgments should be fixed to such a degree that they are never anything but a precise text of the laws."[68] This would become the goal of the nineteenth-century Anglo-American codifiers and those who aspired to what skeptics would call the "slot machine" theory of law: given a particular set of data, all courts should produce predictable and certain outcomes.[69] He went on to say, "Among the three powers of which we have spoken, that of judging is, in some fashion, null. There remain only two."[70]

Juristocracy has claimed too much from Montesquieu. The separate, independent judiciary in a system of separated powers does not feature prominently in his *Spirit of the Laws*. Nowhere, for example, does he mention the Act of Settlement and the greater independence of the eighteenth-century British judiciary. Montesquieu may not have had a clear idea of an independent judiciary, or even of the separation of powers, at all.[71] But many readers, especially the American Founders, interpreted him as advocating them. And able scholars have argued that the Founders interpreted him correctly.[72]

The French baron had a large philosophical-political project in view. He sought to get the French to abandon the vision of "universal monarchy" pursued by the seventeenth- and eighteenth-century Bourbon kings, and to follow Great Britain on the road toward modern, liberal, commercial republicanism. And he believed that judicial institutions could nudge France down this road of moderate reform.[73] Aware that his subversive project might earn him the sort of persecution meted out to Voltaire, he "cloaked" his ideas, and he believed that judges, too, could expand their power and transform their regime without appearing to do so, under the "cloak" of their judicial robes.[74] Some claim that this esoteric teaching appealed to the Founders, who assured Americans that the judiciary would comprise the "least dangerous branch."[75]

William Blackstone influenced eighteenth-century Americans even more than Montesquieu did, especially the lawyers who led the American Revolution, though the "English Montesquieu" virtually plagiarized the baron's work on the British constitution.[76] Blackstone's fame derived from his common-law pedagogy. His *Commentaries* became available in America in 1770 and gave the common law the appearance of logic and order. He became the first professor of English law at a university (Oxford) and began to make the law an academic discipline, providing the foundation for the education of generations of American lawyers. In Parliament, Edmund Burke warned that the colonists ardently defended their rights because so many of them had studied that law, and he claimed that Blackstone had sold as many copies of the *Commentaries* in America as in England. John Marshall and James Kent, for instance, relied on Blackstone. In 1858, Abraham Lincoln, a self-taught lawyer, advised an aspiring law student to begin with Blackstone's *Commentaries,* "get a license, and go to the practice, and still keep reading. That is my judgment of the cheapest, quickest, and best way for [him] to make a lawyer of himself."[77]

Americans did not love all of Blackstone, especially as the conflict with the British intensified. The Tory defender of monarchy and an established church argued that the common law "rights of Englishmen" did not extend to Britain's North American colonies, which he considered conquered dominions of the king. He also held to a restrictive definition of freedom of speech. Some regarded him as an acolyte of the outstanding judicial activist of the eighteenth century, Lord Mansfield. Mansfield eagerly changed English law through his decisions, particularly those in the commercial field, where he integrated the customary "law merchant" (*lex mercatoria*) into the common law. He made decisions with natural law and equity in mind, so that his opponents accused him of "acting as a lord chancellor in the guise of a common law judge," following not the law but his own wisdom and conscience.[78] His most famous decision, *Somerset v. Stewart* (1772), concerned a slave brought from Jamaica to England. Slavery, Mansfield held, violated of the law of nature and could not exist unless some positive law established it. With no such law in England, a slave became free by alighting on English soil.[79] Thomas Jefferson distrusted Blackstone, whom he feared would turn young Americans into Tories by his "honeyed Mansfieldism."

Blackstone's own statements on judicial power appear to reject judicial supremacy. He could not have endorsed parliamentary sovereignty more emphatically:

> The power and jurisdiction of Parliament is so transcendent and absolute, that it cannot be confined, either for causes or persons, within any bounds. It has sovereign and uncontrollable authority in making, confirming, enlarging, restraining, abrogating, repealing, reviving, and expounding of laws, concerning matters of all possible denominations, ecclesiastical, or temporal, civil, military, maritime, or criminal: this being the place where that absolute despotic power, which must in all governments reside somewhere, is entrusted by the constitution of these kingdoms.[80]

Like Coke, he called unreasonable or impossible acts of Parliament "void," but he denied that courts could do anything to check the legislature's will. "That were to set the judicial power above that of the legislature, which would be subversive of all government."[81] "True it is," he wrote, "that what the Parliament does, no authority upon earth can undo." The American revolutionaries would reject this theory of parliamentary sovereignty when they declared independence in 1776. But they would not substitute judicial sovereignty for parliamentary sovereignty.

But some scholars interpret Blackstone, like Montesquieu (and Mansfield), as advancing judicial power while "cloaking" it, and for the same reasons— to promote modern, liberal, commercial republicanism.[82] Despite his apparent rejection of Coke and *Bonham*, he continued to view the common law as the emanation of nature or reason, in accord with American founding ideas of natural right.[83] And his treatment of equity in the *Commentaries* "was in substance a literal summary of Mansfield's views."[84] Whether deliberate or not, at most we can say that Montesquieu and Blackstone advanced judicial power in a cautious and conservative way.[85]

The strong American judiciary derived more from the colonists' own judicial experience than from England's, but the American experience largely recapitulated England's. Colonial governments did not separate governmental powers. Legislatures (often the governor and the upper house) acted as courts of appeal. Thomas Oliver, the governor of West Jersey, "was in the habit of dispensing justice sitting on a stump in his meadow."[86] Courts took on all kinds of executive or administrative functions.[87] The young colonies did not develop the manifold system of specialized courts that England had. Judges served at the pleasure of the king (through his governors) in most colonies.[88] Despite Blackstone, the British common law set down roots in the American colonies, with variations according to local circumstances. Several colonies, suspicious of the common law, attempted to write elaborate codes of law—particularly in New England, where the codes drew from Scripture.[89]

The colonial assemblies often created courts and defined their jurisdiction, though the British authorities believed that this power belonged to the king. (Indeed, the charters that created the colonies, and which guaranteed them the rights of Englishmen, came from crown prerogative. Parliament had nothing to do with them, except in the case of Georgia.) Colonial history saw a series of contests between legislature and governor for control of the courts. For example, the crown rebuffed Massachusetts agents who tried to include legislative participation in court appointments in their new, 1691 charter.[90] In 1754, the crown disallowed a North Carolina court-creation act, emphasizing that the power to establish courts belonged to the king alone, and reprimanded the governor for giving his assent. It similarly vetoed a South Carolina law that provided for good-behavior tenure.[91] The assemblies did have the power of the purse and often refused to guarantee judicial salaries if the judges served at pleasure.[92] The non-extension of the Act of Settlement to America nettled the colonists, indicating that the principles of the Glorious Revolution did not include them.[93]

A number of memorable cases showed the importance of an independent judiciary, but none suggested judicial supremacy. The Salem witchcraft trials took place through a special tribunal, a "kangaroo court." Jacob Leisler, the rebel leader of New York's Glorious Revolution, similarly found himself railroaded by an irregular tribunal, as did the twenty-nine slaves and three whites involved in the horrific 1741 New York slave rebellion.[94] On the other hand, the county courts of Virginia looked de facto independent (of both imperial and popular pressure) and provided the most prominent leaders of the American War of Independence.[95]

The trial of John Peter Zenger for seditious libel, perhaps the most famous case in colonial America, which made truth a defense in libel prosecutions, grew out of a dispute over judicial independence. In 1733, when New York's Governor William Cosby could not bring a suit in a court of equity to recover part of his disputed salary, he brought an equity proceeding in a common-law court. He won his suit, but Chief Justice Lewis Morris dissented, holding that the proceeding violated the constitution. As in *Dr. Bonham's Case,* the governor had practically made himself a judge in his own salary-recovery case. Cosby demanded that Morris give the reasons for his decision. Morris had Zenger publish his opinion, and prefaced it by warning, "If judges are to be intimidated so as not to dare to give any opinion, but what is pleasing to the Governor . . . the people of this province, who are very much concerned both with respect to their lives and fortunes in the freedom and independency of those who are to judge them, may possibly not think themselves so secure in either of them as the laws of his Majesty intended they should be."[96]

Cosby then prosecuted Zenger for seditious libel when he published Morris's dissent. Zenger's acquittal struck a major blow for the freedom of the press. It also provided a case of "jury nullification," whereby juries—the democratic, lower house of the judicial branch—limited the power of judges and legislators.[97]

In 1760, New York governor Cadwallader Colden battled the colony's legal establishment to impose an outsider and at-pleasure judge on the Supreme Court, which he believed conspired with the great landowners and undermined imperial control. He won this fight when, in 1761, royal instructions warned colonial governors that they would lose their jobs if they granted good-behavior judicial appointments.[98] The king removed New Jersey governor Josiah Hardy in 1762 for doing so.[99]

Governor Colden got into another scrape with the New York bench and bar as the British began to impose unpopular taxes in America. He tried to have his council review the award of £1,500 to Thomas Forcey in a civil suit. All colonial authorities believed that the council could review only legal errors, not questions of fact tried by a jury. Though ultimately the Board of Trade forced him to back down, Colden's position provoked pamphlet literature and mob action in defense of jury power and linked the issue of judicial independence with the rising revolutionary cause.[100]

"Judicial review" along the lines of *Dr. Bonham's Case* does not appear in the colonial judicial experience. London's review of colonial legislative acts and judicial decisions looks like the clearest predecessor. Almost every charter permitted the colonies to make laws not "repugnant" to the laws of England, or that "near as possibly" accorded with them. The king's Privy Council would review these acts.[101] This system regarded the colonial governments as municipal corporations, which enacted mere "bylaws." This irritated the colonists, for it implied that they had only those rights and powers that the English deigned to grant them. It signaled that Parliament (or the King-in-Parliament) had power to legislate for the colonies "in all cases whatsoever," in the words of the 1766 Declaratory Act—in other words, that Parliament possessed sovereign power. But before the crisis of the 1760s, the council, reflecting the general policy of "salutary neglect," largely left colonial legislation alone. Indeed, it appeared to fail to do its judicial duty to strike down unconstitutional legislation.[102]

The regular practice of "imperial judicial review," in which the council reviewed both colonial legislative acts and court decisions (some 8,500 statutes and 250 court decisions), established a model of "federal" or "vertical" judicial review under the Constitution—of federal courts reviewing acts of state legislatures and decisions of state courts. But it did not clarify the place of "coordinate" or "horizontal" review, or review by a colonial court of a colonial statute—what Coke may have done in *Dr. Bonham's Case*.[103] We can see some coordinate judicial review at work in the colonial period, though nothing like "judicial supremacy." In 1724, the South Carolina supreme court "refused to follow a statute that established a court rule by which persons claiming to live beyond the jurisdiction of a court that had invoked jurisdiction over them could object to jurisdiction in a variety of ways. . . . The court held that the jurisdiction issue could be raised only by a technical procedure known as 'pleading specially to the jurisdiction.'"[104] One law professor noted that this simply declared that the legislature had usurped the "right of the judiciary to govern the technicalities of its own proceedings." Most early cases of judicial review resembled this one, especially when the legislative body tampered with the right to trial by jury. Early judicial review amounted to little more than institutional self-defense.[105] Even so, the South Carolina legislature had already complained about courts questioning the validity of its acts.[106]

Scholars recently have found more cases of judicial review in the eighteenth century, but the cases did not go very deep. Nearly a century ago, Richard B. Morris identified the only assertion of "judicial supremacy," an overt policy preference, with no appeal to any British or "higher law," by a Maryland county court. But he noted that the court in this case acted in an administrative (tax-assessing) capacity, and its "action cannot serve as a precedent for judicial review strictly considered."[107] Nonetheless, British authorities frowned on even this moderate exercise of judicial power. On the eve of the imperial conflict, the South Carolina court declined to strike down a colonial act as contrary to British law. Only the British Council, not the colonial courts, could enforce the supremacy of British law. Chief Justice James Michie said, "For if this court has a power of judging whether the laws which the General Assembly made are void or not, they have a power superior to the General Assembly. But this is a power which I conceive this court has not." Though not uncontested, the scholarship suggests that "horizontal" judicial review did not develop in colonial America.[108]

THE IMPERIAL CRISIS AND INDEPENDENCE

The imperial crisis brought the issue of judicial power and independence into sharper focus. On the one hand, many American judges stood up for colonial rights against British impositions, and American lawyers led the resistance movement. On the other hand, many colonial courts cooperated with the British, and Americans did not lose their perennial suspicion of the legal profession. (Colonial Massachusetts and Virginia outlawed lawyering for a time.) The bench and bar divided much like the general population—about one in four American lawyers fled the country as a Tory.[109] This crisis established one clear point, that the independent states must free the courts at least from executive power, as in England.

Even before the end of the French and Indian War produced the new policies and taxes that provoked the revolution, litigants called upon American courts to breathe life into the principle of *Dr. Bonham's Case*, that acts of Parliament violated their rights. When a British king died, his successor needed to renew writs in his own name within six months. These included the notorious "writs of assistance"—general search warrants that customs officials could use against suspected smugglers. These writs lasted as long as the life of the king in whose name they ran. They did not need to specify the persons, places, or things that officials could search or seize. The Fourth Amendment would prohibit such general warrants. Its protection against "unreasonable searches and seizures" added that "no warrants shall issue, but upon probable cause, supported by oath or affirmation, and particularly describing the place to be searched, and the persons or things to be seized."

In 1761, after George II died, a group of Boston merchants, represented by James Otis, urged the Massachusetts Superior Court to refuse to issue the writs, claiming that they abridged the fundamental rights of Englishmen. Otis cited Coke's opinion in *Bonham*.[110] The court declined to decide the case until it got instructions from England. When those arrived, it complied and issued the writs. But a young John Adams had heard Otis's argument, and made it famous.[111] In 1817 he said, "American independence was then and there born," in "the first scene of the first act of opposition to the arbitrary claims of Great Britain." A year later he wrote, "Mr. Otis' oration against writs of assistance breathed into this nation the breath of life."[112] A century later, in his search for the origins of judicial review, Professor Edwin S. Corwin wrote, "He might have added that then and there American constitutional theory was born."[113] Adams became one of the staunchest advocates of judicial independence. He may have done for Coke what Coke did for Magna Carta: give "higher law" judicial review a mythical pedigree.[114]

Otis repeated his pleas against the writs of assistance and asserted the *Bonham* principle, and others picked up on it. In 1763, he published a pamphlet, *The Rights of the British Colonies Asserted and Proved*. If one could "plainly demonstrate" that an act of Parliament "was against *natural* equity, the executive courts will adjudge such acts void." Otherwise, "Parliament might make itself arbitrary, which it is conceived it can not by the constitution." Parliament could err. "When such a mistake is evident and palpable," he said, "the judges of the executive courts have declared the act 'of a whole parliament void.'"[115] Here he commended "the grandeur of the British constitution" and "the wisdom of our ancestors," which set the legislative and executive branches as checks on each other.[116]

The next year the city of Boston adopted resolutions that repeated Otis's principles. "The judges of England have declared that acts of Parliament against natural equity are void," they argued. "Acts against the fundamental principles of the British Constitution are void. This doctrine is agreeable to the law of nature and nations, to the divine dictates of natural and revealed religion," they concluded, citing *Dr. Bonham* and related precedents. Similarly, in 1772, a group of Indians sued against a Virginia law that classified them as slaves, using *Dr. Bonham* as an authority. The case was argued by George Mason's brother and reported by Thomas Jefferson. "All acts of legislature apparently contrary to natural right and justice are, in our laws, and must be in the nature of things, considered as void. The laws of nature are the laws of God; whose authority can be superseded by no power on earth."[117]

When the British began to impose taxes on the colonists without their consent, courts responded in a more vigorous fashion. Though Parliament repealed the Stamp Act of 1765 primarily in response to colonial mob action and boycotting of British imports, at least one colonial court—that of Northampton County, Virginia—declared it unconstitutional. Several others shared this sentiment but did not express it officially.[118] While colonial courts did not strike down acts of their coordinate branches (however anachronistic it may have been to call them this before modern separation of powers took hold in the 1770s–80s), here it declared void an act of a superior legislature (albeit one still styled a "high court").

John Adams and James Otis argued the unconstitutionality of the writs before Massachusetts governor Bernard and his council. Bernard punted, calling it a judicial question. The lower courts would have to decide for themselves whether they could conduct business without the stamps (which mobs had made inaccessible). Some lower Bay State courts did operate without them, but the superior court delayed until Parliament had repealed the act.[119]

The colonists especially worried that these acts extended the jurisdiction of the vice-admiralty courts. These vestiges of the pre–Glorious Revolution prerogative courts operated without juries, which colonists regarded as vital institutions of popular participation in lawmaking and law enforcement. (The name "admiralty" shows its origins as a military court.) The idea of "jury nullification," that juries could decide issues of law as well as of fact, continued in colonial America. The jury had redefined the law of seditious libel in the Zenger case, and juries were able to prevent the collection of feudal quit-rents by colonial proprietors and governors.[120]

Likewise, Patrick Henry won the case of the "Parsons' Cause," an important step on the road to religious disestablishment in Virginia, via jury nullification. Virginia had established the Church of England and paid its clergy in a stipulated amount of tobacco. Dissenters (Baptists, Quakers, Presbyterians, and others) had long resented having to support the Anglican establishment. When tobacco prices began to rise sharply in the 1750s, the Virginia legislature enacted a law that paid the ministers in money at the rate of two pence per pound of tobacco when the market price was five to six pence. The king and council vetoed the act. But when ministers sued for back pay, Patrick Henry persuaded the jury to award total damages of one penny, effectively nullifying the veto.[121] These cases, illustrating the power of colonial juries, make the American judicial system resemble what Montesquieu seemed to prescribe.

If juries could not declare British taxes unconstitutional (or at least refuse to convict violators), the colonies had to that extent been deprived of consent to taxation.[122] Thus, the seventh resolution of the Stamp Act Congress asserted, "Trial by jury is the inherent and invaluable right of every British subject in these colonies," and the eighth objected to "extending the jurisdiction of the courts of admiralty beyond its ancient limits." Notably, admiralty courts and courts enforcing navigation acts in England used juries.

The Stamp Act also contained a provision that required stamps on documents issued by "courts of ecclesiastical jurisdiction." No such courts existed in the colonies, and this wording raised the suspicion that London planned to establish the Church of England in America, with bishops, the Book of Common Prayer, and canon law. (One attempt to establish ecclesiastical jurisdiction had failed in Virginia in 1690.)[123] Ecclesiastical courts, like admiralty courts, did not use juries, making them Roman law symbols of despotism.[124]

The new British taxes meant to pay for not only a military establishment (the "standing armies" reviled in English constitutional history) but also a "civil list"—to make judges (and future bishops and clergymen) independent of the colonial assemblies' grudging salary grants. This would eliminate the principal source of the popular assemblies' power—their control of the salaries of governors and judges who served at the king's pleasure. Thus, the Massachusetts General Court impeached Judge Peter Oliver for taking a salary directly from the crown rather than from itself. "Any judge accepting support from the crown would show himself to be an enemy of the constitution," it warned.[125] British payment of colonial salaries threatened to eliminate all of the power that colonial assemblies had built up since the seventeenth century, which had made them the local equivalent of the London Parliament. In short, British policy would undo those parts of the Glorious Revolution that extended to America and plunge the colonies back into the position of absolute dependence that the English faced before 1689.

After Parliament repealed the Stamp Act in 1766, it enacted a new set of taxes in the 1767 Townshend duties. This produced an unprecedented wave of judicial nullification, with courts in seven colonies (plus East Florida) refusing to issue the writs to enforce them.[126] When South Carolina judge Rawlins Lowndes held the writs unconstitutional, the king removed him. When fellow judge William Henry Drayton denounced this removal, he also lost his office.[127] Historian O. M. Dickerson observed, "This unsung record of courage and fidelity to what they believed to be the law of the land must be considered in any appraisal of the colonial judiciary." Tory judges as well as Whigs stood up for the rights of English citizens. "The American determination to keep the courts free from executive control grows in no small degree out of this experience."[128]

As historian Richard B. Morris noted, "This impressive group of colonial decisions should lend considerable weight to the view that the doctrine of judicial supremacy had, under the impetus of the political philosophy of the revolutionary era, gained much more ground than recent writers have been willing to admit."[129] But we should note that such judicial action, like the mob action that coincided with it, came about only in extraordinary, *revolutionary* circumstances.[130] As historian Gordon Wood would later put it, "The uniquely American practices of judicial review and vigilantism were actually two sides of the same legal coin."[131]

The Declaration of Independence made several statements favoring judicial independence, at least against the king. The Second Continental Congress resolved, "He has obstructed the administration of justice, by refusing his assent to laws for establishing judiciary powers." This complaint reflected the long-running struggle between colonial legislatures and governors over the courts. As the revolutionaries went on to say, "He has made judges dependent on his will alone, for the tenure of their offices, and the amount and payment of their salaries," without saying who *should* determine tenure and salary. They assailed the extension of the vice-admiralty courts, and the potential establishment of other prerogative courts, in their complaint that Parliament had passed "pretended legislation . . . for depriving us in many cases, of the benefits of trial by jury."

The Declaration also targeted the Quebec Act of 1774, which established a large colony out of recently acquired French North America. The act provided for no representative assembly and established French civil law, though it adopted the English common law of crimes. The Congress condemned king and Parliament "for abolishing the free system of English laws in a neighboring province, establishing therein an arbitrary government, and enlarging its boundaries so as to render it at once a fit instrument for introducing the same absolute rule into these colonies."

The Declaration also averred that the king had "erected a multitude of new offices, and sent hither swarms of offices to harass our people, and eat out their substance." However exaggerated, this claim clearly reflected the fear that British policy sought to establish a colonial aristocracy—military, civil, and ecclesiastical officers paid by Stamp Act revenue. The act also meant to limit entry into higher education and the learned professions, to keep those spheres exclusively for men of birth and wealth. Americans saw British policy as fundamentally antidemocratic.[132]

As a revolutionary document, the Declaration claimed that British policy justified Americans' rebellion against the imposition of a tyranny. As such, it concluded with an appeal to "the supreme judge of the world." The period between independence and the Constitution of 1789 would mark a new phase in the establishment of the independence, but not the supremacy, of terrestrial judges and courts.

2

THE CONSTITUTION

THE REVOLUTIONARY STATES

T he judiciary of the 1787 Constitution arose largely from the Founders' experience under the state constitutions of the preceding decade. The Second Continental Congress that declared independence also called for a "confederation" of the colonies. It took five years for all of the states to approve their product, the Articles of Confederation. As James Madison astutely observed, the confederation did not establish a *government* at all. He called its lack of judicial power one of its manifest defects. Article IV pledged each state to respect the "judicial proceedings of the courts and magistrates of every other state," but no national body could enforce this provision. The only semblance of a judiciary lurked in Article IX, which provided for national determination of "captures on land or water," and "courts for the trial of piracies and felonies committed on the high seas." The Continental Congress made itself "the last resort on appeal" of interstate land title disputes and in cases between citizens of different states. It established an exceedingly complicated system to arbitrate these disputes, which settled only one case.[1]

The new states showed the Founders how to fit judicial power into republican governments. In general, the new constitutions made the judiciary independent of the executive but more dependent on the legislature. State constitutions presented a variety of judicial systems. Connecticut and Rhode Island changed nothing; these unusually powerful legislatures selected judges who continued to serve annual terms. In these states, as in New Jersey, the upper house of the legislature or governor's council served as the highest court of appeal, like the British House of Lords. Georgia's judges also served entirely at the pleasure of the legislature. New York judges had good-behavior tenure until age sixty. Pennsylvania judges served seven-year terms. Most states adopted lifelong good-behavior tenure with removal by impeachment and "bill of address"—simple majority of the legislature and governor. Only Virginia and North Carolina (and South Carolina, in 1790) went further than this Act of Settlement standard and provided for good-behavior tenure with removal by impeachment only. But the legislatures still chose or nominated the judges, until Massachusetts adopted gubernatorial appointment with conciliar consent.[2]

The first, revolutionary state legislators and constitution drafters wanted above all to make the judges independent—*of the executive,* but not of themselves. Their constitutions also weakened executive power, especially in doing away with gubernatorial power to veto legislation and to appoint officers (including judges). Revolutionary-era popular assemblies tended to suck all power into their "impetuous vortex," as James Madison would later put it. The revolutionary constitution makers separated powers to a point that permitted the legislative branch to overawe the other two branches. These legislators did not see themselves as *representatives* of the people but as the people themselves. They wrote and adopted the new constitutions (until Massachusetts in 1780) and seemed to accept the view of Blackstonian parliamentary sovereignty. The judiciary would benefit from the Federalists' movement from legislative to popular or constitutional sovereignty.[3]

The most interesting institutional innovations providing something like judicial review came in the Pennsylvania and New York constitutions. Pennsylvania provided for a "council of censors," elected to meet every seven years to inquire into whether the government had abided by the constitution. It met only once, to little effect, and Pennsylvanians dropped it in the revised state constitution of 1790. New York adopted a "council of revision," consisting of the governor and several state judges, who could veto acts of the legislature. Madison denounced the former in *Federalist* 50, but repeatedly pressed for the New York model at the Constitutional Convention.[4]

Some writers began to argue for a fully separate and independent judiciary. "The judges ought, in a well regulated state, to be equally independent of the executive and the legislative powers," John Dickinson wrote, in letter 11 of his *Letters from a Farmer in Pennsylvania* (1768).[5] In 1776, John Adams warned against legislative threats to judicial ability to mediate between or balance legislative and executive powers. "Judges, justices, and all other officers, civil and military, should be nominated and appointed by the governor, with the advice and consent" of his council or the whole legislature, he wrote in *Thoughts on Government.* "Judicial power ought to be distinct from both the legislative and executive, and independent upon both, that so it may be a check upon both, as both should be checks upon that." He endorsed life tenure during good behavior and guaranteed salaries, with removal only by impeachment.[6] On the other side, New Hampshire general and future governor John Sullivan doubted the value of empowering a third branch, saying it "is only like two contending powers calling in a third which is unconnected in interest, to keep the other two in awe, till it can gain power sufficient to destroy them both."[7]

STATE COURTS IN THE 1780s

Some judges in the revolutionary states began to resist legislative usurpations. Scholars have long recognized that judges appeared to exercise judicial review before the Constitution and before *Marbury v. Madison*. But they usually regarded the cases as few and murky—historian Richard B. Morris called them "phantom precedents."[8] In recent years, scholars have discovered many more cases of preconstitutional judicial review, and some see them as clearer assertions of judicial power than was earlier recognized.[9]

Nobody can deny that these cases paved the way for judicial review in the 1787 Constitution. Though controversial in some states, the Philadelphia Federalists more or less took judicial review for granted. But these cases of judicial review did not reflect or establish anything like modern judicial supremacy. The judges in these cases remained diffident. And the cases met a hostile reception in the state legislatures even as the Philadelphia Federalist delegates applauded them.[10]

In the 1780 case of *Holmes v. Walton,* the New Jersey state supreme court heard a challenge by someone convicted under a trading-with-the-enemy law that provided for six-man juries. The New Jersey constitution guaranteed "trial by jury" but did not specify the traditional twelve-man version (though earlier charters and legislative resolutions did). The court struck down the act as a violation of the fuller version of trial by jury. As with most eighteenth-century cases, the court issued no written report to ascertain what had actually occurred. Though several counties protested the decision, the next state legislature amended the law to require twelve-man juries. Progressive Era law professor and judicial review critic Louis Boudin claimed that "the mythical nature of this case is demonstrated beyond peradventure of doubt."[11]

The 1782 case of *Virginia v. Caton* also presented an incomplete record (the case was not reported until 1827) but suggested judicial review. The state constitution provided for pardons by *either* house of the legislature in treason cases, but the legislature passed an act that required *both* houses to pardon. Caton got a pardon from the House but not the Senate, and the Supreme Court upheld the unicameral reprieve. Judge St. George Tucker, who would later write an influential treatise on the Constitution, firmly asserted that the legislature could not violate Virginia's written constitution. He contrasted American popular or constitutional sovereignty with English parliamentary sovereignty. He spoke of the court's duty "to protect one branch of the legislature, and consequently, the whole community, against the usurpations of the other." And if both houses combined "to overleap the bounds prescribed to them by the people, I . . . pointing to the constitution, will say to them, here is the limit of your authority; hither shall you go, but no further."[12]

A few years later, the Virginia legislature reorganized the state court system, which imposed new duties on the judges but no salary adjustment. Since the state constitution guaranteed "fixed and adequate" salaries, the judges of the court of appeals objected to this act. Their "Remonstrance" maintained that "to decide between an act of the people [the Constitution] and an act of the legislature" lay "within their line of duty, declaring what the law is, and not making new law." When the legislature did not grant adequate redress, the judges resigned. This episode became known as the Judges Case.[13]

In *Rutgers v. Waddington,* New York judge James Duane held that a state trespass act, meant to permit New Yorkers to recover for damages to their property during the long British occupation, violated the law of nations, part of the common law of New York, particularly as incorporated into the 1783 Treaty of Paris. The law of nations served as an equivalent to natural law, and critics decried its use to aid a British subject against an American claim for damages. Alexander Hamilton represented the party challenging the act, and he appealed to *Dr. Bonham's Case.* In a ruling much like Coke's, Judge Duane held that the legislature *could have* abrogated the law of nations, but the court could not assume that it had done so without an explicit expression of such intent. He abjured judicial supremacy, quoting Blackstone's warning that it "would be subversive of all government."[14] But even Duane's rather modest exercise elicited outrage from the legislature. It called the decision "subversive of all law and good order" and said it "leads directly to anarchy and confusion." Such judicial power "will end all our dear bought rights and privileges, and legislatures become useless."[15] Hamilton no doubt recognized the tenuous value of the decision, and he had his client settle before the legislature or a higher court overturned the decision.

The Rhode Island case of *Trevett v. Weeden* arose out of a paper money law, which compelled creditors to accept depreciated state bills at face value. If they refused, they faced penalties without a jury trial and could not appeal to the state supreme court. It established special courts to hear such cases. For some reason, this case ended up in the regular courts, which said that it contradicted the guarantee of jury trial by "law of the land." Rhode Island's seventeenth-century charter contained no jury guarantee. The charter did guarantee "all liberties and immunities of free and natural subjects" of England, and prohibited laws "contrary and repugnant" to those of England. Some doubt that the court held the act unconstitutional; instead, it accepted a plea that it had no jurisdiction. As in New Jersey and New York, despite the arguably limited expression of judicial disapproval, the Rhode Island legislature impeached the judges. Though the legislature acquitted the judges, it reelected none of them in 1787.[16]

Finally, in the year that the Constitutional Convention convened, the North Carolina supreme court, in *Bayard v. Singleton,* struck down a law depriving Tories of trial by jury in confiscation cases. This case produced an interesting correspondence between James Iredell, the lawyer who argued the case and who would become one of the first US Supreme Court justices, and Richard Dobbs Spaight, a North Carolina delegate to the convention. Iredell defended *Bayard* along the lines of St. George Tucker in *Caton.* Other delegates must have known of Iredell's argument.[17] This case established perhaps the clearest instance of judicial review.

But what *kind* of judicial review did these cases display? Cases array themselves across a spectrum, from minimal to maximal. Minimalist judicial review consists of institutional self-defense. An intermediary version would cover unconstitutional acts. Maximal review would extend to policy judgments, effectively allowing judges to legislate.

Minimally, judicial review preserves judicial power in a system of separated powers. It would allow courts to protect their institutional integrity from encroachments by the legislature or executive. Thus, a court could refuse to perform nonjudicial tasks imposed by the legislature. It could refuse to comply with legislation that curtailed "inherent" judicial powers, like holding parties in contempt of court. Or it could give the courts special guardianship of parts of the Constitution that concern judicial matters—requiring two witnesses in treason cases or trial by jury. Almost all of the pre-Constitution instances of judicial review fit into this minimalist, self-defense category. As we will see, the great case of *Marbury v. Madison* also falls into it.[18] Under minimalist, self-defense judicial review, the courts would have to enforce unconstitutional acts that did not usurp judicial power. An unapportioned income tax or state abortion restriction might violate the Constitution, but this did not affect the judiciary per se.

More broadly, courts could police the constitutional limits of other branches. In the federal system of the Constitution, they could umpire disputes between Congress and the states, to keep Congress from encroaching upon powers of the states and vice versa. The court might also arbitrate disputes between the coordinate branches. At this intermediate level of judicial review, the court could police clear, obvious, and manifest constitutional violations—sometimes called the "doubtful case" standard, by which the court gives the other branches every possible benefit of the doubt. This also introduces the distinction between judicial activism and judicial restraint. It also left open the response that the courts had no greater power of constitutional interpretation than the other branches, the theory of "departmentalism."

The highest and most controversial level of judicial review involves a court's disapproval of the policy of a law or executive act—its wisdom, expediency, or propriety. Almost everyone at the Founding rejected this, and judges only rarely admitted doing so in the twentieth century. Opponents would consistently aver that "unconstitutional" holdings merely masked the policy preferences of the justices—against income taxes, in the example above, or in favor of abortion. But the departmental theory and other constitutional checks on judicial usurpation could check policy-political review.

The presidential veto provides a useful analogy. While the Constitution contains no explicit provision for judicial review, it does for the veto. But it does not say to what the veto extends. A minimal veto extended only to institutional self-defense, to prevent the legislature from impairing executive power. An intermediate veto power would extend to any legislative violation of the Constitution (including those that infringed on inherent judicial power). A maximal veto would extend to policy.

We have become accustomed to a maximal, policy veto, but this remained controversial until at least Andrew Jackson's presidency in the 1830s. George Washington vetoed only two acts of Congress. The first concerned apportionment of seats in the House of Representatives after the 1790 census. The formula that Congress adopted meant that some congressmen would represent fewer than thirty thousand people, a manifest violation of Article I, section 2. Washington had identified a technical, mathematical error, which Congress quickly corrected. It had nothing to do with executive power. Washington also vetoed an act reducing the size of the army. Washington may have considered this a policy disagreement but one concerning an inherent executive power, as commander in chief of the armed forces. Presidents John Adams and Thomas Jefferson vetoed no bills. Fourteen years later, James Madison vetoed a new bank bill on constitutional and policy grounds.[19]

The 1780s cases clearly lie on the border of self-defense and constitutional review, and more toward the minimal end of the scale. Insofar as these courts resisted populist, debtor-relief, and anti-Tory democratic sentiment, they indicated that the judiciary had won more confidence among elites than with the masses.[20] Their opponents would call the Federalists crypto-aristocrats and would see strong courts as their agents.[21]

THE CONSTITUTION

The Federalist reformers sought to address three sets of problems—international (or "federative"), interstate ("federal"), and intrastate ("republican")—and a stronger judiciary had a role to play in all of these. James Madison addressed these in his study preparatory to the convention, "The Vices of the Political System of the United States," in which he argued that the new state legislatures had gotten carried away with the power that democracy gave to the branch most closely connected to the people. They enacted variable and partial laws, changing with every shift of factional control of the assemblies. The legislatures had overawed the governors and often usurped judicial powers—overturning judgments, granting new trials, passing ex post facto laws and bills of attainder.[22]

Madison especially condemned debtor-relief, paper money laws of the kind seen particularly in Rhode Island. In *Federalist* 10 he expressed his hope that the Constitution would deflect the "rage for paper money, for an abolition of debts, for an equal division of property, or for any other improper or wicked project." These laws also constituted "frauds on the citizens of other states, and the subjects of foreign powers." They showed that the Confederation Congress lacked the power to induce the states to comply with the terms of the Treaty of Paris concerning British creditors.[23]

The Federalists sought to strengthen the national government with regard to the states and empower the executive and judicial branches to resist the "impetuous vortex" of the legislature. The stronger central government over the states produced the greatest controversy at the convention (the protracted struggle toward the Great Compromise) and in the ratification debates. The strengthened presidency also caused controversy; fears of monarchy still animated patriots. The stronger judiciary of Article III produced relatively little debate at Philadelphia or in the state conventions. Almost thirty years later Governor Morris, the principal draftsman of the finished Constitution, recalled that he had written "as clear as our language would permit; excepting, nevertheless, a part of what relates to the judiciary." He deliberately made Article III vague. "On that subject," he said, "conflicting opinions had been maintained with so much professional astuteness, that it became necessary to select phrases, which expressing my own notions would not alarm others, nor shock their selflove, and to the best of my recollection, this was the only part which passed without cavil."[24] The final text reads:

> Section 1. The judicial Power of the United States, shall be vested in one supreme Court, and in such inferior Courts as the Congress may from time to time ordain and establish. The Judges, both of the supreme and inferior Courts, shall hold their Offices during good Behavior, and shall, at stated Times, receive for their Services a Compensation which shall not be diminished during their Continuance in Office.
>
> Section 2. The judicial Power shall extend to all Cases, in Law and Equity, arising under this Constitution, the Laws of the United States, and Treaties made, or which shall be made, under their Authority; —to all Cases affecting Ambassadors, other public Ministers and Consuls; —to all Cases of admiralty and maritime jurisdiction; — to Controversies to which the United States shall be a Party; —to Controversies between two or more States; —between a State and Citizens of another State; —between Citizens of different States claiming Lands under Grants of different States, and between a State, or the Citizens thereof, and foreign States, Citizens, or Subjects.
>
> In all Cases affecting Ambassadors, other public Ministers and Consuls, and those in which a State shall be a Party, the supreme Court shall have original Jurisdiction. In all the other Cases before mentioned, the supreme Court shall have appellate Jurisdiction, both as to Law and Fact, with such Exceptions, and under such Regulations as the Congress shall make.

The text of Article III supports Morris's recollection. It made room for either a powerful or an insignificant judiciary. Its first sentence displays this range: "The judicial power of the United States shall be vested in one

Supreme Court, and in such inferior courts as the Congress may from time to time ordain and establish." It provided for a separate judicial branch. Chapter 1 described the relatively modern idea of a judiciary distinguished from the executive. The revolutionary state constitutions often made vigorous assertions of a tripartite separation of powers. Article XXX of the Massachusetts constitution of 1780, for instance, declared that "the legislative department shall never exercise the executive and judicial powers, or either of them: the executive shall never exercise the legislative and judicial powers, or either of them: the judicial shall never exercise the legislative and executive powers, or either of them: to the end it may be a government of laws and not of men."

But the 1780s showed that such formal separation of powers did not prevent legislative hegemony. The Federalists argued that nobody could perfectly define the three powers, and they called for checks and balances among these powers to preserve their independence. The judiciary, especially, needed reinforcement, as Madison explained in *Federalist* 51. The US Constitution presented an implicit, structural separation of powers in its three articles, but it also introduced checks and balances to preserve the independence of the executive and judiciary. Such powers as the veto and appointing officers clearly expressed executive–legislative balance. Article III contained no explicit provision for check by "judicial review," but the separate article itself implied it.

Analysts do not usually call this first sentence of Article III the "vesting clause," as they do the first sentences of Articles I and II. Constitutionalists often note that Article I says that "all legislative powers *herein granted*" belong to Congress, and they stress that this language emphasizes that the Constitution does not grant legislative power *tout court* but only those powers enumerated, especially in section 8. By contrast, Article II entrusts "*the* executive power," not "all executive powers *herein granted*" to the president.[25] Article III also begins with "the judicial power," not "all judicial powers herein granted," but in section 2 it says that "the judicial power shall extend to" a series of cases. This would present a serious potential limitation to federal judicial power, indeed.

The second phrase of the first sentence, "one Supreme Court, and such inferior courts as the Congress may from time to time ordain and establish," left options open. It established judicial power *constitutionally* only to a limited degree; it left most of it to the more clearly constituted political branches.[26] One Supreme Court implied power, as the unity of one president favored executive strength over a plural executive. But the question of whether the Constitution should establish federal courts below it—as opposed to having one Supreme Court hearing appeals from the state courts—became the most controversial question about the federal judiciary at the Philadelphia convention and in the ratifying conventions, and it would continue into the First Congress. Small-state delegates and politicians feared that inferior federal courts would consume all judicial questions and drive the state courts out of existence. The Constitution compromised. Congress "may" establish them, or it may not. Nobody said whether Congress might do away with inferior courts after establishing them. Moreover, Article I gave Congress the power "to constitute *tribunals* inferior to the Supreme Court." How did tribunals differ from courts?[27]

The remainder of Article III's first section beefed up the judiciary. All judges held their offices for life, with good behavior. The convention defeated a proposal by John Dickinson to add bill of address removal.[28] The Constitution guaranteed their salaries; Congress could only raise them. This equaled or exceeded the tenure and salary protections of every state constitution.

Some question of what constituted "good behavior" remained. Did it mean anything short of "treason, bribery, or other high crimes and misdemeanors," for which all civil officers faced impeachment? Article III refers to "judges" but does not specify any number for the Supreme Court. Article I's impeachment provision mentions a "chief justice" but no "associate justices."

In its most important decisions on the judiciary, the convention stepped away from the legislative appointment of federal judges. Article II vests the power to appoint judges and all other officers in the president, "by and with the advice and consent of the Senate." This compromise shared judicial appointment between the executive and legislature.[29] The delegates made the choice at the eleventh hour; for most of the convention they assumed that Congress (or just the Senate) would appoint the judges, as in most state constitutions. Presidential–senatorial appointment made the federal judiciary the most distant from the people. Before the Seventeenth Amendment, the state legislatures chose the senators who confirmed judicial nominees. The Electoral College similarly constituted an intermediate body chosen by the state legislatures or at their direction. Combining an indirectly elected president and senators in the choice of judges put the judges at a fifth- or sixth-hand remove from the people. James Madison, claiming that all of the officers of the new government derived their offices from the people, somewhat sheepishly admitted that federal judges "are the choice, though a remote choice, of the people themselves." He argued that the "peculiar qualifications" of the judicial office made their indirect selection advisable.[30]

Article III's second section gets into the weeds of jurisdiction. *"The* judicial power" of section 1 now extends to several specific types of "cases and controversies."[31] This imposes an important limit on judicial power. The courts cannot initiate exercises of power. They cannot range abroad when interpreting the laws; parties in conflict must present legitimate cases to them. (Cases, as opposed to controversies, entailed criminal matters. The phrase suggests public prosecutions as opposed to private suits.)[32] On the other hand, it says that the power *shall,* not *may,* extend to them. First, it would extend to *"all* cases, in law and equity, arising under this Constitution, the laws of the United States, and treaties made, or which shall be made, under their authority."[33] The courts of the national government would adjudicate cases involving the Constitution and its own laws. It also extended to all cases "affecting ambassadors, other public ministers and consuls," and "to all cases of admiralty and maritime jurisdiction." Nobody contested this grant; a genuinely national government should have its own courts to enforce its own laws. The inability of the confederation to get the states to abide by treaty obligations showed its necessity.

At this point the section establishes a boundary between *all* cases and *not* all cases. Federal judicial power also extended "to controversies to which the United States shall be a party;—to controversies between two or more states;— between a state and citizens of another state;—between citizens of different states;—between citizens of the same state claiming lands under grants of different states, and between a state, or the citizens thereof, and foreign states, citizens or subjects." The question of "sovereign immunity"—whether anyone could sue a state without its consent—would quickly become a political firestorm and produce the Eleventh Amendment, which removed several of these provisions. The jurisdiction in cases "between citizens of different states," known as diversity jurisdiction, had enormous potential. But jurisdiction might not extend to *all* such cases, and the next part of Article III would introduce more important potential restrictions.

Section 2 then defined the original and appellate powers of the Supreme Court. The original jurisdiction (that is, where it would act as a court of first instance, a fact-finding trial court) applied only to a very small set of cases, those "affecting ambassadors, other public ministers and consuls, and those in which a state shall be party." For the bulk of its jurisdiction, the Supreme Court would have appellate jurisdiction, "both as to law and to fact, with such excep-

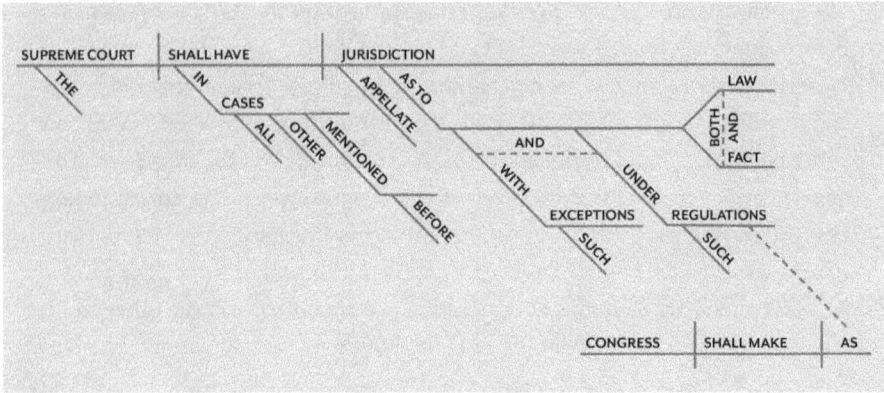

Fig. 1. Grammatical analysis of the exceptions clause.

tions, and under such regulations as the Congress shall make." This language might all but eliminate federal judicial power.[34] It seemed to give Congress the option of denying all appeals to the Supreme Court—the legislature could except and regulate away everything but the meager original jurisdiction. And if Congress opted not to create any inferior courts, one could imagine a lone chief justice (for the Constitution does not establish any associates) waiting for some ambassador or state to bring the rare original suit but otherwise sitting unengaged. So dreamed the antijudicial supremacists, or judicial minimalists, among the Anti-Federalists.

The remainder of section 2 ensured jury trials for criminal cases, but not civil ones. This reflected the colonial era's high regard for juries as popular limitations on government power, including that of the judges.[35] Finally, section 3 defined treason very strictly and limited the punishments that Congress could impose for it.

Article III gave great discretion to Congress to construct the judicial system and to define its jurisdiction. When the First Congress enacted the Judiciary Act of 1789, it practically continued the Constitutional Convention. As we will see, the First Congress compromised, neither maximizing nor minimizing the range of judicial options under Article III but on the whole placing it closer to the maximal end.

Article VI, the supremacy clause, did more than Article III to establish judicial power. It declared the Constitution, federal laws, and treaties "the supreme law of the land; and the judges in every state shall be bound thereby, any thing in the constitution or laws of any state to the contrary notwithstanding." The distinction between Article III "laws" and Article VI "laws *made in pursuance thereof*" implied unconstitutional laws.[36] Article VI's definition of the Constitution as "law" has led many scholars to point out that the shift from regarding the Constitution as a set of political principles to seeing it as law, justiciable and interpretable by courts, is the key to the American judiciary's great power.[37] But even the language of the supremacy clause could keep the federal courts in check. It refers only to "the judges in every state" as the guardians of national supremacy, and those might be only state judges if Congress provided no inferior federal ones. However, the original New Jersey Plan clause referred to "the judiciaries *of the several states*"; the revised language implied that there would be federal judges *in* but not *of* the states.

Ironically, the supremacy clause came from the small-state or New Jersey Plan, which wanted to curb the nationalist Federalist Virginia Plan in favor of states' rights.[38] The Virginia Plan would have enforced supremacy by allowing Congress to use force on recalcitrant states—"to call forth the force of the Union against any member of the Union failing in its duty" under the Constitution. This seemed to recognize the Union as still a confederation of sovereign states, in which the Union would act upon the states as corporate entities in cases of conflict. The New Jersey supremacy alternative opened the prospect of the national government enforcing its laws on individuals within the states, a more national approach, and using courts rather than military force.

The convention's repeated rejection of a New York–style council of revision also revealed its attitude toward judicial review. The Virginia Plan called for "the executive and a convenient number of the national judiciary . . . to compose a Council of Revision with authority to examine every act of the national legislature before it shall operate," with a conditional veto. The delegates voted down this proposal four times. Several delegates took for granted that the federal courts would review congressional acts and so should not play a role in their enactment in such a council—they should not have a "double negative," as Luther Martin put it.[39]

Elbridge Gerry argued that judges should not serve on the council "as they will have a sufficient check against encroachments *on their own department* by their exposition of the laws." This suggested an institutional self-defense view of judicial review. He observed that "in some states the judges had actually set aside laws, as being against the Constitution. This was done, too, with general approbation."[40] (Gerry exaggerated here; the judges had aroused considerable political reaction.)

Other delegates also drew a clear distinction between questions of policy, which such a council, but not a court, should consider, and questions of constitutionality, which belonged to courts. Nathaniel Gorham argued that judges cannot "be presumed to possess any peculiar knowledge of the mere policy of public measures," and Gerry warned against "making statesmen of the judges," undermining the people's representatives as the principal guardians of their rights.[41] George Mason contrasted "unconstitutional" acts to "unjust, oppressive, pernicious" ones. James Wilson noted that a law might be "unjust, unwise, dangerous," yet not "unconstitutional." Judicial participation in the council would enable it to prevent "encroachments on the people as well as on themselves," he said—a call for judicial review beyond institutional self-defense.[42]

Similarly, James Madison wondered whether the grant of jurisdiction to cases "arising under the Constitution" went too far. Rather than a general power to expound the Constitution, the courts should limit review to what he called "cases of a judiciary nature." Madison did not clarify this term, but it certainly expressed a *restriction* on judicial review. The language remained, Madison reported, because the delegates "generally supposed that the jurisdiction given was constructively limited to cases of a judiciary nature."[43]

THE JUDICIARY IN THE RATIFICATION DEBATE

The judicial article did not figure very prominently in the ratification debate, compared to the issues of the relative power of the national and state governments or the power of the presidency. The first significant complaint of those called Anti-Federalists came from the minority of the Pennsylvania ratifying convention, which warned that the new system "would effect a consolidation of the states into one government," and would replace Anglo-American common law with civil law absolutism.[44] Virginia's ratifying convention stood out as paying attention to the judiciary, including a defense by delegate John Marshall. James Madison admitted that the convention could have "better expressed" Article III.[45] Most of the criticism of Article III came from "Brutus," the pseudonymous author of sixteen articles in the *New York Journal* between October 1787 and April 1788.[46]

The Anti-Federalists feared above all that the national courts would swallow up all the judicial business of the country. They "will eclipse the dignity, and take away from the respectability, of the state courts."[47] Brutus noted that the court would abet Congress in exceeding its constitutional limits, for the judicial power would grow in tandem with the legislative power. The courts would "not only carry into execution the powers expressly given, but where these are wanting or ambiguously expressed, to supply what is wanting by their own decisions." He raised the alarm about the "equity" jurisdiction of the Supreme Court. This would allow the courts to interpret the Constitution according to its "spirit" rather than its letter. He particularly suspected that this spirit would be derived from the preamble, especially the "general welfare" clause. This would override the limitation of Congress to the enumerated powers in Article I, section 8 and make them "either expressly or by implication extend to every thing about which any legislative power can be employed."[48]

In a later, more general warning, Brutus claimed that "the Supreme Court under this constitution would be exalted above all other power in the government, and subject to no control. . . . I question whether the world ever saw . . . a court of justice invested with such immense powers, and yet placed in a situation so little responsible." The convention had made the judiciary independent of the executive, as well as "independent of the people, of the legislature, and of every power under heaven. Men placed in this situation will generally soon feel themselves independent of heaven itself."[49]

Another Anti-Federalist critic, the "Federal Farmer," warned that the delegates had not applied precautions about legislative and executive power sufficiently to the courts. "We are in more danger of sowing the seeds of arbitrary government in this department than in any other." He echoed the Federalist claim that "in the unsettled state of things in this country, for several years past, it has been thought, that our popular legislatures have, sometimes, departed from the line of strict justice, while the law courts have shown a disposition more punctually to keep to it." But in the future legislation will settle down and courts become "more severe and arbitrary." Anti-Federalists also decried the lack of jury trial guarantee in civil cases. The Federal Farmer averred that "the common people should have a part and share of influence in the judicial as well as in the legislative." Juries provided "the people at large their just and rightful control in the judicial department."[50] Another pseudonymous "Farmer" noted that the Constitution provided the requisite separation of the judiciary from the executive, but weakened the democratic element of the judicial power, the jury.[51]

Publius, the great defender of the Constitution, addressed Article III in six of the last eight *Federalist* Papers, all attributed to Alexander Hamilton. But earlier numbers pointed out the value of a stronger judiciary in the new system. The old Articles of Confederation essentially had no judiciary—appropriately enough, because the confederation could not really legislate. "Laws are a dead letter without courts to expound and define their true meaning and operation," he noted in *Federalist* 22. (The Articles never mention "laws," but they do refer to "treaties," "rules" in admiralty cases, and some other "regulations.") The confederation failed because it derived its power from the states, not from the people—it thus lacked the element of popular consent necessary for republican government. In the new, real government, "the majesty of the national authority must be manifested through the medium of the courts of justice."[52] In *Federalist* 80, he explained that the courts must enforce the limitations on the states expressed in Article I, section 10; compel states to obey treaty obligations; and enforce Article IV, the privileges and immunities clause, which he called "the basis of the Union" and a "fundamental a provision." The republican, federative, and federal problems that had brought forth the convention would become judicial questions.

James Madison addressed the place of the judiciary in the federal system, touching the fundamental controversy over the respective powers of the national and the state governments. In *Federalist* 39, he described the "compound republic," which he called neither completely national nor completely confederal, but a mixture. "It is true that in controversies relating to the boundary between the two jurisdictions, the tribunal which is ultimately to decide is to be established under the general government," he wrote. We can only assume that the "tribunal" is the Supreme Court. "But this does not change the principle of the case. The decision is to be impartially made, according to the rules of the Constitution; and all the usual and most effectual precautions are taken to ensure this impartiality." We may surmise that these "precautions" lay in the discretionary powers that Congress retained in Article III, especially the "exceptions and regulations" on the Court's jurisdiction. One could see them in the mode of appointment, where the states participated in the choice of the president and the senators who put judges on the bench.[53] Hamilton, in *Federalist* 80, simply called impeachment "alone a complete security" against judicial usurpation.

Federalist 78 made the central argument in defense of judicial review, in one of the most celebrated of all the Federalist Papers. Hamilton began by treating the mode of appointment. "This is the same with that of appointing the officers of the Union in general," he said, "and has been so fully discussed in the two last numbers that nothing can be said here which would not be useless repetition." Even Publius's greatest admirers must see a non sequitur here. The previous papers on executive power had made a compelling case for balancing what we today call "the unitary executive" (the president must have the confidence of his officers for proper administration—what Hamilton called "energy in the executive") with a legislative confirmation check. But one struggles to see how this relates to the appointment of extraordinarily independent federal judges. The Constitution presented a radical shift back to executive judicial appointment, as under the British constitution, after all of the revolutionary states had adopted legislative appointment (until New York and Massachusetts). And the new Constitution did not provide for removal by bill of address, either. Hamilton took it for granted in *Federalist* 9 that lifelong good-behavior tenure ranked among the great improvements recently made in the science of politics.

Hamilton then tried to reassure his readers that they had nothing to fear from this extraordinary independence. In a phrase that would later provide an ironic title to works about judicial supremacy, he said that it would always comprise "the least dangerous branch," because it possessed neither the legislature's purse nor the executive's sword. Its power would depend entirely on its reason, judgment, and persuasion. Here he cited Montesquieu's description of the judicial power as "next to nothing." One can fairly accuse Hamilton of dissembling here, "cloaking" the powerful judiciary that he wanted.[54]

He then presented what many consider to be the most compelling justification for judicial review ever made, and the one that John Marshall would reiterate in *Marbury v. Madison*. The "rights of the courts to pronounce legislative acts void" did not make them superior to legislatures. It simply meant that courts, as much as legislatures, must defer to the people and the people's Constitution, which they had made a higher, fundamental law. It would defeat the purpose of having a written constitution if the judges could ignore it when considering a legislative act that violated it. This logical argument has convinced most students, but some argue that Hamilton begged the question, taking for granted that courts must interpret the Constitution as they would an ordinary law, rather than as a "political" law, which courts have no right to construe. The most celebrated expression of this viewpoint came from Pennsylvania judge John Bannister Gibson in the 1825 case of *Eakin v. Raub*.[55] Hamilton conceded that judges might abuse this power, but he countered that "if it proved anything, [it] would prove that there ought to be no judges distinct from" the legislature.

This part of Hamilton's argument accorded with Madison's views. Madison recognized the threat of judicial power but considered it necessary. He told Thomas Jefferson, on reviewing a draft of a constitution for Virginia, "As the courts are generally the last in making their decision, it results to them, by refusing or not refusing to execute a law, to stamp it with its final character. This makes the judicial department paramount in fact to the legislature, which was never intended, and can never be proper." Years later, when Jefferson had become the archfoe of the federal judiciary, Madison still insisted on the necessity of judicial review. "The abuse of a trust does not disprove its existence," he wrote.[56] As in so many other areas of American politics, Madison clearly grasped the central dilemma of judicial power.

Hamilton went further still. A strong judiciary would provide protections for "the rights of individuals" and against "oppressions of the minor party" from "unjust and partial laws." He gave the clearest contemporary statement of judicial review not just for the courts' self-defense ("cases of a judiciary nature," involving trial by jury or judicial process), or even for general constitutional violations, but for policy reasons—to prevent unwise and partial legislation, especially what nineteenth-century jurists would call "class legislation," or laws enacted not for the public good but to benefit one class at the expense of another. Again Hamilton reassured readers that they need not fear the abuse of this power, as it would take "uncommon fortitude" for judges to stand up to the demands of a determined majority in a democratic society. But he did note that "the benefits of the integrity and moderation of the judiciary have already been felt in more States than one," no doubt with his own case of *Rutgers v. Waddington* in mind.

To Anti-Federalist fears of "equity" jurisdiction running amok, Hamilton simply claimed, in *Federalist* 81, "There is not a syllable in the plan . . . which *directly* empowers the national courts to construe the laws according to the spirit of the Constitution," any more than state courts could. In response to their fears that the new system would wipe out the state courts, he noted that Congress's power to establish "tribunals inferior to the Supreme Court" provided no license to abolish state courts. Indeed, Congress could and probably would share Article III jurisdiction with them. He further noted that nobody could sue a state in the new federal courts. "It is inherent in the nature of sovereignty not to be amenable to the suit of an individual *without its consent*. Unless, therefore, there is a surrender of this immunity in the plan of the convention," they had no cause to worry. In fact, the early Supreme Court would hold that the states *had* surrendered that immunity, which quickly led to the Eleventh Amendment.

In the longest *Federalist* paper (83), Hamilton defended the lack of a guarantee of jury trials in civil, as opposed to criminal, cases. He pointed out that the states used a variety of procedures in civil cases, so the Constitution should not impose one on all of them. Hamilton noted that the Constitution did not *forbid* juries in civil cases, and that Congress might well provide for them. But ultimately "I must acknowledge that I cannot readily discern the inseparable connection between the existence of liberty and the trial by jury in civil cases."[57] The Federalists lost on this point, as the Seventh Amendment would guarantee juries in lawsuits of more than twenty dollars. But this provision of the Bill of Rights still does not apply to the states, and the civil jury has all but disappeared in America.[58]

THE BILL OF RIGHTS

The federal judiciary fared well in the state ratifying conventions.[59] Supporters and opponents both assumed that the federal courts would exercise *some* kind of judicial review. James Wilson expressed one of the first of these assumptions in the Pennsylvania convention, in December 1787: "If a law should be made inconsistent with those powers vested by this instrument in Congress, the judges, as a consequence of their independence, and the particular powers of government being defined, will declare such law to be null and void, for the power of the Constitution predominates." Oliver Ellsworth made the same point a month later in Connecticut: "If the general legislature should at any time overleap their limits, the judicial department is a constitutional check."[60]

At the Virginia convention, Patrick Henry praised the state judges who refused to submit to legislative encroachment in the *Judges Case*.[61] John Marshall went further and argued that the new federal courts would keep Congress within its bounds and thus protect the states. "If [Congress] were to make a law not warranted by any of the powers enumerated," he told the delegates, "it would be considered by the judges as an infringement of the Constitution which they are to guard. They would not consider such a law as coming under their jurisdiction. They would declare it void."[62]

The Federalists had to give way on a bill of rights, and this did involve the judiciary. James Wilson, in one of the first defenses of the proposed Constitution, argued against a bill of rights. Unlike state constitutions, in the federal Constitution "everything which is not given is reserved," and it contained no grants of power that would violate traditional rights.[63] In *Federalist 84*, Hamilton made a similar argument, stressing that the new government had only limited, enumerated powers. In general governments like those of the states, one could assume that the government had the power unless a bill of rights contained an exception. The opposite assumption obtained in the federal Constitution. Here rights remained the rule, power the exception. Indeed, Hamilton argued that a bill of rights presented a hazard, because it would undermine this assumption and "afford a colorable pretext to claim more than was granted. For why declare that things shall not be done which there is no power to do?"

Hamilton presented a compelling structural and logical argument, but he did not strictly adhere to it, for he also argued that the Constitution already contained bill of rights provisions—preserving the writ of habeas corpus and prohibiting ex post facto laws and bills of attainder. Similarly, in *Federalist* 78, Hamilton argued that an independent judiciary was especially needed under a "limited constitution," which he defined as "one which contains certain specified exceptions to the legislative authority." This made the federal Constitution resemble those of the states, which assumed power and made rights the exception. Courts would protect these enumerated rights by their power "to declare all acts contrary to the manifest tenor of the Constitution void."[64]

Some of the Federalists made informal assurances that they would propose a bill of rights after ratification. Though some Federalists wanted to renege on this promise, James Madison (who had agreed with Hamilton's opposition to a bill of rights) took up the project in the First Congress. He believed that a bill of rights would win over Anti-Federalist opponents of the Constitution and give the new system a widespread legitimacy. At the same time, he did not want the amendments to impair any essential power of the federal government. As a result, most of the Bill of Rights appeared anodyne and cosmetic, truly redundant under the original *Federalist* 84 theory. In fact, we can hardly call them amendments, because they did not change anything. The First Amendment, for example, prohibits Congress from establishing a religion, which it never had any power to do. Anti-Federalist Aedanus Burke complained of the insubstantial amendments, calling them "little better than whip syllabub" (a frothy pudding) and "a tub thrown to a whale" (a method by which sailors tried to distract dangerous sea creatures).[65]

A few of the amendments did specify or clarify open questions. As mentioned, the Seventh Amendment required jury trials in civil suits over twenty dollars and made sure that appellate courts could not review any fact tried by a jury. The bulk of the other amendments (four through eight) provided details about criminal procedure. In Congress, Madison said that these amendments would do no harm and would help the federal courts protect rights, a position which Jefferson had urged upon him.[66] Jefferson recommended it for the "legal check which it puts into the hands of the judiciary."[67]

Madison had always had doubts about judicial review—its efficacy, not its legitimacy if appropriately limited. He kept up his campaign for a council of revision because he preferred to prevent enactment of unconstitutional laws rather than to strike them down after enactment. Madison hoped the Bill of Rights would strengthen the second-best option of judicial review.[68] He reiterated to the First Congress Jefferson's point that "independent tribunals of justice will consider themselves in a peculiar manner the guardians of those rights; they will be an impenetrable bulwark against every assumption of power in the legislature or executive."[69]

But the Bill of Rights did almost nothing to empower the federal judiciary, and it remained a constitutional dead letter for over a century because it applied only to the national government. Madison in the House wanted to apply the Bill of Rights to the states as well, but the Senate prevented that. Those who demanded a bill of rights did not primarily want to protect individual rights but to protect state power to regulate rights.[70] Thus, the First Amendment protected the religious establishments in states that maintained them. Madison's draft resolution read, "No state shall violate the equal rights of conscience, or the freedom of the press, or the trial by jury in criminal cases." But the final version read, "Congress shall make no law . . ." Much of the Bill of Rights concerns state *institutions*—churches, militia, and juries. Though not undisputed, almost everyone understood that the Bill of Rights applied only to the national government before and after the Supreme Court declared it so in 1833.[71]

THE JUDICIARY ACT OF 1789

While Madison and the House put together the Bill of Rights, the Senate got the ball rolling on establishing the judicial system under Article III. Oliver Ellsworth of Connecticut and William Paterson of New Jersey mainly drafted the first Judiciary Act.[72] These two delegates at the Constitutional Convention had promoted the Connecticut or Great Compromise and the New Jersey Plan. Like the Bill of Rights, their Judiciary Act provided concessions to the small-state Federalists without crippling the new government.[73] The early Senate met behind closed doors, so we have little legislative history for this landmark statute. Readers would find several of its provisions notably murky.[74]

The first federal judicial system mixed national and state powers.[75] The act established a Supreme Court of a chief justice and five associate justices.

It also established "inferior" courts—thirteen district courts (one for each state). The Supreme Court justices and district court judges would together compose six intermediate "circuit courts." It divided jurisdiction among these courts; district courts had exclusive admiralty jurisdiction, circuit courts heard most criminal and diversity cases and some appeals from district courts. Most important, it shared with state courts many cases to which Article III said that "the judicial power *shall* extend," especially in small suits. High Federalists objected to the sharing of power with state courts, whose judges did not have the independence of federal judges. The justices of the Supreme Court would complain for decades about having to "ride circuit"—to traverse the country over primitive roads to hear cases that they might hear again on the Supreme Court. Some argued that to have Supreme Court justices hear original cases on circuit, beyond those of the limited range outlined in Article III, violated the Constitution.

The Federalists especially cherished section 25, which permitted appeals from the highest court of a state to the Supreme Court, "where is drawn in question the validity of a treaty or statue of, or an authority exercised under the United States, and the decision is against their validity," or where a state court decided in *favor* of a state power in conflict with a federal claim.[76] This put teeth into the supremacy clause and probably did more than any other law to keep the Union together. Over a century later, Justice Oliver Wendell Holmes Jr. would note that the Union depended on this "federal" or vertical judicial review, while it could have done without "coordinate" or horizontal judicial review. For more than a century, nearly all of the controversies over judicial power would concern section 25 review.

Other provisions of the Judiciary Act assuaged Anti-Federalist concerns. Section 11 prohibited suits in federal court "to recover the contents of any promissory note or other chose [debt or bond] in action" that a creditor had assigned to a citizen of another state—in short, to prevent the manufacturing of "diversity" standing to get from state into federal court. (Many Anti-Federalists assumed that state courts would sympathize with small debtors while federal courts would truckle to powerful creditors.) Section 14 prohibited federal judges from freeing prisoners in state prisons by habeas corpus. Other provisions attempted to cabin the much-feared admiralty and equity power of federal courts. Section 9 gave suitors in admiralty cases "a common law remedy, where the common law is competent to give it," and section 16 held that "suits in equity shall not be sustained . . . in any case where plain, adequate and complete remedy may be had at [common] law."

Finally, section 34 appeared to compel federal courts to use state law when hearing diversity cases. "The laws of the several states, except where the Constitution, treaties, or statutes of the United States shall otherwise require or provide, shall be regarded as rules of decision in trials at common law in the courts of the United States in cases where they apply." But this may rather have instructed the federal courts to use American ("several" here meaning "all," not "each") rather than British common law, until Congress promulgated a federal law code.[77] The obscure language of section 34 left uncertain not only what it meant by "the laws of the several states"; it also did not identify the "cases where they apply." A twentieth-century commentator described the wording as "almost perversely uninformative."[78]

Some hail the Judiciary Act of 1789. The eminent legal historian Jules Goebel wrote that of the acts of the First Congress, "none [was] more astutely contrived" than this. James Madison, on the other hand, considered it "defective both in its general structure and many of its particular regulations," but he considered it necessary to get the system in operation immediately.[79]

THE JUDICIARY IN THE 1790S

The new judicial branch labored little and inconspicuously for its first decade, until it got caught up in the highly partisan atmosphere of the late 1790s. George Washington chose prominent Federalists as the first Supreme Court justices in September 1789. He made John Jay of New York, author of some Federalist Papers, the first chief justice. Washington also made sure that the associate justices represented the breadth of the country, choosing William Cushing of Massachusetts, James Wilson of Pennsylvania, John Blair of Virginia, and John Rutledge of South Carolina. Robert Harrison of Maryland declined an appointment; James Iredell of North Carolina took his place.

The High Court decided no cases until 1792; the justices' opinions came only in their circuit court service. Chief Justice Jay drafted (but did not send) a letter to Washington in September 1790 saying that the circuit courts unconstitutionally melded Article III original and appellate roles and also effectively transferred the appointment power from the president to Congress.[80] The justices carried out circuit duty nevertheless, which would become an important precedent.

Although some years transpired before the Supreme Court rendered any important decisions, the Constitution did not remain uninterpreted. Rather, Congress and the president made decisions on the meaning of the document. As Publius put it in *Federalist 37*, "All new laws, though penned with the greatest technical skill, and passed on the fullest and most mature deliberation, are considered more or less obscure and equivocal, until their meaning be liquidated and ascertained by a series of particular *discussions and adjudications*" (emphasis mine). Adjudication—court interpretations—determined part but not all of what the Constitution meant. The "departmental" theory of constitutional interpretation expressed this idea that all three branches had an equal power and duty of constitutional interpretation.

More recently, scholars have distinguished this older tradition of constitutional "construction" as thriving alongside modern judicial "interpretation."[81] Departmentalism and construction have become the principal rivals to judicial supremacy. Madison applied it in the debate over "executive privilege" in 1796. He objected that the president sought to define not just his own power but that of the House of Representatives. "It belonged to each department to judge for itself" what its powers were.[82]

The First Congress had to consider the question of the removal of federal officials. Article II, section 2 prescribed the filling of offices, but the Constitution said nothing about removal except by impeachment. Congressmen presented several theories; ultimately, they decided that the president had plenary removal power. Successor statesmen venerated this decision as the "Rule of 1789." James Madison, in the House, denied that Congress could leave this question to the courts to decide.[83] Congress and the president would wrangle over this issue again, but the Court did not take it up for well over a century. Similarly, Congress considered the extent of its power to "delegate" decision-making to the president or departments in the establishment of postal routes.[84] The Bank of the United States, in Congress, in the administration, and between Congress and the president, presented the most high-profile episode of constitutional construction in the early republic.

George Washington also contributed to several important constitutional constructions, mostly involving foreign policy. His unilateral decision to proclaim neutrality led to a celebrated pseudonymous debate between erstwhile *Federalist* collaborators James Madison and Alexander Hamilton. Washington also established what the twentieth century would call "executive privilege" in thwarting a House attempt to inquire into the negotiation of the Jay Treaty.

The first federal judges tried as much as possible to keep out of political controversy, considering themselves legal rather than political actors. They believed that a distinction existed between law and politics (or right and might, or judgment and will). One does not need to collapse into legal realism (that is, to deny any distinction between law and politics) to recognize that judges cannot escape *some* measure of politics in adjudication, particularly in a high court like that of the US Supreme Court. But constitutional government (government limited by law) depends on minimizing this overlap of law and politics. And even a confessed legal realist judge would have to act as if the difference existed, to give the appearance of keeping out of politics, lest they undermine the raison d'être of a separate, independent judiciary. Judicial supremacy depended upon maintaining this image.[85]

The first important Supreme Court decision involved the justices' refusal to settle Continental Army veterans' claims brought under the Invalid Pension Act of 1792. The act permitted review of their adjudications by the secretary of war. Several of the justices wrote to the president of their unwillingness to serve in a nonjudicial role, notwithstanding their "duty to receive with all possible respect every act of the legislature." When the attorney general sought a writ from the Supreme Court to order the circuit court judges (most of whom sat on the bench before him) to follow the law, the Supreme Court took the case "under advisement," and in the meantime Congress amended the act to its satisfaction.[86]

Insofar as the Court declared the Invalid Pension Act unconstitutional (as the attorney general believed it had), this evinced a minimal, self-defense standard of review, as the act infringed judicial power.[87] This decision reflected the Constitutional Convention's rejection of the council of revision idea, which would have mingled the judicial with the executive power too much. As Hamilton wrote in *Federalist* 73, "It is impossible to keep the judges too distinct from every other avocation than that of expounding the laws."

In the Invalid Pension case, the justices told President Washington that they preferred not to offer an "advisory opinion" rather than deciding an actual "case or controversy." In 1793, the Court made it clear that it would not provide advice to the administration about questions of international law, with regard to the United States' treaty obligations to France. Chief Justice Jay referred to "strong arguments against the propriety of our extra-judicially deciding the questions alluded to, especially as the power given by the Constitution to the president, of calling on the heads of departments for opinions, seems to have been *purposely* as well as expressly limited to the *executive* departments."[88] In the Middle Ages, when judges acted as executive officers, they routinely advised the monarch. But in the eighteenth century, an increasingly independent judiciary ceased to advise the king, and American judges continued that trend.[89]

The first Supreme Court decision to arouse controversy, *Chisholm v. Georgia,* involved a lawsuit by British creditors to recover debts from the state of Georgia. The case arose from the Article III grant of federal jurisdiction in "controversies between a state and citizens of another state." Despite assurances by Hamilton (in *Federalist* 81), John Marshall (at the Virginia ratifying convention), and others, a majority of the Court held that the states had surrendered immunity from suit. Moreover, the majority based its opinion not just on the text of Article III but also on "principles of general jurisprudence" and the nature of the Union—something like the "spirit" of the Constitution.

Intense state reaction quickly ensued. One house of the Georgia legislature threatened death to any federal marshal or other official who tried to enforce the decision. Cooler heads prevailed and Congress proposed an amendment to secure state sovereign immunity. What became the Eleventh Amendment, ratified in 1795, read, "The judicial power of the United States shall not be construed to extend to any suit in law or equity, commenced or prosecuted against one of the United States by citizens of another state, or by citizens or subjects of any foreign state."[90]

The question arises: Did it require a constitutional amendment to overturn this decision? One can argue that the Court got *Chisholm* wrong, and thus that the Eleventh Amendment (like most of its ten predecessors) really did not change anything.[91] If so, the resort to amendment made it seem that the Court had no *equal* in constitutional interpretation. Could Congress have restored the correct meaning of the Constitution by statute, removing such suits from original and appellate jurisdiction of the federal courts? This would have required something close to abolishing all the lower federal courts and leaving the state courts as "ordained" to exercise the judicial power that "shall extend" to cases "between a state and citizens of another state." To misinterpret the Constitution—for a court to declare a rule not in accord with the Constitution, as either against the Constitution or not required by it—resembles unconstitutional legislation. Erroneous court interpretations should not require correction by amendment any more than unconstitutional statutes do. Corrective legislation will do, or even defiance with the acquiescence of other branches (including the states).

In the mid-1790s, the government had enough trouble just keeping the Supreme Court staffed. In May 1791, Justice Rutledge resigned to become chief justice of South Carolina, having heard no cases on the US Supreme Court.

Thomas Johnson replaced him the next year but resigned less than six months later due to ill health. Chief Justice Jay resigned in 1795 to run for governor of New York. He told President John Adams, who tried to get him to return to the chief justiceship in 1801, "I left the bench perfectly convinced that under a system so defective it should not obtain the energy, weight and dignity which are essential to affording due support to the national government." To return would only lend legitimacy to the defective system.[92]

Washington made Rutledge chief justice in 1795, as an interim appointment. Rutledge, though, denounced the Jay Treaty, support for which had become a litmus test for Senate Federalists. Rutledge also showed signs of alcohol abuse and insanity, and the Senate rejected him at the end of the year. Oliver Ellsworth eventually took the center seat. Justice Blair had resigned in the meantime. Corruption forced his likely successor, Attorney General Edmund Randolph, to resign his own office. The Supreme Court vacancy went to Samuel Chase, who would become the only Supreme Court justice ever impeached. In August 1798, Justice Wilson did time in debtors' prison, and he probably would have been impeached and removed, had he lived.[93]

Business, and controversy, began to pick up for the Supreme Court in 1796.[94] The Court struck down a Virginia debt-sequestration law as a violation of the Treaty of Paris. The case made an important assertion of federal supremacy. At the same time, the state solicited federal judicial review to protect state law against what it regarded as an unconstitutional federal act. (Ironically, John Marshall represented Virginia and lost the only argument he ever made before the Supreme Court—argued in the hope that the court would do what he had told the Virginia ratification convention it would do.) Justice Chase noted that Virginia supposed "that this court possesses a power to decide whether this . . . treaty is within the authority delegated to [Congress] by the Articles of Confederation. Whether this court constitutionally possesses such a power is not now necessary to determine. . . . If the Court possesses a power to declare treaties *void*, I shall never exercise it, but in a clear case indeed."[95]

That same term, the Court upheld a federal tax on carriages over a challenge that, as a "direct tax," Congress must apportion it among the states according to population. The parties clearly colluded. They stipulated that the plaintiff owned 125 "chariots," in order to make the case exceed the dollar-amount threshold to get into federal court. They agreed that if he lost his case, he would only have to pay a sixteen-dollar tax, which the government would pay for him. This suggested that the limitation of judicial power to genuine "cases or controversies" would not pose much of an obstacle to judicial review.

The question of what distinguished a direct from an indirect tax would have a long history, culminating in the Sixteenth Amendment (see appendix C). But in this case, the Court simply limited direct taxes to people and real estate and upheld the tax. It implied, though, that the decision could have gone the other way, and that the parties and Court assumed judicial power to overturn acts of Congress.[96] Justice Chase again expressed the "doubtful case" rule, that the Court should only void laws which were clear violations of the Constitution. Justice Paterson relied for his opinion on the history of the Constitutional Convention, noting that the direct tax clause was meant to benefit the southern slave states and "ought not to be extended by construction."

The Court also began to consider whether it had power to resort to natural law principles in its adjudication. The Anti-Federalists had warned that interpreting the Constitution according to its "spirit" would destroy all its limitations (though it might also allow judges to impose their own, rather than the Constitution's limits). Justice Paterson, on circuit in 1795, told a jury that the right to property "is one of the natural, inherent, and inalienable rights of man. . . . The preservation of property is a primary object of the social compact." A state law that took property from one citizen and gave it to another "is inconsistent with the principles of reason, justice, and moral rectitude . . . contrary both to the letter and the spirit of the Constitution."[97] But if a state act violated the letter, nobody need resort to its spirit.

The issue presented itself more clearly in a Supreme Court case of 1798. Considering a Connecticut law overturning the decision of a probate court, Justice Chase said, "An act of the legislature (for I cannot call it a *law*) contrary to the *great first principles of the social compact*; cannot be considered a *rightful exercise* of *legislative* authority," and he gave several examples of such violations. Justice Iredell concurred in the result but disputed Chase's natural law reasoning. "The Court cannot pronounce [a law] to be void, merely because it is, in their judgment, contrary to the principles of natural justice. The ideas of natural justice are regulated by no fixed standard: the ablest and the purest men have differed upon the subject." If positive laws violated natural justice, the Court had no power to annul them. "It is true, that some speculative jurists have held, that a legislative act against natural justice must, in itself, be void; but I cannot think that, under such a government, any court of justice would possess a power to declare it so."[98] He went on to quote Blackstone in opposition to Chase's implied Coke. The many who still denied that courts could consult the text of the Constitution would, even more, excoriate judicial forays beyond the text.

Alexander Hamilton's domestic policies had begun to divide the United States into parties. The wars of the French Revolution further split the country into pro-British Federalist and pro-French Republican parties. The federal judiciary became embroiled in this bitter conflict when the national government began to prosecute its critics for "seditious libel." The Federalists' assumption that they could prosecute under a federal common law of crimes especially alarmed the Republicans.[99] The Founding generation held to the maxim that in any government, the judicial power must extend as far as the legislative. "If there are such things as political axioms," Hamilton had written in *Federalist* 80, "the propriety of the judicial power of a government being coextensive with its legislative may be ranked among the number." A government that can make laws must have courts to enforce them.

A federal common law presented the reciprocal: if the judiciary invoked the common law (which included just about everything under the sun), then Congress's power must extend just as far. (Before the nineteenth century, most legislation adjusted the unwritten, judge-discovered common law.) This would obliterate the idea of a Congress limited to its enumerated powers. Jefferson said, "I consider all the encroachments made on [the Constitution] heretofore as nothing, as mere retail stuff, compared with the wholesale doctrine, that there is a common law in force in the United States." His future antagonist John Marshall agreed, calling it a "strange and absurd doctrine."[100]

The Federalist Congress, anticipating war with France in 1798, enacted a sedition statute to clarify the common law. The act perfectly illustrated Hamilton's prophetic admonition against a bill of rights in *Federalist* 84. "What signifies a declaration that 'the liberty of the press shall be inviolably preserved'?" he asked. "What is the liberty of the press? Who can give it any definition which would not leave the utmost latitude for evasion?"

The Federalists, however, could claim that their act ameliorated the British common law of seditious libel. In 1798, "freedom of the press" in Great Britain meant only "no prior restraint"—no licensing or censorship, but liability for harm done after publication. Truthfulness could not defeat a libel charge. Indeed, England adopted the legal maxim of "the greater the truth, the greater the libel," to inhibit the scandal of publicizing the real faults of the king or his ministry. Also, juries only determined the question of fact: Did the accused publish the piece? The legal question—Does the piece libel?—belonged to the judge.

The Sedition Act allowed truth as a defense and allowed juries to decide on the libelous (false and malicious) nature of the publication. It adopted the standard that the jury had established in the Zenger case in New York in 1735. But these safeguards often proved worthless. Federalist marshals packed juries with Federalist jurors. Judges told those jurors that malicious intent inhered in the act of publication and that the defendant had to prove true every particular in the publication; the slightest false detail vitiated the truth defense. The federal circuit courts convicted about thirty Republican editors and imposed heavy fines and prison sentences. They acquitted only one.

Admittedly, some Republican defendants made inept defenses and seemed to court martyrdom. When Matthew Lyon, a Vermont representative, faced prosecution for denouncing President Adams's "continual grasp for power . . . unbounded thirst for ridiculous pomp, foolish adulation, and selfish avarice," he called Justice Paterson, one of the judges on the bench, as his only witness. Lyon asked Paterson "whether he had not frequently dined with the president, and observed his ridiculous pomp and parade." Paterson replied that he had only rarely dined with Adams and had seen, "on the contrary, a great deal of plainness and republican simplicity." Lyons then asked whether Paterson had not seen at the president's residence "more pomp and servants, than at the tavern in Rutland?" "To this no answer was given. No other witnesses were called." Lyons got four months in prison, a thousand-dollar fine, and court costs, when his witness returned to the bench. Charged again when he complained about his imprisonment, he eluded the federal marshal and returned to Congress.[101]

The Sedition Act (along with other war preparations, especially new taxes and an expanded army) fueled Republican mobilization in the elections of 1800 and made the partisan judiciary a political target. Before the Sedition Act, the Republicans did not oppose judicial power per se. Indeed, many of them criticized the federal courts for their laxity, for failing to overturn the Sedition Act and other Federalist legislation, such as the Bank of the United States. (The Judiciary Act did not provide for appeals to the Supreme Court in criminal cases, so it never ruled on the act.[102] But none of the Supreme Court justices who heard Sedition Act cases on circuit—five of the six—held against it.) The most important expressions of opposition to the Sedition Act, the Virginia and Kentucky Resolutions, ignored the courts, preferring some kind of organized state protest against the act.[103] They defined the Constitution as a compact among the states "with no common judge," and seemed to posit a state role in constitutional construction as an alternative to judicial review.

But Federalist responses to the resolutions made a vocal argument for judicial power, and perhaps even for judicial supremacy. As early as the First

Congress, Elbridge Gerry had said that "the judges are the constitutional umpires. . . . We are not the expositors of the Constitution, the judges are the expositors of the Constitution and acts of Congress."[104] The Rhode Island legislature contended that the Constitution "vests in the federal courts, exclusively, and in the Supreme Court . . . ultimately, the authority of deciding on the constitutionality of any act." Massachusetts declared that "the constructions of all laws made in pursuance" of the Constitution "are exclusively vested by the people in the federal courts." New Hampshire and Vermont also referred to the exclusive power of interpretation by the judiciary.[105] The perceived extremism of the Virginia and Kentucky Resolutions may have augmented judicial power.[106]

The Republicans won the presidency and both houses of Congress in the 1800 elections, though, due to a tie in the Electoral College, the lame-duck Federalist House did not make the choice of Thomas Jefferson over Aaron Burr until February of 1801. In the last weeks of the last Federalist Congress, the party decided to expand the size and scope of the federal, not to say Federalist, courts.

The Judiciary Act of 1801 eliminated the dual Supreme Court justices–district judge circuit court system and established a freestanding set of circuit courts, with sixteen new circuit judges. Adams appointed none but Federalists, the notorious "midnight judges," in the last days of his administration. The act multiplied the number of district courts and broke up their association with state boundaries in what looked to Republicans like an assault on state identity. The act also reduced the Supreme Court from six justices to five, which would deny the incoming president the opportunity to fill the first vacancy. It did away with most of the jurisdictional compromises of the 1789 act, bringing federal judicial power near its Article III maximum. Republicans claimed that wealthy land speculators stood to gain from having their cases heard in federal rather than state courts. But the Federalists had legitimate reasons to reform the federal courts (especially the elimination of circuit riding), and Congress had shaped the bill long before the election.[107] Even so, this last-minute act by a lame-duck president and Congress looked like a clear gambit to entrench a defeated party in the life-tenured branch of the government. A Kentucky representative called it an act "providing pensions for the principals and adherents of a party."[108]

Jefferson had hoped that a bill of rights would enable the judiciary to protect individual rights, and Republicans lamented that the federal courts did not do more to invalidate the Alien and Sedition Acts. Now he said, "The Federalists have retired into the judiciary as a stronghold, and from that battery all the works of republicanism are to be beaten down and erased."[109] Jefferson made a curious, even preposterous, claim. The Republicans aimed to beat down and erase the works of Hamiltonian Federalism (the bank, the army, even the Judiciary Act), if not the Union itself.[110] Normally, courts can tear down better than they can build up. But the new president would find occasions enough to clash with the Federalist courts. Jefferson would threaten the judicial independence that the Federalists had established, not the judicial supremacy that he *feared* they had imposed.

3

THE MARSHALL COURT

JEFFERSON V. MARSHALL

Thomas Jefferson's election led to the first great challenge to federal judicial power and produced recurrent clashes with the new chief justice. Ultimately, Chief Justice John Marshall would save the Founders' independent Court and make a major contribution to preserving the American Union. He would not, however, as many frequently claim, lay the basis for today's sovereign court.[1]

Personalities figured largely in this conflict. The two men (second cousins) shared a mutual dislike. John Marshall's personality contributed to his successful unification and defense of the Court. Good-humored and gregarious, Marshall knew how to lead with a light touch—a skill perhaps acquired as the oldest of fifteen children. Though Jefferson associated Marshall with the aristocratic or monarchical Federalists, most others saw him as a man of the people—unpretentious, even slovenly. He had a common touch that the putatively populist Jefferson lacked. Jefferson derided but perhaps envied the "lax and lounging manner" that made Marshall popular in Richmond society.[2] One Federalist congressman described him as "attached to pleasures, with convivial habits, strongly fixed," and "indolent."[3] His conviviality served him well in small-group leadership, and he would display other traits as he took the Court from the obscurity of the 1790s to the prominence of coordinate equality in the federal system.

The Federalists of 1800 had split into High Federalists, associated with Alexander Hamilton, and moderates, who aligned with President John Adams. The High Federalists did not want Marshall as chief justice but had to accept him, as little time remained for the Adams administration in December 1800.[4] Adams had offered the position to John Jay, but Jay declined to return to a Court that he regarded as insignificant. In retirement, Adams said that "the proudest act of my life was the gift of John Marshall to the people of the United States." Marshall had opposed the Sedition Act and voted for its repeal in his one term in the House of Representatives—though he never called it unconstitutional, and may have written a defense of it.[5] On the Court, Marshall would help keep the High Federalists at bay.

Jefferson's Republicans had fractured as well, between moderates and radicals. Among the radicals—known as Old Republicans or "Quids"—Virginia representative John Randolph stood out. Jefferson would ultimately contain them and arrive, rather despite himself, at an accommodation with Marshall. Although he initially favored Burr over Jefferson, Marshall seems to have anticipated this, regarding Jefferson as a trimmer. He told Alexander Hamilton that Jefferson "will embody himself with the House of Representatives. By weakening the office of President he will increase his personal power. He will diminish his responsibility, sap the fundamental principles of the government" and become a party leader. On inauguration day, Marshall paid the new president a backhanded compliment in a letter to Charles Cotesworth Pinckney: "The democrats are divided into speculative theorists and absolute terrorists. With the latter I am not disposed to class Mr. Jefferson."[6] Marshall would refer to the sage of Monticello as "the lama of the mountains."

Despite his occasional rhetorical excesses, Jefferson became a moderate. Abroad while the Federalists drafted the Constitution, he largely supported it. He did recommend that Virginia withhold ratification until they added a bill of rights. He praised *the Federalist* and prescribed it for the curriculum at the University of Virginia. James Madison would give him ballast, moderating his more extreme expressions.

Jefferson did not underestimate his cousin. He recognized Marshall's great powers of persuasion but regarded him as a cunning casuist. He told Joseph Story, "When conversing with Marshall I never admit anything. So soon as you admit any position to be good, no matter how remote from the conclusion he seeks to establish, you are gone. So great is his sophistry you must never give him an affirmative answer or you will be forced to grant his conclusion. Why, if he were to ask me if it were daylight or not, I'd reply, 'Sir, I don't know, I can't tell.'"[7] Marshall said that Jefferson once called on him and "wrote that he was lucky to find that you were out," and inserted "un-" before "lucky." Marshall called this the one occasion on which "Jefferson came very near to writing me the truth."[8]

Scholars remain uncertain about Jefferson's attitude toward the lame-duck Judiciary Act of 1801 or when he came to favor its repeal. He made a famously mollifying inaugural address in March 1801 ("We are all republicans, we are all federalists"), much to the relief of moderate Federalists like Marshall. The new chief justice administered the oath of office to his cousin and called the address "well judged and conciliatory."[9] The address made no reference to the judiciary. His first message to Congress did not come until it convened in December. Jefferson warned about the expense of maintaining numerous federal officers but said only that "the judiciary system of the United States, and especially that portion of it recently enacted, will of course present itself to the contemplation of Congress," well expressing Jefferson's overt effacement of presidential power and covert control through the party.

The Republicans' act of March 1802 basically repealed the act of 1801 and thus restored the act of 1789. (They made some further amendments in April.) Federalists all opposed it and Republicans were divided; the act passed the Senate by a 16–15 margin. But could Congress constitutionally abolish the new circuit judges' offices? Federalists argued that the repeal violated the good-behavior tenure specified by the Constitution. The Republicans said that they could remove Federalist judges by doing away with their courts. The repeal amounted to a bill of address, removing judges by simple majority vote of the legislature. The April act deferred the next session of the Supreme Court until February 1803, another interesting exercise of congressional control of the Court. Did Congress have this power to suspend the exercise of judicial power? Could it require the justices to convene every tenth year, on Mars?

John Marshall and the incumbent Supreme Court justices could have defied the repeal by refusing to return to circuit riding, the burden of which the 1801 act had relieved them. The High Federalists, spoiling for a fight, advocated this. Marshall caviled, and polled his brethren. All but Justice Chase agreed that even if the circuit duty violated the Constitution, they had accepted it for too long to repudiate it now.[10] The justices soon acted on this understanding. Marshall upheld the repeal act on circuit, and the Supreme Court upheld that decision in February 1803 (Marshall recused himself). "Congress have constitutional authority to establish from time to time such inferior courts as they may think proper," Justice Paterson wrote, "and to transfer a cause from one such tribunal to another." He noted that the claim that it violated Article III for the Supreme Court justices to serve as circuit judges "is of recent date, and it is sufficient to observe, that practice and acquiescence under it for a period of several years, commencing with the organization of the system, affords an irrefutable answer, and has indeed fixed the construction."[11]

MARBURY V. MADISON

The initiation of the case that would become *Marbury v. Madison* apparently induced Jefferson to pursue repeal.[12] In February 1801, Congress passed an act to organize courts for the District of Columbia. It provided for the appointment of some forty-two justices of the peace for five-year terms—more "midnight judges." The president appointed and Senate confirmed these officers, including William Marbury. The president signed Marbury's commission and Secretary of State John Marshall sealed it, but did not deliver it.[13]

This began the next episode in the conflict between the Jefferson administration and the Federalist judiciary. This case has become the cornerstone of judicial supremacy, but it acquired this reputation only relatively recently. Its significance in 1803 really had nothing to do with judicial review of legislation, and the decision all but completely disappeared for decades to come. Beginning in the 1890s, and especially in the late twentieth century, however, the bar and bench turned *Marbury* into the icon of judicial power.[14] Thus, we must establish in some detail what the case really involved and not view it anachronistically.

Marbury brought his suit before the Supreme Court in its original jurisdiction, asking it to issue an order (a *mandamus*) to James Madison, the new secretary of state, to deliver his commission. Section 13 of the Judiciary Act stated, "The Supreme Court shall also have appellate jurisdiction from the circuit courts and courts of the several states, in the cases herein after specially provided for; and shall have power to issue writs of prohibition to the district courts, when proceeding as courts of admiralty and maritime jurisdiction, and writs of mandamus, in cases warranted by the principles and usages of law, to any courts appointed, or persons holding office, under the authority of the United States."[15]

Notably, Marshall did not address the jurisdictional question—"Does this court have the power to decide the case?"—until after he had considered the merits of the case—"Has the applicant a right to the commission?"[16] Had he reversed the order of questions, he could have more quickly and easily disposed of the case. The fact that he chose to order the questions in this way indicated that he wanted to do more than just decide the case. Marshall would go on at some length to establish that Marbury indeed had a right to his commission, that Jefferson and Madison had indeed violated his rights, but that section 13 unconstitutionally extended the Supreme Court's original jurisdiction, so that ultimately Marbury had come to the wrong court.

The Senate had not written section 13 clearly, and one could read it as referring to the Court's appellate rather than its original jurisdiction.[17] This would have enabled the Court to dismiss the suit at the threshold, in keeping with the minimalist principle that judges should never *assume* that the legislature had violated the Constitution.

Neither can one say unequivocally that Article III establishes an upper limit to the Court's original jurisdiction. The exceptions clause might permit Congress to *expand* original jurisdiction as well as to *contract* appellate jurisdiction.[18] In other words, if section 13 *did* extend original jurisdiction, Congress had the constitutional power to do so. Marshall dismissed this possibility, saying it made the jurisdiction clause "mere surplusage." But others have suggested that it may have established jurisdiction for the time being, until Congress should by experience alter it.

Marshall's view admittedly seems more plausible, but he could have avoided the whole question had he made the still more plausible reading of section 13 as not extending original jurisdiction. More important, viewing section 13 as a constitutional extension of original jurisdiction would have compelled Marshall to issue the mandamus to Madison, who would certainly have ignored it (as he did not deign to respond to the order to show cause why the writ should not issue), exposing the powerlessness of the Court.

The bulk of Marshall's opinion addressed the merits of Marbury's case, giving the chief justice the opportunity to berate the Jefferson administration for abuse of power and to remind his cousin of the rule of law.[19] Marshall distinguished between discretionary and ministerial executive power. Courts could not review political or discretionary acts. "By the Constitution of the United States, the president is invested with certain important political powers, in the exercise of which he is to use his own discretion, and is accountable only to his country in his political character, and to his own conscience." This expressed the "political questions doctrine," that some political conflicts cannot become lawsuits.

While this might at first glance appear to be a mark of judicial restraint, it raised the question of who had the power to draw the line between the political and the ministerial.[20] Marshall held that the delivery of a signed and sealed commission involved a merely ministerial duty, which a court could order an executive officer to perform. Unfortunately for William Marbury, he brought suit in the wrong court. (The fact that he did so, and did not attempt to reopen the suit in the correct court, suggests that he participated in a collusive suit.)[21] The case as he arranged it gave Marshall the opportunity to lecture the administration on its duties without issuing an order that Jefferson could spurn.

Having adjudged section 13 to violate the Constitution, Marshall took up the question of whether the courts must still enforce an unconstitutional act or could declare it void. This became the classic statement of judicial review, in the first case in which the Court held against an act of Congress. He largely reiterated the logical argument that Hamilton had presented in *Federalist 78*. "It seems only necessary to recognize certain principles, supposed to have been long and well established, to decide it," he began. The American Constitution established a government of limited powers. "The powers of the legislature are defined, and limited; and that those limits may not be mistaken, or forgotten, the constitution is written."

The people comprised the principals, the government its agent. The ordinary lawmaking discretion of the agent came from the higher law of the Constitution. If an act of the agent appeared to violate the principal's higher law, the Court had no choice but to consult and interpret the Constitution. "It is emphatically the province and duty of the judicial department to say what the law is. Those who apply the rule to particular cases, must of necessity expound, and interpret, that rule." But Marshall made no claim that *only* the Court could interpret the Constitution. He noted that "the framers of the Constitution contemplated that instrument as a rule for the government of *courts,* as well as of the legislature." Nor did he make any claim that the Court's interpretation constituted the last word, or say how a particular decision would apply to future cases. His theory of constitutional interpretation simply expressed his idea of "judicial duty" and really did say nothing new.

At bottom, *Marbury* held that Congress could not extend the original jurisdiction of the Supreme Court. The Court had hardly entered boldly into the political arena and claimed supreme power to interpret the Constitution. Marshall refused to take more power than the Constitution gave the Court. Moreover, the case concerned a judicial writ, mandamus, something that courts had a particular interest in—what Madison had called a "case of a judiciary nature."[22]

The controversial part of the decision involved Marshall's rebuke to the administration, accusing Jefferson and Madison of "sport[ing] away the vested rights of others." He insisted that their behavior threatened the United States as "a government of laws, and not of men." When that storm blew over, the case sank into oblivion, cited only in a few cases concerning technical questions of mandamus. The next time the Court declared an act of Congress unconstitutional, in *Dred Scott* (1857), it did not mention *Marbury*. Congress accepted Marshall's view of section 13 as unconstitutional and amended it to conform to the decision. Twentieth-century jurists turned *Marbury* into a landmark case, a piece of mythmaking equivalent to that of Coke on Magna Carta in the seventeenth century.[23]

Marshall made the law/politics distinction central to the legitimacy of judicial power.[24] Much of the success of his chief justiceship depended on convincing people that the Court did law, not politics. But these terms may mislead us. "Politics" in its classical sense meant the pursuit of justice, not the mere assertion of will or power. The art of politics involved the effort of making will or power *accord* with law or right. Marshall's generation still held firmly to the idea of natural law, and of the Constitution as a "higher law"—not the natural law itself but a kind of intermediary, like the jus gentium or, as Robert Grosseteste defined equity, "halfway between legal and natural justice."[25] The sovereign American people made the Constitution, and judges must abide by that command. To exercise judicial power to change the Constitution, in what would become the "living constitution" view, threatened to make the judges sovereign. Juristocracy resulted from the breakdown in this tension between natural and positive law, as modern political theory destroyed the distinction between law and politics—or defined everything as politics.[26]

IMPEACHMENTS

The Jeffersonian Republicans also resorted to impeachment to curb the courts. Hamilton, in *Federalist* 80, called impeachment "a complete security" against judicial abuse of power. But before long the Jefferson administration would discard impeachment as a mode of political reform—"a mere scarecrow," Jefferson called it. He would have to await vacancies. Though he may not have actually complained that federal judges "seldom retire and never die," this apparently apocryphal quip surely expressed his frustration.

The Marshall Court's acquiescence in the repeal of the 1801 act dampened the Republicans' judicial purge, but New Hampshire district judge John Pickering presented an extreme case. This violently partisan Federalist displayed obvious signs of alcoholic insanity.[27] He administered an admiralty case with apparent bias toward a prominent Federalist shipowner. Article II, section 4 ordained that "all civil officers of the United States, shall be removed from office on impeachment for, and conviction of, treason, bribery, or other high crimes and misdemeanors." Given the good-behavior tenure of federal judges in Article III, impeachment seemed to offer the only way to remove them (although the 1802 repeal amounted to a de facto bill of address removal). In the congressional debate that established the so-called Rule of 1789, some argued that the Constitution made impeachment the only means to remove all civil officers. But that would make the good-behavior provision of Article III redundant.

What constituted an impeachable offense? This question arises in every major impeachment case. Must the House present an indictable (high) crime, or could it impeach for political offenses, an abuse of the power of the office? Hamilton wrote in *Federalist* 79 that "insanity, without any formal or express provision, may be safely pronounced to be a virtual disqualification." One could call alcohol addiction a grave moral failing, but could one classify it as a crime or misdemeanor? Many states criminalized public drunkenness, and the House articles of impeachment said that Pickering "did appear on the bench . . . for the purpose of administering justice in a state of total intoxication, produced by the free and intemperate use of inebriating liquors." (The first three articles of impeachment concerned his administration of the *Eliza* admiralty case, but this fourth article constituted the central charge.) They further condemned him as a blasphemer, "a man of loose morals and intemperate habits," who did "frequently, in a most profane and indecent manner, invoke the name of the Supreme Being, to the evil example of all the good citizens of the United States," and for behaving in a manner "disgraceful to his own character as a judge and degrading to the honor and dignity of the United States." Ironically, a section of the 1801 Judiciary Act that provided for such cases of incapacity had relieved him of his duties, but he returned to the bench after the 1802 repeal.

Pickering did not appear at his trial, nor did he have counsel. Many senators had qualms about defining his behavior as criminal and ousting him in absentia. Could they distinguish between the crimes that justified impeachment and "good behavior"? If so, Federalist control of the ordinary courts, Republicans thought, foreclosed that option.[28] Many senators absented themselves, and the rump Senate convicted him by a 20–6 vote out of a total of thirty-four members. Jefferson bemoaned how long the impeachment process took and despaired that it would take even longer to amend the Constitution to make it easier to remove federal judges. He seemed more willing to tolerate the violation of the constitutional terms of impeachment to oust this dipsomaniacal and partisan district judge.[29]

Supreme Court Justice Samuel Chase then revived the impeachment movement in Congress. Chase began his political career as a radical Democrat and

Anti-Federalist, but he became an especially partisan Federalist judge. He was gruff and overbearing, and even his Federalist colleagues found "Bacon Face" Chase difficult to abide. President Washington nominated him reluctantly in 1796. His conduct of the treason trial of John Fries after the Whiskey Rebellion, and of Republican pamphleteer James Callender for sedition, made him especially hated. He openly campaigned for John Adams in 1800 and did not take the election results as a sign to restrain himself.

In May 1803, he delivered an infamous charge to the Baltimore grand jury. At the time, judges used the charge to instruct jurors about fundamental principles of government and law, and Chase made the most of this pedagogical opportunity. He denounced the 1802 judiciary repeal act as well as the Maryland constitution's adoption of universal suffrage and warned that "our republican constitution will sink into a mobocracy—the worst of all possible governments." He attributed this to "the modern doctrines of our late reformers, that all men in a state of society are entitled to enjoy equal liberty and equal rights." He feared that "peace and order, freedom and property shall be destroyed." Jefferson gave the green light to impeach him.[30]

John Randolph of Virginia, a representative even more volatile and polarizing than Chase, managed the impeachment, to the accused justice's benefit. The issue of what defined an impeachable offense again arose. Randolph and the radicals believed that they need give no reasons. Virginia senator William Branch Giles, who called for the removal of all incumbent Federalist judges, said simply, "We want your offices for the purpose of giving them to men who will fill them better."[31] Even James Madison mused that impeachment might keep judges responsible to the people.

The Federalists insisted on indictable crimes. The articles of impeachment stressed Chase's bias and "oppression" of defendants and counsel. This amounted "to the disgrace of the character of the American Bench, in manifest violation of law and justice." It called the Baltimore grand jury charge "an intemperate and inflammatory political harangue . . . conduct highly censurable in any, but particularly indecent and unbecoming a judge."

In a late addition, the House impeachment managers specified that Chase had violated section 34 of the Judiciary Act, which required the use of state law in federal criminal trials, by his failure to follow Virginia procedure in the Callender sedition trial. The Court had long before decided that it need not follow state court *procedure* (in this case, not trying someone for a noncapital offense in the same term as the indictment), as opposed to substantive law. Hence, all of the justices could face impeachment for this "crime." On the other hand, the Judiciary Act prescribed no punishment for its violation, which could mean either that its violation did not amount to a crime or that the political medium of impeachment constituted the proper remedy.[32]

Remarkably, Vice President Aaron Burr presided over the Senate trial. New York and New Jersey had recently indicted Burr for the murder of Alexander Hamilton. Jefferson had to put aside his personal aversion to his 1800 rival in order to get Burr to help remove Chase. Though he treated Chase disdainfully, Burr inadvertently aided him by making the process judicial and criminal rather than political. Randolph summoned Chief Justice Marshall as a witness. Marshall adopted a notably diffident tone—perhaps fearing to face impeachment himself—again disappointing the High Federalists.[33] The cocky Randolph presented a poor case to the senators, many of whom still caviled about impeachment for political offenses. The effort appears to have unraveled when Jefferson pulled his support, due to a disagreement with Randolph about the settlement of the Yazoo land fraud.[34]

The Senate acquitted Chase on all charges. Even Giles voted to acquit on several of them. Later generations generally saw his case as establishing the criminal-not-political standard of impeachment. But, as with presidential impeachments, judicial ones have occurred so seldom as to leave the question unsettled. Henry Adams concluded that a conviction would have made little difference, since Chase presented such an extreme case. Jefferson reckoned that if Chase could not fall, nobody could. Chase did behave himself in a more decorous fashion after his acquittal, for his remaining six years on the bench, so perhaps the *threat* of impeachment could adequately chasten judicial oppression. The result contributed to Marshall's effort to keep the judiciary on the legal side of the admittedly permeable law–politics divide. John Randolph, the disappointed prosecutor, introduced a bill to allow removal of federal judges by bill of address, but it failed.[35]

MARSHALL V. THE DARK SIDE: FEDERATIVE CASES

After the impeachment mania passed, the federal courts could do important work defending individual rights against what historian Leonard Levy called Jefferson's "darker side."[36] Like the Federalist sedition scare, these threats to civil liberties arose out of foreign policy concerns—Aaron Burr's treason case and the enforcement of the Embargo Act.

After his term as vice president, Aaron Burr, his political as well as financial fortunes in ruins, embarked upon a military–political venture the nature of which remains one of America's unsolved mysteries. He corresponded with

General James Wilkinson, governor of the Louisiana Territory and also in the pay of the Spanish government, to assemble a military force on Blennerhassett Island, on the Ohio River, in today's West Virginia. He might have anticipated a war between the United States and Spain, or perhaps he had plans to conquer Mexico or to foment the rebellion and secession of the trans-Appalachian West. In any case, Jefferson convinced himself that Burr was guilty of treason, and he led a vendetta against Burr. Jefferson pronounced Burr guilty to Congress, issued blank pardons to secure witnesses, and micromanaged the prosecution.[37] Since Blennerhassett Island lay in Virginia, Jefferson had to prosecute Burr in John Marshall's circuit court.

Jefferson also had to tackle the Constitution's strict definition of treason. "Treason against the United States, shall consist only in levying war against them, or in adhering to their enemies, giving them aid and comfort. No person shall be convicted of treason unless on the testimony of two witnesses to the same overt act, or on confession in open court." (History records only about twenty American treason convictions.) Burr had committed no overt act; Jefferson could only claim that Burr *conspired* to commit treason. Ironically, Jefferson endorsed the English common law of treason, which condemned anyone who in any way abetted treason—according to the maxim "In treason, all are principals." Jefferson sought to establish "constructive treason" and wanted a jury to nullify the Constitution's exclusion of it.

Marshall adhered to the constitutionally strict definition of treason—to spite his cousin, his detractors said, and departing from his own earlier interpretation.[38] Though more recent work has defended Marshall against the charge of personal bias, he could not have been unaware of the personal and political stakes of the case.[39] He said, "This court feels many, perhaps peculiar motives, for manifesting as guarded a respect for the chief magistrate of the Union as is compatible with its official duties. To go beyond these would exhibit a conduct which deserves some other appellation than the term respect." He concluded, "However flagitious may be the crime of conspiracy to subvert by force the government of our country, such conspiracy is not treason. . . . The act then should be unequivocal and should have a warlike appearance."[40] To Jefferson's chagrin, Burr walked rather than hanged.

In *Marbury*, Marshall had asked, If Congress had declared one witness sufficient to convict someone of treason, would this not so manifestly violate the text of Article III, a provision that concerns the judicial branch in particular, as to compel the Court to declare it unconstitutional? The Burr case presented the equivalent under the guise of presidential misconstruction of

Article III and thus presented a case of minimal judicial review—involving a clear violation of the constitutional text, which concerned the courts in particular—in what Madison had called a case "of a judiciary nature." Both *Marbury* and *Burr* indicated Marshall's adherence to the Founders' modest standard of judicial review.

The federal courts also frustrated Jefferson's efforts to enforce the Embargo Act, his policy of avoiding war with Britain and France by cutting off trade with them, to compel them to respect the United States' neutral rights.[41] The act fell especially hard on the maritime states of Federalist and Anglophile New England, which gratified their southern Republican political adversaries. The resistance of the "blue-light Federalists" (implying that they signaled embargo-runners with blue lights from the coast) drove Jefferson to distraction.

The cases that arose out of the embargo involved foreign affairs, or the "federative power," the realm least amenable to constitutional restraints, and to judicial ones especially. Foreign policy would become the chief example of the realm of nonjusticiable "political questions." The Court would do all it could to keep out of foreign policy, because a nation at war would hardly scruple about individual rights if its survival hung in the balance, just as belligerent nations would hardly respect neutral rights or the law of nations in the midst of the modern "total war" that followed the French Revolution. War raised the basic question of whether limited or constitutional government could survive in wartime, or if *inter armes leges silent* (in wartime the laws are silent). It raised the problem of preserving a Lockean constitutional domestic regime in a Hobbesian absolutist world. Federalists could call the embargo the Republicans' Sedition Act. Notably, the Federalists defended the Sedition Act on national security grounds, when they faced war with France.

The embargo—a complete prohibition of all foreign commerce—presented constitutional embarrassments. The Constitution gives Congress the power to "regulate commerce with foreign nations." Did regulation include prohibition? Article I, section 9 forbade Congress to *tax* exports; how could it then ban them altogether? But a federal district court upheld the embargo in 1808, noting that commercial and maritime policy must yield to "the grand and ultimate objects [of] the defense and security of the country."[42] A Federalist judge enforced the act where it met most resistance, in New England.

The embargo's unpopularity made it difficult to enforce. Trying to police the maritime and Canadian trade of the entire nation produced an administrative nightmare. Congress let the customs collectors decide whether a ship really meant to voyage to another American port or schemed to trade abroad illegally. When Jefferson, via Treasury Secretary Albert Gallatin, tried to take control of this discretion from the Charleston collector, Justice William Johnson rebuked him in circuit court, stating that Jefferson and Gallatin had acted "without sanction of law" and "were not justified."[43] Jefferson recoiled at this decision by his first appointee to the Court. His attorney general, Caesar Rodney, told him that Johnson had "caught the leprosy of the bench" and had adopted the Federalists' "high-church doctrines."[44] Interestingly, Rodney complained that without unified presidential control of such cases, each federal circuit would have its own law. Advocates of section 25 judicial review would frequently make this same argument against Jeffersonian opponents of the federal courts.[45]

Johnson had to defend his decision against Rodney's letter to customs collectors and also respond to a censure by own his grand jurors. He claimed that Rodney's letter to Jefferson (really *from* Jefferson, as Rodney told Jefferson what the president wanted to hear) constituted "an act so unprecedented in the history of executive conduct [that it] could be intended for no other purpose than to secure public opinion" against the court. As Marshall had in *Marbury*, Johnson defended his exercise of judicial review as necessary to preserve the rule of law. "In a country where the laws govern, courts of justice necessarily are the medium of action and reaction between the government and the governed." He abjured any ambition to usurp power. "The courts do not pretend to impose any restraint upon any officer of the government, but what results from *a just construction of the laws* of the United States. Of these laws the courts are the constitutional expositors; and every department of government must submit to their exposition; for laws have no legal meaning but what is given them by the courts to whose exposition they are submitted" (emphasis mine).[46]

This sounds like the strongest expression of judicial power yet made, probably because we view it through the lens of two generations of judicial supremacy. But Johnson implied that judges could render *unjust constructions of the laws* and left open the question of what the other branches of government might do in case of such misconstruction. *Gilchrist* again concerned section 13 mandamus power. Jefferson and Rodney claimed that the 1789 act did not give the circuit courts power to issue them—that *Marbury* had erroneously denied the Supreme Court's original jurisdiction to grant them. In any event, Congress could alter this arrangement and do away with federal judicial power to issue the writ, or any other writ, altogether. (The exception was habeas corpus, to some degree, as the one judicial writ specified in the Constitution.)

Congress did this with the writ of injunction in labor disputes in the 1932 Norris–LaGuardia Act.

Ultimately, Jefferson did go to Congress to get the power he sought, in amendments to the act. But Gallatin warned him that he needed more: "Congress must either invest the executive with the most arbitrary powers and sufficient force to carry the embargo into effect, or give it up altogether."[47] Anything less would lead to war, which came in 1812.

Jefferson still sought to avoid war by legal enforcement of economic sanctions. New England juries refused to convict embargo-runners, so the administration tried to avoid jury nullification by resort to juryless admiralty courts.[48] Jefferson again tried to broaden the constitutional definition of treason by declaring border zones in rebellion for trading illegally. Justice Henry Brockholst Livingston, Jefferson's second Court appointee, struck down this effort in a Vermont case, along the lines of the treason definition that Marshall had pronounced in the Burr case.[49] Justice Marshall did his part as well, holding that, since the Embargo Act provided only for forfeiture of goods as punishment, Jefferson could not seek common-law criminal penalties.[50] This was another inversion of the 1790s, when Republicans had decried the Federalists' resort to a common law of crimes.[51]

THE GREAT AGE OF THE MARSHALL COURT

Having survived the Jefferson administration, the Marshall Court was able to settle down and make some of its most important contributions to American constitutionalism. James Madison had a much more balanced view about the judiciary than Jefferson. His appointment of Joseph Story to the Court in 1811, when Justice Cushing died, reflected this. This appointment indicated the still relatively low status of the Court—Story was Madison's fourth choice. His first, former attorney general and Massachusetts governor Levi Lincoln, won quick Senate confirmation but declined to serve. His next choice, Alexander Wolcott, had made himself obnoxious as a Massachusetts port collector enforcing the embargo. Many considered him a legal mediocrity. The Senate rejected him by a vote of 9–24, by far the most resounding rejection of a Court nominee in American history. John Quincy Adams, like Lincoln, also declined to serve after confirmation. "Few presidents have had to face such an ordeal or suffer the indignity of so many rebuffs by party and Senate," one scholar noted.[52]

It also indicated that Jefferson had left the office of the presidency weakened, as Marshall said he would. Jefferson called Cushing's death a "circumstance of congratulation" and eagerly sought the "chance of getting a Republican majority in the Supreme judiciary," but he warned Madison that "it will be difficult to find a character of firmness enough to preserve his independence on the same bench with Marshall."[53] He considered Story a crypto-Federalist and tried mightily to prevent his appointment. Jefferson turned out to be correct. Story turned into an even stronger judicial nationalist than Marshall and would carry Marshall's Federalist constitutionalism into the 1840s.

The Senate confirmed Story and Gabriel Duval (nominated when Samuel Chase died) in November 1811, the last additions to the Court for over twelve years, the longest period of stability in the Court's history. This helped Marshall further forge the Court into a solid body and build its espirit de corps. Marshall had the justices live together when in Washington (when not riding circuit) in a kind of fraternity house. They dined and conversed amiably, well supplied with the chief justice's beloved Madeira. An often repeated and perhaps apocryphal story goes that Marshall ruled that the brethren could imbibe only to dispel the gloom of rainy days but that he would construe the rule broadly. "Brother Story, step to the window and see if it looks like rain," he'd say. When Story reported fair weather, the chief justice concluded, "Our jurisdiction extends over so large a territory that it must be raining somewhere."[54]

Most important, Marshall worked to unify the Court's opinions, which were usually unanimous and usually written by himself. This practice also irritated Jefferson. The Court in the 1790s had issued individual (seriatim) opinions. Chief Justice Ellsworth had begun the movement toward unified opinions and Marshall cemented it. Jefferson complained that Marshall "caucused opinions," which were made up in secret conclave and presented as unanimous, "with the silent acquiescence of lazy or timid associates, by a crafty chief justice, who sophisticates the law to his mind."[55]

Justice Johnson told Jefferson how this came about: "Cushing was incompetent, Chase could not be got to think or write—Paterson was a slow man and willingly declined the trouble, and the other two judges [Marshall and Bushrod Washington] you know are commonly estimated as one judge." Johnson felt he had to join the consensus to have any influence.[56] Marshall led but did not dominate the Court; he worked to forge consensus and often compromised his own views for the sake of unity.[57] Even after separate opinions and dissents became more common, Marshall and Story still led the Court.

Jefferson's complaint about the "caucusing" of Court opinions, that it allowed the Court to evade responsibility, sounded ironic coming from the president who governed through the congressional caucus—to the point that, after Jefferson, that caucus effectively chose the president, substituting a parliamentary for a constitutional executive. It also raised the question, If seriatim opinions hid responsibility, *to whom* should the Court answer?

One indication of a more favorable presidential attitude toward the judiciary came in the first months of the Madison administration, with his support of the federal courts against a Pennsylvania challenge. The dispute went back to Gideon Olmstead's capture of the British sloop *Active* during the Revolutionary War. Olmstead, a prisoner of war on the ship, successfully escaped and sailed it toward New Jersey. A Pennsylvania warship then took it to Philadelphia and claimed it. Pennsylvania kept the proceeds from the sale of the prize and ignored a reversal by the Continental Congress's court of appeals for prize cases.[58]

After the war, in 1803, Olmstead sued for the money in federal district court and won. Pennsylvania reacted so belligerently that the district judge, Richard Peters, refused to issue the order enforcing his own decision for Olmstead. Olmstead asked the Supreme Court for a mandamus to Peters to do so, which it granted in 1809. Marshall said that "If the legislatures of the several states may, at will, annul the judgments of the courts of the United States, and destroy the rights acquired under those judgments, the Constitution itself becomes a solemn mockery, and the nation is deprived of the means of enforcing its laws by the instrumentality of its own tribunals."[59] The Pennsylvania governor called up the state militia to prevent enforcement. The federal marshal called up a posse to meet it, and the federal grand jury indicted the state militia general.

On the verge of civil war, the governor appealed to the White House, but Madison sent a strong reply that it he must enforce, not overturn, federal court decisions. The governor backed down, Olmsted got paid, and Madison pardoned the militia officers. The legislature denounced the "unconstitutional exercise of power in the Unites States' courts" and called for a constitutional amendment to provide an impartial tribunal to settle disputes between the states and the federal government.[60] Eleven responded negatively. Virginia, which like Pennsylvania had stood virtually alone in 1798, noted that the Constitution had already established such a tribunal in the Supreme Court.[61]

THE GREAT AGE OF THE MARSHALL COURT: CONTRACTS

Marshall's decisions on the nature of the Union and federal supremacy constituted his greatest contribution to American constitutionalism, but his contract clause cases mattered even more in the everyday lives of Americans and the development of the American economy.[62] The provision of Article I, section 10 that "no state shall . . . pass any . . . law impairing the obligation of contracts" provided the most important constitutional safeguard of the individual rights of citizens in the states. It had appeared in the Northwest Ordinance, the first constitutional provision that concerned relations among citizens, as opposed to between citizens and government. Section 10 forcefully responded to the legislative excesses of the 1780s.[63] Marshall would call it "a bill of rights for the people of each state."[64]

As contract provided the key idea of the political theory of modern constitutionalism (deriving from the covenantal concept in ancient and medieval constitutionalism), so it became the basis of American socioeconomic relations.[65] Only a minor part of English law before 1800, the nineteenth century became the golden age of contract. The maximizing of private ordering and the minimizing of public power defined the classical liberalism of the Founding era. The historian Henry Sumner Maine characterized the modern world as a movement "from status to contract."[66] A democracy considered individuals free and equal, and contract allowed them to govern themselves contracts represented private laws made by individuals. The doctrine assumed that free men could look after themselves and enter into agreements with their equals for their mutual benefit. Government should above all protect citizens from coercion (that is, force, whether from enemies abroad or criminals at home) and fraud—to ensure that everyone kept his hands to himself and kept his promises.[67]

Marshall celebrated this view of contract as the moral basis of society. In several decisions he recalled the evils of legislative abrogation of contracts in the pre-Constitution period, which eroded the "confidence between man and man"—a phrase from *Federalist* 44 that Marshall frequently used—and threatened to demoralize the public. Thus he maximized the potential of the contract clause. Indeed, Marshall saw contracts almost everywhere he looked. For Marshall, this history amounted to "philosophy teaching by example." He would similarly regard the contract clause as a textual manifestation of natural justice.

The first contract clause case concerned the Yazoo land grants of the 1790s. The cash-strapped state of Georgia sold millions of acres of what became the states of Alabama and Mississippi at fire-sale prices. When it became known that the land-company purchasers had bribed every member of the state house (except one, the story goes), a new legislature revoked the grant in 1794. In the meantime, the fraudsters had sold some of the land to "innocent" third parties.[68] At length, a suit challenging the repeal came to the Supreme Court as

Fletcher v. Peck in 1810. Marshall held that the grant, however tainted by fraud, remained a contract that vested rights in the purchasers. To revoke rights once vested would violate both natural justice and the contract clause. The political impact of this decision waned after the federal government paid Georgia and assumed liability for the claims of the purchasers.[69] Notably, claimants could not seek judicial review of the settlement. Congress, more than the Court, had settled the constitutional question.[70]

Two years later, the Court called a grant of tax exemption by the state of New Jersey to an Indian tribe a contract, and held that this obligation continued when the Indians sold the land to whites. In the original grant of 1758, the tribe could not alienate the land. The tribe got the legislature to lift this restriction and allow them to sell; the act allowing the sale said nothing about the tax exemption. "The privilege," Marshall wrote, "though for the benefit of the Indians, is annexed . . . to the land itself, not to their persons."[71] Similarly, in 1819 the Court decided that the grant of a charter by King George III to the trustees of Dartmouth College constituted a contract and thus prevented its takeover by the state of New Hampshire. The contract clause protected a small college ("a private eleemosynary institution") in this case, but also would similarly shelter all American private corporations, so this decision had monumental economic import.[72] The chief justice recognized that his definitions of "contract" stretched credulity. "It is more than possible, that the preservation of the rights of this description was not particularly in the view of the framers of the Constitution," he wrote.[73] But he saw no reason to exclude such institutions from their general language.

Three years later, the Court held as an enforceable contract an agreement between two states. Kentucky broke off from state of Virginia and became its own state in 1792. The agreement creating Kentucky said that the Virginia law of the time would settle disputes about land titles. This became politically contentious because Kentuckians regarded Virginia law as biased toward absentee landowners and against squatters. Kentucky altered Virginia law and gave squatters compensation for the value of any improvements they had made on the land from which the courts had ejected them. The Court again held that this ran afoul of the contract clause.[74]

The Court also ruled on a New York bankruptcy law that allowed a debtor to hand over all of his property to his creditors, though it amounted to less than what he owed, and have no further obligation. First, the Court held that although the Constitution gave Congress the power to "establish uniform laws on the subject of bankruptcies throughout the United States," states could enact their own laws in the absence of a national act.[75] But state bankruptcy laws could not impair the obligation of contracts, as the New York law did.[76]

In contrast to its activism in the area of contracts, the Court finally put to rest the question of the existence of a federal common law. The case that did so came about, ironically enough, from a prosecution of the Jefferson administration for seditious libel. The Sedition Act expired when Jefferson took office; still, federal prosecutors brought libel cases under the common law. Jefferson told them to cease, but one case, against the *Connecticut Courant,* slipped through the cracks and reached the Supreme Court. Justice William Johnson disposed of it quickly. "We consider it as having been long since settled in public opinion" that no federal common law existed. "In no other case for many years has this jurisdiction been asserted, and the general acquiescence of legal men shows the prevalence of opinion in favor of the negative of the proposition."[77] He set aside the question of whether Congress could make libel a crime by statute, for it had not. Remarkably, Johnson seemed to consult only "public opinion," particularly that of "legal men," for his decision. This case concerned criminal law; some years later, the Court also held that no federal civil common law existed.[78]

THE GREAT AGE OF THE MARSHALL COURT: THE UNION

The Marshall Court displayed deference in the foreign policy or federative realm, acted more forcefully in the domestic republican one, and took its strongest stand on federal affairs, stressing the supremacy of the national over state governments. Scholars generally regard Marshall as using the flush of post–War of 1812 nationalism to express this Unionism and then backing away from it after a states' rights reaction set in during the Jackson administration.

Justice Story made the fullest expression of Unionism in the 1816 case of *Martin v. Hunter's Lessee.* This case concerned a dispute over title to the vast lands of Lord Fairfax and his adopted heir, Denny Martin (known as "Fairfax's devisee" in earlier litigation). Virginia had confiscated and sold part of the Fairfax lands, and Martin claimed that these acts violated the 1783 Treaty of Paris and the 1794 Jay Treaty. Many bitter cases involving war damages by the British and American retaliations marked the post-Revolution period.[79] Hamilton's defense of British claimants, as in the *Rutgers* case, did not enhance his popularity; however, Marshall's defense of Virginia confiscators aided his political fortunes, helping him win election to Congress from a predominantly Republican district.[80] At length, the Virginia Supreme Court, led by Chief

Justice Spencer Roane, declared that section 25 of the Judiciary Act violated the Constitution and refused to have its anti-Martin decision reviewed. Marshall had a personal stake in the outcome of the case and so recused himself.

In *Martin v. Hunter's Lessee,* Story exceeded Marshall in his expression of national supremacy.[81] He insisted that the Constitution had come from the American people as a whole—not the people *of* the states, nor even the people *in* the states. He maintained that the federal courts must have all the judicial power that Article III grants and that Congress must establish at least some inferior courts. Federal review of state courts inhered in the Constitution's structure. Far from calling section 25 unconstitutional, Story seemed to call it redundant. "It is a mistake that the Constitution was not designed to operate on the states in their corporate capacities. It is crowded with provisions which restrain or annul the sovereignty of the states in some of the highest branches of their prerogatives."[82]

McCulloch v. Maryland ranks just after, or even ahead of, *Marbury* as the most important Marshall Court decision. *Marbury* had struck down an act of Congress—albeit an awfully insignificant provision that concerned the judiciary in particular. *McCulloch* upheld an enormously important and controversial act of Congress. Thus, it has drawn the fire of small-government constitutionalists both then and now.

The Bank of the United States provoked the first great debate on constitutional interpretation in American history. Treasury Secretary Alexander Hamilton conceived it, and he made an extensive argument for a broad construction of the Constitution (much of which Marshall would incorporate into *McCulloch*). Thomas Jefferson made the "strict construction" argument against it. Madison, then in the House of Representatives, sided with Jefferson. But Jefferson told the president that unless he regarded the constitutional violation as clear, he should defer to Congress's judgment.[83] Washington agreed and accepted the bill.

The charter of the first bank expired in 1811. The War of 1812, which the federal government struggled to finance, demonstrated the need for a bank. Madison, now president, vetoed a bill to create a new bank in 1815, but on policy grounds. He explained that he had come to accept its constitutionality. He set aside his former views as "precluded in my judgment by repeated recognitions under varied circumstances of the validity of such an institution in the acts of the legislative, executive, and judicial branches of the government, accompanied by indications, in different modes, of a concurrence of the general will of the nation."[84] This sounded somewhat like Justice Johnson's view of the question of the federal common law, that popular opinion had a role to play in establishing constitutional meaning.

The second bank became very unpopular in many states, especially among small-state bankers, whom it disciplined by restricting their note issues and insisting that they redeem them in specie. Critics blamed the bank for the depression that began in 1819, alleged that it engaged in fraud, and accused it of using its financial power for political purposes. Maryland imposed a punitive tax on banks not chartered by the state. James McCulloch, the cashier of the Baltimore branch of the B.U.S., sued to recover the tax.

Marshall upheld the B.U.S. and shot down the Maryland tax. He grounded his decision on the thesis that the people of the United States had established a sovereign government, no longer a confederation or league. Marshall conceded that the Constitution had established a "compound republic," noting that "the assent of the states, in their sovereign capacity, is implied in calling a [ratification] convention." But he stressed that the people had ratified the Constitution—that they did so *in* the states did not make the Constitution a product *of* the states. The new government "though limited in its powers, is supreme within its sphere of action."[85]

With regard to judicial power, the centerpiece of *McCulloch* resided in Marshall's defense of "implied powers." A constitution could not specify every particular means that might become necessary and proper to carry out its enumerated ends. Such a constitution "would partake of the prolixity of a legal code, and could scarcely be embraced by the human mind. It would probably never be understood by the public." A constitution articulated certain great ends and objects but left open the means to achieve those objects. "We must never forget that it is *a constitution* that we are expounding."[86]

That last phrase has led many to assert that Marshall claimed the utmost latitude to say what the Constitution means.[87] But since the Court accepted the act, he might as well have said that "it is a constitution that *Congress* had expounded." He claimed no exclusive power for the judiciary to interpret the fundamental law. Nor did he abnegate judicial duty and give Congress a blank check. "Should Congress, in the execution of its powers, adopt measures which are prohibited by the Constitution; or should Congress, under the pretext of executing its powers, pass laws for the accomplishment of objects not entrusted to the government; it would become the painful duty of this tribunal, should a case requiring such a decision to come before it, to say that such an act was not the law of the land."[88] Marshall assumed that the Court might investigate the *motive* of legislation, to distinguish legitimate from pretextual laws. But the return of states' rights Jeffersonianism in the 1820s would provide few opportunities to scrutinize ambitious federal legislation.

The Marshall Court's federalism decisions provoked Virginia supreme court chief justice Spencer Roane, a Jefferson acolyte, and Marshall entered into an extensive pseudonymous exchange with Roane in Richmond newspapers.[89] They really disputed not the bank but the nature of the Union and the limits on Congress's implied powers. As Marshall wrote in *McCulloch*, "Let the end be legitimate, let it be within the scope of the Constitution, and all means which are appropriate, which are plainly adapted to that end, which are not prohibited, but consist with the letter and spirit of the Constitution, are constitutional."

James Madison accepted the constitutionality of the bank but worried that Marshall's "latitudinary mode of expounding the Constitution" left no practical limits on national power.[90] Marshall told Story, "I cannot describe the surprise and mortification I have felt at hearing that Mr. Madison has embraced [the Jefferson–Roane view] with respect to the judicial department."[91] As "A Friend of the Constitution," Marshall went beyond the compound, dual-federalist view of Madison in *Federalist* 39 and his 1800 report to the Virginia Assembly, which had emphasized the "compound" nature of the Union. He sounded more like Justice Story arguing that the Constitution came from the American people as a whole. But Marshall remained cautious enough to avoid claims for federal power beyond the bank.[92]

Marshall could reiterate his principles in the 1821 case of *Cohens v. Virginia.* Congress had authorized a lottery to raise money for the District of Columbia. Virginia prosecuted the Cohen brothers for selling lottery tickets in that state. In an opinion arranged like *Marbury,* Marshall held that Congress *could have* authorized the sale of lottery tickets outside of the district, and overridden state antilottery laws, but had not. Thus, he could reaffirm the superiority of federal over state law without ordering the state to comply.[93] Marshall returned to a Madisonian, compound-republic dual federalism in his interpretation of the supremacy clause. "This is the language of the American people, and, if gentlemen please, of the American states." He concluded that "the United States form, for many and for most important purposes, a single nation. . . . The states are constituent parts of one great empire—for some purposes sovereign: for some purposes subordinate." The Court had a vital role in preserving that system. It had, he said, "no more right to decline the exercise of jurisdiction which is given, than to usurp that which is not given," a fine statement of judicial duty.[94]

The last of the nationalist consensus opinions (*Martin, McCulloch,* and *Cohens* had no dissents) came in Marshall's interpretation of the commerce clause in *Gibbons v. Ogden* in 1824. This appeal challenged a New York law that had granted a monopoly to Robert Fulton for steamboat navigation in state waters. Did the New York law violate Congress's power to "regulate commerce . . . among the several states"? Gibbons claimed that his license under a federal coasting act vitiated the state law.

In the nineteenth century, the commerce clause operated more as a negative restriction on the states than as a positive grant to Congress. It aimed above all to prevent interstate trade wars and economic balkanization. In this view, the framers should have put it in Article I, section 10 rather than among the enumerated powers in section 8. In the twentieth century, the commerce power would become the chief means of national economic regulation, establishing a national police power. Progressives and New Dealers would claim that they simply wanted to restore Marshall's generous interpretation of Congress's power.[95]

Marshall's opinion evinced more complexity than twentieth-century interpreters appreciated.[96] Marshall did define "commerce" broadly: "Commerce undoubtedly is traffic, but it is something more: it is intercourse."[97] Did Congress possess exclusive power to regulate it, or might states legislate (as in bankruptcy) in the absence of congressional acts? Marshall's opinion did not clearly answer this question, which in any event was moot, because Congress *had* acted. Marshall also yielded to state power when he interpreted "among" as "commerce which concerns more states than one," excluding commerce entirely within a state. Strong American animus against monopolies meant that *Gibbons* raised few hackles.[98]

But the great nationalist decisions of the Marshall Court often suffered de facto nullifications by the states. The contractual rights protected in *Fletcher v. Peck,* for example, won out in a political compromise, in which the federal government paid Georgia to forsake its unconstitutional repeal act and established a fund to satisfy the third-party purchasers.[99] After *Green v. Biddle,* Kentucky continued to apply its own land law, rather than Virginia's, until 1831, when the US Supreme Court overruled *Green.*[100] In *Martin v. Hunter's Lessee,* the Virginia court of appeals denied that federal courts could review its decisions under section 25, and Story's opinion to the contrary did not change Spencer Roane's mind on the point. Story simply went around Roane and issued his order to the inferior Virginia district court.[101] In *Cohens,* Marshall reiterated the theory of national judicial supremacy but avoided a clash by holding for

Virginia on the merits. The Ohio legislature denied that the Court had settled the issue in *McCulloch* and enacted its own tax on the Bank of the United States. The Court's decisions, the legislators declared, "have been followed by no effective consequence."[102] As late as 1854, the Georgia supreme court continued to hold section 25 unconstitutional and spurned federal review.[103]

Ohio seized taxes from a branch of the B.U.S. despite *McCulloch*; the Court had to order the state treasurer to return the funds in 1824. Long before John C. Calhoun had spun out his theory of nullification, South Carolina defied a circuit court decision that held its Negro Seamen Act unconstitutional. In the aftermath of the 1822 Denmark Vesey slave rebellion hysteria, the state ordered all free Blacks who entered Charleston to be imprisoned while their vessel remained in port; violators would be sold into slavery. Justice Johnson bravely struck down the act, but the state ignored the ruling. It even defied efforts by the national administration to cease offending the British, whose free Black sailors suffered abuse under the law.[104] Marshall confessed to Story that Virginia had a similar law, "and a case was brought before me in which I might have considered its constitutionality had I chosen to do so. But it was not absolutely necessary, and, as I am not fond of butting against a wall in sport, I escaped on the construction of the act."[105]

Marshall himself, in a case between New York and New Jersey, held that Staten Island belonged to New Jersey. New York ignored the ruling, and the island remains one of the five boroughs.[106] As postwar nationalism faded before the Jacksonian states' rights revival, Marshall despaired. He told Story in 1832, "I yield slowly and reluctantly to the conviction that our constitution cannot last. . . . The union has been prolonged thus far by miracles. I fear they cannot continue."[107]

JUDICIAL POWER IN THE STATES

Though some states resisted federal judicial review, judicial review and judicial power took hold within the states themselves. This may have resulted from the party system, in which parties in power would try to lock in their policies in the courts against the day when they left office.[108] (The Federalists had done this at the national level with the Judiciary Act of 1801, and Republicans would do it later in the nineteenth century.) John B. Gibson, who in 1825 had made what most still consider the most acute critique of the Hamilton–Marshall justification for judicial review, recanted. By 1845 he had accepted it "from experience of the necessity of the case."[109]

But the establishment of judicial review caused political turmoil in many states. New Hampshire had a judicial system much like that of Massachusetts but saw radical structural reforms with each major transfer of party control. When the Jeffersonian Republicans came to power, they impeached or removed Federalist judges by bill of address. Likewise, the attempt to take over Federalist-controlled Dartmouth College arose when the Republicans took over the state government. When the Federalists returned to power in 1813, they abolished the superior court and court of common pleas and created new ones for their own supporters. One of the "midnight judges," whose office the 1802 repeal act had abolished, got one of these. The incumbent Republican judges refused to depart; the next session of the legislature removed the sheriffs who had abetted their resistance. In 1816, the Republicans returned to power and repealed the 1813 Federalist changes. The Know-Nothings in 1855 and Republicans in 1859 did likewise.[110]

The first Ohio constitution guaranteed jury trials, but the legislature dispensed with them in suits of less than fifty dollars. The state supreme court struck the act down, and the legislature impeached, but ultimately acquitted, two justices. The legislature remained defiant and raised the ban to seventy dollars, apparently unchallenged.[111] When Kentucky's high court struck down state debtor-relief and land laws in the 1820s, the legislature abolished the court and created a new one. The old justices refused to retire and the state had two competing court systems. Amos Kendall, who would later write Jackson's court-defying bank veto message, took the "new court" side in this conflict. Francis Blair, who broke into the "old court" building to seize its records, also would join Jackson's "kitchen cabinet." The issue dominated Kentucky politics through the next two elections, and the voters supported the old court. But most of the arguments in favor of it articulated a limited sort of judicial review, making the court equal to rather than superior to the other departments of government, limited to particular cases, and inapplicable in doubtful cases.[112]

State judges also increased their power with regard to juries, which had constituted a sort of lower house of the judicial branch. Juries lost their power to determine law as well as fact, and jury nullification became more anomalous. In 1855, the Massachusetts Supreme Judicial Court rejected a claim that a jury should have the power to judge the constitutionality of a state prohibition law. In an irony not atypical of the Jacksonian period, as the jury became more "democratic" (that is, open to all adult males), its influence declined.[113]

The outstanding control over state judicial power lay in the popular election of judges. Mississippi first adopted an elective judiciary in its 1832 constitution. Fourteen of sixteen state constitutional conventions adopted elective judiciaries between 1846 and 1860, as did every new state admitted to the Union between 1846 and 1912.[114] Elected benches might show deference to the electorate, or they could assert their power because their election gave them democratic legitimacy. Though the later antebellum years saw some abatement of judicial power, other state courts became more forceful, engaging in what amounted to policymaking and using natural law arguments later called "substantive due process."[115] "Court packing" could curb courts in states with appointed judiciaries. Democrats in Illinois disliked their four-justice, majority-Whig supreme court's decisions on alien voting and on the governor's removal power. In 1841, the legislature added five seats to the court and filled them with Democrats, among them future senator Stephen Douglas.[116]

The ambivalence of Americans about the law, the legal profession, and courts seen in the colonial and revolutionary period continued in the antebellum years. Alexis de Tocqueville praised the American legal profession as the closest thing to an aristocracy that the country possessed, and an indispensable counter to excessive democracy. He echoed Hamilton in *Federalist* 35 that the "learned professions" would rise above other competing interest groups and "likely prove an impartial arbiter" in their disputes. In the United States, the unique feature of judicial power made American democracy compatible with constitutionalism. "I do not think that, until now, any nation in the world has constituted judicial power in the same manner as the Americans," he wrote. But American judges knew that they had to stay out of politics and stick to legal questions, though judicial review inevitably led them into political questions. He observed that federal judges, seeing the relative weakness of the federal compared to the state government, more often erred on the side of excessive timidity than usurpation. He adjured American judges to act as statesmen; an irresponsible federal bench could lead to "anarchy or civil war."[117]

But, as in the preconstitutional period, this aristocracy provoked much popular repugnance. The election of judges (which Tocqueville noted)[118] evinced a desire to cabin judicial power, as did the movement for "codification"—codes of law written by the legislature, which would dispel the mysteries of the common law and puncture the pretension of the legal fraternity as the exclusive interpreters of them. States also opened access to the legal profession, steadily eroding any requirements of special training or experience. The Indiana constitution of 1851 provided that "every person of good moral character, being a voter, shall be entitled to admission to the practice of law in all the courts of justice."[119] Abraham Lincoln needed no formal education, standardized test scores, or other credentials to enter the legal profession.

The election of Andrew Jackson led to a new series of challenges to federal judicial power. Though some of his opponents saw him as an even more radical version of Thomas Jefferson, or an American Bonaparte, Jackson would actually pose less of a threat to the federal courts than had Jefferson.[120] He reopened the question of the Bank of the United States when his political opponents, the nascent Whig party, pushed for an early extension of its charter in 1832. Jackson vetoed the bill on constitutional (as well as policy) grounds. His veto message became the classic expression of "departmentalism," the belief that each department of the federal government had the right and obligation to interpret the Constitution for itself. He considered the issue unsettled by either political or judicial precedent. Congress had voted more often against than for the bank. As for *McCulloch*:

[It] ought not to control the coordinate authorities of this government. The Congress, the Executive, and the Court must each for itself be guided by its own opinion of the Constitution. Each officer who takes an oath to support the Constitution swears that he will support it as he understands it, and not as it is understood by others. It is as much the duty of the House of Representatives, of the Senate, and of the president to decide upon the constitutionality of any bill . . . as it is of the supreme judges when it may be brought before them for judicial decision. The opinion of the judges has no more authority over Congress than the opinion of Congress has over the judges, and on that point the president is independent of both. The authority of the Supreme Court must not, therefore, be permitted to control the Congress or the Executive when acting in their legislative capacities, but to have only such influence as the force of their reasoning may deserve.[121]

By the logic of *Federalist* 78, if the supremacy of the Constitution empowered the Court to strike down unconstitutional legislative or executive acts, that same supremacy enabled the president or Congress to overrule unconstitutional Court decisions.

The veto stuck. The Whigs made it the chief issue in the election of 1832. The federal judiciary, they said, "was seriously threatened by the perverse policy of the present administration," which evinced "a settled intention . . . to shake the independence and destroy the efficiency" of the Court.[122] Jackson won decisively. The bank expired in 1836. The B.U.S. veto provoked little controversy, insofar as it claimed that the president could assert his own constitutional views.[123] Though some objected to this, more objected to Jackson's extension of the veto power to policy differences as a usurpation of legislative power. In 1860, Taney told Martin Van Buren that the message did not go beyond the lawmaking stage, that Jackson recognized his obligation to enforce a law once it was made, even if it were enacted over his veto.[124] This veto resembled Jefferson's dropping of prosecutions and pardon of those convicted under the Sedition Act—like the pardon power, veto was a vestige of the royal prerogative.

The closest that Jackson and Marshall came to a direct confrontation involved the Cherokee Indian cases. The state of Georgia had begun taking control of lands inhabited by the Cherokees, who claimed the protection of the federal government, under treaties, against the state. Georgia tried and executed an Indian, ignoring a Supreme Court writ of error to review the case. When the Cherokee nation tried to sue the state, Marshall defined the Cherokees as neither a foreign nation nor as citizens, thus unable to sue in federal court. He denominated them "domestic dependent nations . . . in a state of pupilage. Their relation to the United States resembles that of a ward to his guardian."[125] He noted that the language of the commerce clause distinguished between foreign states and Indian tribes.

Though not an implausible textual reading, one might think that the Indians' "peculiar" status made access to federal judicial protection more, rather than less, appropriate. He began by saying, "If courts were permitted to indulge their sympathies, a case better calculated to excite them can scarcely be imagined." Yet he concluded, "If it be true that the Cherokee nation have rights, this is not the tribunal in which those rights are to be asserted. If it be true that wrongs have been inflicted, and that still greater are to be apprehended, this is not the tribunal which can redress the past or prevent the future."[126]

Marshall, as in Marbury, Cohens, and the Negro Seamen case, tried to avoid an embarrassing political conflict with Georgia, which refused to appear in Court and which had the support of President Jackson. Several pro-Cherokee justices concurred or dissented silently. Marshall encouraged the dissenters (Thompson and Story) to publicize their dissents. The two Jackson appointees (Baldwin and Barbour) concurred in the result but believed that the Indians had no rights.[127]

The issue became less avoidable when Georgia arrested two white citizens for preaching to the Cherokee without a license from the state. Now Marshall attempted to put Georgia in its place. (The state again refused to appear in court, but somehow the state court clerk had sent up the case record.) "The Cherokee nation then is a distinct community, occupying its own territory, with boundaries accurately described, in which the laws of Georgia can have no force, and which the citizens of Georgia have no right to enter, but with the assent of the Cherokees themselves, or in conformity with treaties, and with the acts of Congress."[128]

This case gave rise to one of the most frequently told stories in American constitutional and political history, that Jackson defiantly said, "Mr. Marshall has made his decision. Now let him enforce it."[129] Though quite in character, no evidence indicates that Jackson did so. In fact, the president had nothing to *enforce* anyway. The Judiciary Act required that Marshall remand the decision to the Supreme Court of Georgia. Only if the state refused to comply could the Supreme Court have issued a writ for the president to execute. But Jackson had induced Georgia's governor to pardon Worcester et al., and they dropped the case. Marshall certainly did not want push to come to shove. He especially wanted to avoid pushing Georgia into alliance with the South Carolina nullifiers. One scholar calls the decision an advisory opinion and an "improper election manifesto."[130]

The chief constitutional crisis of the Jackson years, South Carolina's attempt to "nullify" the protective tariff, did not involve the federal courts directly.[131] Calhoun's larger theory of the nature of the Union did deny the power of the Supreme Court to review state laws.[132] As the Federalists had, in response to the Virginia and Kentucky Resolutions, defenders of national supremacy argued that the federal courts should settle the dispute. In his famous Senate debate with Robert Hayne (fronting for Calhoun), Daniel Webster argued that "the people have wisely provided, in the Constitution itself, a proper, suitable mode and tribunal for settling questions of constitutional law." The supremacy clause and the Article III grant of jurisdiction "in all cases" arising under the Constitution, laws, and treaties "cover the whole ground."[133] Senator John Clayton of Delaware agreed, saying that "We have no other direct resource, in the cases we have been considering, to save us from the horrors of anarchy, than the Supreme Court."[134] Hayne denied that the Constitution "expressly" granted such review and argued that "questions of sovereignty are not the proper subjects of judicial investigation"—that is, they presented "political questions." Like the Anti-Federalists, Hayne argued that courts of the national government would take sides in national–state contests, to aggrandize national power. Moreover, a national legislature that violated the Constitution would not curtail the jurisdiction of a court that abetted its own powers.[135] Senator John Rowan of Kentucky concurred, saying that the states would not "be subjected to a judicial aristocracy."[136]

The political branches settled the conflict over nullification, mostly on South Carolina's terms, as Henry Clay arranged a compromise that lowered the tariff. South Carolina merely "repealed" its secession ordinance.[137] Jackson, in his forceful defense of the Union given in his Proclamation on Nullification, seemed to accept the congressional judicialist argument, observing, "There are two appeals from an unconstitutional act passed by Congress—one to the judiciary, the other to the people and the states"—that is, elections and constitutional amendment.[138] Though he may not have fully embraced Webster and the Whig nationalists' view of the nature of the Union and federal powers, his proclamation strengthened the nationalist case.[139] One scholar called the proclamation a "stunning defense of the Court."[140]

In the meantime, states' rights advocates, angry about the Georgia Cherokee case and others, induced the House Judiciary Committee to recommend the repeal of section 25. The repealers argued that federal review of state courts contradicted the nature of the Union, which they regarded as "a league or treaty." Representative James Buchanan wrote a report for the minority of the committee against it, relying mostly on *Cohens v. Virginia*.[141] The full House overwhelmingly defeated the committee's repeal bill. Most Jacksonians preferred to take over the courts rather than to curb their power.[142]

In the wake of the nullification controversy, Justice Joseph Story published his *Commentaries on the Constitution of the United States,* a landmark of nationalism and perhaps the first clear statement of judicial supremacy.[143] He expressed this claim in a chapter entitled "Who Is the Final Judge or Interpreter in Constitutional Controversies?" He conceded Jackson's point that each oath taker must interpret the Constitution, and that in many "political questions" those would prevail. (This again presented the catch-22 of defining a question as political.) In justiciable cases, "the case is not alone considered as decided and settled; but the principles of the decision are held, as precedents and authority, to bind future cases of the same nature." But even Story conceded that, if a court decided wrongly, "it might require the interposition of Congress, or, in the last resort," constitutional amendment. This perhaps recognized the "usual and most effectual precautions" to which Madison alluded in *Federalist* 39.[144]

Marshall had treaded cautiously when the Jeffersonian Republicans came to power, and he ably navigated the controversies over the Judiciary Act repeal, impeachments, and other potential threats to the Union and the federal judiciary's place in it. He became more assertive when Jefferson left office, and especially after the War of 1812 had stoked American nationalism. In his last years he appeared to "follow the election returns" and to trim his sails in the face of Jacksonian democracy.

The Court's fragmentation predated the Jackson election, as the trend toward seriatim opinions by the newer justices developed. In 1827, Marshall wrote his only major dissenting opinion for a closely divided Court in *Ogden v. Saunders*. *Sturges* had held that state bankruptcy laws could not alter the terms of contracts already made.[145] Four justices in *Ogden* held that a state could alter contractual obligations made after its bankruptcy law went into effect. Marshall wrote an impassioned dissent, in which he resorted to natural law or vested rights principles that he had subordinated to the text of the contract clause since *Fletcher v. Peck*. He appealed to the distressing history of the 1780s, when similar state laws threatened "to destroy all confidence of man in man" and "sap the morals of the people."[146] The chief justice perhaps overreacted, for the majority agreed that such state laws could not alter obligations to out-of-state creditors. As the economy became more extensive and interstate, such debtor relief laws would amount to little.

In its 1829 term, the Court began to qualify its broad interpretation of the commerce power, in *Willson v. Blackbird Creek Marsh Company*. The state had dammed a creek in order to drain a pestiferous swamp. The attorney general called the creek "one of those sluggish reptile streams, that do not run but creep, and spread their venom." Willson claimed that the act rendered worthless his coastal license (the same that prevailed over the New York steamboat monopoly in *Gibbons*). Marshall held that the coastal licensing act did not apply, and he now interpreted the Delaware act as an exercise of the "police power," or the general state power reserved (per the Tenth Amendment) to legislate for the safety, health, welfare, and morals of the people.[147] The line between the national commerce power and the state police power would become one of the most enduring questions in American constitutional history.

That same term, the Court gave the states greater power to regulate corporations than its robust contract clause cases suggested. Rhode Island had chartered a bank in 1791, and in 1822 it enacted a tax on bank stock. The Court rejected the bank's plea that the original charter implied exemption from taxation, since a ruinous tax could destroy the contract. "The Constitution of the United States was not intended to furnish the corrective for every abuse of power which may be committed by the state governments," Marshall decided.[148]

But Marshall bucked the Jacksonian election trend in the 1830 case of *Craig v. Missouri.* Short of cash, the state issued interest-bearing notes and made them legal tender for public debts. The Court, by a 4–3 vote, struck them down as "bills of credit" prohibited by Article I, section 10.[149] This straitjacketing of state ability to borrow money contributed to the movement to repeal section 25 of the Judiciary Act. Marshall predicted that the repeal movement would succeed or that the dissenters on the Court would effectively "nullify" it.[150] Section 25 survived, but this boldly nationalistic decision did not.[151]

Finally, in 1833 Marshall held that the Bill of Rights applied only to the federal government and not to the states. This decision almost certainly accorded with the intent and understanding of the framers and ratifiers of the amendments.[152] But not everyone accepted it. Some state courts held their governments to the federal Bill of Rights.[153] Here, Marshall had more material with which to work a nationalist interpretation than he had in the salad days of his contract clause cases, but he demurred in the face of the Jacksonian states' rights resurgence. To some degree, this decision enhanced federal judicial power by keeping individual rights cases out of federal courts and forestalling a political backlash from southern slaveholders or their abolitionist opponents.[154] Ironically, the newest Jackson appointee, the eccentric Henry Baldwin, who did not participate in the case, would have dissented; he continued to apply the Bill of Rights to the states in his circuit.

John Marshall died in July 1835. It is hard to deny that he did more than anyone to preserve the Founders' Union from the centrifugal forces of Jeffersonian and Jacksonian democracy and states' rights. Doing so from the vulnerable position of the "least dangerous branch" was extraordinarily deft, and undeniably statesmanlike. His opinions met Jackson's standard—that court interpretation of the Constitution merited only "such influence as the force of their reasoning may deserve." Few could resist his reasoning, and he usually won over his brethren and the citizenry. Without doubt, he often crossed the law/politics line, for the American Constitution's establishment of the "judicial power" makes it impossible to do otherwise. But Marshall did so with profound prudence, exercising a distinctly *judicial* statesmanship—keeping law and judgment within bounds—by which all his successors would be judged.[155] He exercised *juris* prudence, not political prudence.[156] Many of Marshall's successors would maintain the appearance of jurisprudence while using it as a Trojan horse for juristocracy.

4

THE COURT AND THE CRISIS
OF THE UNION

THE TANEY COURT

The fifth US chief justice, Roger Brooke Taney, little resembled his predecessor. Most remember him today only for his infamous decision in *Dred Scott*. In 2017, the state of Maryland removed Taney's statue from the statehouse grounds in Annapolis. This recalled his depressed reputation at the time of his death, in 1864. When Senator Lyman Trumbull moved to place a bust of the recently deceased chief justice in the Senate, Massachusetts senator Charles Sumner led the campaign against it. Taney's legacy, he said, would "be hooted down the page of history."[1] His reputation recovered in the early twentieth century, before his stock began to decline again during the "second Reconstruction" of the 1950s–60s. If we remembered Taney only for the first twenty years of his chief justiceship, we might consider him a worthy successor to the great chief justice. While the "political branches" bear some share of responsibility for making slavery "a judicial question," *Dred Scott* (and Taney's behavior after it) fit into a pattern of judicial supremacism that Lincoln and the Republicans checked and that did not resume until near the end of the century.

Andrew Jackson and his party did not object to judicial power in the way that Jefferson had.[2] The Jacksonians happily took over the federal bench by attrition and replacement. Old Hickory benefited from a wave of vacancies and never had occasion to complain that justices "seldom retire and never die." Congress also increased the size of the Court from seven to nine, as it tried to keep up with the territorial expansion of the nation.[3] By the end of his presidency, every justice except Joseph Story bore the Jackson stamp.[4] Politicians still did not consider the Court particularly important, and they chose justices for party purposes.

Jackson first chose his postmaster general, John McLean. An exemplary PG, McLean scrupled to go along with Jackson's policy of "rotation in office"— that is, use of the Post Office for patronage purposes. In particular, McLean did not want to fire incumbent Adams appointees whose support he would need to win the next presidential nomination. So Jackson "kicked him upstairs" to the Court. McLean became a de facto Whig and continued to angle for the presidency until his death in 1860.[5]

Jacksonian politics also complicated Taney's path to the Court. A prominent Maryland Federalist until the 1820s, his support for Jackson made him attorney general in 1829. He earned his stripes in Jackson's war against the Bank of the United States. After his recharter veto triumphed, Jackson decided to go further and destroy the bank by removing the federal government's deposits from it. His Treasury secretary, Louis McLane, believed that the withdrawal violated the law and refused to pull the money out. Jackson transferred McLane to the State Department and replaced him with William Duane. Duane got cold feet and also refused to remove the deposits, so Jackson fired him. Jackson then moved his attorney general to the Treasury and Taney pulled the trigger on the bank. Jackson's affronted Senate opponents "censured" the president and refused to confirm Taney's recess appointment, so the Marylander returned to private practice. When Associate Justice Gabriel Duval retired in 1835, Jackson named Taney for that seat, and the lame-duck anti-Jackson Senate rejected him 24–21. Chief Justice Marshall died that summer, and the Jacksonian Senate elected in 1834 confirmed Taney's appointment to the center seat in December.[6]

Taney did not have Marshall's winning personality, and his Court differed greatly in style, though less so in substance. Marshall has attracted dozens of biographers, many of them eminent; Taney not so many. In his history of the *Dred Scott* case, Donald Fehrenbacher described him upon his swearing in as rather unprepossessing:

Taney was already 59 years old . . . and because of chronic ill health it seemed unlikely that he would enjoy a long tenure. President after president took office with the mistaken expectation that before the end of his term he would have the naming of a new chief justice. Taney's ailments were real enough, but he fussed about them excessively and wore an air of invalidism that grew more pronounced with advancing age. Six feet tall, stooped, with homely features and irregular, tobacco-stained teeth, he was an unimpressive figure until he began to speak.

Then, without oratory or gesture, he held his audience by the force of his reasoning and conviction.[7]

Taney would not try to marshal the Court as Marshall had; seriatim opinions became the norm. He ended the practice of charging grand jurors, believing that American democracy had matured enough to do without the traditional instruction.[8] (Senator Charles Sumner said that this displayed a "jacobin" attitude.)[9] Taney expressed his populism by the trousers he wore, as opposed to Marshall's "small clothes."[10]

But Taney would in no wise become a judicial sansculotte. Notwithstanding the fears and impressions of conservatives like Joseph Story, the Taney Court did very little to alter the course of Marshall's jurisprudence, especially insofar as Marshall had already curbed his Federalist nationalism. Confirmed in December 1835, Taney did not participate in the Court's 1836 term that began the next month. A year later, however, he decided several significant cases. Its most famous, the *Charles River Bridge* case, gave the states more power to promote economic development at the expense of established corporate charter contract holders, but Marshall had implied this in his *Providence Bank* opinion. Despite Story's claim, Marshall himself probably would have concurred with Taney.[11] The Court maintained the ethos of sanctity of contract as essential to republican self-government.[12] The Court also gave a wider berth to the state police power when it abutted interstate commerce, but Marshall adumbrated this in *Willson v. Black Bird Creek Marsh Co.*[13] A tedious tug-of-war to define the commerce–police power line would continue into the next century.

The only flat-out repudiation of his predecessor in the 1837 cases came in *Briscoe v. Bank of Commonwealth of Kentucky,* a 4–3 decision that overturned a 4–3 Marshall opinion in *Craig v. Missouri.*[14] The notes of the Bank of Kentucky more resembled constitutionally prohibited "bills of credit" than had the Missouri state loan certificates in *Craig.* The state wholly owned the bank but denied paternity, and here the Jacksonian justices found a sufficient loophole. Kentucky went further than Missouri and made its bank notes legal tender, in effect, not just for debts owed to the state but also for private contracts. If creditors refused to accept the notes, they could not recover for two years. Story dissented bitterly, and again claimed that he spoke for the late chief justice, this time more plausibly. *Briscoe* marked the last battle of the Bank War, freeing states to take over the monetary system of the nation.

If the Taney Court tipped the balance of federal power toward the states, it did so by augmenting national *judicial* power. Nemesis smote the Taney Court after its assertion of national judicial power to strengthen slavery, to the point of imposing slave-state law on the entire nation. But most of its earlier exercises of national judicial power had to do with the integration of the national economy, as the Court tried to keep out of centrifugal slavery-related questions. It impressively resurrected a federal common law less than a decade after the Court had repudiated it. Credit for this belongs to Joseph Story, and in many ways Story dominated the Taney Court until his death in 1845.

Without a federal common law, how could federal courts to exercise the Article III judicial power that extended to "controversies [but not *all* controversies] . . . between citizens of different states"—its "diversity" jurisdiction? Section 34 of the Judiciary Act provided that "the laws of the several states, except where the Constitution, treaties, or statutes of the United States shall otherwise require or provide, shall be regarded as rules of decision in trials at common law in the courts of the United States in cases where they apply."[15] But what defined "the laws of the states," and "the cases in which they apply"?

Justice Story gave innovative answers to these questions in the 1842 case of *Swift v. Tyson*. John Swift (of Maine) lent money to Nathaniel Norton, who then sold to George Tyson (of New York) land that he did not own. Tyson paid Norton with a "bill of exchange" (essentially, an IOU), which Norton then signed over to Swift to repay his loan. Could Swift, the holder of a negotiable bill of exchange owed by Tyson, collect if Tyson had been defrauded when he had negotiated the bill to a third party (Norton), who then paid his own debt to Swift with Tyson's note? Did the Norton–Tyson fraud relieve Tyson of the obligation to pay Swift? Or should Swift bear the burden of tracking down Norton?[16]

New York had no statute regulating such transactions, and one could read its common law court decisions either way. In any event, Story concluded that the federal courts need not follow state common law in cases like this. "In the ordinary use of language, it will hardly be contended that the decisions of courts constitute laws. They are, at most, only evidence of what the laws are, and are not, of themselves, law." Rather, the federal courts could consult the "general commercial law," or "law merchant," a kind of common law of commercial nations, which had found it commercially beneficial to make bills of exchange as much like cash as possible.[17] Bills of exchange and other commercial instruments would lose value if creditors had to ascertain the purity of every transaction through which they had passed.

Story held that the federal courts could adopt their own legal rules in cases beyond strictly local concern. (The category of "strictly local" became ever narrower over the years, eventually reduced mostly to immobile real estate.) Story hoped that the state courts would adopt the federal rules, which the Supreme Court could oversee for the entire nation. Some states did, and some did not, so the law often differed when the parties came to court from the same state or from different states. But the Taney Court unanimously acceded to this significant expansion of federal judicial power.

Many historians have seen *Swift* as a class-based effort to benefit increasingly large and multistate corporations against smaller local concerns. It encouraged sharp operators like Swift and Norton at the expense of the less canny—a bias that would ensure that the race went to the swift. (Whether or not Swift and Norton had conspired, the *Swift* rule opened the door to such chicanery.) Many state judges followed suit and altered common-law rules to benefit entrepreneurs.[18] Others have stressed the legitimate concern about local bias against out-of-state concerns and do not see much class bias at all.[19]

Whatever the merits of the motives and results of these changes, they clearly represented a large increase in judicial power in nineteenth-century American economics and society. Jacksonian-era constitutions limited state legislative power and, as we have seen, increased judicial review from popularly elected judges. The new political parties that arose became the chief conduits of popular power, organizing the new democratic political system and making nineteenth-century America, in political scientist Stephen Skowronek's celebrated phrase, a "regime of courts and parties."[20]

Story also eagerly extended the Court's admiralty jurisdiction. Article III provided that the judicial power extended to "all cases of admiralty and maritime jurisdiction," but the 1789 Judiciary Act gave concurrent power to state courts and tried to get disputes settled by common law whenever possible, reflecting colonial distrust of juryless admiralty courts such as those that had enforced British navigation laws. But "it was once said of Justice Story that 'if a bucket of water was brought into his court with a corn cob floating in it, he would at once extend the admiralty jurisdiction of the United States over it.'"[21] Traditionally, admiralty jurisdiction extended only to tidal waters, and the Marshall Court had upheld this rule in the 1825 case involving the ship *Thomas Jefferson*. As commerce extended to the inland waters of America, Congress in 1845 extended federal admiralty power to all navigable waters, presumably as part of its power to regulate interstate commerce.

The Court accepted this extension in 1852 but asserted that it derived not from the act of Congress but by its own redefinition of the tidal water limit.[22]

That limit had made sense in England, where almost all waters ebb and flow with the tides, but not in America, where vast bodies of water, like the Great Lakes, do not. From now on, navigability rather than tidal impact would supply the standard. The Court held that Congress could not extend the Court's jurisdiction under the guise of regulating commerce, but it overruled the *Thomas Jefferson* precedent and accepted the jurisdiction.

During that same term, the Court held that a railroad bridge spanning the Ohio River interfered with interstate commerce and ordered it raised or removed. Congress then denominated the bridge a "postal road" and "lawful." In 1854, a storm destroyed the bridge, and steamboat operators tried to prevent its reconstruction. The Court grudgingly upheld the act that declared it lawful, but on commerce, not postal, grounds.[23]

The Court also made access to federal forums easier for corporations. The Marshall Court had held that every member of a corporation (its shareholders) must reside in a different state in order for "diverse citizenship" to permit moving a case to federal court.[24] Now the Court would consider a corporation a citizen of the state from which it got its charter.[25] As with *Swift*, some say this decision favored large, multistate enterprises, but one study concluded that "corporations seem to have tried as hard to escape [federal] jurisdiction as to have it confirmed."[26]

The Taney Court also decided what became the ur-source of the "political questions" doctrine, *Luther v. Borden*. In the early 1840s a group of Rhode Island citizens established a rival government because the established government severely limited the right to vote. (Rhode Island had maintained its 1664 royal charter and did not adopt a new constitution in the 1770s. The most democratic state now ranked among the least, as it retained a property qualification for voting.) These advocates of "popular constitutionalism" initially disdained the strategy of appealing to the state courts. But when the state authorities clamped down on them, they turned to the US Supreme Court.

One of the rebels sued a militiaman who had arrested him, and claimed that the charter government violated Article IV, section 4 of the Constitution, which provided that "the United States shall guarantee to every state in this Union a republican form of government." The Court called the recognition of the legitimate government of the state a "political question." Congress would determine the legitimate government when it chose to admit representatives and senators from the state, or the president would, if (pursuant to acts of Congress) he responded to a state's request to "protect each [state] . . . against domestic violence," which also is provided for in Article IV, section 4.[27]

Although President Tyler had not intervened, Taney asked, "Could the court, while the parties were actually contending in arms for the possession of the government, call witnesses before it and inquire which party represented a majority of the people? . . . If the judicial power extends so far, the guarantee . . . is a guarantee of anarchy, and not of order."[28] Outright rebellion might provide an obvious example of a "political question," but it still largely raised the question of who had the power to define questions as political. Taney's "abrogation of positive action had the effect of positive action," as one historian pointed out. *Luther v. Borden* "paved the way for judicial supremacy by enhancing the authority of the Court to settle questions concerning the allocation of powers under the Constitution," said another. "As happened frequently in the history of the Supreme Court, an apparent abdication of power in actuality manifested an assertion and accession of power."[29] A law professor would later observe that the Court "does not actually decide *everything*. . . . But the Court may decide *anything*. . . . The Justices reserve plenary authority to decide who decides."[30] This case, with its apparent fear of revolution or out-of-doors exercise of popular sovereignty, may again have reflected the Taney Court's concern for slave-state security.[31]

SLAVERY AND *DRED SCOTT*

By the 1850s, the Court enjoyed great public prestige, having faced no significant opposition from the dominant Democratic Party that had staffed it.[32] Today, we define Taney's Court by the *Dred Scott* case, the most infamous decision in US history. Though hardly anybody today defends the merits of the decision, its expression of judicial supremacy has become the norm.[33] In retrospect, it did fit into a pattern of Taney Court activism, but the Court had avoided taking on the issue of slavery for quite a long time. One can fairly criticize John Marshall for avoiding it—he did not apply to slavery the kind of imagination that he did in contract clause cases. He might have utilized the emancipatory potential of the natural law and law of nations, as Justice Story tended to do. The Court could not avoid dealing with cases that arose out of the international slave trade, for example. And while Marshall, along with Story, called slavery contrary to the law of nature, he made more room for it under the law of nations—the United States, for example, could not extend its own definition of slaving as piracy to other nations that had not.[34] We have seen Marshall's evasion of the issue of South Carolina's Negro Seamen Act and that state's effective nullification of Justice Johnson's decision. The Taney Court twisted itself into knots on the potentially explosive issue of treating slaves as articles of commerce subject to Congress's commerce power.[35]

The Court avoided dealing with the issue of fugitive slaves until 1842. Article IV, section 2 of the Constitution (the fugitive slave clause) provided that "No person held to service or labor in one state, under the laws thereof, escaping into another, shall, in consequence of any law or regulation therein, be discharged from such service or labor, but shall be delivered up on claim of the party to whom such service of labor may be due." But the text did not specify who would enforce the clause. The Founders wrote the clause in the passive voice and placed it in Article IV, which had to do with "comity"—obligations that the states owed to one another. It gave no specific power to Congress in Article I, section 8, nor did it withhold any from the states in Article I, section 10.

Congress passed a Fugitive Slave Act in 1793, which allowed slave owners to "recapture" their runaway slaves (if they could do so in a peaceful and orderly way) and obliged state authorities to assist them. The act caused little controversy until the 1820s, as the slavery issue became more divisive and free state–slave state comity began to erode. Many free states began to enact "personal liberty laws" to protect their free Black citizens from kidnapping.

Pennsylvania prosecuted Edward Prigg, a Maryland slave catcher, under Pennsylvania's personal liberty law, and Prigg challenged his conviction. Justice Story rendered a very enigmatic decision. He upheld Congress's power to enforce the fugitive slave clause and held that state laws like Pennsylvania's could not obstruct it. He went on to say that the Constitution empowered Congress alone to enforce the clause. States might help to enforce it if they wished, or they could refuse. Taney objected to this potentially antislavery part of Story's opinion (which, incidentally, would have struck down part of an act of Congress for the first time since *Marbury*). He misinterpreted it as an invitation to states to foil national enforcement efforts, and northern antislavery zealots followed his misinterpretation.[36] Disgruntled southerners thus got Congress to enact a more stringent Fugitive Slave Act as part of the Compromise of 1850, enforced by federal commissioners.

Another interstate matter that the Court had to address concerned the status of slaves taken voluntarily into a free state. States distinguished between "transit" through a state, a "sojourn" visit of a few days or weeks, and the establishment of a permanent "domicile." As interstate comity broke down, free states began to liberate slaves who tarried in their domain for ever briefer periods, and eventually (*Dred Scott* was the first time) slave states would insist that even domicile in a free state did not prevent reenslavement upon return to a slave state. In *Strader v. Graham* (1850), the Supreme Court held that a slave's status depended upon the courts of the state and that the federal courts had no power to review their decisions. If the Negro happened to reside in a free state and his status became disputed, he went free; if he chanced to find himself in a slave state, its courts could declare him a slave. Story seemed to regard slave status as so peculiarly local as to not be subject to the expansion of a federal common law since *Swift v. Tyson*.[37]

As the sectional conflict became focused on the issue of slavery in the territories, the Court entered the fray and attempted to settle it in the *Dred Scott* case. One could say that the Court had merely responded to an invitation to determine an issue frequently proffered by politicians. The Kansas–Nebraska Act, for example, which repealed the Missouri Compromise and opened the Louisiana Purchase territory to slavery, had a provision that expedited appeals to the US Supreme Court in disputes over slavery. One senator wryly observed that Congress had enacted "not a law but a law suit." Stephen Douglas, the act's sponsor, refused to say whether or when a territorial legislature could prohibit slavery, calling it "a judicial question." *Dred Scott* well displayed the marks of "the political foundations of judicial supremacy."[38]

In the 1830s, John Emerson, an army doctor, took his slave, Dred Scott, into the free state of Illinois and to parts of the Louisiana Purchase territory where the Missouri Compromise had prohibited slavery. They returned to Missouri. After Emerson died, Scott became the property of John Sanford of Massachusetts.[39] Scott sued for his freedom in the Missouri courts, claiming that his time domiciled in Illinois and Wisconsin territory freed him. He won his first suit, in 1846, the court applying the principle of "once free, always free." In 1850, the Missouri supreme court reversed. For the first time, a slave state repudiated the "once free" principle and allowed the "reattachment" of slavery. The Court said that this change in policy resulted from increasing hostility to slavery in the free states. "Times now are not what they were," the Court warned. "Not only individuals but states have been possessed with a dark and fell spirit in relation to slavery, whose gratification is sought in the pursuit of measures, whose inevitable consequence must be the overthrow and destruction of our government."[40]

Strader prevented an appeal from the Missouri supreme court to the US Supreme Court, so Scott then brought suit in federal circuit court, presenting himself as a citizen of Missouri suing a citizen of New York.[41] In 1854, the circuit court rejected his freedom suit. Scott then appealed to the US Supreme Court, which heard arguments in February 1856 and rearguments in December. The easy way out would reaffirm *Strader* and let the Missouri high court decision stick. Apparently, the Court initially took this route, with Justice

Nelson drafting a brief opinion. But Justice Wayne wanted the decision to go further and take on the issues of Congress's power over slavery in the territories and of Black citizenship. This provoked Justices Curtis and McLean to prepare extensive dissenting opinions. Their dissents led Chief Justice Taney to take over writing the majority opinion.[42]

Meanwhile, Justice Catron kept his friend President-Elect James Buchanan abreast of the case's progress, and Buchanan cajoled fellow Pennsylvanian Justice Grier to join the five southern justices so that the Court did not divide exactly along sectional lines. Tipped off about the pending decision, Buchanan said in his inaugural address that the question of prohibiting slavery in the territories "is a judicial question, which legitimately belongs to the Supreme Court . . . before whom it is now pending, and will, it is understood, be speedily and finally settled. To this decision, in common with all good citizens, I will cheerfully submit, whatever this may be."[43]

Lincoln aptly called Taney's decision "an astonisher in legal history." We remain uncertain about its import since, in Taney Court fashion, it issued nine separate opinions—seven agreeing with the outcome, though for various reasons, and two dissenting. A majority clearly held that Blacks could not claim US citizenship (and therefore could not sue in federal courts), and that Congress had no power to prohibit slavery in the territories. As in many cases of judicial muscle, Taney addressed extensively the merits of the case rather than simply dismissing it for lack of jurisdiction. This led many Republicans to call his decision on the merits obiter dictum—literally "said in passing," or just "by the way"—not necessary for the decision and of no force.[44] Taney insisted that Blacks composed no part of "the people" who had ordained and established the Constitution, and that the Founders regarded them as "a subordinate and inferior class of beings, who had been subjugated to the dominant race and, whether emancipated or not, yet remained subject to their authority, and had no rights or privileges but such as those who held the power and the government might choose to grant them." States might choose to make Blacks citizens and extend to them rights, but that did not make them citizens of the United States.[45]

The denial of Black citizenship provoked the lesser controversy, given white racial attitudes of the time, including those of antislavery Republicans. Taney's denial of congressional power over slavery in the territories raised more hackles, for it held unconstitutional the fundamental raison d'être of the Republican Party. Generations had assumed (though some had disputed this since the Missouri Compromise) that this power was derived from Article IV, section

3, paragraph 2, which said, "The Congress shall have power to dispose of and make all needful rules and regulations respecting the territory or other property belonging to the United States." Taney concluded that Congress's power came, rather, from the preceding paragraph, which said that "new states may be admitted by the Congress into this union." The "all needful rules" paragraph applied only to territory in American possession in 1787, which made the Northwest Ordinance's prohibition of slavery acceptable. Taney held the Missouri Compromise unconstitutional (though Congress had repealed it in the 1854 Kansas–Nebraska Act). The Republican Party called for its restoration.

Taney went further and maintained that the Fifth Amendment also meant that Congress could not prohibit slavery in the territories. He articulated what later commentators would call "substantive due process," the idea that the legislature cannot abridge some fundamental rights by *any* process.[46] "An act of Congress which deprives a citizen of the United States of his liberty or property, merely because he came himself or brought his property into a particular territory of the United States, and who had committed no offense against the laws, could hardly be dignified with the name of due process of law," Taney said.[47]

Taney looked upon slaves not just as property but as a kind of superproperty, one that he claimed the Constitution "distinctly and expressly" protected (though the Constitution in fact never used the word "slave" or "slavery" and always refers to slaves as "persons"). Since Congress could not prohibit slavery, neither could a territorial legislature established by Congress. (Though only Taney's opinion made this point, it eliminated the option of "territorial sovereignty" championed by Stephen Douglas, a middle-of-the-road position that sidestepped the question of congressional power by arguing that even if Congress *had* the power, it should not exercise it but should leave it to the people of the territory.)

Taney went all the way to the most extreme proslavery position, that Congress had an obligation to protect slave property in the territories. "The only power conferred is the power, coupled with the duty, of guarding and protecting the owner in his rights."[48] He implicitly adopted the Calhounite theory that saw the general government as only the agent or trustee of all of the states, which could not discriminate against the property of some of them.[49] In effect, the Court exercised the kind of sectional veto or concurrent majority that Calhoun's theory called for.[50]

The decision engulfed the nation, politicizing the Court as never before. Justices Taney and Curtis became so angry at each other's opinion that Curtis resigned. Republicans denounced *Dred Scott,* and its embrace became a litmus test for Democrats. It provided the central issue in the famous debates between Lincoln and Douglas in the Illinois Senate race of 1858. Douglas defended the decision; Lincoln rejected it.[51] Douglas claimed that *Dred Scott* did not annihilate his own policy of territorial sovereignty because even if a territory could not positively prohibit slavery, it could refuse to enact the necessary laws (slave patrols and the like) without which slavery could not survive. Lincoln pointed out that Douglas could not logically claim that *Dred Scott* established a constitutional right that lawmakers who took an oath to support the Constitution could nullify.

Though Lincoln denounced *Dred Scott,* he did not say *precisely* how the Republicans would undo it. Senators William Seward and Zechariah Chandler said that they would "reorganize" the Court, Chandler calling the decision a Taney "stump speech" and "mere fanfaronade."[52] It seems most likely that the Republicans planned to elect a Republican president who would appoint judges to overturn *Dred Scott.* Douglas accused Lincoln and the Republicans of embarking on "a crusade against the Supreme Court" and of appealing its decisions to "a tumultuous town meeting" or "a Republican caucus sitting in the country," threatening mob rule over the rule of law.[53] He went so far as to say that "that decision becomes the law of the land," as if the Court's interpretation of the Constitution equaled the Constitution.[54]

Lincoln of course denied this. Republicans accepted the decision of the particular case, *Dred Scott v. Sanford.* However erroneous the decision, Dred Scott remained legally a slave. Republicans would not "raise a mob and free Dred Scott." Lincoln rather denied the decision as a precedent or authority, applicable to all future cognate cases. "We know that the Court that made it, has often overruled its decisions, and we shall *do what we can* to have it overrule this one" (emphasis mine).[55] Lincoln steered a middle course between juristocracy and anarchy.

The value of a case as a precedent varied, Lincoln argued. "If this important decision had been made by the unanimous concurrence of the judges, without any apparent partisan bias, and in accordance with legal public expectation, and with the steady practice of the departments throughout our history, and had been in no part based on assumed historical facts which are not really true," it would have considerable authority. But *Dred Scott* failed on all of these counts. Precedents also acquired authority if "affirmed and re-affirmed through a course of years," precisely what the Republicans aimed to prevent.[56] "We oppose the Dred Scott decision in a certain way," he explained. The

Republicans would not forcefully defy the outcome of any particular case, but "[we] do not propose to be bound by it as a political rule. . . . We propose so resisting it as to have it reversed if we can, and a new judicial rule established on this subject."[57]

Lincoln had some fun pointing out that Douglas's hero was Andrew Jackson, the president who had repudiated the idea of the Supreme Court as final arbiter of constitutional interpretation in the Bank War. Better yet, he reminded Douglas that Douglas had participated in the Illinois Democrats' court packing of 1841. "I know that Judge Douglas will not deny that he was in favor of overslaughing that decision by the mode of adding five new judges, so as to vote down the four old ones." Indeed, Douglas himself became one of the five. "It was in this way precisely that he got his title of judge." Lincoln made sport of Douglas's newfound respect for precedent and his expression of horror at court packing. "When the Judge tells me that men appointed conditionally to sit as members of a court will have to be catechized beforehand on some subject, I say, 'You know best, Judge; you have tried it.' When he says a court of this kind will lose the confidence of all men, will be prostituted and disgraced by such a proceeding, I say, 'You know best, Judge; you have been through the mill.'"[58]

As the Civil War approached, some northern states took up the "nullification" strategy with regard to the Fugitive Slave Act, or reverted to the Virginia high court's resistance to US Supreme Court review in the 1820s. Federal slave catchers held a fugitive slave, Joshua Glover, in a Milwaukee jail, and Wisconsin abolitionists did "raise a mob and free" Glover. The federal government prosecuted editor Sherman Booth for aiding the Fugitive Slave Act nullifiers, but the Wisconsin courts refused to respond to review orders by the US Supreme Court, and the legislature revived the language of the Virginia and Kentucky Resolutions in favor of state power to decide constitutional controversies.[59]

The Court in *Ableman v. Booth* resoundingly and unanimously upheld the constitutionality of the Fugitive Slave Act and, per Marshall and Story, the section 25 federal review power. Now abolitionists in Congress called for the repeal of section 25.[60] But this apparent blow to states' rights (courts would use it to put down southern state resistance to desegregation in the 1950s) really enlisted national judicial power to make slave-state law apply nationwide, giving local slave codes extraterritorial effect, reversing the rule of "freedom national, slavery local."[61]

In a related case, Kentucky asked the Court to issue a mandamus to Ohio authorities to extradite a fugitive slave. Taney could not bring himself to issue an unenforceable order, so, à la Marshall in *Marbury*, he scolded the Ohio-ans for dereliction of duty but begged off on jurisdictional grounds.[62] With seven states having already seceded, this apparently antislavery decision really aided *secession*, paralleling lame-duck President Buchanan's unwillingness to use force to preserve the Union. The war would soon make these questions moot anyway.

Lincoln's first inaugural address provided the classic statement against judicial supremacy. He explained his theory of the permanence of the Union, rejecting secession as unjustified revolution. Nobody had violated any "plainly written provision" of the Constitution concerning the rights of the slavehold-ing states. "But no organic law can ever be framed with a provision specifically applicable to every question which may occur in practical administration," he said, echoing John Marshall's description of "a constitution" in *McCulloch*. "No foresight can anticipate, nor any document of reasonable length contain express provisions for all possible questions." The people could only settle disputes about issues like fugitive slaves and slavery in the territories by elec-tions and majority rule. "The Constitution does not expressly say" one way or the other on these issues. Thus, Lincoln argued, they presented political questions, not judicial ones.

"I do not forget the position assumed by some," he continued, "that consti-tutional questions are to be decided by the Supreme Court." Lincoln conceded the finality of its decisions in particular cases, and called them "entitled to very high respect and consideration, in all parallel cases, by all other departments of the government." An erroneous decision like *Dred Scott* still must stand, as "the evil effect following it, being limited to that particular case, with the chance that it may be overruled, and never become a precedent for other cases, can better be borne than could the evils of a different practice"—cold comfort, perhaps, for Dred Scott. As Publius had remarked, "Individual oppression may now and then proceed from the courts of justice," but "the general liberty of the people can never be endangered from that quarter."[63] But, Lincoln concluded, "At the same time, the candid citizen must confess that if the policy of the government, upon vital questions, affecting the whole people, is to be irrevo-cably fixed by decisions of the Supreme Court, the instant they are made, in ordinary litigation between parties, in personal actions, the people will have ceased to be their own rulers, having to that extent practically resigned their government into the hands of that eminent tribunal."[64]

Nonetheless, Lincoln did not deny the coordinate power of judicial review, and even came to the Court's defense, somewhat. "Nor is there, in this view, any assault upon the Court, or the judges. It is a duty, from which they may not shrink, to decide cases properly brought before them; and it is no fault of theirs, if others seek to turn their decisions to political purposes."[65] Indeed, considering the colossal overreach of the *Dred Scott* decision, the Republicans showed remarkable restraint, limiting their scrutiny to that particular decision and not extending it to the justices, nor to the Court, nor to judicial review per se.

Before any court reconsidered *Dred Scott,* the Republican administration began to disregard it as a precedent and to pursue its own "construction" of the Constitution. For instance, federal law limited passports and patents to US citizens, but Lincoln's State Department issued them to free Blacks. Congress also abolished slavery in the territories in 1862. After the war, when the Emancipation Proclamation or the Thirteenth Amendment had freed all Blacks, the Civil Rights Act of 1866 declared them to be citizens, *Dred Scott* notwithstanding.[66] Most say that the Fourteenth Amendment in 1868 overturned *Dred Scott,* but the administration and Congress had already been done that. The amendment just made it more difficult to undo.

THE COURT AND THE CIVIL WAR

Taney continued to oppose the Republicans and assert judicial power after the war began and Republicans took control of the government. Of the five slave-state justices, only one (John A. Campbell of Alabama) went with his state. Virginian Peter V. Daniel died in May 1860, and lame-duck President Buchanan could not replace him because southern Democratic senators had walked out. Justices Catron and Wayne remained loyal to the Union. The chief justice turned Copperhead and preferred to let the Confederates secede in peace.[67] His situation on the Court limited his ability to frustrate Lincoln's conduct of the war.

The Civil War presented a host of quintessentially political controversies that were nonjusticiable, or at least were not adjudicated until after the war ended. Taney had prepared opinions striking down Union measures like conscription, but he had no opportunity to promulgate them.[68] The administration tried to keep controversial issues out of court, often "running out the clock" and taking advantage of the slower pace of litigation. When it had to, it abolished uncooperative courts like the District of Columbia's circuit court.[69] Justice Miller noted that the Court made "strenuous efforts" to avoid embarrassing the administration.[70]

Lincoln took several controversial steps in the four-month period between his inauguration and the meeting of Congress in special session on Independence Day of 1861.[71] Lincoln spent and borrowed millions of dollars without congressional appropriation, though Article I, section 9 says, "No money shall be drawn from the Treasury, but in consequence of appropriations made by law," and Article I, section 8 gives Congress the power "to borrow money on the credit of the United States." He also expanded the regular army and navy without congressional authorization (despite the constitutional statement that "Congress shall have power . . . to raise and support armies [and] to provide and maintain a navy"). As Lincoln put it to Congress that July, "These measures, whether strictly legal or not, were ventured upon under what appeared to be a popular demand and a public necessity; trusting then as now that Congress would readily ratify them. It is believed that nothing has been done beyond the constitutional competency of Congress."[72] Congress did indeed retroactively ratify his acts. It remains hard to imagine how steps like these could have become court cases. Nobody then imagined today's custom of legislators suing executives.

The first direct clash between the administration and the courts concerned Lincoln's suspension of the writ of habeas corpus. This writ (literally, an order to produce or present the body) allows a prisoner to petition a judge to compel his captors to give reasons for his detention. Nineteenth-century Americans called habeas the "great writ." In the Founding generation, every Anglo-American would place it on his short list of the essential "rights of Englishmen," along with consent to taxation and trial by jury. Parliamentary control of the writ in the Habeas Corpus Act of 1679 helped to advance the English constitutional revolution. Article I, section 9 of the Constitution reads, "The privilege of the writ of habeas corpus shall not be suspended, unless when in cases of rebellion or invasion the public safety may require it."

But *who* could suspend it? As with the fugitive slave clause, the framers wrote in the passive voice. Almost no precedent could guide Lincoln. General Andrew Jackson had suspended the writ during the war of 1812, and the governor of Rhode Island had done so during the Dorr Rebellion.[73] Jefferson asked Congress to consider suspending the writ in the Burr treason imbroglio. In dicta and treatises, Marshall and Story seem to have believed that the power belonged to Congress as it had to the British Parliament.[74]

Lincoln suspended the writ to prevent sabotage along the railroad line from Philadelphia to the District of Columbia. The army detained John Merryman, a Maryland secessionist and suspected saboteur, in Fort McHenry. Chief Justice Taney, as a judge in the Maryland circuit, issued a writ of habeas corpus, which the fort commander rebuffed. Taney then issued a writ for the commander to appear and explain himself, but guards would not admit the writ-bearing federal marshal. In his opinion, *Ex parte Merryman*,[75] Taney expressed his surprise that anyone would suppose that the president rather than Congress possessed the power to suspend the great writ. He placed much emphasis on the clause's location in Article I, and on English history and American commentators.[76]

Taney went on to make an extraordinary statement of judicial supremacy. Article II declares that the president "shall take care that the laws shall be faithfully executed"—indeed, Lincoln would justify many of his controversial acts on the basis of this provision. But, Taney claimed, "he is not authorized to execute them himself, or through his agents or officers," but only "as they are expounded and adjudged by the courts." The executive can only act "in subordination to judicial authority, assisting it to execute its processes and enforce its judgments."[77]

Taney accused Lincoln of usurping legislative and judicial powers, but it looked more like Taney had grasped executive power. He concluded that "I have exercised all the power which the Constitution and laws confer upon me, but that power has been resisted by a force too strong for me to overcome." He transmitted a copy of his opinion to Lincoln, and said, "It will then remain for that high officer, in fulfillment of his constitutional obligation to 'take care that the laws be faithfully executed,' to determine what measures he will take."[78] Lincoln ignored Taney's opinion and persisted in his policy.

Many critics claim that in the habeas fracas, Lincoln defied the court, as Jackson had done in the Cherokee cases. The analogy applies only because Lincoln appears to have defied the Court no more than Jackson had. Taney's opinion in *Merryman* was just that—an opinion, even an "advisory opinion," and not an enforceable (or defiable) order.[79] Lincoln certainly did stand for independent, coordinate construction of the Constitution, or "departmentalism," a point elaborated in his attorney general's more extensive opinion.[80] Lincoln did not call the suspension power exclusively presidential. He told Congress, "Whether there shall be any legislation upon the subject, and if any, what, is submitted entirely to the better judgment of Congress."[81]

Congress did in fact pass the Habeas Corpus Suspension Act in 1863, and the fact that it took until 1863 to do so lends considerable support to Lincoln's argument that the president must possess the power to suspend in sudden emergencies. The act said, "During the present rebellion, the President . . . whenever, in his judgment, the public safety may require it, is authorized to suspend the privilege of the writ of habeas corpus."[82] But Lincoln could read this as merely declaratory, if the president's power derived from the Constitution rather than from Congress, as if Congress had declared that he a had a four-year term of office.[83] The act then required the administration to provide to the federal courts lists of people held without the privilege of the writ, and that the administration should release them unless the federal grand jury's next session indicted them. This satisfied Lincoln's needs, since most detentions did not last long and were undertaken for preventative rather than punitive purposes ("not so much for what has been done," as Lincoln put it, "as for what probably would be done").[84] The administration only provided one list of political prisoners. It also interpreted the act as inapplicable to irregular combatants ("aiders and abetters of the enemy . . . amenable to military law"), and the dispute over the status of such parties continues into our own century.[85]

Lincoln's Supreme Court appointments indicate the relative unimportance of the institution and the continued influence of regional and especially party considerations in its composition. His first choice, Noah Swayne of Ohio, ranks among the most forgettable justices who served as long as he did— twenty years. We may know his second choice, Samuel Miller of Iowa, the first trans-Mississippian justice, as the "justice of shattered dreams" who crippled the Fourteenth Amendment in the *Slaughterhouse Cases*.[86] David Davis of Illinois had managed Lincoln's presidential campaign and would resign from the Court in 1877, when he was chosen as US senator by the Illinois legislature. (His shift simultaneously removed him as the deciding vote in the electoral commission established to settle the 1876 presidential election.)[87] Lincoln chose his Treasury secretary, Salmon P. Chase, as chief justice, to "kick upstairs" a political rival and provide a reliable vote on controversial Civil War measures. Chase would display a lamentable lack of judicial temperament during his brief tenure in the center chair.[88] In 1863, Congress added a tenth seat to the Court, to accommodate California. Stephen J. Field, a loyal, or "war," Democrat, did establish a significant jurisprudential record in his thirty-four years on the bench. Unfairly, however, he became a symbol of conservative or "laissez-faire" judicial activism. Field also maintained hopes of rising to the presidency.[89]

The new personnel sustained the administration in the first important war-related case, recognizing the president's power to impose a blockade on the rebel states. Justices Wayne and Grier joined the three new Lincoln men in a 5–4 decision. The dissenters held that only Congress could declare a rebellion and blockade, which it did some three months after Lincoln.[90] The Court also refused to review the cases of civilians tried by military commissions. Commissions did not qualify as Article III courts, and the Judiciary Acts had given the Supreme Court no power to review their decisions.[91]

THE JUDICIAL AND POLITICAL QUESTIONS OF RECONSTRUCTION

The Court became somewhat more assertive after the war ended, but it displayed considerable prudence in observing the line between law and politics in cases related to Reconstruction. As a result, the institution emerged from the crisis of the Union stronger and more prestigious than ever. The *Dred Scott* disaster turned out to have done no lasting harm. The Republicans largely confined their critiques to that particular decision and did not extend it to the judges, much less to the Court itself or to judicial review.

The Court dismissed as frivolous suits brought by the states of Georgia and Mississippi to enjoin the president from enforcing the Reconstruction acts. These desperate gambits presaged today's everything is-justiciable attitude.[92] The Court struck down both state and federal acts that limited certain public offices and professions to those who could swear that they had never betrayed the Union. The Court regarded these "ironclad oaths" (as opposed to an oath of *future* loyalty) as ex post facto laws or bills of attainder. These decisions provoked no legislative reaction.[93]

The Court's decision in *Ex parte Milligan* would become the brightest star in the civil libertarian judicial firmament. The Court overturned the prosecutions by military commission of several antiwar Indiana Democrats. Insisting that the Constitution applied "equally in time of war and peace," Justice Davis said that "no doctrine, involving more pernicious consequences, was ever invented by the wit of man than that any of its provisions can be suspended during any of the great exigencies of government."[94] Though it aided former rebels and their allies and imperiled the freedmen, many regarded the *Milligan* case as a great statement of civil liberty and a courageous decision by the Court in defiance of the dominant political coalition. But this view needs some discounting. Courts find it easier to defend individual rights after a war ends. The Court would effectively repudiate *Milligan* during World War II, when the issue of military commissions came up again.

The *Milligan* case alarmed Republicans, who believed that it would imperil the system of military rule that they had designed for the defeated but recalcitrant rebel states. They apparently believed the Democratic politicians and editors who hoped that it would.[95] To prevent this, Congress repealed a recently enacted expansion of the Court's power to grant habeas petitions on appeal from the circuit courts.[96] The Court then dismissed an appeal pending from a Mississippi newspaper editor, William McCardle, who had published articles opposing Reconstruction. The Court recognized Congress's plenary power to regulate and make exceptions to its appellate jurisdiction.[97] Justice Grier accused his brethren of dereliction of duty in delaying and finally dismissing the case. Navy Secretary Gideon Wells wrote that "the judges of the Supreme Court have caved in, fallen through, and failed," cowed by congressional radicals.[98]

Many see *Ex parte McCardle* as the most important example of the seldom-used "jurisdiction-stripping" power of Congress to keep the Court within bounds. The case itself amounted to little and marked the outer limit of congressional reaction—though some radicals wanted to abolish the Court entirely, to require supermajority or unanimous opinions, or to forbid judicial review of the Reconstruction Acts or prohibit all judicial review.[99] The House resolved to investigate a press rumor that some justice (most fingers pointed to Stephen J. Field) had openly declared the Reconstruction program unconstitutional.[100]

The Court could still entertain petitions for habeas via certiorari under the original Judiciary Act, which it did later that year. The jurisdiction repeal act, the Court said, intended "to oust the Court of its jurisdiction of the particular case then before it on appeal." It called such an act, virtually an order from Congress to dispose of one case only, "unusual and hardly to be justified except upon some imperious public exigency." By this time, though, most cases had become moot through the restoration of civil government in the last rebel states.[101]

Moreover, when Congress passed a law that ordered the Court not to consider presidential pardons, it held that this did not constitute a legitimate "exception" under Article III but rather an encroachment on executive power.[102] However minor, a century later, Justice William O. Douglas doubted whether his day's fully supreme Court would put up with the McCardle limitation.[103] Alexander Hamilton had called impeachment "a complete security" against judicial usurpation, but the Chase episode turned it into Jefferson's "scarecrow." The exceptions clause offered an even greater means to control the Court, but *McCardle* made it almost as useless as impeachment.

The most controversial exercise of judicial power during the Reconstruction period came in the *Legal Tender Cases*. As secretary of the Treasury, Chase fought to destroy state paper money and establish a national currency. He won this in the National Banking Act of 1863, which established a Jacksonian version of the Bank of the United States. (A hard-money advocate before the slavery issue turned him into a Republican, Chase maintained fond hopes of winning the Democratic presidential nomination while on the Court.) He also had to accept congressional authorization of almost half a billion dollars of greenbacks—paper money or national bills of credit not redeemable in gold or silver, which must be accepted as legal tender for all debts except import duties and interest on the national debt. Chase privately expressed his hatred of this policy.[104]

The greenback issue conjured up memories of the paper money inflation of the 1780s, singled out by Madison as the sort of "improper and wicked project" that the Constitution would prevent. But the Constitution did not say anything about whether the *national* government could emit bills of credit or make anything but gold and silver legal tender. Massachusetts congressman George Boutwell recalled that Lincoln thought Chase's position on greenback issue factored in his decision to put him on the Court. "We want a man who will sustain the Legal Tender Act and the Proclamation of Emancipation," Lincoln said, according to Boutwell. "We cannot ask a candidate what he would do; and if we did and he should answer, we should only despise him for it. Therefore we must take a man whose opinions are known."[105]

But in the first legal tender case (*Hepburn v. Griswold*), Chase declared the act void, at least with regard to debts contracted before its enactment. The act carried "the doctrine of implied powers very far beyond any extent hitherto given to it." He also resorted to the "spirit" of the Constitution or natural law, including the due process clause of the Fifth Amendment, which Taney had used in *Dred Scott*. As to his own role in the law's enactment, he could only plead the distortions of wartime. "Amid the tumult of the late civil war," he said, "the time was not favorable to considerate reflection. . . . Some [he named not himself] who were strongly averse . . . were constrained to acquiesce in the views of advocates of the measure." But "under the influence of calmer times," they had "reconsidered their conclusions."[106]

Some see *Hepburn* as "one of the most dubious examples of judicial review in the Court's history," but it proved ephemeral.[107] On the day that the Court announced it, President Grant sent two nominations to the Senate—one to replace Grier, whom many regarded as *non compos mentis and* whom Chase had wheedled into joining his opinion, and one to fill a vacancy due to Congress's reexpansion of the size of the Court to nine.[108] Chase tried desperately to prevent a reconsideration of the case; Justice Miller wrote that he "resorted to all the stratagems of the lowest political trickery" to do so. But in 1870 the Court reversed *Hepburn* and upheld the act.[109]

The Court's reputation suffered less by the original opinion than by the appearance that Grant had packed the Court and had appointed Justices Bradley and Strong particularly to overturn it.[110] Though we usually associate monetary inflation with democratic and populist movements, in this era it also benefited railroads, then heavily indebted. The widespread revulsion at this apparent manipulation settled the number of justices at nine from then onward.[111]

Indeed, the Chase Court acquired a reputation for "activism," paving the way for late nineteenth-century entrepreneurial or "laissez-faire" jurisprudence.[112] The Court struck down two acts of Congress in the seven decades before 1864, and ten in less than two decades under Chase. But numbers do not tell the whole story. Marshall and Taney had few occasions to strike down federal legislation, because the Jeffersonian Republican and Jacksonian Democratic parties embraced federal minimalism. The new Republican Party revived the nationalist ambitions of the Federalists and Whigs. Thus, the Democratic holdovers on the new Court suddenly became activated.[113]

The Chase Court asserted its power in matters unrelated to Reconstruction. When Congress created a court of claims to relieve itself of petitions for payment by US creditors, the Court refused to review its decisions until Congress amended the act to guarantee the finality of its own decisions.[114] But this only reiterated *Hayburn's Case* of 1792, when the Court declined to adjudicate Revolutionary War pension claims. The justices refused to ride circuit in states under military control so as not to risk civilian subordination to the military.[115] The justices regarded themselves as nothing less than supreme but nothing other than a court. The Court also struck down a prohibition of the sale of naptha, a volatile hydrocarbon used as illuminating oil. The government claimed that the prohibition aimed to increase the revenue from taxes on legal petroleum products, but the Court found that justification "too remote and uncertain," in fact a pretext for what they considered "plainly an exercise of police."[116]

The Court very energetically protected investment in the largest industry in antebellum America, the railroads. Many states and localities had taken on large debts to promote railroads and other "internal improvements" before the Civil War. Many came to regret it. One city, Dubuque, Iowa, denied its obligation to pay its railroad promotion bonds because railroads did not serve a "public purpose" for which a municipality could levy taxes. The US Supreme Court overturned the Iowa high court's acceptance of this argument in 1864, in what one historian called "one of the most strong-handed chapters of judicial policymaking."[117] Justice Swayne wrote that the Iowa decision violated "the plainest principles of justice. . . . We shall never immolate truth, justice, and the law, because a state tribunal has erected the altar and decreed the sacrifice."[118] Justice Miller dissented, privately calling his brethren "if not monomaniacs, as much bigots and fanatics on that subject as is the most unhesitating Mahomedan in regard to his religion." But Miller's dissents pretty clearly expressed his own antirailroad biases, born from his personal and home-state economic failures.[119] Though some other state courts, including Michigan's esteemed supreme court under Thomas McIntyre Cooley, continued to allow railroad bond repudiation, the US Supreme Court ensured the securities of foreign bondholders.[120] The Court also upheld the great federal promotion of the transcontinental railroads.[121]

Reconstruction presented quintessentially "political questions," left to the elected, political branches, not to litigation. The legislative–executive conflict climaxed in the impeachment and trial of President Andrew Johnson in 1868. Chief Justice Chase presided over that trial, but the Senate majority set the rules.[122] In the last episode of Reconstruction, the presidential election of 1876, Congress also set the rules but brought in the justices. Congress established an electoral commission of fifteen: five senators and five representatives, with five from each party, plus two Democratic and two Republican justices, who would choose a fifth. All expected the justices to choose Justice Davis, a disillusioned Republican. But the Illinois legislature (controlled by Democrats and Independents) suddenly elected Davis to the US Senate. He resigned and the justices chose the reliable Republican Joseph Bradley. The commission, on a party-line vote, gave the presidency to Rutherford B. Hayes. In a sense, the Supreme Court chose the president. But in contrast to the 2000 election, the Court did not do so as an institution, and did not do it by litigation.[123]

In one of the best-known Supreme Court decisions of the Reconstruction era, *Texas v. White*, the Court defined the United States as "an indestructible union, composed of indestructible states."[124] "The nature of the Union" presented the ultimate "political question" of the Civil War and Reconstruction period. It concerned political theory, federalism, and sovereignty. Before the war, Americans disputed whether the states remained sovereign and could secede. After the war, they asked whether they had ever existed out of the Union, and how they could regain their proper relation to it. Though Lincoln expressed a coherent and justly celebrated theory of the Union in his first inaugural address, as the war neared an end and he faced the practical problem of restoring the Confederate states, he dismissed the theoretical question of their ever-out status as "a pernicious abstraction" that would only impede the task of reunion.[125]

When the Court faced the issue in *Texas v. White*, it adopted the practical compromise of the moderate Republicans: it considered the rebel states to be states for some purposes but not for others. For example, they could not send representatives and senators to Congress, as states could, until they ratified the Fourteenth Amendment, which only states can do. The particular case concerned the effort of the restored government of Texas to recover bonds that the rebel government had sold during the war. Texas remained unreconstructed, without congressmen or presidential electors. The Court decided that it could reclaim the bonds because the rebel government had sold them in furtherance of the rebellion, making the sale void. On the other hand, the Court validated "acts necessary to peace and good order among citizens," like acts and judgments concerning marriage, inheritance, contracts, and torts.[126]

Thus the Court followed the party line on the ultimate political question and implicitly upheld the Military Reconstruction Act of 1867, which had recognized the state government that brought the suit. Justice Grier, among the most hostile to the Republican Reconstruction policy, dissented and pointed out the inconsistency: "I am not disposed to join in any essay to prove Texas to be a state of the Union, when Congress have decided that she is not." As a nonstate, she could not sue in federal court. Worse yet, once in court, "having relied upon one fiction, namely, that she *is* a state in the Union, she now relies upon a second one . . . that she was not a state at all during the . . . rebellion. She now sets up the plea of *insanity*, and asks the Court to treat all her acts made during the disease as void."[127] Grier misled a bit, as the Court had not voided *all* her acts but only those abetting the rebellion. Even so, Grier had a legitimate point.

Historians no longer depict the post–*Dred Scott* Court as disgraced and cowed, as they did a century ago.[128] But the current generation of historians has gone overboard in the other direction, seeing judicial supremacy, or at least its foundation, in the 1860s. It looks more like the Chase Court returned to the moderate, coordinate, politically prudent position of Marshall, after the drift toward judicial supremacism that exploded in *Dred Scott*, though Marshall navigated the law/politics rapids more deftly and smoothly than did Chase.[129] Congressional Republicans confidently believed that the courts, now full of Republicans, would remain faithful to their policies, so when they lost control of Congress after fourteen consecutive years, in 1875, they expanded the federal courts' jurisdiction to near the maximum that Article III allowed (or required, as the High Federalists of 1789 had maintained).[130]

5

THE COURT IN THE INDUSTRIAL AGE

The period between Reconstruction and the New Deal represents a transitional or intermediate period in the rise of judicial supremacy. For a long time historians depicted it as the "laissez-faire era," in which a conservative Court defended entrepreneurial liberty against progressive socioeconomic reform. It is often called the "Lochner era," after the 1905 case in which the Court struck down a maximum hours law for bakers. It has become clear that such cases did not occur frequently and did not have great impact. Indeed, public support for the judiciary appears to have increased in this period, and this would help the Court survive challenges from the progressives and New Dealers.

THE END OF RECONSTRUCTION

After the preservation of the Union and the abolition of slavery, the United States faced the challenge of the industrial and urban revolutions. Generations of historians have said that the Supreme Court under Chief Justices Waite and Fuller (1873–1910) destroyed the Fourteenth Amendment as a protector of Black civil rights and recrafted it as a shield to big business against regulation. The first charge they exaggerated somewhat, and the second very much. It reflects a twentieth-century progressive and New Deal–liberal preference for "personal" over "economic" rights in reverse.[1]

The Fourteenth Amendment poses a frustrating enigma for the historian. The whole original Constitution contained very little of *substance*—terms like "the privileges and immunities of citizens" in Article IV, section 2. The bulk of the Constitution consisted of structural and procedural terms—establishing institutions, terms of office, mode of election, and the like.[2] Yet we have voluminous records of debates over its provisions, in both the Constitutional Convention and the state ratification conventions. Elliot's *Debates* runs to five volumes, and the Wisconsin documentary history of ratification contains twenty-seven.

The Fourteenth Amendment, on the other hand, contains *much* of substance—the privileges or immunities, due process, and equal protection clauses of section 1. Yet the scanty and often incoherent debate in Congress offers little interpretive guidance. Alfred Avins could fit it all into one (over-sized) volume.[3] Even more aggravating, most of the congressional debate addressed sections 2, 3, and 4, which concerned temporary problems that were soon and permanently forgotten.[4] Debate in the state legislatures on ratification hardly exists.[5] Contemporary newspapers and journals offer little additional help.[6] The Court would have very little assistance as it interpreted what would become a whole new Constitution.

The Reconstruction Republicans faced the (probably impossible) task of protecting the freedom of the former slaves while maintaining as much as possible of the dual federalist system of the antebellum years. By one theory, the abolition of slavery in the Thirteenth Amendment did everything necessary. That amendment made the freedmen citizens and entitled them to the privileges and immunities of citizens. Legislators wrote the Civil Rights Act of 1866 on this view, declaring the freedmen to be citizens (*Dred Scott* notwithstanding) and enumerating their civil rights: "to make and enforce contracts," especially; "to sue, be sued, and give evidence in court; to marry, bequeath, and inherit; and to be subject to the same criminal law as whites."[7]

We can best understand the Fourteenth Amendment as an effort to make the Civil Rights Act permanent. Congress had enacted that statute over President Johnson's veto, and a future Congress might repeal it by a simple majority. The chief sponsor of the amendment, Senator John A. Bingham of Ohio, believed it necessary because Congress had no power to enforce the privileges or immunities clause (just as many abolitionists had believed it had no power to enforce the fugitive slave clause). Section 1 grants no specific power to Congress. It reads "no state shall make or enforce any law which shall abridge the privileges or immunities . . . nor shall any state deprive any person of life, liberty, or property, without due process of law; nor deny to any person . . . the equal protection of the laws." This language would have put it in Article I, section 10 of the original Constitution, along with the contract clause and other restrictions on the states, rather than in Article I, section 8, which granted power to Congress. Section 8 gives Congress the power to regulate commerce, which means more than just providing for courts that will strike down obstructions to interstate commerce—though that court-negative rather than Congress-positive approach predominated until the late nineteenth century. Thus, the federal government would have to show "state action," not just offenses against individuals by private actors. But one could argue that state *failure* to protect Blacks from private offenses constituted state action—state inaction, or state dereliction, could trigger federal enforcement.

The Court's first Fourteenth Amendment case surprised the public. It concerned not the freedmen but the butchers of New Orleans, who objected to a Louisiana law that forced them to conduct their trade in a state-franchise slaughterhouse, located downriver from the city, ostensibly for public health reasons.[8] The Crescent City Livestock Company had thoroughly bribed the legislature to award it this valuable monopoly. Opposition to the act also fed on white Louisianans' hatred of the mixed-race "carpetbag" Republican government.[9]

John A. Campbell, the former Supreme Court justice, made the butchers' case. His pleas showed the potential versatility of the substantive provisions of the Reconstruction amendments. They claimed that the act amounted to involuntary servitude in violation of the Thirteenth Amendment, abridged a privilege or immunity of US citizens, deprived them of liberty and property without due process of law, and denied them the equal protection of the laws.

Justice Miller wrote the majority opinion in a 5–4 decision that hordes of critics inevitably said "eviscerated" or "gutted" the Fourteenth Amendment. He quickly dismissed the Thirteenth Amendment claim; that provision eliminated only chattel slavery. He made a sharp distinction between one's rights as a citizen of the United States and as a citizen of a state. US citizenship conferred few and insignificant rights—to use the navigable waterways of the nation, to petition Congress, or have access to American consuls when abroad. Thus, the privileges or immunities clause, probably the one that the framers of the Fourteenth Amendment expected to do most of the work, was reduced to virtual oblivion.

Of the substantive due process claim, Miller said, "Under no construction of that provision that we have ever seen, or any that we deem admissible," could the act "be held to be a deprivation of property." He saw equal protection, like the Thirteenth Amendment, as a principally race-based guarantee for the freedmen. Unless it was thus narrowly read, Miller feared that the amendment would destroy the federal system and turn the Court into "a perpetual censor" of the state legislatures. Four dissenters embraced a more robust interpretation of the amendment, which would prevail in the 1890s, after the nation had abandoned the freedmen's cause.[10]

Nor did the Court help much when it considered positive acts by Congress to secure civil rights. In a series of cases, it hobbled the Enforcement (or Ku

Klux Klan) Act. The Court insisted on a federal showing of state action in Fourteenth Amendment cases. While it considered the idea that state dereliction could constitute state action, it required the government to demonstrate rather than assume it. Thirteenth and Fifteenth Amendment cases did not require state action, but it did need to prove a racial motive—a kind of "hate crime" law avant la lettre.[11]

On its way out, the Republican Congress in 1875 passed a Civil Rights Act that prohibited discrimination in places of public accommodation. This act memorialized the recently deceased radical senator Charles Sumner; few congressmen considered it enforceable.[12] The Court struck it down in the *Civil Rights Cases* of 1883. The Court reiterated that the Fourteenth Amendment did not give Congress the power to enact laws and impose them on the states—to "create a code of municipal law for the regulation of private rights." It could only enforce the amendment by providing remedies when states violated those rights. The common law of all the states required proprietors "to furnish proper accommodations to all unobjectionable persons who in good faith apply for them." If the states altered the common law to discriminate, "Congress has full power to afford a remedy"—presumably, by providing access to federal courts.[13] Even when the Court upheld state requirements of segregation—theoretically "equal but separate" accommodations—in *Plessy v. Ferguson* in 1896, it confirmed what had long been accepted in law and custom.[14] That decision raised little controversy at the time, though undoing it in the 1950s would mark the beginning of modern judicial supremacy.

Critics have unjustly fingered the Court as the principal cause of the failure of Reconstruction, and scholars in recent years have corrected this distortion.[15] Our own assumption of judicial supremacy has anachronistically caused us to attribute the failure of Reconstruction primarily to the Court. Though the Court did not help much, Reconstruction failed primarily for political reasons, including the exhaustion of northern whites with regard to policing race relations in the South and the perduring determination of white southerners to maintain white supremacy.[16] Republicans' loss of Congress in 1874 meant the end of federal enforcement. Even a radically Republican Court could only have done so much in the long run—again showing that courts can better strike down than make policy. When Democrats won control of the whole federal government in 1892, they repealed many of the Reconstruction acts. Notably, though the Court had sustained some Reconstruction-era voting rights enforcement acts, the sponsors of the repeal legislation asserted that Congress could "reverse the Supreme Court on a constitutional question."[17] The Court at least left a doctrinal legacy that lawyers could—with some imagination—revive in the Second Reconstruction of the 1950s–60s.

Perhaps the hoariest fable in the tale of the late nineteenth-century Court's transformation of the Fourteenth Amendment involves Roscoe Conkling bamboozling the justices into treating corporations as persons under it. The story goes that as attorney for the Southern Pacific Railroad, Conkling, a powerful US senator and twice appointed to the Court (declining both times), fed the Court a distorted account of the deliberations of Congress's Joint Committee on Reconstruction, on which he had served. Conkling claimed that the committee moved from the term "citizen" to that of "person" in order to include corporations, "artificial persons," under its coverage.[18] In fact, none of this mattered. Corporations had long been considered "citizens," a status that had given them access to federal courts since the Marshall era. Howard Jay Graham exploded this "conspiracy theory" of the Fourteenth Amendment in the 1930s, but it continues to resurface.[19]

The real question concerned whether the amendment's due process clause—emerging as the substitute for the vitiated privileges or immunities clause—was merely procedural or was substantive. The Court had rejected the substantive interpretation of due process in the *Slaughterhouse Cases,* and did so again four years later in the first important economic regulation case, *Munn v. Illinois.* The case concerned the attempt by the "granger movement" (farmer cooperatives) to control prices set by railroads and grain elevators. The Court upheld the law over Fourteenth Amendment challenges, announcing a very permissive standard for state regulation: "Property does become clothed with a public interest when used in a manner to make it of public consequence. . . . When, therefore, one devotes his property to a use in which the public has an interest he, in effect, grants the public an interest in that use." Moreover, the Court said that it would not second-guess legislative determinations that private property had become public. We "must assume that, if a set of facts *could* exist that would justify such legislation, it actually *did* exist" (emphasis mine).[20] This standard sounded like what we today call "rational basis" review, and it would go far toward the elimination of judicial review. Justices Field and Strong dissented, as in *Slaughterhouse,* and their view would gain support by 1890.

JUDICIAL REVIEW AFTER RECONSTRUCTION

But judicial review waxed stronger in the post-Reconstruction period, and judicial power generally became more important as the nation entered a long period of divided government, in the states as well as at the national level.

Between 1875 and 1897, one party almost never controlled the presidency and both houses of Congress. In a system dominated by "courts and parties," this made the courts more influential. Republicans recognized this when, like the Federalists in 1801, they augmented judicial power to lock in their policies.[21] This produced the first of a new wave of critiques of the peculiar American doctrine of judicial power.

Legal scholar William M. Meigs wrote one of the first analyses, in the *American Law Review* in 1885. He noted that this unique feature of American constitutionalism had received little attention and had a very flimsy pedigree. He attacked the "courts and their adulators" who propounded claims for judicial review that he called "utterly wrong and based on no sound principle." He pointed out that the "fungus-like idea of the omnipotency of courts" appeared first in defense of the Alien and Sedition Acts, and more recently in works by foreign scholars like Herman Von Holst who hailed from militarist police states.[22]

In 1890, Judge Charles E. Shattuck took aim at novel claims that "due process of law" had a substantive content (the view of the dissenters in *Slaughterhouse*). Like Meigs, he claimed that this had little basis in history or principle and denounced the "manifest tendency to regard constitutional prohibitions as a panacea for moral and political evils, to look upon courts of law, as distinguished from legislatures, as the only real protectors of individual rights."[23] Seymour Thompson, a former Missouri judge and the editor of the *American Law Review,* also regularly wrote and published articles critical of the federal judiciary in these years.

In 1893, James Bradley Thayer of the Harvard Law School wrote perhaps the most important essay ever on judicial review, "The Origin and Scope of the American Doctrine of Constitutional Law." Though he admitted that the Founders had accepted judicial review, he argued that the Constitution mainly defended liberty through its structural features—widespread suffrage, frequent elections, short terms of office, bicameralism, and the executive veto. He saw judicial review as a necessary evil and wanted to keep it as limited as possible. (Like most observers, Thayer grappled mainly with the problem of coordinate or horizontal judicial review and permitted a looser standard in federal or vertical cases.) Courts should only overturn legislative acts in cases that left "no room for reasonable doubt," which one could call "plain and clear," "very clear," "clear and unequivocal," "as obvious to the comprehension of everyone as an axiomatic truth," "manifest," or "so obviously repugnant [that] all men of sense and reflection . . . may perceive it." He likened it to the standard in criminal prosecutions, where twelve men had to agree to guilt "beyond a reasonable doubt." Thayer saw the "political questions" doctrine as useless, as judges had "perverted" it in such a way as to "really operate to extend the judicial function beyond all bounds." Judicial review insulted the dignity that legislators deserved. It demoralized them and made them lazy and irresponsible, allowing them to pass laws carelessly with the assumption that the courts would sort them out.[24]

Notably, these condemnations of judicial supremacy appeared before the mid-1890s, when historians usually see the first truly controversial cases of conservative or "laissez-faire" judicial activism.[25] Later scholars identified the chief justiceship of Melville Fuller in 1888, and an extensive personnel turnover on the Court around that time, as ushering in the laissez-faire era. The dissenting views of Justice Field would become majority ones, abetted by additions to the Court such as his nephew, David Josiah Brewer. The critics of the late nineteenth-century judiciary displayed an affinity for the British system of legislative sovereignty advanced in Woodrow Wilson's first book, *Congressional Government*, and in British jurist A. V. Dicey's *Law of the Constitution*.[26]

James B. Weaver, the Populist candidate for president in 1892, echoed Woodrow Wilson's argument that the United States no longer needed the Constitution's restraints on democracy for an American people who had transcended the Founding-era problem of faction and become fully capable of governing themselves.[27] Weaver and Wilson essentially embraced Waite's "rational basis" standard in *Munn*, which would all but eliminate judicial review. Philosopher Felix Cohen later said that this standard "makes of our courts lunacy commissions sitting in judgment of the mental capacity of legislators and, occasionally, of judicial brethren."[28] As law professor Richard A. Posner added, Thayer's theory "had no stopping point—once you embraced it, you cannot explain why a law would ever be declared unconstitutional."[29] But Congress only augmented the Court in these years. In 1886, it began to pay the justices to employ a clerk. More important, the 1891 Evarts Act all but ended "circuit riding" by creating a new set of circuit courts, as had the Judiciary Act of 1801.[30]

NEW INDUSTRIAL PROBLEMS

As American politics returned to normal after Reconstruction, the most important cases of the Waite Court involved the negative commerce clause, or striking down state laws that discriminated against growing "foreign" corporations and threatened to balkanize the national market. By the end of the 1880s, the great size and power of American corporations, first the railroads and then the manufacturing "trusts," had outgrown the ability or willingness of the states to regulate and forced Congress to step in. But when Congress legislated on the railroad and trust problems, it avoided making difficult policy choices and enacted laws that opened the door to judicial policymaking. As in the lead-up to *Dred Scott*, politicians found it in their interest to let the courts legislate.[31]

The railroad problem combined ruinous competition on long-haul routes between large cities with a railroad monopoly that squeezed shippers on short-haul routes between small towns. The railroads needed to gouge small shippers to make up for losses in the larger, competitive markets. They sought permission among themselves to limit rate competition—to "pool" or establish cartels—on the long hauls, but obviously shippers would not like that. Small shippers, on the other hand, wanted maximum rates on short hauls, which worked against the interests of the railroads and large shippers. Congress rejected clear statements on either pooling or rate discrimination. The Interstate Commerce Act of 1887 mandated "reasonable and just" rates, prohibited pooling, and prohibited rate discrimination only in cases of "substantially similar circumstances and conditions."[32]

The act's greatest innovation was to create the Interstate Commerce Commission, the first "independent regulatory agency," to enforce it.[33] The act seemed to make the commission *in* but not *of* the executive branch. The president appointed five commissioners (no more than three of whom could represent the same political party) for a staggered term of six years, with the advice and consent of the Senate, but he could remove them only for cause. The commission would attempt to exercise the legislative power of rate-making and would adjudicate particular cases, in apparent violation of the separation of powers.

The federal courts, and the Supreme Court, looked askance at what they saw as a competitor. As with Reconstruction, it goes too far to hold the Court primarily responsible for the failure of the Interstate Commerce Act, but it certainly didn't help.[34] It would not treat the commission's findings of fact as conclusive, but it considered appeals de novo. It would not let the commission set rates, calling that a legislative function that Congress had not delegated.[35] It also held that the "reasonableness" of a rate remained a judicial question. It would not cooperate with the commission's effort to promote pooling, instead applying the Sherman Antitrust Act to railroads. It also frustrated the commission's efforts to relieve short-haul rate discrimination. The commission had undertaken a "cooperative" approach in which the railroads would have to give up discrimination and shippers would have to accept pooling. One analyst concluded, "Despite its initial success, the [Interstate Commerce Commission]'s effort to institutionalize cooperation was dashed by a judiciary armed with an adversarial model of regulation."[36]

The Court did ease up on the commission as the years went by, but it helped to render it ineffective for almost two decades. When Congress gave the commission a clearer legislative mandate, in the 1906 Hepburn Act, the Court did not stand in the way. Toward the end of the Fuller years, the Court showed itself more accommodating to the progressive administrative state. One could criticize the Court for failing to do its judicial duty to keep Congress under control. The Court rose to supremacy in the twentieth century through its ability to let the regulatory state expand while keeping it under the Court's ultimate control. This explains the gist of a famous statement by Charles Evans Hughes in 1907—then governor of New York, later associate justice (1910–16), and then chief justice (1930–41). Hughes had championed a public service commission in New York to regulate railroads and other public utilities. He noted that utility owners eagerly sought judicial review of commission rulings and expressed his high regard for courts. "We are under a Constitution, but the Constitution is what the judges say it is, and the judiciary is the safeguard of our liberty and of our property under the Constitution." But he warned that courts would lose public esteem if they meddled in regulatory matters and impeded public demand for public administration. "No more insidious assault could be made upon the independence and esteem of the judiciary than to burden it with these questions of administration," that is, questions of technical difficulty and detail that better belonged to specially trained experts than to generalist judges. "Let us keep the courts for the questions they were intended to consider," he said—to "real judicial questions" rather than "matters of detail."[37] Medieval clerics made similar arguments, that priests could, but should not, exercise secular power beneath their sacerdotal dignity.[38]

Congress addressed the general monopoly problem in the Sherman Antitrust Act of 1890. Congress had to choose whether to protect consumers from monopolistic prices or to protect small producers from their larger competitors.[39] Unlike the Interstate Commerce Act, the Sherman Act relied on regular court enforcement and seemed simply to adopt the old common-law prohibition of "conspiracies in restraint of trade." But the common law had held monopolistic conspiracies unenforceable; the new act made them criminal. Controversy would also arise over whether the act applied to labor unions and agricultural cartels.

Over time, the Court interpreted the Sherman Act primarily to promote efficiency and consumer welfare, adopting the "rule of reason" in 1911. It held

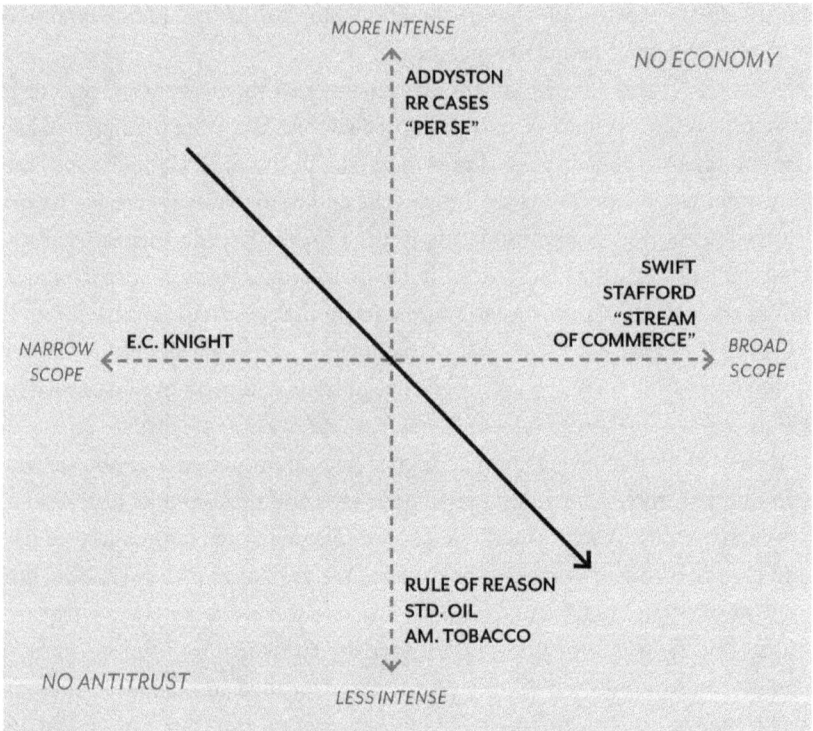

Fig. 2. The trend of Supreme Court antitrust doctrine.

not *all* combinations unlawful (despite the plain text that read "all"), but only "unreasonable" ones that harmed consumers. It moved from a very broad view of the *intensity* of the act (*every* combination) and narrow view of its *scope* (interstate commerce), to a narrow view of its intensity (unreasonable combinations) and a broader scope (the "stream-of-commerce") (see Fig. 2).

The Court's first Sherman case involved the "sugar trust," which controlled more than 90 percent of sugar refining in the country. The Court defined sugar refining not as commerce but as manufacturing that took place completely within one state and thus was beyond Congress's power to regulate. The Court would only accept intrastate or manufacturing regulations that had a "direct" effect on interstate commerce. Though the antimonopolists seemed to have in mind combinations exactly like the sugar trust, most analysts regarded the decision as having rendered the act useless.[40] A few years later the Court decided that the act did apply to railroad combinations, frustrating the cartel-promoting work of the Interstate Commerce Commission and stressing that the act applied to *every* combination that was truly interstate commerce.[41] In 1905, the Court loosened its strict definition of interstate commerce. In a case against the beef trust, it held that though the trust consisted of discrete acts of intrastate manufacturing, these acts together constituted an interstate "stream (or current) of commerce."[42] Finally, in suits against the tobacco and oil trusts, the Court broke them up but announced the new standard of the rule of reason.[43]

The Court had boldly stepped in to make the tough policy decision that Congress had dodged. At the most stringent, the Court could have read the law to apply to every contract, since every agreement between two contracting parties excludes everyone else. If A agrees to buy a pound of sugar from B, C can complain that their agreement prevented him from buying that pound. Such an absurdly intense interpretation would destroy the economy, especially if the Court combined it with a maximally broad scope—to include all economic activity, reading "commerce among the states" as we read the commerce power today. At the other extreme, the Court could read the act with such low intensity and narrow scope as to nullify it. As it happened, the Court began with high intensity and narrow scope and moved toward lower intensity and broader scope (see Fig. 2).

Industrial crisis and labor unrest brought the Court to consider the applicability of the antitrust act to labor conspiracies, and the overall relationship of strikes and interstate commerce. Beginning in the 1870s, American courts began to use injunctions to control labor strikes. Courts of "equity" issue injunctions—orders to perform or refrain from some activity. The labor injunction (as with all equitable remedies) assumed that an aggrieved party had no adequate remedy at law and would suffer irreparable harm without extraordinary relief. Plaintiffs could obtain injunctions quickly, without jury trial—or even, in their early proceedings, without the defendant's testimony. Courts treated injunction defiance as contempt and could produce a jail term up to six months (see appendix A).

In 1894, Eugene V. Debs led the American Railway Union, the nation's largest industrial union, in a secondary boycott or "sympathy strike" against the Pullman Palace Car Company. ARU workers all over the country refused to handle trains with Pullman cars on them and thus shut down the national transportation system. The Justice Department got an injunction from a circuit court in Illinois, ordering the union to stop interfering in the operation of the railroads by "threats, intimidation, force, and violence." Debs and other ARU leaders violated the order and appealed from jail.

The circuit court granted the injunction because the Union had violated the Sherman Act. Debs appealed to the Supreme Court for a writ of habeas corpus. The Court refused the appeal and upheld the injunction. It did not address the antitrust issue but instead made a broad statement of national power. "The entire strength of the nation may be used to enforce in any part of the land the full and free exercise of all national powers and the security of all rights intrusted by the Constitution to its care," Justice Brewer wrote for a unanimous Court. "The strong arm of the national government may be put forth to brush away all obstruction to the freedom of interstate commerce or the transportation of the mails."[44]

Coming in the same term as the sugar trust decision, it appeared that the Court had nullified the Sherman Act as it applied to big business and then applied it to organized labor, exposing its class bias in the conflict of the 1890s. The Populist–Democratic party platform of 1896 condemned "government by injunction as a new and highly dangerous form of oppression by which federal judges, in contempt of the laws of the states and rights of citizens, become at once legislators, judges, and executioners." Though until 1908 the Court would not explicitly hold that the Sherman Act applied to labor, federal courts continued to issue injunctions against strikes, and relief from injunction for any reason became one of the leading causes of organized labor.

At about this time, another indication of probusiness and antilabor bias from the Court came in the more arcane realm of tort law. In a railroad accident case in Ohio, the Court imposed the "fellow servant" rule of liability instead of the state's "vice principal" rule.[45] The fellow servant rule exempted employers from liability for injuries to employees if their fellow employees caused them, while the vice principal rule often considered them liable if the fellow employee really acted as a supervisor. The Court's imposition of the pro-employer rule followed from the "federal common law" that had begun with *Swift v. Tyson* in 1842, and it contributed to the impression that federal courts provided a refuge for strong corporate defendants against weak worker plaintiffs. As one scholar has argued, the decades of the Progressive Era saw recurrent attacks on this bias. "The image of the federal courts as probusiness forums," and "the belief that federal judges tended to favor business was a widely shared part of American political culture, particularly among the less well-to-do and members of the working class, especially those affiliated with or sympathetic to labor unions. Whether or not the belief was well founded, either generally or in any particular instance," it periodically turned the Court into a political issue.[46]

The income tax decisions became the most notorious of the 1895 cases, easily the most controversial cases since *Dred Scott* and widely regarded as "egregious decisions, to say the least."[47] In 1894, the Democrats won control of both houses of Congress and the presidency for the first time since the Civil War. In addition to repealing most Reconstruction civil rights statutes, they reduced the protective Republican tariff. To recoup the revenue lost by the tariff reduction, and to shift the burden of taxation onto the wealthy of the urban and industrial Northeast and Midwest, Congress adopted an income tax. Congress made it both modest and progressive—a 2 percent tax on income above $4,000, which touched only about 2 percent of the population, and on corporation income. Congress had adopted an income tax during the Civil War. Regarded as an extraordinary war levy, it expired in 1872. In 1881, the Supreme Court affirmed its constitutionality—at least as applied to the earnings of a lawyer.[48]

The Constitution's taxing provisions consist of a grant of power and a restriction in Article I, section 8, and a further restriction in section 9. Section 8 says, "Congress shall have power to lay and collect taxes, duties, imposts, and excises . . . but all duties, imposts and excises shall be uniform thorough the United States." Section 9 says, "No capitation, or other direct, tax, shall be laid, unless in proportion to the census or enumeration herein before directed to be taken." Most evidence indicated that the Founding generation defined a "direct tax" as a tax on persons and land. When James Madison asked at the Constitutional Convention what defined a direct tax, "nobody answered." When the Court considered the tax on carriages in *Hylton,* in 1796, Justice Paterson, a member of the Constitutional Convention, said that the apportionment clause was meant to benefit the southern states, which had large amounts of land, much of it less valuable, and large numbers of slaves. It would prevent the northern states, with less but more valuable land and few or no slaves, from onerously taxing the slave states. But he called apportionment "radically wrong; it cannot be supported by any solid reasoning [and] ought not be extended by construction."[49] Yet even Representative James Madison had regarded the carriage tax as a direct tax.

To declare the income tax a direct tax would not make it unconstitutional per se. But requiring it to be apportioned would render it a practical impossibility (see appendix C). Apportionment would defeat its purpose as a progressive "class tax" on the wealthy urban-industrial America and make it a burden on the agrarian South and West, which sought relief from the tariff. *Pollock v. Farmers' Loan & Trust Company* challenged the act in 1894. The parties clearly colluded—it was a stockholder purporting to stop his company from paying a tax. On some marginal points, such as taxes on the income from land and the taxation of state and municipal bond interest, clear majorities held the tax unconstitutional.[50] But the major issue concerned the tax on the income from *personal* property—stocks and private sector bonds—and on the $4,000 exemption. On these the Court divided 4–4, Justice Jackson being ill.[51] The full Court heard reargument in 1895, and this time the Court held 5–4 that Congress must apportion a tax on personal property, too. That left only wages and salaries, and the Court surmised that Congress did not intend to tax only these and so held the entire act void. It did not address the question of whether the exemption violated the uniformity clause.[52]

Pollock ranks among the most contentious decisions in American history. The Court seemed to go out of its way to invite a reaction—it chose, as one scholar put it, "the path of most resistance."[53] Many saw the income tax as a weapon in a looming war of classes. Senator John Sherman had said "the attempt to array the poor against the rich is socialism, communism, devilism."[54] Pollock's lawyers, among the most prominent members of the American bar, appealed to this sentiment and called the act "communistic in its purpose and tendencies, and . . . defended here upon principles as communistic, socialistic—what should I call them—populistic as have ever been addressed to any political assembly in the world."[55] Populists would shriek that the Court had taken sides in the class conflict, indeed acting like a "political assembly."

Justice Field's concurring opinion noted that "the present assault upon capital is just the beginning. It will be but the stepping-stone to others, larger and more sweeping, till our political contests will become a war of the poor against the rich—a war constantly growing in intensity and bitterness."[56] In dissent, Justice Harlan wrote that "it is not possible for this court to have rendered any judgment more to be regretted," saying that the majority had launched "a judicial revolution that may sow the seeds of hate and distrust among the people of different sections of our common country."[57] Justice Brown said that "it approaches the proportions of a national calamity."[58] Seymour Thompson, in the *American Law Review,* claimed that "our judicial annals do not afford an instance of a more unpatriotic subserviancy to the demands of the rich and powerful classes."[59]

Collusive, closely divided, and strident in tone, *Pollock* became the lightning rod of the 1895 term. (Nobody dissented in *Debs,* and only Harlan dissented in *E. C. Knight.*) Since Justice Jackson voted to uphold the act, it appeared that one of the justices "switched" to vote against it in the second case.[60] But, in the end, the Court got away with it. *Pollock* launched the *"Marbury* myth," which conservative lawyers had built up since the 1880s.[61] They convinced the

Court that striking down the tax would gratify John Marshall.[62] But *Pollock* indicated a new kind of judicial review—not for institutional self-defense or a clear textual transgression, but for policy preferences.

The Court became an issue in the 1896 election as never before.[63] In addition to denouncing "government by injunction," the Populist–Democratic platform claimed that the income tax case had overruled an act made "in strict pursuance of the uniform decisions of that court for nearly 100 years, that court having in [*Springer*] sustained constitutional objections to its enactment which had previously been [presided over] by the ablest judges who ever sat on that bench." It called on "Congress to use all the constitutional power which remains after that decision, or which may come from its reversal by the courts as it may hereafter be constituted."[64]

But the decision may have had more popular appeal than Populists in the 1890s and later scholars made out.[65] The Populist–Democratic candidate, William Jennings Bryan, had to handle the issue gingerly to avoid association with anticourt radicals.[66] "They criticize us for our criticism" of the Court, he said in his "Cross of Gold" nominating speech. But, he said, "we have not criticized; we have simply called attention to what you already know," and he directed his auditors to the dissenting opinions of the Court itself.[67] The Republicans defended the Court and law and order generally.[68] The conservative National, or "Gold," Democrats, who left when the party fused with the Populists, emphatically condemned "all efforts to degrade" the Court.[69] And, however unpopular *Pollock* was, the Republican defenders of the Court won the election.

Ultimately, a constitutional amendment, the Sixteenth, overruled the *Pollock* decision, in 1913. This would make it arguably the first *erroneous* Court decision undone by amendment, and thus quite a statement of judicial power. As we have seen, the Eleventh Amendment overturned a *correct* interpretation of the Constitution, and it did not take a constitutional amendment to overturn *Dred Scott.*

One small but interesting illustration of both the unimpaired prestige of the Court and its limits after the crisis of the 1890s concerned the "retrocession" of part of the District of Columbia to Virginia in 1842. Congress got serious about fulfilling Pierre L'Enfant's original plan for a grand, imperial capital city, and some regretted the loss of the area south of the Potomac. Congress asked the attorney general to consider the constitutionality of the retrocession, but attorney general replied that the courts had not considered it. Congress then instructed him "to bring suit to determine" the question. But Judiciary

Committee chairman George F. Hoar insisted that Congress had posed "a political question and not a judicial question" and killed the motion.[70] If the "political questions" doctrine could limit judicial power, the political branches could not leave it to the Court to define political questions.

LEGAL MODERNISM AND DUE PROCESS

A fascinating paradox marked the late nineteenth-century American legal world. On the one hand, the academic world rejected the principles of the Founding, and on the other, the judiciary reasserted them. The academic movement fed "the revolt against formalism." "Formalism," often loosely translated as "idealism," saw the law as real and existing, discoverable by human reason and applied to everyday situations. Law in this sense came from God and/or nature; men discovered or declared it rather than made it. This natural law tradition went back to Plato, Cicero, and Coke. The Founders expressed it most clearly in the Declaration of Independence, which spoke of "self-evident truths," God-endowed rights, and governments limited to the protection of those rights.

The nineteenth century saw a set of repudiations of the natural law idea. They had always existed alongside it—elaborated, for instance, by Thrasymachus in Plato's dialogues, William of Ockham in the scholastic Middle Ages, and Thomas Hobbes in modern political thought. These formulations went by various names, including positivism (law as simply the will of the sovereign), relativism, pragmatism, historicism (law as the product of the ever-changing social, economic, and cultural context), Darwinism or "living constitutionalism," and utilitarianism (individual rights don't stand in the way of maximizing social utility). Harvard Law School dean Roscoe Pound provided a particular American version of these themes in his "sociological jurisprudence."[71]

"Legal modernism" has become a general term for these ideas.[72] Though significant differences existed among them, they shared a common disdain for logic, metaphysics, and a priori or axiomatic reasoning. Philosopher William James cobbled them together and called it "pragmatism," a distinctive kind of American pseudo philosophy. All of these theories displayed hostility to constitutionalism, leaving no room for fixed, higher law as a limit to political power.

How would the American judiciary adapted to these new theories? One found it difficult enough to justify judicial review in a constitutional system—some remained unconvinced by the logic of *Federalist* 78 and *Marbury v. Madison* that a fixed, written constitution necessitated judicial review. What could legitimate it under a plastic constitution? In Britain, the informal, evolving, common-law constitution eschewed judicial review. In America, the idea of human-made law fed the rise of judge-made law. No longer confined to deciding according to natural law or the Constitution, judges could fashion decisions to fit their own policy preferences.

One of the first and most important rejections of formalism came in Oliver Wendell Holmes's 1881 book *The Common Law,* with its famous aphorism that "the life of the law has not been logic: it has been experience. The felt necessities of the time, the prevalent moral and political theories, intuitions of public policy, avowed or unconscious, even the prejudices which judges share with their fellow-men, have had a good deal more to do than the syllogism in determining the rules by which men should be governed."[73] Judges kept the law up to date and did in fact legislate—though wise judges legislated tactfully, discreetly, "interstitially." This posed no problem in the English common law system, where Parliament could correct erroneous judicial rules. But when jurists applied this Holmesian view of law to *constitutional* law, it produced a "living" or "common law" constitution.[74] In America, without parliamentary supremacy, the judicial word would become final, except for formal amendment—and the difficulty of amendment provided one of the principal arguments for the need for a living constitution—or the court-curbing tools rusting in the Article III shed.[75]

Holmes occupied an especially important place in American legal education. The revolt against formalism began in the academy, at a time when higher education affected a select few and did not yet shape American society. The universities certainly did not produce most American judges, very few of whom had any formal legal education, let alone taught law, as Holmes did. They did not incubate judges through the law school graduate–judicial clerk nexus that we have today. Not until Levi Woodbury, appointed in 1845, did a justice attend a law school; Benjamin Curtis in 1851 became the first law school graduate on the Court. As late as the 1940s, Robert Jackson and James F. Byrnes reached the Court without a law degree. The justices did not employ law school clerks before Justice Gray began to do so in 1882, and Congress did not pay for them until 1886. William Howard Taft could have gone to Harvard or Columbia Law School but returned to Cincinnati, for the quality of the degree remained unimportant to professional success.[76] The development of the modern law school accompanied the American adaptation of the modern German research university, which made its first impression in the United States with the establishment of Johns Hopkins in 1876. Well into the twentieth century, American judges came through traditional, usually Christian church–affiliated, liberal arts colleges.[77]

The legal academy grew alongside the rise of the legal profession. This movement, seen in the formation of the American Bar Association in 1878, ran in a contrary direction. The ABA remained a relatively conservative organization well into the twentieth century. As we have seen, leaders of the American bar promoted the *Marbury* myth to put down the income tax. Edward S. Corwin, a progressive critic, called the ABA "a sort of juristic sewing circle for mutual education in the gospel of laissez-faire."[78] They also had a professional interest in promoting legal education. Requiring more credentials did more than just improve professional standards. (Until the 1930s, Indiana only required "good moral character" to practice law.) Education and testing also acted as economic barriers to entry, reducing the number of practitioners and preserving the cartel that the association sought. In the twentieth century, the association would look askance at the proliferation of part-time and night school legal education, which tended to open the profession to Blacks and new immigrant groups.[79]

Among judges, a retrograde revival of natural law took place. Americans did not endure as great a reaction as Europeans did against rationalistic natural law principles associated with the French Revolution, but they did retreat from them early in the century. Natural law concepts made a comeback the 1850s and got their greatest potential boost from the Fourteenth Amendment. The new amendment's open-ended privileges or immunities, due process, and equal protection clauses provided broad avenues for judicial interpretation. The Court had minimized privileges or immunities in the *Slaughterhouse Cases,* but the butchers had made their case on all three clauses. All of them suggested that the government could not abridge some fundamental rights—originally the national government, under the Article IV privileges and immunities clause and the Fifth Amendment due process clause; maybe the states, under Article IV; and now both, under the Fourteenth Amendment, with the addition of the equal protection clause for the states. One need only define a right as a privilege or immunity, or as a liberty or property interest, or to define the group targeted by the law (butchers, bakers, candlestick makers, women, Blacks, homosexuals) as subject to unequal treatment. Though *Slaughterhouse* killed privileges or immunities, due process could fill in for it. Equal protection might have done just as well.[80] One could call the three clauses of the Fourteenth Amendment fungible.

The due process clause had its origin in the "law of the land" provision of Magna Carta and appeared in many state constitutions. "Equal protection" introduced a new phrase, but some commentators called it redundant, arguing that due process included equal protection.[81] Some state courts had applied the due process clause in a substantive way before the Civil War. Natural law language adorned early US Supreme Court decisions, but Chief Justice Marshall preferred to use the text of the contract clause as an equivalent to protect "vested rights." The US Supreme Court picked it up again shortly before the Civil War, most notably in *Dred Scott*'s defense of slave property. The antislavery movement likewise claimed that the liberty provision of the due process clause of the Fifth Amendment prohibited slavery in the territories.

After the war, the Court suggested on several occasions that a substantive reading of due process had more life than *Slaughterhouse* and *Munn* indicated, even as it sustained state regulations challenged as violating due process. In 1890, the Court finally struck down a state railroad regulation under the Fourteenth Amendment.[82] Legislatures could set railroad rates and could delegate that power to state railroad commissions. But the judges called the *reasonableness* of a rate a judicial question, and states could not deprive the regulated of a judicial hearing. Due process, in other words, guaranteed judicial process. If a commission set a rate so low that the railroad could not make a profit, this would amount to confiscation—a taking of private property without just compensation. The dissenters quite rightly observed that this case repudiated *Munn*.[83]

Many see this case as anticipating the Court's application of the Bill of Rights—here the takings clause of the Fifth Amendment—to the states, a process called the "incorporation" of the Bill of Rights. But the Court really just equated an uncompensated "taking" with the denial of due process and identified some overlap or similarity between the provisions of the Bill of Rights and the due process clause.[84] Substantive due process and incorporation would furnish very similar tools of judicial power (see appendix B).

Before the Court explored whether due process included any of the other specific provisions of the Bill of Rights, it devised a right of its own, "liberty of contract." Though the first expression of this right seems to have occurred in 1895, historians most often trace it to the 1897 case of *Allgeyer v. Louisiana*, in which the Court held that Louisiana could not prohibit its citizens from purchasing insurance from other states.

The 1905 case of *Lochner v. New York* provided the most infamous example of substantive due process/liberty of contract.[85] That state passed a law, purportedly a public health or police power measure, which limited the number of hours that bakers could work to ten per day and sixty per week. The Court upheld the public health provisions of the law (sanitary code, tile floors, and the like), but a 5–4 majority struck down the labor regulations. Justice

Rufus W. Peckham could not see baking as a particularly hazardous occupation. As adult males in their right minds, these workers could look after themselves. Peckham saw the law as a labor regulation masquerading as a public health measure, "in reality, passed from other motives." This part of the statute interfered in liberty of contract without warrant. Peckham may have correctly suspected that the act was promoted by larger, old-stock, organized bakers to reduce competition from small, recently immigrated, nonunion ones.[86] Even the most conservative laissez-faire courts accepted most labor regulations, but they often drew the line at union-driven "class legislation."

Though *Lochner* gave its name to the entire period from 1890 to 1937, it did not typify the era. Law professor David Bernstein has done exhaustive research on the case and recently pointed out its anomalies: the legislature placed the purportedly health regulation in the state's labor code, enforced it with criminal sanctions, and made no provision for overtime pay. One could call Peckham's decision idiosyncratic at best. The more moderate concurring justices did not give their own reasons for supporting his conclusion. As in the income tax cases, a narrow 5–4 majority made the decision, and one of the justices may have "switched" his vote here, too.[87] Rather than narrowly scrutinizing such state laws, the Court more often accepted the flimsiest police power justifications, as when it accepted racial segregation as a valid means to prevent racial friction, in *Plessy v. Ferguson*. Even in its most conservative phase, the Court never presented as much of an obstacle to progressive reform as many critics at the time and since have portrayed it.[88]

Oliver Wendell Holmes's dissent in *Lochner* became a progressive touchstone. He averred that the Court had adopted its own Social Darwinian views as constitutional law. "The Fourteenth Amendment does not enact Mr. Herbert Spencer's *Social Statics*," he quipped. Holmes mischaracterized his brethren, and his statement looked like the pot calling the kettle black, as Holmes was the only Darwin-influenced justice on the Court. *Lochner* rested on the political theory of the Founding, and liberty of contract, in particular, had a close connection to the Civil Rights Act of 1866 (whose list of rights began with the right "to make and enforce contracts"), which provides the best guide to interpreting the Fourteenth Amendment. Holmes went on to say that the Court should only strike down laws that obviously violated "fundamental" principles as they have been understood by the traditions of our people and our law." The right to make contracts in ordinary occupations of life certainly ranked among those. But progressives latched on to Holmes's claim that the decision rested on a particular "economic theory which a large part of the country does not entertain."[89]

The high point of conservative, laissez-faire judicial activism, what one scholar calls "almost a replay of 1895," came during the 1908 term.[90] In 1906, Congress passed the Employers' Liability Act, which made railroads liable for injuries sustained by their employees, doing away with the "fellow servant" rule that the Court had imposed in the *Baugh* case. The Court struck down the act because it went beyond interstate and into intrastate commerce.[91] It also struck down that part of the 1898 Erdman Act that was meant to encourage collective bargaining by forbidding discrimination against union workers.[92]

In this case, Justice Harlan gave classic expression to the liberty of contract doctrine, that employer and employee had equal freedom to hire, fire, work, or quit on whatever terms they desired. In another case that seemed to evince a particular animus against organized labor, the Court made it explicit that the Sherman Antitrust Act did apply to labor union activity.[93] Finally, the Court held that federal courts could enjoin state officers to prevent them from enforcing unconstitutional acts (here, allegedly "confiscatory" railroad rates). The Court got around the Eleventh Amendment ("sovereign immunity") by saying that a state officer lost his state immune status when he undertook to enforce unconstitutional acts.[94]

In this "intermediate" phase of judicial review—more active than before the Civil War but not yet fully modern judicial supremacy—almost all of the controversial Court cases met some political response and did not become permanent. Congress's attempt to abolish the fellow servant rule of *Baugh* in the first Federal Employers' Liability Act went down in 1908, but soon Congress amended the act and the Court accepted it. The Court did, however, continue to oversee questions of reasonableness, engaging in valuation cost-analysis, until 1944.[95] Thus, Congress could use its interstate commerce power to amend the Court-devised "federal common law" by statute.[96] The Court also accepted state alterations to the federal common law.[97]

It took longer to curb the labor injunction, but Congress finally did so in the Norris–La Guardia Act of 1932. Congress and the states overturned the income tax cases the hard way, by the Sixteenth Amendment, in 1913. When Congress gave the Interstate Commerce Commission more explicit power to set railroad rates in the 1906 Hepburn Act, the Court yielded. Congress also established a special system of three-judge panels for injunctions of state officers, which arose from the Young case.[98] The Court's reinterpretation of the Sherman Act and adoption of the "rule of reason" in 1911 survived. When Congress had the opportunity to amend the act, it did not disturb the new rule.[99] Substantive due process/liberty of contract would never die, and it remains the most powerful tool of judicial activism, but progressives on the Court would turn it away from protecting economic property rights and toward non-economic rights and the rights of minorities.

Conservative defenders of the federal courts won the election of 1896, but most preferred not to repeat the trauma of the decade, and thus the early twentieth-century progressive movement arose. Presidents Theodore Roosevelt and William Howard Taft contributed to this by their appointments to the Supreme Court. Throughout the twentieth century, movements would emerge to curb judicial power—to strip jurisdiction, to make judges elective or subject to recall, to require unanimity or supermajorities—but these would largely amount to nothing. The route to judicial supremacy came through reformers' preference for changing judicial *personnel*, educating lawyers and judges, staffing bar and bench, and using them to promote rather than to impede progressive reform.

Roosevelt had defended the old order in the 1890s, then became a moderately progressive president and ultimately a radical third-party leader in 1912. In 1902, he appointed Oliver Wendell Holmes to the Court. Roosevelt particularly liked Holmes's military background, as he was looking for a justice who would support American imperialism and not worry too much about the extension of rights to Filipinos or Puerto Ricans. He also liked the reputation that Holmes had for defending organized labor. The president did not seem to consider Holmes's rather radical legal philosophy.

Considered one of the fathers of American legal realism, Holmes embraced legal positivism and sought the complete separation of morality and law. He admitted that his philosophy came "devilish near to believing that might makes right." This meant that Holmes had no sentimental sympathy for the underdog or for social justice, though somehow he acquired that reputation, which scholars have only recently corrected.[100] Nonetheless, this revolutionary appointment stirred no controversy. "The amazing thing about the entire episode of Holmes's appointment," one historian noted, "was that neither the press nor the figures who played any important part in it appreciated the significance of what was happening."[101]

Roosevelt ended up repudiating Holmes. He had no real reason for this, apart from Holmes's dissenting opinion in the *Northern Securities* case, TR's marquee antitrust prosecution. Roosevelt simply took amiss Holmes's independent "attitude." Yet Holmes did deliberately strike a posture of independence. Scholars sometimes hold him out as an example of the perils of predicting post-appointment behavior. But for thirty years on the Court, Holmes regularly issued progressive opinions. His dissent in *Lochner* became a progressive bumper sticker, accusing the Court of reading its own laissez-faire, Social Darwinist policy preferences into the Constitution. Holmes bore false witness against his brethren, among whom he alone, in 1905, flirted with Social Darwinism.[102]

He also gave expression to the minimalist judicial review standard of *Munn* and *Thayer*. In his view, the Constitution barred only laws that "a rational and fair man necessarily would admit . . . would infringe on fundamental principles as they have been understood by the traditions of our people and our law." The Sage of Beacon Hill here offered another throwaway line, as Holmes did not himself follow this standard, which as one commentator has observed, "amounted to an abnegation of judicial responsibility."[103] He seems rather to have followed the intuitive rule that he suggested to his clerks: when someone challenges a law's constitutionality, ask yourself "Does it make you puke?"[104] Roosevelt's next appointee, William R. Day, had a more mixed record, contributing to an early twentieth-century progressive trend but becoming more conservative in his later years. His third, William H. Moody, served for only three years.

Historians usually depict William Howard Taft as the conservative chief justice of the reactionary 1920s, or as the antiprogressive presidential candidate of 1912, but in fact he considered himself a progressive, as did other politicians. Suspicious conservative party chieftains considered Taft to Roosevelt's left in 1908.[105] As a federal judge in the 1890s, Taft, like TR, defended the old order. He told his brother that organized labor hated him for having issued injunctions against strikers "almost by the bushel."[106] Over several days during the 1894 Pullman strike, he told his wife of the necessity to "kill some of the mob . . . [U]ntil they have had much bloodletting, it will not be better." He expressed disappointment that only six strikers had been killed by federal troops, as this was "hardly enough to make an impression."[107] He made an extensive and thoughtful defense of the courts in the midst of the crisis, explaining the essentially conservative nature of the judiciary.[108]

But he joined Roosevelt and the Republican progressives in their effort to ameliorate the conditions that had provoked the unrest of the decade. Taft had to defend his own record as a circuit judge (1892–1900) in the election of 1908, against Bryan's third attempt to win the presidency. The Democrats had moderated their criticism of the federal courts since 1896.[109] The 1904 Democratic nominee, Alton Parker, a relatively progressive judge on the conservative New York Court of Appeals, criticized Roosevelt's adoption of judicial reform proposals by North Dakota's progressive federal district judge, Charles Amidon.[110] Taft feared that he could not survive the opposition of organized labor, but he defended his record and claimed, "There is not an issue in this campaign comparable in importance to the attack on the courts—the insidious attack on the courts that is being made by Mr. Samuel Gompers [president of the American Federation of Labor] and his partner, Mr. William Jennings Bryan."[111] Taft easily won the election, the usual reward for the incumbent party in a period of peace and prosperity. But Taft's presidency would produce a progressive rebellion that again raised the issue of the compatibility of judicial power—and of constitutionalism generally—with democracy.

Progressives, New Dealers, and their modern liberal successors depicted the Fuller, laissez-faire, *Lochner* era as the originator of judicial supremacy. They would claim that they had restored the Court to its proper constitutional role or had turned judicial power to good rather than bad ends.[112] As we will see, many of the great liberal activists so feared appearing to imitate the Lochnerites that they concocted ridiculous dodges like the "right to privacy." The early intermediate/Fuller era did indeed take steps toward judicial supremacy. *Pollock* and other cases proved difficult to defend. But it is clear that such cases were few, and had little impact. The political branches retained vigor and overturned most of them. Above all, the "old fools" seem to have sincerely believed that they were doing law, not politics, because they still believed that such a distinction existed. When judges embraced "legal modernism," collapsing law and politics, judicial supremacy really kicked in.

6

THE PROGRESSIVE AND
NEW DEAL PERIOD, 1910-53

The later intermediate, or progressive New Deal, era of judicial power spanned the chief justiceships of White, Taft, Hughes, Stone, and Vinson. Earl Warren stands out as the midwife of modern judicial supremacy, but one could make a strong case for Taft, who symbolized the ambivalence of the Progressive Era. After helping to make the Court more progressive as president, he made it more conservative as chief justice in the 1920s. But above all, he built its institutional power. More than anyone but perhaps John Marshall, he enabled the Court to withstand the most severe challenge it faced in the 1930s, when Hughes caved in to New Deal statism in order to save its institutional power. The progressive sense that a powerful Court could promote progress got a brief rehearsal under Stone—a period better and more accurately known as the Roosevelt Court. But after a few volatile years, the Court returned to one of its most restrained periods under Vinson and his (that is, Truman's) cronies.

TAFT, WILSON, THE WHITE COURT AND
THE PROGRESSIVE ERA, 1910-21

Taft had defended the judiciary in his 1908 campaign for the presidency, and he continued to do so as president. As pressure mounted in Congress to enact an income tax in defiance of the Court's 1895 decision, Taft negotiated a compromise by which Congress would enact a tax on corporation income and propose a constitutional amendment to tax incomes without apportionment. The story usually goes that the conservatives mistakenly assumed that the states would never ratify the amendment, which the states quickly did. In any case, Taft credited himself for sparing the Court the embarrassment of having to overturn *Pollock*. The Court also signaled its flexibility when it upheld the tax on corporate income, though nothing substantial distinguished this tax from the one that it had struck down in 1895. The Sixteenth Amendment made the whole question moot.[1]

Taft had always wanted to serve on the Court. As president, he filled five vacancies in one term. Only Presidents Washington and Lincoln, under unusual circumstances, had that many openings. Taft, now in his midlife, progressive phase, recognized the problem of the old, conservative Court. He told Tennessee judge Horace Lurton, "The condition of the Supreme Court is pitiable, and yet those old fools hold on with such a tenacity that it is most discouraging." He called Chief Justice Fuller, whom Taft resented for refusing to resign so that he could take Fuller's place, "almost senile." In addition, he said, "Harlan does no work; Brewer is so deaf that he cannot hear and has got beyond the point of the commonest accuracy in writing his opinions; Brewer and Harlan sleep almost through all the arguments. I don't know what can be done. It is most discouraging to the active men on the bench."[2] The old conservatives had run afoul of Theodore Roosevelt as well and determined to hold out as long as possible. Justices Harlan and Fuller allegedly made a pact not to resign "until they have to take us out feet foremost."[3]

Taft crossed party lines and appointed Lurton (whom TR had made a district judge) to the Court in 1910. As with Taft, one could call Lurton a "progressive conservative," willing to accept more active government but denying that the Court should act as "a continuous constitutional convention" or allow the rule of men to replace the rule of law. While sharing the progressive view of law as the means to promote public welfare, he particularly wanted to repudiate the idea that judges should actively shape the law themselves. His appointment drew criticism from both organized labor and state bar associations, an odd combination.[4]

Taft next appointed New York governor Charles Evans Hughes, a leading Republican progressive. Some speculated that Taft put him on the Court to eliminate a rival for the presidency in 1912. Though Taft strongly intimated that he would make Hughes the chief justice, when Melville Fuller died later that year Taft instead promoted Edward D. White. Willis Van Devanter took White's associate seat. This influential Wyoming Republican would become known as one of the archconservative anti–New Deal "four horsemen" in the 1930s, but in these early years he represented a run-of-the-mill party man with some progressive signs. Charles Evans Hughes remembered him as at least "certainly not an ultraconservative."[5]

John Marshall Harlan, the last of the old generation—or as Holmes called him, "the last of the tobacco-spittin' judges"—passed away in 1911. Taft ran into the most trouble when he proposed to replace him with Mahlon Pitney, who had aroused the opposition of organized labor, again on the issue of injunctions against strikes. Many progressives of his day shared Pitney's animus against unions.[6] The Senate confirmed him, with the helpful endorsement of his Princeton classmate Woodrow Wilson, who was then compiling a progressive record as the governor of New Jersey.[7] Harvard law professor Charles Warren published two articles defending "the progressiveness of the Supreme Court"; he became Woodrow Wilson's assistant attorney general the next year.[8] In 1914, one popular magazine used Warren's work to demonstrate that the Court "has caught the present-day infection. It is progressive." The author quite confidently asserted that the Court "has come to be the most powerful, perhaps, in some respects, of all the institutions" of American government, whose decisions are accepted "without protest."[9] By 1914, even TR was praising the increased progressivism of the Court, and in 1917, the *New Republic* described laissez-faire formalism as "generally discredited."[10]

Taft's influence extended to the appellate courts as well and belied his later reputation as a hidebound conservative. He endorsed the promotion of Learned Hand from a district court to the second circuit. Taft had appointed him to the district court but smarted when Hand supported TR in 1912 and became a celebrated progressive. But Taft got over these ideological and personal affronts and supported Coolidge's elevation of Hand in 1924. Similarly, in 1922, Taft counseled against the appointment of James M. Beck to the Supreme Court, though Beck ranked among the leading constitutional conservatives of the postwar period.[11]

These Taft justices did not last long, except for Van Devanter; Woodrow Wilson would replace three of them in his first term. They did move the Court in a more progressive direction, but they nettled some progressives by their adoption of the "rule of reason" in the *American Tobacco* and *Standard Oil* cases of 1911.[12] (Ironically, the "old fool" laissez-faire justices had taken a hardcore, "every combination" trust-busting stance.) In a sense, the antitrust decisions became the principal issue in the 1912 election. Taft defended them, and the federal judiciary generally, against a left-progressive attack that Roosevelt eventually latched on to.

Republican senator Robert La Follette of Wisconsin, who sought the Republican nomination in 1912, led this anticourt movement. "Battling Bob" wanted to bring the German-statist Wisconsin Idea to the United States. (North Dakota district judge Charles Amidon was another TR adviser on judicial issues. North Dakota, like Wisconsin, had a large German population with inclinations toward Prussian statism, but Bismarck, the city named for the architect of the German welfare state, lacked a major university cheek-by-jowl with the statehouse.) His former law partner and adviser, Gilbert Roe, wrote *Our Judicial Oligarchy* in 1912. The courts, La Follette asserted in the introduction, posed the principal obstacle to progress, having taken the side of wealthy interests against the poor. Roe urged the American people to recognize that the Court had usurped the legislative role, as when it rewrote the Sherman Act. They should treat it as a legislative body, with judges elected for brief terms, to be "recalled" by the people, like other elected officials in progressive states.[13]

Roe built upon a rising crop of academic and legal criticism of the federal judiciary and the entire constitutional system. The conservatives' inflation of the significance of *Marbury* and judicial review provoked a progressive iconoclasm.[14] Seymour Thompson, the former Missouri judge and editor of the *American Law Review,* continued his criticism of the federal courts from the 1890s. Walter Clark, chief justice of the North Carolina supreme court, called judicial review itself, never mind its abuse, a usurpation, never intended by the Constitution's framers and ratifiers.[15] Political scientist J. Allen Smith added to the argument that the Constitution thwarted democracy, and claimed that its most antidemocratic feature, judicial review, served as a post-ratification addition to the Founders' plutocratic plan.[16] This represented the last gasp of scholarly rejection of judicial review per se.[17]

This serious debate about the most basic feature of judicial power showed its relatively weak status a century after *Marbury.* Charles Beard, who would soon publish the most famous progressive critique of the Constitution, *The Economic Interpretation of the Constitution,* made a convincing argument that the Founders built judicial review into the original constitutional design. But this only made the Constitution worse, as Beard argued that the courts did exactly what the Founders wanted them to do, protecting property against majority rule.[18] Edward S. Corwin, whom Woodrow Wilson had brought from the University of Michigan to Princeton and who would become one of the most influential interpreters of the American Constitution, switched from the judicial usurpation to Beard's view, and along the way coined the term "judicial review."[19]

This period also saw the first popular history of the Supreme Court, by muckraking socialist Gustavus Myers. Myers focused on personnel rather than judicial power, presenting an overtly corrupt bench, arguing that the judges wielded the law as a weapon on behalf of capitalists in the class struggle.[20] He had little to say about judicial power per se, other than calling it a "usurpation" (established in the state courts before the Constitution), smuggled in by the Founders, who cleverly averted public notice of its potential. Myers averred that the justices of his day mostly shilled for the railroads. Fuller, for instance, owned railroad stock and prevented mutilated workers from recovering damages for their injuries.[21] Chief Justice White probably got his post as a reward to the American Catholic hierarchy for its defense of plutocracy.[22] He never pleaded the cause of a poor litigant, and "his clients were mainly Jewish merchants of wealth." Horace Lurton stood for the "constitutional right to be killed," and won the moniker "Private Car Lurton" for taking free railroad passes.[23] More sophisticated progressives, like Roscoe Pound, also emphasized the personal background of the justices, but in a subtler, more indirect way. They argued that the judges had unconsciously absorbed the interests of their socioeconomic class and the overall zeitgeist and that an archaic, scholastic mode of legal training blinkered them.[24]

Theodore Roosevelt had many personal and policy grievances with his anointed successor, and he added judicial reform to his independent campaign for president in 1912. As part of his radically progressive New Nationalism campaign for "direct democracy," TR called for enabling the people to recall unpopular judicial decisions. He did not endorse the recall of judges, though he approved of bill of address removal by legislatures. Most important, he limited his proposal to state, not federal, courts. Astute progressives saw the state courts as often more conservative than the federal, and the US Supreme Court as the least conservative of all. Harvard law professor Charles Warren tried to illustrate this in a series of articles defending the Court.[25]

Roosevelt particularly had in mind a New York Court of Appeals case, *Ives v. South Buffalo Railway*, which held New York's workmen's compensation law unconstitutional. (The voters soon amended the state constitution to overturn the decision.) Taft said that Roosevelt's judicial proposals made him unfit for another term as president and would "suspend the Constitution."[26] In his renomination acceptance speech, Taft called TR's recall proposal "grotesque" and said that judicial independence presented "the supreme issue" in the campaign.[27]

The judicial recall provided the principal issue between Taft and Roosevelt in 1912. (Taft hardly campaigned at all. He stuck to the tradition that the man, especially the incumbent president, did not seek the office and that parties, not personalities, ran election campaigns.) Taft took this threat so seriously that he largely ignored Woodrow Wilson and preferred a Democrat to the schismatic Roosevelt.

The real contest in 1912 pitted Roosevelt against Wilson, and neither emphasized the Court. TR called Wilson a conservative, and he often did sound the least progressive of the three. On unions, for example, Wilson allegedly wrote, "I am a fierce partizan of the open shop and of everything that makes for individual liberty."[28] Wilson's diffidence about the Court was on display in one of the centerpieces of his first-term New Freedom program, the Clayton Antitrust Act. He had rather vaguely campaigned against the Court's "rule of reason" decisions of 1911, which his party's platform "regretted." He gave the impression that he wanted to break up the trusts while Roosevelt wanted to regulate them. Wilson claimed that lawmakers had become familiar enough with the unfair methods that produced monopoly to define and outlaw them.

But when Congress began to do so, small businessmen, especially, feared that these prohibitions would make it impossible to carry on ordinary affairs. So the act only prohibited practices like tying and interlocking directorates if they "substantially lessened competition or tended to promote monopoly"— essentially a statutory expression of the rule of reason.[29] Neither Wilson nor Congress wanted to extend special privileges to organized labor, despite the American Federation of Labor's increasing support for the party.[30] The labor provisions of the Clayton Act did not give unions exemption from the antitrust laws or prohibit injunctions against strikers. They declared that the act did not "forbid or restrain individual members of [unions] from lawfully carrying out the legitimate objects thereof" and permitted injunctions "to prevent irreparable injury to property, or to a property right."[31] The AFL "gambled that it could win from the courts what it could not from the Congress," one study concludes, indicating that unions faced less judicial hostility than the federation often claimed and that the courts did not range too far from mainstream public opinion.[32]

The New Freedom Congress extended the jurisdiction of the Supreme Court. The original Judiciary Act's crucial section 25 allowed the Court to review state court decisions, but only if the state court held *against* a federal constitutional claim and in favor of a state law. If the state court struck down a state law as in conflict with the federal Constitution, the Supreme Court could not review. Thus, in the *Ives* case, the New York court held that the state workers compensation law violated the Fourteenth Amendment, so the US Supreme Court could not review its decision. In 1914 Congress amended the Judiciary Act to allow such appeals. This again showed that critics regarded the US Supreme Court as more progressive than the lower federal courts, and much more progressive than many state courts.

Wilson used the Court to launch his 1916 reelection campaign attempt to win over progressives who had voted for TR in 1912. In January, he nominated Louis Brandeis to the Court, beginning the first substantial or ideological nomination fight in Supreme Court history.[33] Previous Senate battles had arisen over party faction or patronage. The legal establishment considered Brandeis a radical and a maverick. A host of powerful interests, many of whom he had bested in court, organized an opposition campaign.[34] The Senate Judiciary Committee held hearings for months. Brandeis himself did not appear. Harlan Fiske Stone became the first nominee to do so, in 1925.

The controversy hardly concerned Brandeis's "judicial philosophy" at all. Only near the end did he respond to a charge that he "did not believe in a written constitution." Brandeis replied that his constitutional views resembled "very much those of Justice Holmes." He embraced sociological jurisprudence, perhaps best seen in his extensive presentation of social science data in the "Brandeis brief" that prevailed in *Muller v. Oregon,* a 1908 case that upheld an Oregon maximum-hours law for women. This marked an important step in the rise of judicial supremacy, a sign that progressives would try to use rather than reduce judicial power for reform purposes. He had recently expressed his Holmesian progressive beliefs in an essay, "The Living Law."[35]

Rather, opponents felt that Brandeis did not fit into the elite legal establishment, especially that of his adopted home, Boston. Several past presidents of the American Bar Association, including Taft, declared that Brandeis did not qualify for the Court. Brandeis had embarrassed Taft by exposing his antedating of a report exonerating his interior secretary, Richard Ballinger, during a controversy about conservation during his presidency. Taft privately expressed in bitter terms what he considered the personal affront of Wilson's appointment.[36] Brandeis was of course the first Jew ever nominated,[37] and though his opponents made no overt or even subtle expressions of anti-Semitism, such sentiments perhaps inhered in the elite bar's criticism of Brandeis's methods and legal ethics. Oddly, criticism centered on the fact that "the people's lawyer" often compromised his clients' interests for the sake of his social reform agenda—that he acted more like a judge than an advocate. This suggested a view of the legal system as a form of social engineering rather than as a forum for the resolution of disputes in the traditional Anglo-American adversarial mode. But the specifics amounted to little more than a generalized sense that they considered him untrustworthy, and certainly not "clubbable."

In the end, Wilson got the Senate Democrats to toe the line, and the body confirmed Brandeis on a party-line vote. Wilson never expressed any desire to alter the Court, to pack it with progressives. In his final appeal he said that Brandeis would "ornament the high court of which we are all so justly proud."[38]

Brandeis's appointment marked an important step in the rise of judicial supremacy. It signaled that progressives had decisively moved away from the Populists' approach of curbing judicial power toward judicial personnel—taking judicial power for granted and using it for their own purposes. Brandeis, and his acolyte, Felix Frankfurter, would also further the cultivation of clerks, usually the brightest graduates of Harvard Law School, as a way to build a progressive judicial bench.

Moreover, despite his assertions of social science "facts," Brandeis really evinced more of an emotional, quasi-religious orientation. (Franklin Roosevelt would call him "Old Isaiah.") He would display what Benjamin Cardozo called *Gefühlsjurisprudenz*, "a jurisprudence of sentiment or feeling."[39] He departed from judicial norms in his covert exercise of political influence, again largely through Frankfurter. "Brandeis's primary standard for action was his own conscience. If he believed he was right, that settled the matter for him, no matter what others might think," one analyst observes.[40] Another notes, "Brandeis allowed his own prejudices to affect his judging."[41] As the standard text in American constitutional history puts it, "Zealous, self-righteous, and concerned with improving politics and society, Brandeis, far more than Holmes, gave the progressive reform impulse tangible expression in constitutional law and anticipated the judicial liberalism of the mid-twentieth century."[42]

The Court in Wilson's years largely continued the progressive trend begun under Roosevelt and Taft. Wilson's first appointee, James C. McReynolds, became a notorious conservative on the Court, the most antiprogressive of the "Four Horsemen" of reaction in the 1930s. But nobody expected this when Wilson appointed him, with apparently little thought, in 1914. When Charles Evans Hughes resigned to run for president against Wilson in 1916, Wilson chose John Hessin Clarke, whom he identified as the most progressive candidate. In 1917, the Court appeared to overrule the *Lochner* case (though it did not mention it) when it approved a ten-hour-workday law for all workers in Oregon.[43] The majority continued to look upon organized labor with a gimlet eye, but many progressives shared this attitude during this period. In 1915, it struck down a Kansas law that prohibited "yellow-dog contracts" under the Fourteenth Amendment, as it had for the federal government under the Fifth Amendment in *Adair*.[44] Two years later it affirmed that employers could get court injunctions to prevent union organizers from appealing to workers to breach their yellow-dog contracts.[45]

As the nation neared the brink of war, the Court upheld an extraordinary act to meet the demands of several railroad unions for an eight-hour day with no reduction in pay. The four powerful railroad brotherhoods threatened to walk if the owners did not meet their demand, which would cripple the national defense preparedness effort. Wilson made a special address to Congress to pass the Adamson Act. This apparent capitulation to union extortion became the central domestic policy issue of the 1916 election. Wilson narrowly prevailed in that contest, and the Court upheld the Adamson Act by a tortuous 5–4 decision.[46] Hughes would probably not have turned the minority into a majority had he remained on the Court, despite his opposition to the act as a political candidate.[47]

The Adamson Act, and the eventual war, made the Court more conservative. The radical implications of the act alarmed Justice Day especially.[48] Day wrote the opinion in the 5–4 decision that struck down Congress's attempt to eradicate child labor, in one of the progressives' greatest disappointments. Since the 1890s (as in its antitrust decisions), the Court had adopted a more permissive view of Congress's efforts to use its power to regulate interstate commerce to cloak essentially police power goals. It had upheld the prohibition of the interstate shipment of obscene literature, lottery tickets, adulterated foods, and prostitutes, because almost everybody condemned these. One scholar has traced "the evangelical origins of the living Constitution" in these cases.[49] Alcohol would not admit of a nationwide policy until the Eighteenth Amendment, so Congress took the extraordinary step of divesting alcohol of its character as a commercial article, over President Taft's veto of what he considered an unconstitutional delegation of legislative power. The Court accepted this, too.[50]

But in *Hammer v. Dagenhart* the Court drew the line. President Wilson, too, had only recently come to support the child labor prohibition, previously saying that it would take an "absurdly extravagant" interpretation to sustain it. Justice Day made the strained but not altogether implausible argument that in the earlier cases, Congress had targeted inherently harmful articles. Here it targeted innocuous things (textiles or furniture) in order to regulate labor in the states. Day further misread a provision of the act as if it permitted mill owners to ship goods manufactured by child labor after thirty days.[51] He also misread the Tenth Amendment as giving Congress only powers "expressly" granted.[52] Congress responded by imposing a punitive tax on the profits of companies that employed children, since the Court had upheld apparently regulatory taxes when Congress imposed them on artificially colored oleomargarine, phosphorous matches, and narcotics. In 1922, the Court struck down this attempt to use the taxing power to do what it could not do by the commerce power.[53]

World War I brought up many of the constitutional issues of the Civil War, and the Court again largely upheld government power. The government used conscription much more widely in the Great War, and the Court upheld it under Congress's power to raise and support armies. Congress enacted a Sedition Act in 1918, and the Court unanimously validated it that year. It also accepted national price controls in the Lever Act. In 1920, the Court upheld an ambitious program of state socialism by North Dakota's Nonpartisan League, against a challenge that taxation to establish state-owned banks, farm manufacturing and marketing companies, grain elevators and mills, and housing did not constitute a "public purpose."[54]

THE TAFT COURT, 1921-30

A reaction against progressive statism had set in as early as the 1918 elections, when the Republicans regained control of Congress. That Senate then rejected the Treaty of Versailles, and the Republicans won the presidency and Congress in the landslide of 1920. For a long time, historians have taken pains to point out the persistence of progressivism in the 1920s and to not exaggerate the reactionary aspects of the decade. But it did see at least a hiatus during the Progressive Era, and saw it clearly in the new Supreme Court under William Howard Taft.

Taft ranks among the most influential chief justices in American history. Nobody can rival John Marshall, who did for the Court what George Washington had done for the presidency. But none of Marshall's successors tried to build the institution until Taft. If Melville Fuller's Court made bold assertions of laissez-faire ideology, it did so with an almost admirably reckless disregard for political reaction. Taft, on the other hand, showed political sensitivity and acumen. He actively helped in judicial personnel selection, tried to keep the Court from appearing too conservative, lobbied Congress about its docket, and worked to give it a building equal to its dignity and power.

Ex-president Taft told the electorate that the future of the Supreme Court presented the most important issue in the 1920 election.[55] Wilson had put men on the Court who would not resist "socialistic raids upon property rights."[56] Taft's influence on the composition of the Court began with himself, when Chief Justice Edward D. White died two months into the Harding presidency. Taft had long aspired to the chief justiceship. Indeed, some suggest that Taft, who had called for new blood to replace the "old fools" on the Court, chose to elevate the elderly White to the center chair to set up a vacancy for himself. He got President Harding to appoint him, and he guided Harding in the appointment of two new justices, Edward Sanford and Pierce Butler. Conservative ex-senator George Sutherland stood in line already, something of a rival to Taft for the center chair. These three, along with McReynolds and Van Devanter, composed a solid conservative majority. Holmes and Brandeis became the regular progressive dissenters. Harlan Fiske Stone, Calvin Coolidge's appointee, drifted to their side, and by the end of his term Taft regretted that he had pressed for Stone.

Doctrinally, the Taft Court presented a very mixed bag. Its interpretation of the labor provisions of the Clayton Act dashed whatever hopes the AFL and unionists had for relief from injunctions and antitrust liability. The Court interpreted the diffident language of the statute as if it had done nothing more than codify earlier Court interpretations.[57] Taft must have enjoyed striking down an Arizona law that prohibited injunctions in labor disputes. Taft had vetoed the bill for Arizona statehood in 1911 because it provided for the recall of judges. The state dropped the provision, entered the Union, restored the recall, and restored the labor injunction prohibition. Brandeis privately called Taft's rare application of the equal protection clause in this case "fantastic." He told Felix Frankfurter that the Court "is malleable on almost everything but trade unions. Then its prejudices become active."[58] Organized labor had few political allies in the economically prosperous 1920s.

Taft struck down the congressional tax on the profits of manufacturers who used child labor, but even Holmes and Brandeis concurred, presumably on stare decisis grounds: what Congress could not regulate by the commerce power it could not regulate by the taxing power.[59] In 1923, the Court tried to rein in the definition of businesses "affected with a public interest" against state regulation.[60] But during that same term it unleashed the federal "spending power" against a taxpayer claim that a federal program promoting maternal health through a "grant in aid" to the state exceeded the enumerated powers of Congress.[61] Taft recoiled, though, when the Court struck down a congressionally enacted minimum wage law for women in the District of Columbia. Justice Sutherland noted that the Court had never explicitly overturned *Lochner* and that liberty of contract remained the rule (here under the Fifth Amendment, but in most cases under the Fourteenth Amendment for state regulations). Taft ardently dissented with Holmes. *Adkins v. Children's Hospital* caused the most hostile reaction of all Taft Court opinions; the decision ostensibly was 5–3 but really was 5–4, because Brandeis recused himself.

The Court haphazardly revived liberty of contract/substantive due process. Indeed, critics saw the lack of a clear rationale for its application as one of the chief shortcomings of the Taft era.[62] Progressive justices sometimes joined, and conservative justices sometimes dissented, in due process cases. Holmes wrote a landmark decision that held that state regulation could amount to a "taking" in violation of the Fifth Amendment.[63] Conservative leader Sutherland wrote the opinion that upheld the progressive program of land-use "zoning" for urban planning.[64]

The application of substantive due process for non-economic or civil liberties in the 1920s, and the concurrent expansion of the "incorporation" of the Bill of Rights, stood out. The first came into view as early as 1917, when the Court voided state and local laws that tried to segregate housing by forbidding real estate sales to minorities.[65] The Taft Court struck down an Oregon law that outlawed nonstate schools and a Nebraska law that outlawed the teaching of (modern) foreign languages.[66] Both of these reflected the nativist, Klan-organized distrust of foreigners and Catholics. (At about this time, an ambitious young Alabama politician, Hugo Black, joined the Klan.) Justice McReynolds wrote these opinions, arguing partly on property rights (private schools) grounds and partly on the natural right of parents to educate their children. The Taft Court also took the first step in moderating the summary treatment of Black criminal defendants, ordering a federal court to review an Arkansas trial that resembled a lynching.[67] It also struck down Texas's "white primary" law, sustaining a suit by a Black voter who was disfranchised under it.[68] Taft knew that these decisions would help the Court and Republican Party appeal to Blacks, Catholics, and other ethnic minorities.[69] He also helped get another Catholic, Pierce Butler, appointed to the Court, in 1923.

In 1925, the Court for the first time held that a provision of the Bill of Rights (freedom of speech) applied to the states. Though it upheld the conviction of a leader of the Communist Party under New York's criminal anarchy law, *Gitlow v. New York* marked the first step in what came to be called the "incorporation" of the Bill of Rights.[70] But in the meantime, the Court generally gave both the states and the federal government a wide berth in social engineering and the policing of morals. Over the silent dissent of the "Catholic seat," Justice Butler, the Court upheld state power to sterilize the "feeble-minded," a campaign that would ultimately mutilate some sixty thousand Americans and provide a model for Nazi Germany.[71] The Justice Department turned the Mann "white slave act" from a prohibition of coercive prostitution into a moral crusade, applicable to gangsters and public figures such as boxer Jack Johnson who transgressed racial norms.[72] The Court found itself at sixes and sevens about the enforcement of Prohibition, many fearing that its flagrant and widespread violation threatened the rule of law.

Taft succeeded in preserving public support for the Court. In 1924, Robert La Follette undertook a third-party progressive campaign that offered the last serious summons to curtail the power of the Court. He called federal judges "petty tyrants and arrogant despots."[73] La Follette wanted to permit Congress to overrule Court decisions by a two-thirds vote.[74] Senators George Norris and William Borah similarly proposed to abolish lower courts and require Supreme Court supermajorities.[75] Republicans made the La Follette judicial proposal a key issue in their 1924 campaign.[76]

John W. Davis, the Democratic nominee, also condemned the La Follette plan, as he had Theodore Roosevelt's judicial recall in 1912. As president of the American Bar Association in 1923, Davis called the proposals for judicial reform "naked and undisguised as an attack upon our theory of government under a written constitution." But he came to condemn the Republicans for exaggerating its significance.[77] Republican vice presidential candidate Charles Dawes especially enthusiastically defended the Court.[78] Republicans reminded ethnic and religious minorities that the Court had vindicated their liberties. Meanwhile, the Democratic Party's 1924 convention could not agree to condemn the Ku Klux Klan. Chief Justice Taft urged a newspaper editor to highlight recent minority rights decisions. La Follette's proposal became a "political albatross" that he tried to ignore or weakly explain away.[79]

Coolidge won in a landslide. In his inaugural he said, "The expression of popular will in favor of maintaining our constitutional guarantees was overwhelming and decisive. There was a manifestation of such faith in the integrity of the courts that we can consider that issue rejected for some time to come."[80] Most recent treatments argue that the 1924 campaign "chilled the anti-Court movement for a decade."[81] Judicial power had figured in the elections of 1896 and 1912, with similar results. One historian has aptly titled the attacks on the courts "a muted fury," unable to rally deep political support. Populists had tended to focus more on the institutional power of the courts, many still denying the legitimacy of judicial review itself. More advanced progressives, like Roscoe Pound and Felix Frankfurter, saw greater potential in altering judicial personnel rather than judicial power. They emphasized the education and training of lawyers who would become the next generation of judges.[82] As Louis Brandeis put it just before he joined the Court, "What we need is not to displace the courts, but to make them efficient instruments of justice; not to displace the lawyer, but to fit him for his official or judicial task."[83] The most prescient of them saw beyond putting down judicial obstacles to progressive reform, toward enlisting the courts in advancing that agenda. Progressive ex-senator Albert Beveridge's four-volume biography of John Marshall, in which he depicted the chief justice as the father of living constitutionalism and judicial policymaking, took a step in this direction.[84]

Taft shaped the structure and procedure of the courts as well as their personnel. The chief justice tried to rationalize and centralize the federal judicial system, seeing himself not only as the chief justice of the Supreme Court but also as the administrative head of the whole federal judicial system.[85] He induced Congress to increase the number of federal district judges and to move them to jurisdictions with heavier workloads, in 1922. Taft above all put over the 1925 "Judges' Bill," which enabled the Supreme Court to control its docket. Heretofore almost anybody with enough time and money could compel the Court to review their case by a writ of error. These included the bevy of ordinary tort and contract cases under Article III diversity jurisdiction. Taft's bill allowed the Court to choose which appeals it would hear via the writ of certiorari rather than error. Taft "went to the cusp of appropriate judicial conduct" in pushing the bill through Congress. (Congressmen called it the Judges' Bill not just because it concerned the judges but also because the judges wrote it.) He astutely kept himself out of the limelight, aware that he still had old political enemies in Congress, especially in the Senate.[86]

The Judges' Bill allowed the Court to focus on "important" cases—cases of high constitutional import rather than run-of-the-mill litigation. As one scholar recently noted, the Court would no longer provide "a simple dispute settlement mechanism." It would now have to explain why "it was selecting its own cases to serve ends extrinsic to the cases themselves."[87] It would inevitably steer the Court toward, rather than away from, "political questions." "Docket control" featured prominently in the growth of judicial power in other countries in the late twentieth century.[88]

Finally, Taft lobbied for a new home for the Court, which had convened in the cramped basement of the Capitol for decades. The justices did most of their work from their home offices, circulating draft opinions by messenger. Taft secured $10 million of a $50 million congressional pot for new public buildings and recruited the eminent architect Cass Gilbert to plan the truly monumental courthouse that we see today, which occupies more than a football field in area, is four stories high, and is encased in gleaming marble and trimmed in oak and bronze. One could liken it to Solomon's temple, which fit Taft's idea of heaven as a perfect court. Taft had to do some deft politicking here, too, for many of his brethren saw no need for a new setting.

Taft died before the groundbreaking and never saw the completion of the colossal edifice, in 1935, and some of the old justices refused to use the new facilities—what Robert Jackson called the "marble mausoleum." Taft's most visible and lasting legacy provided an apt metaphor for his Court—a building for a modern Court, designed in a deliberately antimodern style, no longer under but separate from and on the same plane as the legislative edifice.[89]

Taft's health deteriorated in the late 1920s, and he became anxious about the future of the Court that he had put together. He lamented that Justice Stone had become a regular dissenter, with Holmes and Brandeis—the "Bolsheviki," as he privately called them. The prospect of future appointments by President Herbert Hoover did not encourage him. "Hoover is a progressive just as Stone is, and just as progressive as Brandeis is."[90] He hoped to serve long enough to collect his pension in 1931, or as long as he needed "to prevent the Bolsheviki from getting control," he told his brother in 1929. But ill health forced him to resign in February 1930. He died a month later, on the same day as his jurisprudential twin, Edward Sanford.

THE NEW DEAL, THE HUGHES COURT, AND THE COURT-PACKING CRISIS

Progressive historians long mischaracterized Herbert Hoover as the last laissez-faire conservative when in fact he had supported TR's Progressive campaign in 1912 and moved the Court in a more progressive direction.[91] A solid six-man conservative majority contracted to what progressives called the Four Horsemen after 1930. Hoover nominated Charles Evans Hughes as chief justice. Since losing the presidential race to Woodrow Wilson in 1916, Hughes had held several public offices, most notably serving as secretary of state. But Senate progressives objected to his private practice representing large corporations. (Stone had drawn similar fire, as the first nominee to appear before the Senate, in 1925.)

Hughes's 52–26 confirmation vote stood out as remarkably close for a former associate justice whose president's party had a Senate majority. According to a widely told but disputed story, Hoover really wanted to elevate Justice Stone to the center chair and fill his place with the very progressive Learned Hand. Hoover felt that he must at least make the gesture of offering the chief justiceship to Hughes. He expected Hughes to decline, since his son was the solicitor general and could not continue in that office with his father on the bench. To the president's chagrin, Hughes accepted his offer over the phone, with no hesitation.[92]

The Senate rejected Hoover's nominee for associate justice, John J. Parker, by the narrowest possible margin, 39–41. The AFL and the National Association for the Advancement of Colored People opposed him, because he had upheld the application of an injunction in a labor dispute and had expressed his opposition to Black suffrage in a 1920 North Carolina gubernatorial race. The AFL complaint weighed more, politically, and concerned the judiciary in particular. Washington senator Clarence Dill accused Parker of adhering to "the doctrine of property rights as superior to human rights" and warned that if the judges "do not watch their step . . . we will find a way to change the Constitution and upset the judiciary itself."[93] Parker's defenders said that he had to abide by the most recent decision of the Supreme Court on the matter, in the *Hitchman* case. "Shall the legislative branch control the decisions of the Supreme Court?" Hoover asked. The progressives, he worried, wanted "to subordinate the Court, not merely to the legislative branch but to the prevailing views of the Senate alone."[94] The chief chronicler of Supreme Court appointments concluded that the rejection is "now all but universally regarded not only as unfair and regrettable but a blunder," as Parker served another twenty-eight years on the Fourth Circuit Court of Appeals and compiled a progressive record, especially in labor cases.[95]

Hoover chose the more conservative Owen J. Roberts, who had no track record to which the progressives could object. He would become a jurisprudentially befuddled and vacillating wild card in the coming New Deal conflicts on the Court. Finally, when the venerable Oliver Wendell Holmes retired in 1932, Hoover decided to give the progressives one of their own, Benjamin Cardozo. Cardozo came out of the legal realism movement, a more radical version of Roscoe Pound's sociological jurisprudence. He had expressed the progressive view of law as made (and especially as judge-made) and an explicitly relativist pragmatism in his most famous work, *The Nature of the Judicial Process*, in 1921. But one scholar aptly calls Cardozo a "small-r Realist," and Cardozo repudiated its more radical adherents in a 1932 address to the New York Bar Association.[96] He recognized the danger of what he called *Gefühlsjurisprudenz*, but his successors would show less caution.[97]

By 1932, Hoover had lost control of Congress, so he sought to avoid another contentious nomination fight. That year, progressives finally passed a bill to prohibit injunctions in labor disputes. The Norris–La Guardia Act clarified the ambiguous language of the Clayton Act and appeared to give the AFL what it had sought for a generation, including an implicit exemption from the anti-trust laws. Hoover fought the bill, but in the end he conceded and signed it. He appended the opinion of his attorney general, William Mitchell, who expressed his constitutional doubts about the act. (The Taft Court had struck down a similar Arizona law in the 1921 *Truax* case.) But the attorney general punted: "It seems to me futile to enter into a discussion of these questions. They are of such a controversial nature that they are not susceptible of final decision by the executive branch of the government. . . . These questions are of such a nature that they can only be set at rest by judicial decision."[98] *Marbury* had rejected the addition of jurisdiction to the Supreme Court. Mitchell's opinion seemed to say that the Court could reject congressional power to limit its jurisdiction.[99]

Nobody made an issue of the Court in the 1932 presidential election. Near the end of the campaign, FDR maladroitly blamed the Depression on the Republican Party, which had controlled the presidency, Congress, "and, I might add for good measure, the Supreme Court as well."[100] In fact, Republican presidents had appointed two of the most progressive justices, Stone and Cardozo, and Brandeis had identified as a Republican until 1912. The two most conservative justices, Butler and McReynolds, were Democrats. Hoover called the charge "atrocious" and said that it suggested that Roosevelt wanted a subservient judiciary. He called it "the most destructive undermining of the very safeguard of our form of government yet proposed by a political candidate."[101]

Roosevelt won the presidency in a landslide, with overwhelming majorities in both houses of Congress. In his call for "bold experimentation" to meet the Depression, he expected few constitutional obstacles. "Our Constitution is so simple and so practical that it is possible to meet extraordinary needs by change in emphasis and arrangement without loss of essential form," he said.[102] Congress quickly enacted a sweeping program of industrial reform in the National Industrial Recovery Act, which allowed trade associations to adopt "codes of fair competition" to control output, prices, and labor standards without fear of the antitrust laws. The Agricultural Adjustment Act did the same for farmers, in hopes that reduced output would raise crop prices. It also taxed processors to subsidize the farmers if prices did not rise.

Concerning the Court, the Economy Act was meant to redeem the Democrats' pledge to reduce Hoover's extravagant spending and balance the budget. A 1932 act cut the pensions of retired Supreme Court justices by fifty percent. At least two incumbent justices, conservatives Van Devanter and Sutherland, wanted to retire but now could not afford to.[103] Thus, FDR would go his entire term without any vacancies on the Court, which had not happened to any president since James Monroe.

The Court gave Roosevelt little trouble during his first two years as president. Many progressives believed that the Court had a reliable majority.[104] But others in the administration worried that the president's programs stood on shaky constitutional ground and deliberately avoided enforcement litigation.[105] In two important state cases, the High Court showed a high tolerance for New Deal–type programs. It accepted a New York milk price–fixing law, broadening the category of businesses "affected with a public interest" to virtually the anything-goes *Munn* standard.[106] It also upheld a Minnesota farm mortgage moratorium law against a textbook challenge under the contract clause. "While emergency does not create power," Chief Justice Hughes said, "emergency may furnish the occasion for the exercise of power." He went far toward adopting the "living constitution" view against the argument that the contract clause meant the same thing in 1934 as it had in 1787. The claim that "the great clauses of the Constitution must be confined to the interpretation which the framers, with the conditions and outlook of their time, would have placed upon them," he said, "carries its own refutation."[107]

In three dramatic cases in 1934, he upheld Congress's abrogation of "gold clause" contracts, in which debtors (including the US government, with its "gold bonds") promised to repay in gold of the "present weight and fineness." These contracts became common in response to Civil War–era greenback cases as a way for creditors to defend themselves against inflation of the currency. In 1934, the government reduced the gold value of the dollar by 60 percent, saving the federal Treasury some $10 billion—and private debtors perhaps $60 billion more. In a maneuver similar to Marshall's in *Marbury*, Chief Justice Hughes decided that Congress had broken the law but that the creditors had suffered no remediable loss.[108]

Even the liberals who concurred found this hard to swallow; Justice Brandeis privately called it "terrifying in its implications."[109] Roosevelt had prepared for an adverse ruling and had composed a radio address to explain why he would defy the Court. Public approval of the New Deal in the 1934 midterm elections, which increased Democratic majorities from 60–35 to 70–23 in the Senate and from 309–113 to 322–113 in the House, further encouraged him.

The Court crisis began on what New Dealers called Black Monday, May 27, 1935. The Court had struck down the enforcement of the National Industrial Recovery Act petroleum code earlier in the month; now it unanimously trashed the entire act. *Schechter v. U.S.*, known as the "sick chicken case," held that the NIRA had delegated legislative power from Congress to the president, and from the president to private interests. It called the economic activity involved here, slaughtering chickens, completely local and beyond Congress's power to regulate. Even the most liberal of the justices, Benjamin Cardozo, who endorsed administrative discretion, conceded that the act displayed "delegation running riot."[110] Brandeis likewise told the president's chief adviser, "We're not going to let the government centralize everything." Stone told former president Hoover that he opposed the "steady absorption of power by the President" and the "failure of Congress to perform its legislative functions."[111] That day, the Court also unanimously struck down a federal bankruptcy act for taking property without just compensation.[112] The most galling of the Black Monday decisions allowed Congress to limit the president's power to remove members of the "independent regulatory commissions," in this case the Federal Trade Commission.[113]

Roosevelt expressed dismay that the liberals had abandoned him in these cases. He had expected Brandeis's cooperation, but Brandeis called May 27 "the most important day in the history of the Court and the most beneficent."[114] In a press conference, Roosevelt chided the Court for adopting a "horse-and-buggy definition" of interstate commerce. The hostile public reaction to this criticism of the Court also surprised him.[115]

It appeared that Roosevelt shared Woodrow Wilson's and other progressives' disdain for the separation of powers and checks and balances of the original Constitution, considering them outdated obstacles to reform. President Roosevelt brought to Washington an expectation that he would have the cooperation of the US Supreme Court as he had secured the cooperation of the New York Court of Appeals when he was governor in Albany. When elected, he told Justice Cardozo that he looked forward to a continuation of the relationship that they had enjoyed when Roosevelt was governor and Cardozo was on the New York high court.[116] He said that president, Congress, and Court should work together as a "three-horse team." His Congress had rubber-stamp administration bills, sometimes sight unseen. But this produced careless and sloppy legislation that could not survive the judicial review of even sympathetic justices.

Roosevelt responded to Black Monday by promoting an even more ambitious domestic policy program in the "second New Deal." This involved the Social Security Act, higher taxes, and the breaking up of public utility holding companies. It also tried to restore the NIRA through more specific and targeted legislation and new methods. Congress tried to establish cartels in particular industries, like oil and coal production. Above all, FDR accepted New York senator Robert Wagner's National Labor Relations Act to promote collective bargaining. The Wagner Act went beyond the exemptions from antitrust laws and injunctions of the Norris–La Guardia Act. It required employers to bargain collectively with whatever independent union a majority of its employees chose, and it listed a range of "unfair labor practices" that employers could not commit.

These acts deliberately challenged the Court. Many in Congress voted for them on the assumption that the Court would strike them down.[117] Republicans alleged that the new farm bill was designed to embarrass the Court and stoke the administration's campaign against it.[118] Roosevelt advised Congress to enact the Bituminous Coal Conservation Act regardless of their doubts about its constitutionality. "All doubts should be resolved in favor of the bill, leaving to the courts, in an orderly fashion, the ultimate question of its constitutionality. I hope your committee will not permit doubts as to constitutionality, however reasonable, to block the suggested legislation."[119] Felix Frankfurter told Roosevelt, "Let the Court strike down any or all of them . . . especially by a divided Court. *Then* propose a constitutional amendment." FDR told his cabinet that he was "not at all adverse to the Supreme Court declaring one New Deal statute after another unconstitutional," as that would provide "a real issue . . . on which we can go to the country" in the 1936 election.[120]

The Court obliged in several 1936 cases. It struck down the Agricultural Adjustment Act, holding that its attempt to control agricultural production lay beyond Congress's power to regulate interstate commerce and involved "the expropriation of money from one group [processors] for the benefit of another [farmers]." Justice Roberts's defense of the Court's exercise of judicial power galled legal progressives. "The Constitution is the supreme law of the land ordained and established by the people," he wrote, and "all legislation must conform to the principles it lays down." Facing an allegedly unconstitutional act, "the judicial branch of the government has but one duty—to lay the article of the Constitution which is invoked beside the statue which is challenged and to decide whether the latter squares with the former." Echoing Hamilton in *Federalist* 78, Roberts claimed that the Court had no political power. "The only power it has, if such it may be called, is the power of judgment."[121]

Progressive critics mocked this traditional description of judicial review as risibly naive at best, and more likely a transparent mask for the imposition of the judge's reactionary policy preferences. In his bitter dissent, Justice Stone made a bold statement of judicial supremacy. "While unconstitutional exercise of power by the executive and judicial branches of the government is subject to judicial restraint, the only check upon our own exercise of power is our own sense of self-restraint."[122] A year later, Justice Sutherland repudiated this call for "self-restraint" as "both ill considered and mischievous. Self-restraint belongs in the domain of will and not judgment."[123]

The Court also rebuked the methods of the new Securities and Exchange Commission, likening the administrative agency to the arbitrary Star Chamber court.[124] It held the Bituminous Coal Act unconstitutional, as "legislative delegation in its most obnoxious form."[125] The most controversial decision of this term struck down a New York minimum wage law for women.[126] Unlike many of the Black Monday decisions, these sharply divided the Court in 6–3 or 5–4 decisions.

The president now set the stage for the greatest conflict in the Supreme Court's history. FDR won an overwhelming reelection in November 1936, all but eliminating the Republican Party from Congress; Democrats enjoyed greater than four-to-one majorities in both houses. But Roosevelt did not so much as mention the Court in his campaign. Montana senator Burton Wheeler advised him to avoid the issue, which had gone so badly for him as La Follette's running mate in 1924. Roosevelt himself recalled that the Republicans had used the defense of the Court to great advantage in that election.[127] Nor did the Democratic Party platform address the problem. It called for "clarifying amendments" if New Deal programs required them.

On February 5, 1937, FDR shocked the nation with his proposal to pack the Court.[128] Roosevelt claimed that the justices had become too old to keep up with their workload, and he asked Congress for the power to appoint a new justice for each incumbent over the age of seventy who did not retire. This would give him six new appointments right away. Roosevelt devised this scheme with his attorney general, Homer S. Cummings. They kept the secret remarkably well. He consulted and alerted none of the rest of his cabinet or any members of Congress. They tipped off John L. Lewis, head of the Congress of Industrial Organizations, and Charlton Cogburn, the AFL general counsel. Roosevelt cryptically told his adviser Felix Frankfurter to prepare himself for a shock.

The insider status of these labor leaders indicated something about Roosevelt's plan. In December, a group of militant auto workers had begun a "sit-down strike" of General Motors plants in Flint, Michigan. Governor Frank Murphy, a prominent New Dealer, had pledged not to use force to oust the strikers and ignored a state court's order to do so. Few doubted that the governor acted at the behest of the president. The court-packing plan thus looked like the national-level counterpart to this state-level assertion of executive and mob power over courts. The public and politicians roundly condemned both the strikes and the plan. They would engross the country and vex FDR for the next six months.

The deviousness of Roosevelt's proposal stood out for all to see, and he very quickly had to shift the basis of its justification—from the infirmity and inefficiency of the justices to their usurpation of legislative power. But he had already waited too long. The controversy soon became less about the Court's abuse of power and more about the president's. Roosevelt's plan did not violate the Constitution per se, but it clearly affronted the constitutional principle of the separation of powers. Roosevelt, like many progressives, had scant regard for this principle. He rather envisioned a fusion of powers, of the three branches pulling in tandem, yoked together, as he put it, as a "three-horse team."

Members of Congress, especially senior senators, took this as a threat to their own power and independence. All the leaders of the House immediately refused to consider the bill; the Senate held extensive hearings, but these served more as a platform for the opposition than to build support for the bill.[129] But Roosevelt persisted. His landslide reelection convinced him that "the people are with me." He would go over the heads of the legislators and compel them to follow—much as Woodrow Wilson had done on the Treaty of Versailles, facing a hostile Senate in 1919, and with much the same result.

The president's surprise left his party nonplussed; his gambit embarrassed many veteran progressive court curbers. Roosevelt's personnel-packing approach did not address the fundamental problem of judicial power. *The Nation* noted that it "clearly does not meet the issue of the judicial power as an obstruction to democratic action."[130] It provided "a poultice where surgery was required," one critic later said.[131]

Burton Wheeler, who had run for vice president in 1924 on an anti-Court ticket, led the Senate opposition. New Deal interest groups like farmers and labor offered at most tepid support, and opposition senators brought forth an array of Court supporters. They especially highlighted the Court's defense of minority rights, which Chief Justice Taft had begun to cultivate in the 1920s. The Republican congressional minority prudently kept quiet and let the Democrats take down the administration. The justices also came to their own defense. Opposition leaders got Chief Justice Hughes to present a letter affirming that the Court had kept abreast of its work, and that a larger Court would actually impose more of a burden than a relief. Justices Brandeis and Van

Devanter, representing the liberal and conservative wings of the Court, signed the letter, which Hughes called "in accord with the views of [all] the Justices."[132]

More wind left the president's sails when the Court appeared to drop its opposition to reform legislation. Shortly after the Hughes letter, the Court reversed itself and upheld a Washington minimum wage law for women. Justice Roberts had provided the fifth vote to strike down New York's virtually identical law a year earlier; he now joined the progressive majority.[133] Roberts had made his decision well before the president's February proposal, so he could not have responded to it. But this chronology remained hidden until years later, so the Court *appeared* to have capitulated to the president's threat—a "switch in time'll save nine" the media quipped.[134] But Roosevelt continued to press for his bill. He said, with some justification, "I do not think there is any news in it," for the Court had employed liberty of contract/substantive due process in cases like *Lochner* (1905), repudiated it in *Bunting* (1917), and resurrected it in *Adkins* (1923). Roberts might well "switch" back.

The Court made a more decisive switch in April, when it upheld the Wagner Act.[135] Though the Court had liberalized its definition of interstate commerce since 1895, after this decision Congress would face almost no limits on its power to regulate the economy. The Court did not explain why the principles of its lead case, involving an enormous steel company clearly engaged in interstate operations, applied to the much smaller companion cases. Nor did it account for the problem of delegation of legislative power to the National Labor Relations Board (assuming Congress had the power in the first place). Though some scholars have argued that 1937 represented no sharp break with precedent, almost nobody saw it as anything other than a political decision in response to Roosevelt's proposal.[136] (The Court did not hear the five "Labor Board cases" until after the plan had been announced.) The conservative Four Horsemen continued to dissent, but Hughes and Roberts joined the liberals.

In the end, Roosevelt packed the Court the conventional way as the old justices began to retire and die. While House Judiciary Committee Chairman Hatton Sumners forcefully rejected the court-packing plan, he devised an act that allowed the justices to "retire" with secure pensions. Conservative justice Van Devanter took retirement in May 1937; Sutherland, the next year. Roosevelt continued to press the Senate for a compromise bill that would create four new seats, but the death of Senate Majority Leader Joseph Robinson in July ended that possibility. The fact that Roosevelt, who said that the Court needed young liberals, had promised the first position on the Court to Robinson, an old conservative, further exposed the president's disingenuousness. One journalist observed that the Senate Judiciary Committee's report against the proposal read like a bill of impeachment.[137] The Court had weathered its most severe storm since the 1800s.

THE ROOSEVELT COURT

Roosevelt's court-packing plan ended up inoculating the Court from future political challenges.[138] Neither the president nor Congress came close to adopting any significant proposal to limit the Court's power after 1937. As a Senate Judiciary Committee report put it, the scheme had been rejected so emphatically that "its parallel will never again be presented."[139] But if the Court weathered Roosevelt's plan, it barely survived his personnel alterations. Ex-president Hoover called Roosevelt's staffing of the new Court worse than the "cowing" that his proposal had produced in the old Court.[140] He seemed determined to make the Court a political institution by appointing political justices.

His first nominee, Senator Hugo Black, a populist demagogue, shocked his colleagues. But Roosevelt knew the Senate could not reject one of its own members. A journalist revealed Black's membership in the Ku Klux Klan shortly after his confirmation. As an Alabama defense attorney, he had blatantly manipulated racial and religious prejudice when he defended a man who had killed a Catholic priest who performed the marriage ceremony for the man's daughter and a Puerto Rican. After winning his Senate seat in 1926 with Klan support, Black ensured that he could later deny his membership. His Klan sponsor provided him with a letter of resignation and told him "I'll keep it in my safe against the day when you'll need to say you're not a Klan member."[141] Black gave a national radio address to this effect, and tried to depict himself as the *victim* of religious bigotry. In his first term on the Court, he would embarrass his colleagues with his homegrown constitutional doctrine and reckless activism. Black seemed to express Roosevelt's contempt for the Court.[142]

Stanley Reed, Roosevelt's next appointment, though a cipher, evoked no scandal. Roosevelt next chose Felix Frankfurter, who would become a polarizing figure on the Court, alienating many of his brethren with his professorial, condescending, and manipulative personality. The justices' background in the legal academy fed the contentiousness. They frequently cited law review articles and seemed to curry favor with the law schools, a trend that Chief Justice Taft had worried about.[143] One academic history of the Stone and Vinson Courts got its title, *Division and Discord,* in no small part from Frankfurter.[144] The discord also derived from differing views of the judicial function. Despite his reputation as a progressive and even a radical, Frankfurter called for judicial self-restraint and would lock horns with the liberal activists whom Roosevelt appointed.

Of these liberal activists, William O. Douglas offered the most outlandish profile. Legal historian G. Edward White classified him as an "anti-judge."[145] Judge Richard Posner nicely summarized his biography, calling Douglas "one of the most unwholesome figures in modern American political history. . . . A liar to rival Baron Munchausen." Douglas falsely claimed to have served in the army in World War I, and said he had recovered from polio to do so. He neither served nor had polio. "Apart from being a flagrant liar, Douglas was a compulsive womanizer, a heavy drinker, a terrible husband to each of his four wives, a terrible father to his two children, and a bored, distracted, uncollegial, irresponsible, and at times unethical Supreme Court justice who regularly left the Court for his summer vacation weeks before the term ended."[146] A thoroughgoing realist who closely followed Black's lead, he would become the Court's longest-serving member.

Roosevelt next filled the "Catholic seat," opened by Pierce Butler's death, with his attorney general, Frank Murphy. Murphy had refused to enforce a court order during the 1937 sit-down strike crisis, and it seemed remarkable that he would become the nation's chief law enforcement officer and now a justice. Many (including Murphy himself) believed that Roosevelt had "kicked him upstairs" to remove him as a potential presidential candidate in 1940 or to relieve certain Democratic city bosses from corruption investigations. Like Black, Murphy had also prepared an exculpatory letter, a "law-and-order" lecture to Congress of Industrial Organizations chief John L. Lewis from 1937.[147] Many saw the appointment as another expression of Roosevelt's contempt for the Court. Historians have almost all regarded Murphy as clearly unsuited to the job.[148]

Murphy had no hesitation about reading his own liberal inclinations into law—the Court would now "temper justice with Murphy," they joked. Even more clearly than Brandeis, he brought to the Court a *Gefühlsjurisprudenz.* "I write the law as my conscience bids me," he said in 1946. As one commentator later wrote, "If any Justice uses the 'gastronomical' approach to decisions—that is, votes by the nausea or pleasure he gets from hearing the case—it is Murphy."[149] This accorded with the skeptical realist view that decisions could depend on what a judge had for breakfast on any given day, or with Holmes's famous statement of his standard of unconstitutionality: "Does it make you puke?"[150] Murphy anticipated Earl Warren, though his untimely death in 1949 cut short his career.

James McReynolds, the last of the Four Horsemen, retired in 1941. Roosevelt's third term overcame his determination not to resign so long as "that crippled son-of-a-bitch was in the White House."[151] Chief Justice Hughes also stepped down later that year and Roosevelt elevated Harlan F. Stone to the center chair. This further undermined the Court, as Stone proved to be an abysmal administrator who could not prevent the scorpions from spewing their venom. Taft had urged President Hoover to pass him over in 1930.[152]

Robert Jackson, the attorney general, took the associate justice seat. An ardent New Deal liberal and Roosevelt loyalist, he had said in 1937, "If you're going to pack the Court, you've really got to pack it."[153] When Jackson took his oath as FDR's seventh appointee, the president said, "It may not be proper to announce it, but today the Court is full."[154] But Jackson would end up aligning with Felix Frankfurter as an advocate of judicial restraint.

The other associate justice slot went to South Carolina senator James Byrnes. But he soon resigned, in 1943, to join the administration's war management team, and was replaced by Dean Wiley Rutledge of the Iowa College of Law. With Black, Douglas, and Murphy, Rutledge would compose the core of a liberal activist bloc that Frankfurter called "the Axis." The Court passed a milestone in 1943, when for the first time in its history a majority of its decisions fell short of unanimity. The number of dissenting opinions tripled during the Roosevelt Court years. Though they shared a progressive New Deal ideology, the new justices (Black went from junior to senior associate justice in four years) "ultimately viewed one another as 'political animals' whose judicial objectivity could not always be trusted."[155]

The first decision heralding the activist "Roosevelt Court" came in the 1938 case *U.S. v. Carolene Products*. Here the Court upheld a 1923 congressional prohibition of the interstate shipment of "filled milk," a cheap milk substitute that the powerful dairy lobby wanted to eliminate from their market. As with the Labor Board cases, it indicated that Congress could regulate just about anything under the guise of the commerce power. But the case became famous for its fourth footnote, in which Justice Stone wrote that the Court would presume constitutionality "for regulatory legislation affecting ordinary commercial transactions," unless the act lacked "some rational basis." This recapitulated the standard of *Munn* and Holmes's dissent in *Lochner*, the "rule of clear mistake" from James Bradley Thayer, but applied to *one set of* interests and rights. However, the Court would not presume constitutionality "when legislation appears on its face to be within a specific prohibition of the Constitution, such as those of the first ten amendments," or in cases involving discrimination against "discrete and insular minorities." This became known as the "preferred freedoms" doctrine, the "double standard" of "bifurcated review."[156] The progressive New Deal state thus reversed the rights assumed/ power enumerated standard for the federal government. Some groups, and some rights, would enjoy greater judicial protection than others.[157]

Carolene Products (or at least its famous footnote), though little noticed at the time, became the blueprint for postwar American judicial liberalism. The double standard let the New Dealers dilute the unvarnished legal realism of the academic world without completely sacrificing the benefits of judicial power for good purposes. Justices Black, Douglas, Murphy, and Rutledge embraced unrestrained legal realism. Justices Frankfurter and Jackson advocated the "legal process" or "process restraint" school. For them, the Court should intervene especially in areas where the political process broke down, leaving vulnerable individuals and groups unable to defend their own interests—the ones excluded from what political scientists would describe as America's "polyarchy" or "interest group" system.

The legal process theory helped to extricate judicial review from its antidemocratic morass. In the process view, judicial review reinforced democracy.[158] It attempted to make legal realism more palatable and to preserve the potential of judicial review to forward social change by making sure that judges did not overuse it. The double standard established a latter-day "cloaking" of judicial power.[159] It required, for example, the claim that the New Deal Court had not innovated but had simply restored the original constitutional doctrines on issues like the commerce power or due process. They called the pre-1937 laissez-faire judges, not themselves, the activists.[160]

This little-noted footnote incubated the germ of modern judicial supremacy. An equally obscure act, the 1938 Federal Rules of Civil Procedure, provided another significant source of judicial power in that year. Twentieth-century jurists meant to simplify procedure by "merging" law and equity (see appendix A). In fact they produced what one scholar called "the triumph of equity."[161] Common-law rules tried to cabin, narrow, and contain litigation, and that helped to keep judicial power within bounds; equity stepped in when the law became too strained and technical. Equity and related procedural innovations—the extension of standing, joinder of parties, pretrial discovery, and class action suits—encouraged litigation and empowered judges by giving them more flexibility and discretion. This would build upon the *Carolene* double standard. Judges would deny injunctions (an equitable remedy) to employers in labor disputes, for example, but would liberally use equitable procedures and remedies for minority group plaintiffs in civil rights suits.[162]

On the same day as the *Carolene Products* decision, the Court also made a dramatic expression of its new agenda. In *Erie Railroad v. Tompkins,* the Court repudiated the entire federal common law, dating back to the 1842 case of *Swift v. Tyson,* stating that the federal courts had no power to fashion their own common law but must take the common law of the states as their rule (as the text of section 34 of the first Judiciary Act suggested). Observers saw this as an unprecedented act of judicial self-denial. For the first time in its history, the Court declared one of its own precedents unconstitutional. But really the case reflected the old progressive belief that federal courts had favored big business and that state courts would be more likely to succor the weak. This charge reflected another progressive exaggeration of the "laissez-faire" era. In the instant case, the state rule favored the railroad and the federal rule favored the injured plaintiff. And in later years the Court would have to reconstruct a federal common law, which would often reflect its new liberal agenda.[163]

The Court expressed its anything-goes standard of national socioeconomic regulation most fully in the 1942 case of *Wickard v. Filburn.*[164] It upheld a fine imposed on an Ohio farmer, Roscoe Filburn, who had grown eleven acres of wheat beyond what the Agricultural Adjustment Administration had allotted him. Filburn did not sell his wheat across state lines; it never left his farm. But the Court held that by growing wheat that he would otherwise have had to purchase, he depressed, however infinitesimally, the market price of the crop. With the last of the Four Horsemen off the bench, the Court spoke unanimously. Justice Jackson told his clerk that "in order to be unconstitutional . . . the relation between interstate commerce and the regulated activity would have to be so absurd that it would be laughed out of Congress."[165] This expressed the "rational basis" standard of *Munn* and James Bradley Thayer, and of Holmes's *Lochner* dissent, the one that Felix Cohen said "makes of our courts lunacy commissions sitting in judgment of the mental capacity of legislators and, occasionally, of judicial brethren."[166]

The president of the American Bar Association called the post-1937 shift in decisions "the most devastating destruction of constitutional limitations upon federal power, and the most unprecedented expansion of that power over the everyday affairs of individual citizens, witnessed in the century and a half of the existence of the United States." He asked, "Can a government which may arbitrarily control the individual's economic freedom be relied on permanently to keep safe his civil and political liberties?" But he had not taken note of the *Carolene Products* footnote.[167] Today's standard textbook in constitutional history observes the seismic shift of the late 1930s. The New Deal "created a regulatory welfare state . . . that revolutionized the federal system and went far toward displacing the regime of the framers." The 1937 decisions began "momentous changes in constitutional law that lay to rest the doctrines of substantive due process, liberty of contract, and dual federalism."[168] The wave of overrulings introduced a great deal of uncertainty into the law, what an ABA critic would later call "the new guesspotism."[169]

After the failure of the court-packing plan, a conservative coalition in Congress began to resist the extension of the New Deal. With the political branches deadlocked, the Court now led rather than impeded the progressive cause. The new Roosevelt Court abetted organized labor above all. It upheld the Norris–La Guardia Act as well as state anti-injunction laws (small potatoes after the surprise of the Wagner Act validation).[170] Led by Justice Murphy, the Court defined picketing as free speech protected by the First Amendment, but in less than a year it began to curtail this doctrine, as picketing almost always involved intimidation and force beyond speech or lawful expression.[171]

The Court also (in defiance of the Roosevelt Justice Department) all but exempted unions from the antitrust laws. "No Court has ever undertaken so radically to legislate where Congress has refused to do so," Justice Roberts remarked.[172] It further classified New York teamsters who hijacked or extorted payment from nonunion truckers as engaged in "traditional labor union activity," which was exempt from federal racketeering laws.[173] The Court displayed more deference to the Labor Board than it did, for example, to the Interstate Commerce Commission, "an administrative agency at present somewhat out of favor in so-called liberal circles," one commentator observed.[174] In 1941, Edward S. Corwin, long a champion of progressivism but now having second thoughts, called the Court "a sort of superlegislature in the interests of organized labor."[175]

The Court also got out of the way of the plethora of new administrative agencies created by the New Deal, beginning what administrative law scholars call "the era of deference."[176] As Charles Evans Hughes had observed in 1907, the Court's power to control constitutional interpretation depended on not overdoing it by getting stuck in the weeds of administrative detail. So the Court abandoned its own methods of public utility valuation and left it to the commissions. One observer called this "one of the dullest and least-publicized and most important of Roosevelt's victories over the old court."[177] It defined the "substantial evidence" required to defer to agency decisions as *any* evidence. Congress, in the 1946 Administrative Procedure Act, instructed the courts to accept any agency decision that they could not call "arbitrary and capricious." The courts interpreted this as equivalent to the Thayer standard of "anything short of insanity."[178]

The Court's supervision of the Securities and Exchange Commission's enforcement of the Public Utilities Holding Company Act of 1935 displayed the new attitude toward the regulatory state. The PUHC Act required the breakup of elaborate public utility structures built in the 1920s. The act imposed, in popular parlance, a "death sentence" on the "power trust." The holding companies had to submit reorganization plans for SEC approval. The Chenery Corporation, which managed the Federal Water Services Company, began to purchase shares in the newly organized company, which accorded with the plan that the SEC had approved. But then the commission prohibited the purchases as a violation of common-law principles. Chenery sued, and the Court held that the commission had improperly interpreted the common law, and it overturned the SEC's ruling in 1943. The commission then again forbade the Chenery acquisition and forced it to surrender the purchased shares at a loss, this time on the basis not of the common law but of the PUHC Act. The company had not illegally made the purchases; the commission and the Court had approved them. But now the Court permitted the commission to apply its interpretation retroactively—that is, to make an *ex post facto* law.[179]

Justices Robert Jackson and Felix Frankfurter, both dedicated advocates of administrative government, dissented. "It is clear that there has been a shift in attitude" in the Court, Jackson wrote, because the facts in the two cases were identical. The majority's deference "makes judicial review of administrative orders a hopeless formality." The majority could only aver that somehow the expertise of the commission justified an *ex post facto* penalty. "Now I fully realize what Mark Twain meant when he said, 'The more you explain it, the more I don't understand it,'" he said of the Court's opinion. "This is the first instance in which the administrative power is sustained by reliance on that disregard of law which enemies of the [administrative] process have always alleged to be its principal evil."[180]

Though even the Labor Board did not always get what it wanted (the Court overturned its pro-union rulings on sit-down strikers and replacement workers), sometimes the Court tried to advance labor interests when the administrators would not. The low point in the Roosevelt Court's public image arose out of the *Jewell Ridge* or "portal-to-portal" case. The United Mine Workers claimed that the 1938 Fair Labor Standards Act (largely the work of then-senator Hugo Black) required owners to pay miners for the time that it took them to get to and from their jobs—it could take coal miners, for example, some time to get from the mine head to the coal seam. In the *Jewell Ridge* case, the Court overturned a Labor Department determination that it did not.[181] The UMW retained Black's former law partner (and Klan mentor), Crampton Harris. Justice Jackson took umbrage that Black had not recused himself, and he wrote a dissent that alleged that Senator Black had interpreted the FLSA in a way contrary to Justice Black. The "Jackson–Black feud" reignited when Chief Justice Stone died in 1946 and Jackson publicly denounced Black to prevent his elevation to the chief justiceship. This tirade instead convinced Truman not to promote Jackson, whom the president described as having "surely gone haywire." The president called his predecessor's Court appointments "somewhat disgraceful."[182]

The drama and personalities of the Jackson–Black feud obscured the real significance of the *Jewell Ridge* case, which was the union's attempt to win in Court what it could not win in Congress.[183] With millions of dollars of potential back pay liability at stake, Congress explicitly overruled the *Jewell Ridge* decision. In May 1947, it declared that the FLSA had been "interpreted judicially in disregard of long-established customs, practices, and contracts between employers and employees, thereby creating wholly unexpected liabilities, immense in amount and retroactive in operation," which would gravely harm interstate commerce.[184] The act went on to cut off lawsuits under the FLSA, one of the few occasions in which Congress exercised its power to limit the jurisdiction of the federal courts.[185] Justice Jackson said that "the Supreme Court has never had such a rebuke at the hands of Congress."[186] With the Court acting like what *Newsweek* called "Santa Claus to labor unions," the same Congress also made significant revisions to the Wagner Act with the 1947 Taft–Hartley Act.[187] Congress had corrected the Court's rewriting of the Fair Labor Standards Act. Now it amended its own irresponsibly drafted and enacted National Labor Relations Act, since the Court had not, as expected, held it unconstitutional in 1937.

The volatility and activism of the Roosevelt Court spilled over into its wartime decisions. As the "good war," World War II did not generate the domestic opposition of earlier wars, but it presented its own challenges to civil liberty. As the nation prepared for war in 1940, the Court reviewed a case in which a Pennsylvania school district required public school pupils to salute the American flag. Some Jehovah's Witnesses, who would become the plinth of the Court's religious freedom jurisprudence, refused to do so, and the Court upheld the board's power to expel them. Only Justice Stone dissented.

A wave of ugly harassment against the Witnesses ensued, and three years later the Court reversed this decision, with only Justice Frankfurter, its author, dissenting. What explained the volte-face? Justice Douglas told Frankfurter that "Hugo [Black] thinks maybe we made a mistake." "Has Hugo been reading the Constitution?" Frankfurter asked. "No, he's been reading the newspapers," Douglas replied.[188] The chief justice implored Justice Jackson to omit reference to the attacks in the decision.[189] The justices did not want to appear to follow the election returns, let alone the headlines.

During the war, the Court maintained its usual deference to the executive, now commander in chief of the armed forces. War has always posed the greatest challenge to constitutional government, and it raises the question of whether a nation can maintain constitutionalism in wartime. Cynics often say that, in fact, *inter armes leges silent*—"in war, the laws are silent."[190]

The Roosevelt Court did not keep silent but rather sought to add its voice to the war effort. In the Nazi saboteurs case, it curtailed its famous (postwar) declaration in *Milligan* (1866) that civil liberties did not hibernate in wartime. In 1942, a number of German agents disembarked from a submarine on Long Island, New York. The FBI quickly apprehended them, and President Roosevelt established a military commission to try them. The Court upheld the proceedings in July but did not announce its decision until October, by which time the army had put six of the saboteurs to death. The Court took until October "to craft a decision that would avoid any concurrences or dissents, even though the justices were well aware that Roosevelt had violated several Articles of War."[191]

The Court hit one of its all-time lows in the 1944 *Korematsu* case, upholding the detention of tens of thousands of Japanese American citizens solely on account of their race. As a technical matter, the Court held that the government had punished Fred Korematsu for remaining in a restricted area—that is, for failing to report to a relocation center/concentration camp. Years later, Black insisted that the government could have achieved the same result by suspending the writ of habeas corpus.[192]

Though Black's theory appears not altogether implausible, it still seemed unnecessary and counterproductive to lend the Court's imprimatur to the government's policy. Justice Jackson in dissent admitted rather frankly that a civilian court could do nothing to interpret or stop military orders and so argued that they should simply refuse to participate in their enforcement. He objected to Black's opinion as a "distort[ing] of the Constitution to approve all that the military may deem expedient." Such judicial misinterpretation "is a far more subtle blow to liberty than the . . . order itself." An unconstitutional military order would pass away with the war, but the Court's decision "for all time has validated the principle of racial discrimination." Jackson made a strong assumption of judicial supremacy here, claiming that "if we review and approve, that passing incident becomes the doctrine of the Constitution. . . . The principle then lies about like a loaded weapon ready for the hand of any authority that can bring forward a plausible claim of urgent need."[193] Jackson here sounded like Stone in his *Butler* dissent, expressing an exaggerated sense of judicial infallibility. The Court finally overruled *Korematsu* in 2018, but a hot, existence-threatening war would probably produce a similar expedient, with or without the Court's blessing.

Shortly after the war, President Truman began to reconstitute the Court, hoping to make it more harmonious.[194] Law professor Louis Jaffe, sympathetic to the new orientation of the Court, noted that the justices' feuding had "done disservice to the Court" and imperiled its liberal agenda.[195] Truman's appointments did not noticeably curb the Roosevelt Court's rancor, but they did make it more conservative (see Fig. 3). In 1946, he replaced the two remaining pre-Roosevelt members, Chief Justice Stone and Justice Roberts. (Roberts's resignation occasioned another ugly intramural spat, as Black refused to sign a letter that credited Roberts's "fidelity to principle." This petulance so disgusted Jackson that he offered to resign.)

The real change came in 1949, when two members of "the Axis," Murphy and Rutledge, died. Truman's replacements were less ideological and peevish—but thoroughly mediocre nevertheless. Not just disappointed liberals regarded Truman's appointees as cronies and hacks. The new chief justice, Fred Vinson, allegedly lobbied for the nomination of Tom Clark, "because Vinson wanted *someone* on the Court who knew less law than he did."[196] Truman would later say of Clark, "It isn't so much that he's a bad man. It's just that he's such a dumb son of a bitch. He's about the dumbest man I think I've ever run across."[197] Though the Court remained faithful to the regulatory freedom side of *Carolene,* it disappointed civil libertarians, as when it upheld convictions of American Communist Party leaders under the Alien Registration Act of 1940 (the Smith Act) and did not review the death sentences of Julius and Ethel Rosenberg under the Espionage Act.[198] The new chief justice, Fred Vinson, had no more success than his predecessor at marshaling the Court.

Two 1947 decisions indicated the *Carolene* agenda. In *Adamson v. California,* the Court held that the Fourteenth Amendment did not "incorporate" a right against self-incrimination, allowing a prosecutor to call attention to the defendant's refusal to testify. Black, for the Axis dissenters, laid out his case

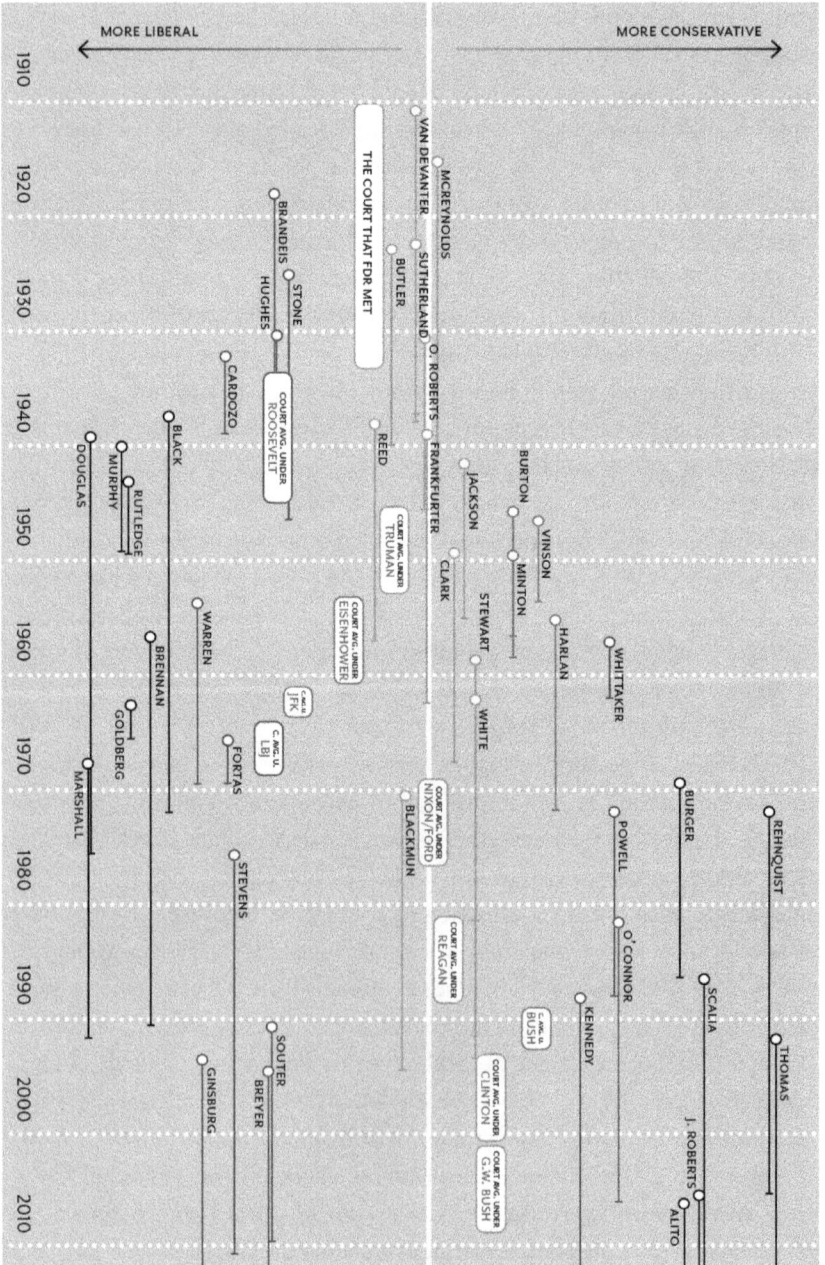

Fig. 3. Judicial Behavior and the Ideological Makeup of the Supreme Court from Franklin Delano Roosevelt to George W. Bush. William M. Landes and Richard Posner, "Rational Judicial Behavior: A Statistical Study," Olin Law and Economics Working Paper, 404 (2008).

for "total incorporation," the idea that the Fourteenth Amendment applied each and every provision of the Bill of Rights to the states. This provoked an extensive debate in the legal academy, spurred by Justice Frankfurter, on the intent of the framers and ratifiers of the Fourteenth Amendment.

Civil libertarians would cherish "incorporation," since the twenty-six rights specified in the first eight amendments almost all concerned "non-economic" or "personal" rights. Incorporation could thus do for personal rights what substantive due process had done for economic rights. (Indeed, what we usually regard as the first incorporation case, from 1897, involved one of the few "economic" rights in the Bill of Rights: the takings clause of the Fifth Amendment. But this case really involved old-fashioned substantive due process.)[199] Black, however, claimed that total incorporation would promote judicial restraint, in that it would prevent judges from selecting those rights that they favored as fundamental, or "implicit in the concept of ordered liberty," as the Court had put it in 1938.[200] This did not limit Black. As law professor Louis Jaffe noted, he "resourcefully manipulates the specifics of the Bill of Rights. He reads a clause literally or broadly as is expedient."[201] Much of the work of the Warren Court would involve the incorporation of ever more of the Bill of Rights (*Adamson* was overruled in 1965) and then adding to those rights (see appendix B).

During that same term, the Court announced its most important religious freedom decision, *Everson v. Ewing Township.* The Court had incorporated the free exercise provision of the First Amendment in a 1940 case involving the right of Jehovah's Witnesses to proselytize.[202] In *Everson,* it held that the establishment clause also applied. *Everson* involved a subsidy given by a New Jersey town for the transportation of students to Catholic schools. Justice Black announced that the establishment clause imposed a "wall of separation between Church and State," using a phrase from an 1802 letter by President Thomas Jefferson to a group of Connecticut Baptists. In years ahead, secularists would repeat that phrase so often as to eclipse the actual text of the First Amendment.

Here Justice Black's Klan background resurfaced, particularly in the postwar context of the revival of anti-Catholicism seen in writers like Paul Blanshard and organizations like Protestants and Other Americans United for the Separation of Church and State.[203] As one scholar notes, "Black had long before sworn, under the light of flaming crosses, to preserve . . . the separation of church and state," and he had administered oaths to thousands of others to do likewise.[204] Curiously, Black held that the transportation subsidy did not breach this wall. Justice Jackson, for the dissenters, pointed out that he could not reconcile the "wall of separation" standard with the result in the case. In the long run, this decision would prove a Pyrrhic victory for the religious, as the Court would build up the wall of separation to a nearly total prohibition of any public support for religion. Ultimately, insofar as morals legislation had a religious basis, it would do away with the states' "police power" to legislate for the morals part of the "public safety, health, welfare, and morals."

Everson also showed one of the fundamental problems of the incorporation of the Bill of Rights. The eighteenth-century proponents of the Bill of Rights mostly wanted to preserve the power of the states to regulate rights, not to protect individual rights per se. The opponents of the 1798 Sedition Act did not object to laws punishing seditious libel, but they objected to the federal government's punishing it. Thus, the First Amendment states that "Congress shall make no law respecting an establishment of religion"—no law, either in favor of or against religious establishments. This protected religious establishments in those states that had them (New England) as much as it prevented the federal government from establishing churches in those that did not.[205] In Everson, the Court took a provision that was meant to protect state power and turned it into a limitation on that power.

One cannot help but suspect that Black channeled Marshall in Marbury or Cohens, conceding the result in the instant case for the long-run sake of the principle. And the run proved not too long, for in the next term the Court struck down an Illinois law that permitted religious instruction in public school facilities, though privately funded. Only Justice Reed dissented, observing that "a rule of law should not be drawn from a figure of speech."[206] The reaction of local school boards varied; some complied and some ignored the decision. Four years later, the Court narrowly upheld a program almost indistinguishable from the Illinois released-time program, and Justice Douglas intoned, "We are a religious people whose institutions presuppose a Supreme Being. . . . When the state encourages religious instruction . . . it follows the best of our traditions."[207] Many years elapsed before the implications of the separationist principle fully blossomed.[208]

The 1947 term also produced the remarkable case of Shelley v. Kraemer, in which the Court held that state court enforcement of "restrictive covenants"—promises by purchasers of real estate not to resell to members of particular races—amounted to "state action" prohibited by the Fourteenth Amendment. In 1917, the Court had struck down local segregation ordinances on substantive due process/liberty of contract grounds.[209] But in 1926 it held that restrictive covenants could achieve the same result, since such private agreements did not constitute "state action."[210] The Court now held that publicly enforced private discrimination violated the Fourteenth Amendment.[211]

This decision had tremendous implications. Again the Court had reached the right result for the wrong reasons.[212] As Robert Bork would later comment:

The impossibility of applying the state action ruling in *Shelley* in a neutral fashion may easily be seen. Suppose a guest in a house becomes abusive about political matters and is ejected by his host. The guest sues the host and the state courts hold that the property owner has a right to remove people from his home. The guest appeals to the Supreme Court, pointing out that the state, through its courts, has upheld an abridgement of his right to free speech.[213]

By this logic, nearly any form of discrimination, by state governments or by private individuals, violated the Constitution, which would have made all future civil rights legislation unnecessary. In consequence, *Shelley* became an enigmatic, one-off dead end, what Philip Kurland called "the *Finnegan's Wake* of constitutional law."[214]

Shelley added to the "guesspotic" criticism of New Deal Court overrulings. After having struck down apartheid in 1917, the Court accepted it in 1927 and now had returned to its 1917 position. Similarly, in 1926 the Court had struck down a Texas law that limited primary election voting to whites. The Texas Democratic Party then reconstituted itself as a private organization, and the Court accepted the racial restriction in 1935. In 1944, the Court undid this and returned to its 1927 position. In a dissenting opinion, Justice Roberts objected to the "present policy of the court freely to disregard and to overrule considered decisions and the rules of law announced in them." He saw in this an "intolerance for what those who have composed this court in the past have conscientiously and deliberately concluded, and [this] involves an assumption that knowledge and wisdom reside in us which was denied to our predecessors." He likened the majority's opinion to "a restricted railroad ticket, good for this day and train only."[215]

Near the end of Vinson's tenure, the Court made one of its most remarkable decisions, declaring President Truman's 1952 seizure of the nation's steel mills unlawful. The industry owners faced a strike by the United Steelworkers, and President Truman claimed that a strike would imperil the war in Korea. Congress had given the president the power to impose an eighty-day "cooling off" strike-deferral period in cases of emergency, but Truman did not want to invoke this provision of the Taft–Hartley Act, which he had vetoed as a "slave-labor bill."[216] So he instructed his secretary of commerce to operate the mills for the government.

Rarely does the Court take on presidential action so squarely, and even more rarely during wartime. The Court trimmed the almost limitless extent of "inherent" executive power over foreign affairs that it had declared in the 1936 *Curtiss-Wright* case. Above all, Congress had considered and rejected giving the president the power here exercised. The Steel Seizure case became a landmark separation-of-powers case, but as the ever-acerbic Fred Rodell put it, "purporting to protect Congress under the old separation-of-powers theory, [it] actually appropriated the top power and the last word, as usual, for itself."[217] *Youngstown* presented an unusual direct confrontation between the president and the Court, but the "cold," limited nature of the war, the weak status of the president, and the dubious claim about the strike's potential impact, somewhat weaken the Court's assertion of power.

The totalitarian regimes of the mid-twentieth century and the horrors of World War II produced a reaction against progressive legal theory, as many attributed the recent calamities to relativism and positivism.[218] Especially in Catholic universities, intellectuals traced the connection from "Hobbes, Holmes, and Hitler."[219] But this had little impact on American jurisprudence. The twentieth-century postwar years displayed the reverse of the nineteenth-century postwar period. In the nineteenth century, the academic world rejected natural law while the courts picked it up. In the twentieth, the academic revival of natural law made little impression on the courts. Rather, judges seemed to follow the philosophy of "emotivism," which viewed moral judgments as expressions of an individual's preferences and dislikes.[220] What Cardozo called *Gefühlsjuriprudenz* had arrived. As the legal realist Hessel Yntema put it, judging was "an emotive experience in which principles and logic play a secondary part."[221]

About a year after Dwight D. Eisenhower won the presidency in 1952, Chief Justice Vinson died. Felix Frankfurter acidly commented that this presented "the first indication that I have ever had that there is a God." This provided a fitting epitaph for the mood of the waning Roosevelt Court. After its abortive foray into liberal judicial activism, the Court under Chief Justice Earl Warren would permanently establish judicial supremacy as we know it today, to flesh out what the Roosevelt Court had adumbrated.

7

JUDICIAL SUPREMACY ARRIVES
The Warren Court

BROWN AND THE FIRST WARREN COURT, 1953-62

Nobody expected Earl Warren to become the father of modern judicial supremacy and liberal activism. He cut his teeth as a California Progressive, following Theodore Roosevelt, who excoriated the courts. He supported the La Follette–Wheeler presidential bid in 1924, the last presidential campaign to call for a curb on judicial power.

Warren cracked heads as the state attorney general. One of his most celebrated cases, nailing communists for murdering a ship engineer in their campaign to gain control of the Oakland waterfront unions, featured many prosecutorial methods that his Supreme Court would declare unconstitutional. In 1936, he denounced the New Deal as "a totalitarian state wherein men are the pawns of a dictator." As governor, he foiled the effort to put noted legal realist Max Radin on the California supreme court, and he waffled on the issue of loyalty oaths to keep subversives out of state government.

Above all, Warren actively abetted the internment of Japanese Americans during World War II, and although he never expressed any regret for it prior to his posthumously published memoirs, many saw his civil libertarian record as chief justice as an effort to atone for this, like Hugo Black making up for his Klan background. ("Hugo used to wear a white robe and scare Black people, now he wears a black robe and scares white people," they quipped.) Warren acted as a fairly liberal governor, endorsed by Republicans, Democrats, and Progressives alike, calling for a state fair employment law, and giving the state a public health insurance system.[1]

Though the details remain disputed, it appears that Warren's support for

Eisenhower at the 1952 Republican national convention won him the first opening on the Court. Eisenhower had entered that race to keep the party from being taken over by the conservative and isolationist wing represented by Joseph McCarthy and Robert Taft. He regarded Warren as a middle-of-the-road Republican like himself. But Eisenhower's five appointments moved the Court back toward its Roosevelt-era liberal orientation (see Fig. 3). The relatively liberal "first Warren Court" (1953–62) would hit its stride in the Democratic administrations of the 1960s. The arch-realist Fred Rodell, who called the dysfunctional Roosevelt Court "the most brilliant and able collection of Justices who ever graced the bench together," said that Warren "seems essentially a direct, plain-spoken politician who knows that his is a fundamentally political job."[2]

Warren would revive the intuitive, personal, subjective *Gefühlsjurisprudenz* of Frank Murphy, as indicated when he would ask counsel in oral argument, "Yes, but is it *fair?*" As one biographer concluded, "If one takes away Warren's ethical premises, his opinions evaporate. No overarching doctrinal unity binds them; they are individual examples of beliefs leading to judgments . . . [O]ne can never divorce Earl Warren's opinions from Earl Warren." Much the same characterized his predecessor Frank Murphy, "but the same posture that invoked ridicule in Murphy was the source of Warren's strength as a judge."[3]

The Warren Court's first important case—five cases headed by *Brown v. Board of Education of Topeka* but called at the time the Segregation Cases—provided the proximate source of modern judicial supremacy and was the most important Court decision in American history. Though controversial at the time, desegregation has since acquired all but unanimous public approval. The Court did the right thing ("simple justice," in the half-ironic title of the standard narrative history of the case) when no other part of the American political system would—not the president, not Congress, and certainly not the states. "We must never forget," wrote liberal activist icon Justice Stephen Reinhardt of the ninth circuit court of appeals, "that it was the Court, not Congress or the president, that put an end to official segregation. . . . It was the Court, not any other branch of government that for the first time gave meaning to the phrase 'with liberty and justice for all.'"[4] Yale law professor Ralph Winter observed that even if judges considered *Brown* itself illegitimate, "Once it was handed down, they felt relieved from constitutional restraints."[5] The Court would live for decades on the moral capital it gained in *Brown*. Opposition to judicial supremacy became associated with the defense of white supremacy.[6]

The Court first heard *Brown* in 1952, with Fred Vinson still in the center chair. The case capped a long campaign by the National Association for the Advancement of Colored People to litigate against Jim Crow. Public interest groups like the NAACP led the way in bringing about the "rights revolution" of the twentieth century, providing the support structure that opened the courts to marginal actors.[7] The justices scheduled the case for reargument mostly at the behest of Felix Frankfurter, who feared that the Court would sustain the separate but equal doctrine or overturn it by a narrow margin. In particular, the Court asked the parties to address the question of the intent of the framers and ratifiers of the Fourteenth Amendment.

Brown rested upon a generation of progressive legal philosophy, of sociological jurisprudence, legal realism, and living constitutionalism. A generation of Black organizations and legal advocates had matured since the Great Migration of the early twentieth century. They—the NAACP and its general counsel, Thurgood Marshall, especially—had absorbed the principal insight of legal realism, that law simply served as a tool or weapon wielded by the dominant powers in a society—big business in the first stage; now the white race; later, men, heterosexuals, and others. Charles Hamilton Houston, the dean of Howard University Law School, trained his students to become "social engineers," to use the legal system to gain what they could not win through politics.[8] One scholar described the premises of "Houstonian jurisprudence" thus: "Given an immoral America, the NAACP campaign required that lawyer–social engineers use the Constitution, statutes, and 'whatever science demonstrates or imagination invents'" for social change. Another said he represented a significant step in legal liberals' overcoming their fear of "Lochner era" judicial power.[9]

This utilitarian view of law also applied to history. The NAACP sought a useable past—believing, as Marshall's deputy, Robert L. Carter, put it, that "all history is distortion."[10] As we say today, power derives from controlling the narrative. Almost all scholars admitted that the Fourteenth Amendment did not mean to prohibit segregation, especially in public schools. The same Congress that sent the amendment to the states provided for segregation in the schools of the District of Columbia and segregated spectators in the congressional galleries. Even the Civil Rights Act of 1875, the most radical Reconstruction statute, did not prohibit school segregation. Before *Plessy v. Ferguson,* lower federal courts accepted "equal but separate" under the Fourteenth Amendment.[11] Even Justice John Marshall Harlan, the lone dissenter in *Plessy,* who insisted on the "color-blind Constitution," accepted a Virginia law that provided for high schools for whites only.

Repeatedly, therefore, the Court upheld the separate but equal doctrine, though since the 1930s it had begun to insist on real, substantial equality in segregated facilities. Felix Frankfurter's clerk, Alexander Bickel, researched the history and could only conclude that the framers of the amendment left it open to future "growth," on "living Constitution" lines.[12] The NAACP retained a constitutional historian, Alfred H. Kelly, to make its historical argument. Kelly later confessed that he had traduced his professional standards as a historian for the sake of social justice. He did not lie, he said, but by "using facts, explaining facts, bearing down on facts, sliding off facts, quietly ignoring facts, and above all interpreting facts," tried to reframe the narrative.[13] Later, in an article entitled "Clio and the Court: An Illicit Love Affair," he confessed to engaging in "law-office history." In fact, distorted history consistently characterized Warren Court jurisprudence. One liberal legal scholar confessed the "notorious fact" that the Warren Court had "flunked history."[14]

Warren worked assiduously to pull the justices together on *Brown*, regarding unanimity as essential in such a controversial case. He would insist that the Court devise an opinion "short, readable by the lay public, non-rhetorical, unemotional, and, above all, non-accusatory."[15] Unanimity required a number of political compromises, however, which would severely weaken the final opinion. Black, Douglas, Minton, and Burton posed no problem. Frankfurter particularly fretted about the implementation of the decision. His fears would lead to its virtual evisceration in the *Brown II* case. Justice Clark initially opposed Warren but finally agreed when he became convinced that desegregation presented "a question of politics and, as a political decision, I can go along with it."[16] Jackson wanted a frank admission that the Court had made a political choice, and he prepared a concurring opinion along these lines. "Our problem is how to make a judicial decision out of a political conclusion," he said.[17] He succumbed to a heart attack shortly before the decision came out and did not complete his concurrence. Warren got him to agree to the unanimous opinion while visiting him in the hospital. The chief justice got to the last holdout, Stanley Reed, with a personal appeal: "Stan, you're all by yourself in this now. You've got to decide whether it's really the best thing for the country." He also assured Reed that the Court would permit gradual implementation.[18]

The decision came down May 17, 1954. Warren punted on the question of original intent. He found the history "inconclusive." He suggested that it would not have mattered anyway, for "we cannot turn back the clock . . . we must consider public education in the light of its full development and its present place in American life." A luxury in the nineteenth century, formal education now determined success in life. (This suggested, on "living constitution" lines, that public education had *become* a right or, in modern progressive terms, an entitlement that all could claim.)[19] Segregation impaired the ability of Black children to benefit from education. "To separate them . . . solely because of their race generates a feeling of inferiority as to their status in the community that may affect their hearts and minds in a way unlikely ever to be undone."

Here Warren cited sociological and psychological studies that claimed to show this effect. In the most controversial of these (footnote 11), psychologist Kenneth Clark claimed to show that Black children in segregated schools preferred white dolls to Black ones when asked which ones were "nice." Footnote 11 of *Brown* would become the second-best-known footnote in Court history, after footnote 4 in *Carolene Products.* Warren concluded that "in the field of public education the doctrine of 'separate but equal' has no place. Separate educational facilities are inherently unequal," and thus violated the equal protection clause of the Fourteenth Amendment.[20]

The District of Columbia case posed a peculiar problem, since the Fourteenth Amendment applied only to the states and the Fifth Amendment lacked an equal protection clause. So the Court relied on the due process clause of the Fifth Amendment, notwithstanding the fact that liberals celebrated the internment of "substantive due process" in the constitutional revolution of 1937. Warren added, "Segregation in public education is not reasonably related to any proper governmental objective." Either of these doctrines could have worked as well in *Brown.* The Court finally claimed that since it had just found that the states could not segregate schools, "it would be unthinkable that the same Constitution would impose a lesser duty on the federal government." This inverted the obvious historical argument that since the Thirty-Ninth Congress had imposed segregation in the District, it could not have forbidden the states to adopt it.[21]

As in *Shelley v. Kraemer,* the Court in *Brown* reached the right result on the wrong grounds.[22] Warren wanted a "non-rhetorical" opinion. He used the term "rhetorical" in its contemporary sense which, like "political," has a negative connotation, implying "unnecessarily wordy or overstated." But *Brown* suffered most of all from a lack of "rhetoric" in the classical sense of persuasive speech. Even after nearly everyone came to celebrate its result, *Brown* has few defenders as jurisprudence.[23] It did not forthrightly take on the issue of the Fourteenth Amendment, or even its own precedents in interpreting the amendment. It did not, for example, overrule *Plessy v. Ferguson,* because its decision applied only to public education. Many found the social science basis of the decision indefensible. Its evaluation of the social benefits of education and analysis of the "feelings" and "hearts and minds" of children raised quite a few eyebrows. It embodied Cardozo's *Gefühlsjurisprudenz,* or emotivist judging.

The Court had never before offered this near-caricature of "sociological jurisprudence" and it would never do so again. Later psychological emotivist decisions in abortion and homosexuality cases cited no "authorities." Its weakness as legislation masquerading as a judicial decision manifested itself in its final order, or lack thereof.[24] Neither Linda Brown nor the other named plaintiffs in the cases, let alone the millions of other Black children in segregated schools, would attend integrated schools in the fall of 1954, and in fact most of them would not for many years to come. Even the Court knew this: "Because these are class actions, because of the wide applicability of this decision, and because of the great variety of local conditions, the formulation of decrees in these cases presents problems of considerable complexity." The Court ordered another round of arguments about appropriate remedies, which came over a year later.

The implementation decision, known as *Brown* II, came down on the last day of May 1955.[25] It left enforcement to the federal district courts in conjunction with local school boards. Its order extended only to the plaintiffs in the five cases (actually four, as Delaware had already desegregated) of *Brown* I. Over the objections of the NAACP, the Court left the other school districts to reform themselves. Failing that, the NAACP would have to sue them seriatim. The Court told even the *Brown* I defendants only to comply "with all deliberate speed."

This cryptic phrase, conjured up by Felix Frankfurter, fulfilled the promise of "gradualism" that Warren had made to several reluctant justices; it was the price of unanimity. It also would produce more deliberation—evasion, really—than speed. Though some border states desegregated, almost no Deep South schools complied. *Brown* II instructed the lower courts to "be guided by equitable principles" in shaping remedies. Years later, the flexibility inherent in equity would give courts great power to compel desegregation; in the near term, it allowed them to connive with "massive resistance" by whites of the Deep South.[26]

The *Brown* decisions did not produce an immediate reaction from the white South. One scholar describes the response as "stunned silence," and several prominent politicians called for calm and compliance.[27] The nation as a whole divided rather evenly. A majority overall and outside the South approved of desegregation, but only 53 percent of Blacks did nationwide.[28] The virtual nullification of *Brown* II also soothed segregationist concerns. But they still denied the legitimacy of the decision. In March 1956, nineteen senators and seventy-seven representatives signed the "Declaration of Constitutional Principles," usually called the Southern Manifesto.[29]

Though denounced then and since as an intemperate expression of racist defiance, the declaration in fact displayed a measured and moderate appeal to fence-sitting northern whites.[30] It did not use the language of nullification or interposition, thus not even going as far as the Virginia and Kentucky Resolutions, which themselves did nothing more than appeal to other states to demand repeal of the Sedition Act. Instead, it pledged "to use all lawful means to bring about a reversal" of *Brown,* which sounded like Lincoln on *Dred Scott.* It exhorted southerners "to scrupulously refrain from disorder and lawless acts," aware that violent resistance would backfire. It suggested that even if the Court had erred in *Plessy v. Ferguson,* its permission of segregation had become customary in the South over six decades, "part of the life of the people. . . . and confirmed in their habits, customs, traditions, and way of life." However reasonable it tried to sound, however, the manifesto failed to deflect the racially egalitarian zeitgeist that had been waxing since World War I, and especially after World War II. Southern congressmen with national aspirations, like Lyndon Johnson and Estes Kefauver, did not sign. Nor did any congressman outside the former Confederacy.

In July 1957, President Eisenhower said, "I can't imagine any set of circumstances that would ever induce me to send federal troops . . . to enforce the orders of a federal court." But the resistance of state elected officials to a desegregation plan for Central High School in Little Rock, Arkansas, compelled Eisenhower to send in regular army forces and to nationalize the Arkansas National Guard. Little Rock anticipated the violent resistance of southern whites in the 1960s, the "backlash" that would finally compel Congress to act in 1964.[31]

This dramatic episode stands out as the only action taken to enforce *Brown* during the Eisenhower years. Historians have excoriated Eisenhower for giving no public support to the Court after *Brown,* which decision he privately criticized. Nevertheless, his Justice Department had argued for desegregation, called for a more forceful implementation in *Brown* II, and zealously desegregated the District of Columbia. He allegedly expressed regret for his appointment of Earl Warren and William Brennan, but all of his post-*Brown* appointments supported the decision.[32]

Eisenhower clearly emphasized his duty as president to enforce particular court *orders*—as in Little Rock—but not wide-ranging, nonspecific *opinions* like *Brown*.[33] He said in September 1957 that "it was not his responsibility to keep order everywhere, but only to see that the orders of a federal judge were carried out."[34] This sounded very much like Taney's view of presidential power in the *Merryman* case, and Eisenhower seemed to accept some version of judicial supremacy. He told his brother, "The meaning of the Constitution is what the Supreme Court says it is," and he said publicly that it made "no difference whether I endorse [*Brown*]. The Constitution is as the Supreme Court interprets it."[35]

With presidential support, the Court made an unprecedented statement of judicial supremacy in the September 1958 case of *Cooper v. Aaron*. It upheld the order of the eighth circuit court of appeals to implement the Little Rock desegregation plan immediately. *Cooper* went beyond unanimity; the Court took the novel approach of reporting the opinion in the names of all nine justices.[36] It claimed that *Marbury v. Madison* "declared the basic principle that the federal judiciary is supreme in the exposition of the Constitution, and that principle has ever been respected by this Court and the Country as a permanent and indispensable feature of the constitutional system." The Court now solemnly uncorked the "*Marbury* myth," fermenting since the 1890s. "It follows that the interpretation of the Fourteenth Amendment enunciated by this Court in the *Brown* case is the supreme law of the land," and bound the states.[37] The Court had now claimed for itself what others had claimed for it.[38] Critics of the Southern Manifesto had alleged that there could be no "lawful" opposition to a Supreme Court decision because of the identical status of that decision and the Constitution. Senator Wayne Morse of Oregon had immediately responded to the manifesto in this way.[39] Senator Price Daniel of Texas said, "You can't call any action of the Supreme Court unconstitutional," notwithstanding the fact that the Court had declared one its own decisions unconstitutional in 1938.[40]

Felix Frankfurter, who had pressed as ardently as the chief justice for unanimity in *Brown*, insisted on publishing a separate, concurring addendum to *Cooper*. He wanted to educate the bench and bar of the South, upon whose cooperation he believed desegregation would depend. He stressed that opponents could not call *Brown* "the dubious pronouncement of a gravely divided Court" but must see "the unanimous conclusion of a long-matured deliberative process." He reminded them that "local customs, however hardened by time, are not decreed in heaven" and that "the constructive use of time will achieve what an advanced civilization demands and the Constitution confirms." He concluded with Lincoln's inaugural appeal to "the better angels of our nature."[41] Warren fumed at Frankfurter's insistence on getting in the last word. Frankfurter's didactic pep talk made irreparable the growing rift between them and drove the chief justice toward the activist side of the bench.[42]

When Eisenhower withdrew the bayonets from Little Rock, the Court moderated its tone. One detects an element of bravado in *Cooper's* declaration of judicial power. The Court heard no more desegregation appeals for several years, and nothing beyond token compliance took hold in southern schools for another decade. Since *Brown* prohibited segregation but did not require integration, states adopted "freedom-of-choice" plans, giving students the option of school attendance. Usually, no whites would choose to transfer to the historically Black school, and only a handful of intrepid Blacks would attempt to cross over.

The Court was also cautious about extending *Brown*, which only applied to public schools. It declined to review state miscegenation laws; Felix Frankfurter warned that doing so "would seriously embarrass the carrying out of the Court's decree" in *Brown*. One commentator counted a woman imprisoned for five years for interracial marriage among the "unfortunate people whose personal fates had to be sacrificed as part of the more momentous institutional task of protecting *Brown* from outright defiance or evisceration."[43] When the Court ordered desegregation in other realms, it did not provide any reasons for doing so but simply said that the laws violated the principles of *Brown*. But if Brown condemned segregation because of its psychological effect on Black educational attainment, what did that have to do with segregation in public parking garages or on buses? These declarations also had little effect on segregation and raised more questions about the Court's jurisprudence.[44]

COLD WAR HIATUS: REACTION AND RETRENCHMENT

In the midst of the Little Rock desegregation crisis the Court issued a number of opinions on Cold War internal security matters that produced more of a reaction than *Brown*. In 1956, President Eisenhower appointed William Brennan to the Court. He wanted a conservative Democrat to fill the "Catholic seat," vacant since Frank Murphy's death in 1949.[45] Brennan would become as liberal as Murphy, and much cannier, reinforcing the liberal bloc now that the chief justice had migrated from the restrained to the activist side. Brennan possessed a remarkable ability to construct Court majorities. He told his clerks that a justice need only know how to count to five. "With five votes, we can do anything." Some commentators have argued that we should more accurately call the Warren Court the Brennan Court. Brennan's impact began to show in the 1956 term, during which the government lost eleven out of eleven cases concerning anticommunist policy, culminating in four cases announced on June 17, 1957, which FBI director J. Edgar Hoover called "Red Monday." The cases involved federal and state sedition laws, legislative investigative powers, government employee loyalty programs, and related internal security questions. It held, for example, that the federal sedition act (the 1940 Smith Act) "preempted" state sedition laws.[46] It then interpreted the Smith Act as applicable only to speech or writing that approximated action more closely under earlier applications of the "clear and present danger" standard, making convictions virtually impossible. It held that the House Un-American Activities Committee could not simply expose disloyalty; its investigations had to have some genuine legislative purpose. The Court also vindicated the free speech claims of leftish state employees, especially teachers, who faced dismissal. It also held that defendants should have access to secret FBI dossiers.[47]

Red Monday gave rise to the last serious attempt by Congress to limit the jurisdiction of the Court. Indiana senator William Jenner pushed a bill that would have eliminated appeals to the Supreme Court in five categories of cases. But the bill had little chance. Although it only concerned communist/internal security cases, many saw it as a Trojan horse for opposition to *Brown*.[48] Liberal Democratic senator Paul Douglas called for a resolution approving *Brown*, since the Jenner bill targeted specific Court decisions. The moral capital of that case had already paid dividends for the Court. Senate Majority Leader Lyndon Johnson helped prevent passage, and the Eisenhower administration, though upset about the rulings, did not support Jenner. Vice President Richard Nixon, presiding over the Senate, helped defeat it with a procedural ruling.[49] In August, the Senate voted to table the bill, 49–41.

As political scientist Walter Murphy observed, since Jefferson, "the President and Congress never joined together to press a serious assault on judicial power."[50] The waning of the Cold War and the election returns also helped, with a surge of liberal Democrats elected in 1958 and Jenner unseated. Another political scientist noted that opposition to the Court had never achieved consensus or momentum. "Only a part of the population is at odds with the Court at any time. . . . No sizeable sector with an identifiable common interest has ever maintained a persistent and consistent opposition."[51] Political scientist Robert Dahl had made a similar argument in 1957, noting that given the social origins of the justices, they would never remain long out of step with prevailing elite opinion.[52]

Outside of Congress, other voices expressed concern about the Warren Court, even if they did not call for a reduction of judicial power. Justice

Robert Jackson, in his posthumously published Harvard lectures, which he had drafted while the Court debated *Brown,* warned that "a cult of libertarian judicial activists" expected the Court to provide a "bulwark against all dangers and evils that today beset us internally." He called this a "vicious teaching" that promoted exactly the kind of judicial supremacy that liberals had fought before 1937.[53] The 1958 Conference of State Chief Justices complained about the "centralizing" effect of US Supreme Court decisions weakening state governments. But this expression of old Anti-Federalist concerns did no more than call on the Court to "exercise one of the greatest of all judicial powers—the power of judicial self-restraint."[54]

Some observers noted that the state court justices themselves hardly evinced self-restraint. Judicial activism at the state level did rise in tandem with the Warren Court.[55] John Dethmers, the chief justice of the Michigan supreme court, repudiated the congressional effort to curb the Court; "that would mark the beginning of parliamentary, and the end of constitutional, government." Dethmers took care to point out that the state chiefs did not "criticize the Supreme Court's decisions in the troublesome segregation cases." He primarily blamed "writers and professors of law, dedicated to judicial activism," while his own court had embarked on an activist, centralizing campaign.[56] The American Bar Association issued a report critical of the Court in February 1959, but it also repudiated the Jenner proposals.

Some judges and law professors expressed their unease with modern judicial supremacism, but their proposals ended up just as diffident as those of Congress, the state chief justices, and the ABA. These reflected the "process restraint" approach associated mostly with Felix Frankfurter. The most severe rebuke of the Warren Court came from Judge Learned Hand of the second circuit court of appeals, a liberal icon and widely regarded as the ablest judge not on the Supreme Court. In February 1958, he gave a series of lectures at Harvard, published as *The Bill of Rights.* He asserted that no textual or historical basis existed for judicial review, but he accepted it as a practical necessity to have a place for final decision on constitutional controversies. Hand chided the Warren Court for acting as a "third legislative chamber." He repudiated the *Carolene* "preferred freedoms" or "double standard" as a liberal fabrication, and could see *Brown* only as a "coup de main." Hand concluded, "For myself, it would be most irksome to be ruled by a bevy of Platonic Guardians, even if I knew how to choose them, which I assuredly do not."

Segregationists and anticommunists warmly received his critique, but Hand disavowed them and the Jenner bill. Outside of the South, the lectures drew condemnation from mostly liberal academic reviewers.[57] Some saw it as sour grapes from the great jurist who never made it to the high court where lesser lights like Earl Warren (whom Hand called "the dumb Swede") sat.[58]

Columbia law professor Herbert Wechsler followed up on Hand's argument, criticizing the Warren Court for failing to make decisions according to "neutral principles." Legal, as opposed to political or legislative, officers cannot make "value judgments" but must decide cases according to some principle not aiming at a particular outcome, "reasons that in their generality and their neutrality transcend any immediate result that is invoked." Instead, "the Court has been decreeing value choices in a way that makes it quite impossible to speak of principled determinations or the statement and evaluation of judicial reasons, since the Court has not disclosed the grounds on which its judgments rest."[59]

This was a fairly standard critique of the shoddy reasoning of *Brown,* but Wechsler added a more idiosyncratic claim that the real issue in that case involved freedom of association and that the Court had privileged Black desire to associate over white preference *not* to associate. Like Hand, Wechsler accused the Warren Court of doing for its preferred interests what the old "laissez-faire Court" had done for property rights. Also like Hand, he offered no response other than an exhortation to give better reasons. But his concerns did not bother the realists, who rejected the possibility of neutrality. They comfortably embraced a liberal Court that acted as the "conscience" of the nation.[60]

Finally, in 1962 Yale law professor Alexander Bickel made the most comprehensive and enduring analysis of the judicial power problem in his ironically titled *Least Dangerous Branch.* Bickel took the legitimacy of judicial review for granted and reiterated his support for the result in *Brown*—that, even if the framers and ratifiers of the Fourteenth Amendment had not intended to prohibit segregation, "they did not foreclose such policies as may indeed have invited" it. He also embraced the "living Constitution," drawing from the ancient philosopher Heraclitus and Justice Brandeis the belief that the only abiding thing is change.

But he conceded that such decisions posed a problem—what he called the "countermajoritarian difficulty" of unelected judges trumping the political branches in a democracy. As his mentor, Felix Frankfurter, had put it, "Because the powers exercised by this Court are inherently oligarchic, Jefferson all of his life thought of the Court as 'an irresponsible body' and 'independent of the nation itself.' The Court is not saved from being oligarchic because it professes to act in the service of humane ends."[61] If the Constitution needs updating, why do the judges get the job of doing it? The countermajoritarian difficulty would indeed become an academic obsession for the next several decades.[62]

Bickel also called for self-restraint by the cultivation of the "passive virtues"—the use of technical dodges such as mootness, ripeness, and vagueness to avoid deciding cases. Thus, he credited the Court for dismissing a challenge to miscegenation laws in the aftermath of *Brown*. "The Court should declare as law only such principles as will—in time, but in a rather immediately foreseeable future—gain general assent." The Court should lead the people but not get too far ahead of them. "It is at once the shaper and the prophet of the opinion that will prevail and endure." The nation—or enough of it—would accept the abolition of segregation in 1954, but it would not yet countenance the abolition of capital punishment, for example.[63] But, like other recent critics, Bickel did no more than advise the Court to clean up its act and make its decisions more cautious and convincing. Law professor Gerald Gunther jocularly said that Bickel called for "100% insistence on principle, 20% of the time."[64]

The Warren Court emerged from these reactions unscathed. Along with the cooling of the Cold War and electoral resurgence of Democratic liberalism at the end of the decade, the Court helped by exercising some of the restraint that these critics counseled. In 1959, it rendered two decisions that blunted some of its Red Monday cases, mostly due to the caution of Felix Frankfurter.[65] *The New York Times*, lamenting these concessions to anticommunism, wrote with considerable exaggeration, "What Senator Jenner was unable to achieve the Court has now virtually achieved on its own."[66] The justices continued to avert their eyes from the non-implementation of their desegregation decisions. With the failure of efforts like the Jenner bill to curb the Court's power, its critics focused instead on the men nominated to the bench. After Earl Warren, Eisenhower's appointees became the first to face substantive, doctrinal questions in their confirmation hearings.[67] The last years of the "first Warren Court," 1958–62, proved its most quiescent.

THE SECOND WARREN COURT, 1962-69

Brown had planted a seed for further activism. Though it produced few immediate results, the Court met no substantial reaction, and public opinion seemed to follow it. "Whether they knew it or not they had crossed a watershed," political scientist Robert McCloskey observed. "A body of men who had attacked with telling effect perhaps the most difficult social problem in America were not likely to be overly modest about their powers thereafter."[68]

The trajectory of the second Warren Court emerged in its cases on legislative apportionment. Congressional and state legislative districts often contained vastly different numbers of constituents. In the US Senate today, for example, California's roughly 40 million people have the same representation as Wyoming's 600,000, a population variance ratio of 67:1. Some state variance ratios ran into the hundreds and thousands because legislators from the older, more rural, and conservative parts of the state did not redistrict to reflect population growth in cities, which tended to vote more liberally. Federal courts consistently rejected challenges to these malapportioned systems under the "political questions" doctrine.

In 1946, Felix Frankfurter, for a divided Court, refused to address an Illinois apportionment case, warning against "enter[ing] this political thicket."[69] In *Baker v. Carr* (1962), he and Justice Harlan dissented from a decision that made apportionment cases justiciable. Frankfurter suffered a stroke and retired soon after *Baker* (if not because of it), and his replacement, Arthur Goldberg, provided the fifth vote for a liberal activist bloc.

Baker only began the "reapportionment revolution." The Court told the lower courts to consider the question as a violation the equal protection clause. The next year, the high court imposed the standard of "one person, one vote."[70] One year later, the Court held that states must apportion congressional districts along these lines, despite the fact that the Constitution gave to Congress the power to regulate the "time, place, and manner" of congressional elections.[71]

The apportionment cases signaled the end of the "political questions" doctrine, which had always done little more than ask the justices to restrain themselves. These cases showed that the Warren Court would abjure such "passive virtues." Warren "systematically dismantled the complex web of rules and constraints that had limited the scope of judicial power," two scholars observed, including "political questions."[72] As one critic would later put it, the Court "does not actually decide *everything*. . . . But the Court may decide *anything*. . . . The Justices reserve plenary authority to decide who decides."[73] As in *Brown*, the Court gave no plausible textual or historical reasons for its decisions, which as Justice Harlan said, "[flew] in the face of history." But the outcome struck most Americans as intuitively fair. (Colorado citizens voted by referendum to approve a state Senate not apportioned strictly on the basis of population. The Court also struck this down.)[74]

These cases clearly illustrated the *Carolene* principle: the Court stepped in to rectify a breakdown in the democratic process in which the elected officials had an interest in maintaining a less than democratic system and so would not likely fix it.[75] Elected officials, rather than their constituents, reacted unfavorably, afraid that reapportionment would cost them their jobs. The House of

Representatives passed a bill to remove Supreme Court jurisdiction in apportionment cases, but it failed in the Senate. In a wonderful bit of irony, Senate liberals defeated it by filibuster—using a minority rule tactic in the one body that could never abide by the new rule, as Article V states that "no State, without its Consent, shall be deprived of its equal Suffrage in the Senate."[76]

But liberals who hoped that reapportionment would advance progressive government by giving more power to urban, liberal populations gained little. This might have occurred, had the shift been made earlier in the century, but by the 1960s the demographic center of gravity had shifted to the moderate suburbs. This provided another example of what one critic would later call "the hollow hope"—the inability of courts to bring about constructive social change.[77]

The Court also stoked controversy in its next set of religious freedom cases. In 1962, it held unconstitutional the New York State "Regents' Prayer," which read, "Almighty God, we acknowledge our dependence upon Thee, and we beg Thy blessings upon us, our parents, our teachers, and our country." The state did not compel students to recite this anodyne invocation, but the Court nevertheless classified it as an unconstitutional establishment of religion.[78] The next year, the Court held that a Pennsylvania law requiring the reading of ten Bible verses and the Lord's Prayer every day (again with student freedom to opt out) was likewise impermissible.[79]

These decisions rank among the most unpopular in American history and the Court easily could have avoided them, since the plaintiffs lacked anything usually recognized as "standing" to sue. They appeared to be ad hoc, given the Court's precedents that upheld transportation subsidies to religious schools and released-time programs for religious instruction. But Justice Black's opinion cited no precedents anyway. Justice Douglas, who had said, "We are a religious people whose institutions presuppose a Supreme Being," now claimed that even "In God We Trust" on US currency violated the Constitution.

The cases produced a movement for a constitutional amendment to permit school prayer, in what self-described secular humanist Leo Pfeffer called "a one-man crusade" by New York representative Frank Becker. But the public outcry did not last long, and the amendment never got out of Congress, due in part to divided sentiments among evangelical Protestants.[80] *Brown* still paid dividends. When Alabama segregationist representative George Andrews remarked that the Court "put the Negroes in the schools and now they've driven God out," it only bolstered Court supporters.

The Court's wave of criminal procedure decisions stoked a popular and more consequential reaction. These involved the "incorporation" of most of the provisions of the Fourth, Fifth, and Sixth Amendments. Incorporation had appeared on the constitutional horizon since the late nineteenth century (see appendix B), and it began to make progress with the First Amendment in the 1920s. Under Warren, it became a flood. The chief justice said "the bill of rights is the heart of any constitution,"[81] yet this perspective arose only very recently. The Founders had adopted the Bill of Rights as an afterthought—as an appendix, not the heart of the document—in 1791. For most of the next century and a half, the heart of the Constitution remained its institutions and structures. To make the Bill of Rights its heart put the Court at the center of American constitutionalism.[82]

The incorporation wave began with the 1961 case of *Mapp v. Ohio*, in which the Court applied the exclusionary rule to the states: prosecutors could not use evidence gathered illegally by the police in criminal trials, and the Court would overturn convictions based on such evidence. The Fourth Amendment reads, "The right of the people to be secure in their persons, houses, papers, and effects, against unreasonable searches and seizures, shall not be violated, and no warrants shall issue, but upon probable cause, supported by oath or affirmation, and particularly describing the place to be searched, and the persons or things to be seized." In 1914, the Court had imposed the exclusionary rule on the federal courts, but this rule certainly did not present the only way to enforce the amendment. Traditionally, officers' personal liability for violations kept them in line, and warrants protected *them*, not the accused.[83]

The Court chose not to impose the rule on the states in 1949.[84] Now the Court not only applied the Bill of Rights to the states but also told them exactly *how* they must enforce it. These orders grew quite detailed, as in the high-profile case of *Miranda v. Arizona*, which spawned a set of warnings that police had to give to suspects in custody: "You have the right to remain silent; if you give up the right to remain silent, anything that you say can and will be used against you in a court of law; you have the right to speak to any attorney and have one present during questioning; if you cannot afford an attorney, one will be appointed to represent you." Judges would use the exclusionary rule to overturn confessions made without the warning.

The Warren Court indicated its legislative rather than adjudicative bent when it announced that the new criminal rules would apply only to *future* cases.[85] It would hardly do to release or retry thousands of prisoners convicted on the basis of illegally seized evidence. We define legislation as prospective and general, while judges make retrospective and individual decisions, but here the Court announced a general rule for the future. It had adumbrated this in *Brown*, where it sacrificed relief to individual plaintiffs for the sake of future desegregation policy. The increasingly overtly political–legislative nature of the Warren Court also surfaced in the de facto lobbying that took place before it in the amicus briefs of public interest groups, which the Court encouraged.[86]

The Court's criminal procedure cases especially provoked criticism because they coincided with urban race riots and a tripling of the violent crime rate that began in the 1960s. Though many social scientists denied that the Court's decisions had the effect of "handcuffing the police," the public saw the correlation.[87] Congress reacted with the Crime Control Act of 1968, which allowed federal prosecutors to relax the *Miranda* rules. (They chose not to do so until the 1990s; the Court would later void this part of the act.)[88] Richard Nixon made "law and order" the theme of his 1968 presidential campaign, and his victory would blunt liberal judicial activism.

But in the mid-1960s, the Court rode the wave of political liberalism that crested in the election of 1964. The unusually conservative Republican nominee, Barry Goldwater, criticized the Court's school prayer, criminal procedure, and reapportionment decisions but steered clear of its civil rights cases, another step in *Brown's* progress toward canonization.[89] He went down in the greatest landslide since 1936. Incumbent Democrat Lyndon Johnson did not defend the Court; he simply said that he did not consider it a fit issue for a political campaign. This implied an endorsement of the Court as suprapolitical and sacrosanct.

Ironically, Johnson had made his entry into national politics in 1937 by branding himself as the only one of seventeen Democrats in a special primary election to defend Franklin Roosevelt's court-packing plan.[90] Johnson moved the Court further left (see Fig. 3). He coaxed Arthur Goldberg out of the "Jewish seat," making him ambassador to the United Nations and suggesting the vice presidency for 1968. He replaced Goldberg with his crony Abe Fortas. A leading legal realist, Fortas decided by instinct and then told his clerks to find citations. Thus was another adherent of *Gefühlsjurisprudenz* added to the Court. "He considered law indeterminate and did not care much about it," a biographer notes. In his hands, "realism licensed crude instrumentalism."[91]

Johnson inaugurated the "Black seat" by inducing the whimsical Tom Clark to resign and make room for NAACP general counsel Thurgood Marshall. Johnson told Clark that he could only make Clark's son, Ramsey, attorney general if his father stepped aside.[92] Johnson intended the Marshall appointment to symbolize racial progress.[93] He remained an advocate rather than a judge, in keeping with the realist conflation of law and politics, and simply followed the lead of the liberal wing.

In his classic statement on judicial power in *Federalist* 78, Publius had assured his readers that the judiciary would constitute the "least dangerous branch." But, he added, we could expect this only "so long as the judiciary remains truly distinct from both the legislature and the executive." In the mid-1960s, the federal courts looked more like an arm of the Great Society Democratic coalition. Circuit court justice J. Skelly Wright, a leading liberal activist judge, praised the Warren Court for this. While the old laissez-faire Court wrongly used judicial power to thwart "a revolution in the role of government," the Warren Court rightly exercised it "to further that effort."[94]

The Court also creatively reformed American libel law in the 1964 case *New York Times v. Sullivan.* Civil rights groups had taken out an ad in the *Times* that contained several minor factual inaccuracies, but under Alabama law such falsehoods enabled the plaintiffs to win several million dollars in damages. In this case, the Court voided the Alabama libel law and imposed a more liberal national standard—that public figures must prove "actual malice" (knowledge of falsehood or reckless disregard of truthfulness) to win a libel suit.[95] The Court depicted its decision as a First Amendment case, but it concerned the private or civil law that protected individuals from damage by other individuals, not to the state.[96]

The pre–New Deal Court had done this sort of thing for a century, displacing state common laws with a federal common law. The Court suddenly repudiated this in 1938, even holding one of its own precedents unconstitutional.[97] As with substantive due process, liberal jurists believed that judges had used the federal common law to protect large, out-of-state corporations from their in-state victims. But now progressive judges could use it to promote good causes like the civil rights movement as well as to gain the approval of major media like the *Times.*

The unacknowledged return to pre–New Deal constitutional doctrine stood out clearly in the famous right-to-privacy case, *Griswold v. Connecticut,* the next year, in which the Court struck down a state law that prohibited the distribution of contraceptives. The Court had twice previously declined to review the law, using Bickel's passive virtues of lack of standing and ripeness. The law had long lain dormant; the birth control advocates had a difficult time finding a prosecution that they could challenge.[98] The Court now took the case, and Justice Douglas announced that the law violated a constitutional right to privacy. He began with a restatement of the *Carolene* double standard, saying, "We do not sit as a super-legislature to determine the wisdom, need, and propriety of laws that touch *economic* problems, *business* affairs, or social conditions. This law, however, operates directly on an intimate relation of husband and wife and their physician's role in one aspect of that relation" (emphasis mine). Douglas weaved together a right to privacy from various provisions of the Bill of Rights, such as the Third Amendment's prohibition on the quartering of troops in private homes. "Specific guarantees in the Bill of Rights have penumbras, formed by emanations from their guarantees that give them life and substance."[99]

Griswold parodied the sloppy, subjective, result-oriented *Gefühlsjurisprudenz* of the Warren Court. To the old debate between "selective" and "total" incorporation, the Court now added a "selective-plus" option. The Court overlooked some specific rights, like grand jury indictment, jury trials in civil cases, and the right to bear arms (until 2010), while it concocted and imposed unspecified ones like "privacy."[100] Three justices concurred in the result but preferred to emphasize the Ninth Amendment assertion that "the enumeration in the Constitution, of certain rights, shall not be construed to deny or disparage others retained by the people." Justice Harlan preferred a restatement of old-fashioned substantive due process that most liberals still disparaged as *Lochner*esque. Justice White also concurred; the reasons for his separate opinion remain unclear.

Justices Black and Stewart dissented, fearful of the power that Douglas claimed, to invent rights. "I like my privacy as well as the next one," Black wrote, "but I am nevertheless compelled to admit that government has a right to invade it unless prohibited by some specific constitutional provision." The Ninth Amendment and substantive due process, he argued, amounted to just two names for the same thing, a "natural law due process philosophy" that the Court had repudiated after 1937. He rejected the claim that the Court had the duty to keep the Constitution up to date, and he called such hubris "no less dangerous when used to enforce this Court's view about personal rights than those about economic rights."

Since public opinion overwhelmingly favored married couples' access to contraceptives and agreed with Justice Stewart's description of the Connecticut statute as "an uncommonly silly law," *Griswold* elicited almost no opposition. But a few years later the Court would jettison its emphatically repeated limitation to "marital" privacy and extend the right to privacy to unmarried couples.[101] In this case, Justice Brennan declared that the right included that of deciding "whether to *bear* or beget a child" (emphasis mine). A few months later, this would become the endlessly controversial right to abortion.

The Warren Court's decisions on obscenity and pornography similarly exposed its seat-of-the-pants policymaking penchant. In several cases the justices struggled to define the bounds of the First Amendment's protection. They tried "whether to the average person, applying contemporary community standards, the dominant theme of the material as a whole appeals to prurient interests." They excluded "material characterized by patent offensiveness and indecency." Matter "utterly without social importance" or "utterly without redeeming social value" also went down. Justice Stewart summed up the shifting, subjective standard pithily when he declared that he could not define illegal pornography but "I know it when I see it."

The law of obscenity became a matter of case by case, or "look by look," judicial scrutiny.[102] This produced the institution of "movie day" at the Supreme Court, when the justices screened the disputed smut. Since Black and Douglas embraced First Amendment absolutism, their view was that the amendment protected everything, and so they absented themselves from movie day. Harlan's clerks had to apprise the nearly blind justice of the on-screen action. Justice Marshall only objected when he found the challenged films insufficiently salacious.[103] As in its sedition decisions, the Court never held that no standard existed, but it also never held against a challenged work, so state prosecutors abandoned the futile effort to win convictions.

THE END OF THE WARREN COURT

The Warren Court avoided civil rights cases for most of the decade after *Brown*. But when the civil rights movement entered a more militant phase in the early 1960s, as protesters began to exercise the rights that the Court said they possessed, Congress finally acted, in the Civil Rights Act of 1964 and the Voting Rights Act of 1965. With the political branches now on its side, the Court began to take further steps. It made the transition from prohibiting segregation to requiring integration in public schools, holding freedom-of-choice plans inadequate. Due in part to a sense that the Court's nineteenth-century precedents had neutered the Fourteenth Amendment, Congress based the Civil Rights Act on its power to regulate interstate commerce. The Court accepted this under the anything-goes *Wickard* standard, though Justices Douglas and Goldberg preferred a straightforward Fourteenth Amendment equal protection rationale.[104]

The Court also held that Congress, rather than the Court, could define the substance of equal protection. Justice Harlan objected to this, insisting, "That's for us to say."[105] In 1968, the Court went further and held that the Civil Rights Act of 1866 made it illegal for a private real estate owner to refuse to sell to Blacks.[106] This marked a return to the all-encompassing nondiscrimination rule of *Shelley v. Kraemer.* It transformed the *right* to make and enforce contracts into an *entitlement,* compelling people to contract. As in many other Warren Court cases, this decision rested on fanciful and deliberately distorted history.[107] It made the 1964 act unnecessary—indeed, it made redundant the Fourteenth Amendment itself, since the old Civil Rights Act derived from the Thirteenth Amendment. But, as with *Shelley,* the Court would not follow this case to its logical conclusion.[108]

The Warren Court reached its final frontier in its attempt to establish a right to welfare. The New Deal had transformed the entire political theory of the United States. Liberals no longer limited government to the protection of natural rights; they now expected it to provide positive benefits or entitlements—collective bargaining for union members, crop subsidies for farmers, old-age and disability pensions, and the like. In one of the most widely cited law review articles ever written, Yale law professor Charles Reich called this "the new property."[109] While the Court could not directly mandate benefits, it could make them easier to obtain and harder to curtail.[110] It held, for instance, that states could not impose residency requirements for migrants to receive welfare payments.[111] Similarly, it required that states only cut off benefits via due process—formal notice and time to respond with counsel.[112] It appeared that the Court wanted to make income or wealth a "suspect classification," like race or sex. As the laissez-faire Court had adopted substantive due process, this trend reflected substantive equal protection. But the post-Warren Court of the 1970s would draw back on this point.

As law professor Scott Powe has observed, the Warren Court mostly imposed the social and cultural standards of the national elite on what it saw as benighted local majorities for the sake of victimized local minorities. It principally targeted southern whites and urban Roman Catholics, whom the justices regarded as racist and obscurantist "deplorables." They sought to liberate Blacks, the poor, secular freethinkers, porn producers and consumers, petty criminals, and vagrants from Victorian cultural norms.[113]

Race was the flagship, as the Warren Court revolution began with *Brown* and advanced with the civil rights movement. Almost every major area of Warren Court jurisprudence had some connection to Black Americans. The reapportionment cases were meant to empower urban voters, as Blacks had for decades migrated en masse from the rural South into the urban North, Midwest, and West.[114] Likewise, most of the Court's criminal procedure cases displayed a racial concern. In the *Miranda* case, Justice Brennan had to persuade Warren not to express it so overtly.[115] One did not have to identify as an ardent liberal to recognize that the criminal justice system often acted as a means of racial subordination.[116] Most states outside the South had already adopted the rules that the Court imposed nationwide.

The new national law of libel derived from the effort of the Alabama authorities to hound the *New York Times* out of the state and prevent it from reporting on the brutal suppression of the civil rights movement. With regard to the nascent right to welfare benefits, the justices well knew that anything that benefited[117] the poor generally would benefit Blacks especially. This perhaps explains the Court's obscenity "jurisprudence," for, as one historian notes, "it is hard to discern the Court's policy goal in the obscenity cases.... It may have ... acted on the egalitarian idea that pornography ought to be made publicly available to everyone, not merely to the wealthy, who could indulge their tastes privately."[118]

The school prayer and right-to-privacy contraception cases primarily targeted northern, urban Catholics, but the latter had a racial aspect, as poor people generally, and Blacks especially, had less access to birth control (and later, to abortion) than the affluent. Though an ugly racist eugenic strain had long contaminated the birth control movement, the mainline Protestant American establishment sincerely believed that the quality of Black life would be improved by reducing the number of Black people.

The Warren Court also fleshed out the *Carolene Products* agenda in what it did *not* do. The Court became famous for defending the "personal" rights of "discrete and insular minorities," but it also adhered to the other premise of *Carolene*, leaving economic regulation or "property rights" to the political branches. Thus, the Court maintained the "age of deference" to administrative agencies that had begun with the New Deal. But even here it showed its preferences, deferring more to agencies like the Labor Board, which was prolabor, and being more critical of the Interstate Commerce Commission, which it considered pro-railroad, as the Court had in the 1940s.[119]

Everyone could see the Court's willingness to let the states regulate without stint in the *Lee Optical* case. Here the state's ophthalmologists got the legislature to prohibit the fitting of glasses by opticians without a prescription from the ophthalmologists. This displayed a classic piece of rent-seeking, of one profession trying to limit competition from another, just as *Carolene Products* resulted from the dairy lobby's campaign against "filled milk."[120] Justice Douglas admitted that the "law may exact a needless, wasteful requirement in many cases." But he left that decision to the legislature, not the Court. "The day is gone when this Court uses the due process clause . . . to strike down state laws, *regulatory of business and industrial conditions,* because they may be unwise, improvident, or out of harmony with a particular school of thought" (emphasis mine).[121] The Court provided an anything-goes standard for the state police power, equivalent to *Wickard v. Filburn*'s limitless commerce power for Congress, and the states responded with a bevy of special interest regulation.[122] Statists also loved antitrust law under the anti–big business Warren Court. It adopted the simple principle, as Justice Stewart put it, that "the government always wins."[123]

The end of the Warren Court provided an almost poetic illustration of its political nature. Chief Justice Warren wanted to retire in 1968, confident that Robert Kennedy, the Democratic front-runner, would choose his successor. Kennedy's assassination in June 1968 made Warren fear that his long-despised fellow Californian, Richard Nixon, might win. Warren and President Johnson tried to fix it so that Johnson could replace Warren. Warren submitted a letter of resignation, "effective at your pleasure." Johnson replied, "With your agreement, I will accept your decision to retire effective at such time as a successor is qualified."[124]

Several justices had put off retirement because they disliked the current president. The senile Nathan Clifford despaired of being replaced by a Democrat and at last retired when Garfield upset Winfield Scott Hancock in 1880.[125] Justices Harlan and Fuller pledged to remain on the Court "until they have to take us out feet foremost." Taft held on to prevent the "Bolsheviki" from getting control of the Court. McReynolds said he would never leave while "that crippled son-of-a-bitch" FDR was in the White House. But no incumbent justice had ever tried to secure his successor. Johnson then proposed to elevate his old friend Abe Fortas from associate to chief justice. Johnson also chose a Texas chum, Homer Thornberry, to fill Fortas's associate justice seat. In the Senate, the question arose whether a vacancy really existed, since Warren remained in office.

The Fortas nomination hearings soon turned into an assault on the Warren Court, particularly its criminal procedure decisions.[126] Public opinion had turned sharply against the Court, with its public approval rating reaching a low point in 1968.[127] Conservatives assailed Fortas as a Johnson crony, and Fortas indeed continued to act as a political adviser to the president. In the face of a Senate filibuster, Johnson had to withdraw the nomination. The press then revealed that Fortas had a number of ethically dubious financial connections, and he had to resign from the Court altogether.

Warren had stated that he wanted to retire solely on account of age. So, as he was not getting any younger, he had no choice but to let Nixon replace him—as well as Fortas. The Warren Court had come to an end, but it had established a new and apparently permanent kind of judicial power. Despite the controversial nature of many of its decisions, none of them met any serious response from the political branches—quite a contrast to the laissez-faire Court, whose unpopular decisions often met successful political reaction.[128]

8

THE METASTASIZING OF
JUDICIAL SUPREMACY

Under Earl Warren, the Court finally became supreme, transcending the fits and starts of the alleged bids for power in the intermediate periods of the laissez-faire, progressive, and New Deal eras. It had now undeniably won supremacy—"more supreme than court," in one commentator's view.[1] It remains to see how it *stayed* supreme. That it succeeded is clear, especially when progressives, erstwhile defenders of the liberal supremacism of the Warren Court, began to question the power of the more conservative post-Warren era in the late twentieth century, and especially after *Bush v. Gore* settled the 2000 presidential election. Republicans made ten unanswered appointments to the Court from 1969 to 1993. Though these ten justices often disappointed conservatives, they certainly moved the Court somewhat to the right (see Fig. 3). The Court remained supreme largely as it had become so: by leading public opinion toward elite policies but not getting too far ahead of the hoi polloi, and by retracing its steps when necessary.

THE BURGER COURT

The national elite for whom the Warren Court spoke detested Richard Nixon to an extraordinary degree, as reflected in the chief justice's gambit to replace himself before Nixon's election. That stratagem failed, and now liberals feared losing the judicial as well as the presidential wing of the Great Society. Sixties liberals rather sanctimoniously regarded themselves and the Court as the conscience of the nation.[2] Nixon and the yahoos threatened all that they had accomplished. As conservatives hounded him off the bench, Abe Fortas whined that "every decent constitutional decision of the last three years, and for some years prior thereto, has been denounced."[3] The Left regarded Nixon's law-and-order campaign theme as thinly veiled racism. They classified "law and order" as code words for white supremacy and backlash, a dog whistle that rabid racists could hear. Racial self-righteousness had defined the Warren Court since *Brown*, and it came to define post-1960s liberalism.

Warren Earl Burger of the DC circuit court of appeals had attracted Nixon's attention as a vocal critic of the Warren Court's criminal procedure decisions. Burger even prodded the Nixon campaign team to hit the Court harder, though Nixon's advisers counseled more caution. One warned that "any condemnation of the Court will be interpreted as fascist," since resistance to judicial supremacy implied support for white supremacy.[4] Nixon thus vaguely said that he would seek "strict constructionists" for the federal bench. Burger had locked horns with the leading Washington, DC, circuit court liberal, David Bazelon. Analysts classify Burger as a moderate conservative (see Fig. 3), and he had neither the ideological zeal, the political touch, nor the fundamental jurisprudential chops to reorient the trajectory of his predecessor's Court. No serious opposition arose to his appointment as chief justice.

Nixon ran into more trouble when he tried to replace Fortas with a southerner. Liberals saw this as part of his nefarious southern strategy, trying to win over traditionally Democratic southern whites by exploiting their racial animus, and especially courting those who had supported the overtly racist George Wallace when he ran as an independent in 1964 and 1968.[5] When Nixon appointed Clement Haynsworth of Virginia, Senate Democrats avenged the Fortas takedown. They emphasized ethical/financial lapses, or at least the appearance of impropriety, as tit for tat. But they primarily labeled the nominee segregationist and antilabor. Most commentators have come to see Haynsworth, like John J. Parker, as an unfortunate victim of partisan politics.

Nixon's next choice, Floridian G. Harrold Carswell, more fairly invited defeat. History will forever remember him by the endorsement made by Nebraska senator Roman Hruska. Conceding that Carswell had but slender qualifications, Hruska said, "Even if he were mediocre, there are a lot of mediocre judges and people and lawyers. They are entitled to a little representation, aren't they, and a little chance? We can't have all Brandeises and Frankfurters and Cardozos and stuff like that there."[6] Louisiana senator Russell Long also complained about overeducated judges who had imposed wild polices from the bench and said, "It might be well to take a B student or a C student who was able to think straight."[7]

These senators had more of a point than perhaps they realized. At least one critic of juristocracy has recognized that we should not expect judges recruited from the top of a competitive legal system to limit themselves to conserving.

They will rather "want to be architects of the legal system and engage with high-level philosophy, political theory, economics, and sociology." They aspire to social engineering and rule rather than to mere judging.[8]

Nixon at last gave in. He blamed antisouthern prejudice for the Haynsworth and Carswell rejections and took Burger's advice to nominate Burger's child-hood friend and best man, Harry Blackmun. The Senate easily confirmed him. The administration then mounted an effort, via Representative Gerald Ford, to impeach Justice Douglas, partly as revenge.[9] The next year, Justices Black and Harlan left the Court within a week of one another. The Senate readily accepted Virginian Lewis Powell. Nixon's other choice, William Rehnquist, ran into trouble because of a memo that he wrote against *Brown* as Justice Robert Jackson's clerk in 1952. Rehnquist claimed that Jackson had instructed him to produce an argument in favor of segregation and disclaimed its views as his own.[10] The 68–26 Senate vote indicated the sacred character of the Warren Court's signature case.

THE COUNTERREVOLUTION THAT WASN'T

Nixon appointed four justices; only Rehnquist stood out as a clear conserva-tive among them. The Burger Court marked no counterrevolution. It curbed some Warren Court trends but advanced others. Above all, Burger nurtured the judicial supremacy that Warren had established. The Court drew the line most clearly on welfare rights, or the "new property." In 1973, the Court held that Texas schools could be funded on the basis of local property taxes, though this usually meant that wealthier families would enjoy better-funded schools. Stewart joined the four Nixon justices; White and three liberal Warren Court veterans dissented.[11]

The Court also took several steps to permit broader latitude for the police in criminal procedure cases, in keeping with Burger's criticism of Warren Court coddling of criminals. But these technical and marginal adjustments did little to deflect the incorporation of the Bill of Rights and the imposition of national standards on the states. In many cases, Burger Court adjustments actually *favored* criminal defendants.[12] Likewise, Burger maintained the princi-ple of "one person, one vote" apportionment, but gave the states greater math-ematical latitude.[13] The Court finally tried to extricate itself from the morass of Warren Court obscenity jurisprudence. It let local communities prohibit depictions of "patently offensive 'hard core' sexual conduct."[14]

In two important areas, school desegregation and capital punishment, the Court took two steps forward and one step back in the face of popular protest.

School desegregation did not really begin until ten years after *Brown*, when the Civil Rights Act of 1964 prohibited discrimination in programs receiving federal financial aid, and especially after the Elementary and Secondary Education Act of 1965 began serious federal funding. In 1968, the Court held that freedom-of-choice plans that produced only token integration did not meet the *Brown* standard and began, along with the Office for Civil Rights in the Department of Health, Education, and Welfare, to erase the distinction between *de jure* and *de facto* segregation.[15] Federal judges ordered northern and western cities such as Boston and Denver to integrate, and in 1971 the high court approved busing as a means of overcoming residential segregation.[16]

However, the bureaucrats and judges ignored the text of the Civil Rights Act, which said that "'desegregation' shall not mean the assignment of students to public schools in order to overcome racial imbalance."[17] "White flight" to the suburbs or to private schools made it difficult to integrate increasingly minority urban school systems, so cities began to bus city students to the suburbs and vice versa. "Forced busing" aroused disapproval of whites and Blacks alike and produced serious riots in South Boston. Joseph Biden, a young US senator in the 1970s, led an unsuccessful effort to restrain the federal courts about busing, and a half century later he got grief for it from his primary challenger and ultimate running mate, Kamala Harris. Populists resented the fact that elite policymakers—including the high-profile federal judges who issued the integration orders—sent their own children to private schools.

In 1974, the Court drew the line and struck down a metropolitan Detroit integration plan. Judges or officials could only bus in cases of intentional discrimination. The Court divided along the same lines that it had in the school property tax case. Justice Marshall surmised that the majority had catered "to a perceived public mood that we have gone far enough in enforcing the Constitution's guarantee of equal justice."[18]

Liberals had long wished for the abolition of capital punishment. The claim that executions displayed racial bias added to the cause. Since the Constitution refers to capital crimes in several places, this would require a good deal of "living constitution" legerdemain. In 1972, the Court, again 5–4, with the four Nixon appointees in dissent, condemned capital punishment as administered by the states as arbitrary and standardless, thus violating the Eighth Amendment as an instance of unusual punishment. Randomly applied execution could hardly serve as a deterrent.[19] Justice Brennan believed that "evolving standards of decency," disclosed to himself and four brethren by some sort of Urim and Thummim, had made capital punishment unconstitutional. In an interesting version of the claim that judicial review reinforced rather than frustrated democracy, Justice Marshall asserted that most Americans *would* oppose the death penalty if they knew more about it. But the people overwhelmingly supported it. Those states that wanted to continue capital punishment adopted new laws and procedures to make the process less arbitrary, such as mandatory sentencing and separate juries to determine punishment, and the Court upheld these in 1976.[20] Ironically, the number of executions increased as a result of the Court's intervention.[21]

The Court also played a prominent role in Watergate, the greatest constitutional crisis of the postwar generation. The lower courts, particularly Judge John Sirica of the District of Columbia district court, helped crack the case, and the Supreme Court unanimously held that Nixon must turn tape recordings over to the special prosecutor investigating the Watergate burglary.[22] Some contended that nineteenth-century presidents like Andrew Jackson or Abraham Lincoln would have defied the Court, with the intervening years showing how powerful the judiciary had become.[23] The prosecutors appealed to the justices' self-importance, telling them that the case would determine whether they or the president ultimately interpreted the Constitution. On the other hand, Nixon occupied an extremely weak position; Congress probably would have impeached him, had he defied the Court, and the justices would not have acted so confidently without support in Congress. But they did claim that the extent of "executive privilege" constituted to some degree a justiciable rather than a completely political question.[24]

Though the Court did prohibit the censorship of the Pentagon Papers over administration claims that their publication would threaten national security, the Burger Court kept out of foreign affairs. It overruled, for example, the extravagant efforts of lower federal courts to issue injunctions to stop military action in Indochina. Justice Douglas's characteristically outré forays into personal diplomacy, and his outspokenly antiwar views, contributed to the campaign to impeach him in 1970.[25]

"HARRY'S ABORTION"

The greatest innovation and most controversial of all Burger Court decisions came in *Roe v. Wade*. This, more than any other case, made the judiciary a political lightning rod for the next fifty years. The chief justice assigned the opinion to Harry Blackmun. This produced a great deal of internal dissension, as Justice Douglas accused Burger of trying to manipulate the decision and especially bristled at a reargument to accommodate the two new Nixon appointees.[26] Blackmun proved insecure, dilatory, and inept. He called himself "old number three," having been Nixon's third choice for the slot and often derided as Burger's "Minnesota twin." He also had just published a legendarily embarrassing baseball antitrust decision.[27] He did not have Warren's or Brennen's gift for consensus building and he possessed below-average logical and moral reasoning ability. (Brennan helped, but as a Catholic, he did not want to appear to help too much.) In 1972, Blackmun preferred not to have the Court license the killing of the unborn at the same time that it outlawed the execution of murderers and rapists.[28] The Court clerks recoiled at the justices "so openly brokering their decision, like a group of legislators," two journalists reported. "There was something embarrassing and dishonest about the whole process." Inevitably, they called the decision "Harry's abortion."[29]

The Court decided two cases. A Texas statute permitted abortion only to save maternal life. Most states had similar laws. Georgia's law, more recent and liberal, permitted abortion to preserve maternal life or "health," with approval by a hospital board and with carte blanche for pregnancies that resulted from rape or incest.

"Standing" presented the first problem. Normally, an abortionist would challenge his criminal conviction under one of these laws. Instead, the Court heard a plea to enjoin the enforcement of the state laws from two pseudonymous women, Roe and Doe, who had already given birth, and from the abortionists who felt threatened by these laws.[30] The Court had recently limited federal judicial power to enjoin the enforcement of state criminal laws outside of the appeal of real cases from state courts. It ignored this stricture in *Roe,* and the case went up with no factual record.[31] The Burger Court here followed the Warren Court tendency to put aside procedural and structural safeguards against judicial lawmaking. *Roe* attracted criticism as much for its legislative rather than adjudicative nature as for the substance of the decision. A host of honest liberals confessed that they liked the result but blushed at the means by which it arrived.

"Harry's abortion" provided a labored, lengthy, and discursive opinion. It began with a fake contraction, an explicit disavowal of *Lochner,* though the decision would never shake its reputation as the liberal *Lochner.* Blackmun claimed that abortion statutes "are of relatively recent vintage" and provided a long, tendentious account in the worst Warren Court tradition of distorted "law-office history."[32] After reviewing the Pythagoreans and Aristotelians and English common law, he came to the Texas statute, which resembled the statute in most American states in the nineteenth century. He held that the statute could not claim to uphold Victorian moral standards, since it made no distinction between married and unmarried women. Insofar as it intended to protect maternal rather than prenatal life, it failed, because surgical abortion had become much safer—in early stages, it was safer than full-term delivery.

Moreover, its goal of protecting the unborn must give way to the woman's right to privacy. Blackmun explicitly rejected the argument that the unborn could claim the status of "persons" protected by the Fourteenth Amendment. "We do not resolve the difficult question of when life begins," he said. The privacy right—whether derived from the liberty clause of the Fourteenth Amendment or the catchall Ninth Amendment—included the right to abortion. Blackmun denied that he had promulgated an absolute right; states could require that only physicians perform abortions.[33]

Blackmun went on to devise a three-stage standard for the states. During the first trimester, states could impose no restrictions. During the second trimester, states could regulate abortion only for the sake of maternal health. "With respect to the State's important and legitimate interest in potential life," he said, "the 'compelling' point is viability" or "capability of meaningful life outside the mother's womb." Only during the third trimester or after viability could the state limit or prohibit abortion, but it still must allow for abortion for "maternal health."[34]

The companion *Doe* case provided more detail. The Georgia law permitted abortion in a broader range of cases but only with the approval of a multiple-member hospital committee. The Court had answered the claim that the list of permitted conditions was overly vague in a 1971 District of Columbia case, where the Court upheld an abortion law that included a health exception as long as that term included "psychological as well as physical well-being . . . medical judgment may be exercised in the light of all factors—physical, emotional, psychological, familial, and the woman's age—relevant to the well-being of the patient."[35] Justices Douglas and Stewart concurred in the result but continued to spar over whether abortion derived from the right to privacy (Douglas) or due process liberty (Stewart).[36]

New arrival Justice Rehnquist dissented. He caviled at the "standing" issue, chiding the Court for taking the case unnecessarily. Rehnquist would have applied the "rational basis" or anything-goes standard of *Lee Optical* with regard to the state police power. He noted what many would recognize, that Blackmun's trimester scheme "partakes . . . of judicial legislation."[37] Justice White pointed out that the decision amounted to abortion on demand, available for any reason "or no reason at all, and without asserting or claiming any threat to life or health, any woman is entitled to an abortion at her request" if she could procure a provider.[38] Chief Justice Burger, who had somewhat reluctantly concurred, disputed this claim. He trusted that "the vast majority of physicians observe the standards of their profession. . . . Plainly, the Court today rejects any claim that the Constitution requires abortion on demand."[39] But professional ethics would matter little. While most physicians and hospitals shunned abortion, a small number of specialists in freestanding "clinics" aborted millions.[40] The decision did not produce new abortionists, nor did it pay existing ones. *Roe* made abortion a right, not an entitlement.[41]

Roe did not cause an immediate uproar. It took some time for the enormous extent of the abortion license to become apparent and for an opposition coalition to form. As with the *Brown* decision, some years ensued before a backlash set in. The media deliberately downplayed the decision's reach.[42] The *New York Times* headline (below the fold) read, "High Court Rules Abortion Legal in First Three Months."[43] *Time* stood out as one of the few outlets to explain that the case meant "abortion on demand."[44] It remains common to this day to read that *Roe* outlawed "most" state abortion laws or legalized only first-trimester or previability abortions. In fact, it voided *all* state laws, even the most permissive, such as New York's, which permitted abortion up to twenty-four weeks for any reason, but only maternal-life-saving ones after that point.

States that continued to prosecute abortionists soon discovered this. For instance, Dr. Kenneth Edelin performed a hysterotomy (Caesarian section) abortion at twenty- to twenty-eight weeks, but a pathologist testified that the child had survived outside the womb. A jury convicted Edelin of manslaughter, but an appellate court reversed on the grounds of insufficient evidence. Commentators interpreted the decision as a vindication of the physician's discretion that the Court had emphasized in *Roe*.[45]

At about the same time, the prosecution of abortionist Jesse Floyd in South Carolina showed the extent of the abortion license. Floyd had failed to preserve the life of a child who survived his abortion and lived for twenty days. Federal judge Clement Haynsworth (the failed Supreme Court nominee) noted that "viability" presented a question of fact for physicians to determine "on a fetus-by-fetus basis." Haynsworth chided the prosecutor for bringing the case. The prosecutor did not understand *Roe*, which "he had read about in a magazine, and he had a digest of it prepared by a first-year law student which, in several respects, was quite misleading." He should have known "that the fetus in this case was not a person whose life the state law could legally protect."[46] *Roe* guaranteed the "right to a dead fetus."[47]

Many secularists saw opposition to abortion as a religious issue, and many religious saw it (like contraception) as a particularly Catholic issue. The Southern Baptists, among the most conservative Protestant denominations, did not come to oppose the decision for some time.[48] Justice Douglas called attention to religious opposition in a concurring opinion in *Roe*.[49] Justice John Paul Stevens would later emphasize the religious basis of anti-abortion laws, saying that they amounted to a violation of the First Amendment establishment clause. Former justice Tom Clark had written an influential law review article along these lines.[50] Law professor Louis Lusky, the Stone clerk most responsible for the *Carolene Products* footnote, had become a critic of freewheeling liberal judicial activism. But he made allowances where "taboo-laden social attitudes (often rooted in religious dogma) . . . make it politically difficult for legislatures to do what most of their constituents really want."[51]

The national parties had not yet aligned on the issue. Liberals such as Jesse Jackson and Ted Kennedy, along with many blue-collar (especially Catholic) Democrats, opposed abortion. Mainline Protestant and reformed Jews as well as many evangelical Protestants endorsed the decision. "Country club" Republicans such as Nelson Rockefeller, Gerald Ford, and most Burger Court justices approved it. When Gerald Ford became president a year and a half after *Roe*, he chose as his vice president Rockefeller, who as governor had saved New York's permissive abortion law from repeal. Ronald Reagan, the Goldwaterite governor of California, who would turn the party from eastern liberalism toward southwestern conservatism, signed California's abortion liberalization law in 1967.[52] The two 1976 party platforms skirted the issue. When President Ford appointed John Paul Stevens to the next vacancy on the Court in 1975, nobody asked him about abortion. He not only would embrace *Roe* but also came to exercise a crucial influence on the next new justice, Sandra Day O'Connor, recruiting her to the cause.[53]

Many liberals stood by *Roe* as they had stood by *Brown*, saying that they applauded the result but still found the Court's reasoning indefensible.[54] Yale law professor John Hart Ely offered the most noted critique, and would provide the most serious effort to justify the *Carolene* double standard,[55] but he could not justify *Roe*. "Were I a legislator I would vote for a statute very much like the one the Court ends up drafting," he wrote. But "what is frightening about *Roe* is that this super-protected right is not inferable from the language of the Constitution, the framers' thinking respecting the specific problem at issue, any general value derivable from the provisions they included, or the nation's governmental structure . . . a charge that can responsibly be leveled at no other decision of the past twenty years." *Roe,* he said, "is bad because it is bad constitutional law, or rather because it is *not* constitutional law and gives almost no sense of an obligation to try to be." He called it a left-wing *Lochner,* and opined that it "may turn out to be the more dangerous precedent."[56] Scholars of a conservative and libertarian orientation agreed.[57]

Unlike *Brown, Roe* did not quickly and permanently gain public approval and become sacrosanct. If anything, the decision intensified opposition to abortion, a backlash opposite to *Brown's.*[58] Years later, Ruth Bader Ginsburg, the feminist icon and ironclad advocate of abortion rights, lamented the Court's role. She claimed that the Court had short-circuited the democratic process, which had been moving toward greater acceptance of abortion, and might have stressed women's rights rather than physicians'.[59]

She got the story half right. The Court did usurp the legislative function, but legislatures did not evince a clear proabortion direction. Thirteen states had adopted Georgia-style "therapeutic" laws (based on a model proposed by the American Law Institute in the 1950s). But these laws had little impact, since medical advances had made hardly any abortions medically necessary.[60] Four states (Alaska, Hawaii, New York, and Washington) had adopted more liberal laws between 1967 and 1970, allowing abortion on demand up to a certain point (viability, or twenty-four weeks in New York). But New York's 1970 law had passed by one vote in the legislature, which then repealed the act in 1972. (Governor Rockefeller successfully vetoed the repeal.) No states adopted more liberal laws after 1970, and several rejected proposals to do so. The people of Michigan rejected a New York–style law just a few weeks before *Roe,* by a wide margin. North Dakota did likewise by an even wider margin.

Federal and state courts also split. Five federal courts had sustained state abortion laws and six struck them down, while sixteen state courts upheld them and five voided them.[61] When a federal judge ruled Connecticut's abortion law obsolete because it was meant to protect pregnant women rather than the unborn, the legislature immediately reenacted it with a prenatal-life preamble.[62] One federal court went so far as to declare the unborn constitutional persons protected by the Fourteenth Amendment.[63]

Also on the eve of *Roe,* the Michigan supreme court declared that the unborn possessed personality in tort law—as cases of injury or death to children in utero. Many states had moved in this direction in the twentieth century. The leading tort authority, William Prosser, called the first federal case to do so "the most spectacular and abrupt reversal of a well-settled rule in the whole history of torts." As legislatures liberalized their abortion statutes during the 1960s, commentators noted the retrograde movement in the courts and the anomalies it produced. For instance, a woman hit by a car on her way to an abortionist could sue the driver for the death of the child. Some pro-life advocates hoped that the Warren Court liberals would add the unborn to their roster of victim groups, as politically defenseless, discrete, and insular minorities.[64] But the US Supreme Court dedicated itself to the establishment of the abortion right and would become the battleground for those trying to preserve and overturn it.[65]

AFFIRMATIVE ACTION

After abortion, the Burger Court's boldest and most controversial assertions of judicial power came in the promotion of race-based affirmative action, particularly in the field of employment. Affirmative action arose from a series of presidential orders that prohibited discrimination by contractors doing business with the federal government. President Franklin Roosevelt had issued the first of these in 1941. The Johnson administration began to require contractors in certain construction trades in designated cities to provide statistical data and "goals and timetables" for increasing minority employment. President Nixon extended this program, known as the Philadelphia Plan, to all federal contractors.[66] Contractors challenged the plan as a violation of the Fourteenth Amendment and the 1964 Civil Rights Act, but the lower federal courts upheld it and the Supreme Court did not review.[67]

At the same time, the Court upheld the Equal Employment Opportunity Commission's adoption of the "disparate impact" definition of discrimination. If an employment standard, racially neutral on its face and not intended to discriminate, screened out a disproportionate number of minorities, the Court would hold it illegal unless the employer could prove "business necessity."[68] The difficulty of demonstrating business necessity led most employers to adopt racial quotas. The commission had radically reinterpreted the Civil Rights Act, which in several places expressed disapproval of race-conscious or proportional policies. But the Court granted the commission "great deference."

The breadth of the commission's victory astonished the civil rights community. Law professor Alfred W. Blumrosen, the chief architect of the commission's policy, wrote an analysis of the case entitled "Strangers in Paradise."[69] Burger called *Griggs* the most important decision of his chief justiceship,[70] but an NAACP lawyer said, "We always suspected Chief Justice Burger really had no idea at all what he was doing when he wrote *Griggs*."[71] Nonetheless, one could say that the Burger Court did no worse than its predecessors on the civil rights front. One scholar notes that, since 1896, it is "impossible to identify in the opinions of the Supreme Court a constitutional law of racial classifications that may usefully be distinguished from the ad hoc policy preferences of a majority of the Court."[72]

From 1978 to 1980, the Court extended affirmative action still further. The University of California medical school at Davis set aside sixteen of one hundred places for Black applicants. Four justices accepted this quota and four forbade it. Justice Powell split the difference. He held the hard-and-fast quota unconstitutional but said that the school could take race into account for the legitimate purpose of the educational benefits of a "diverse student body."[73] "Diversity," hardly mentioned in the case, became the foundation of race-conscious policies for the next generation.[74]

The next year, the Court approved "voluntary" quotas, when the Kaiser Aluminum Company set aside half of its apprentice training slots for Blacks. The plan was hardly voluntary, having resulted from pressure from the federal government. The company agreed to it under an ongoing court-supervised consent decree. The Court mused that though the Civil Rights Act did not *require* preferential treatment, it did not *prohibit* it. The Court blessed such programs if they did not "unnecessarily trammel the interests of white workers."[75] The decision insulated employers from "reverse discrimination" suits by white workers. The next year the Court upheld a ten percent quota for minority-owned firms, which Congress had adopted in the Public Works Employment Act.[76]

Public approval that followed *Brown* did not recur in the abortion or affirmative action cases. Public opinion waffled in both areas. As one commentator noted, most Americans disapproved of abortion on demand but they supported policies that resulted in it.[77] Likewise, Americans tended to approve of "soft" affirmative action—outreach programs to recruit minorities and make them aware of opportunities, hiring procedures that broke out of the "old boy network." But they objected to double standards and hard-and-fast "quotas." "Hard" affirmative action depended on judicial and bureaucratic power.[78] It almost never won a popular referendum or legislative vote.[79]

The Court's jurisprudence on women's rights and sex discrimination also revealed its variegated strategy of activism. The Court had never held sex classifications subject to the same strict scrutiny as racial ones, requiring a "compelling state interest" and a law tailored as narrowly as possible to meet that interest. The Court accepted "rational basis" for sex discrimination claims until 1971. That year, the Court held that an Idaho law that favored men as administrators of estates violated the equal protection clause.[80] Liberals on the Court relished the chance to go all out and hold all sex classifications unconstitutional, but they stayed their hand because they assumed that the Equal Rights Amendment, sent by Congress to the states in 1972, would do it for them. To their surprise, the requisite number of states did not ratify, due in no small part to their own abortion decisions.[81] So the Court invented a new level of judicial review, "intermediate scrutiny," for sex discrimination.[82] After two decades of attrition, the Virginia Military Institute case did about all that the amendment would have done anyway.[83]

THE ADMINISTRATIVE JUDICIARY

The affirmative action cases showed that the federal judiciary wanted to abet the new array of administrative agencies that the New Deal and the Great Society had spawned. The Court had initiated school desegregation in *Brown;* after ten dormant years, it reinforced the administrative transformation of desegregation into integration. In Title VI enforcement, the primary role of the Office for Civil Rights "morphed from termination of funding for programs engaged in court-defined discrimination to using its rulemaking authority to define standards that could be enforced through injunctive relief," notes one scholar, who describes this judicial–bureaucratic cooperation as "institutional leapfrog."[84] In the Title VII cases, the bureaucrats initiated the statutory redefinition and the Court confirmed it. Far from hobbling federal agencies, the courts increasingly followed their example. The judicial process no longer contrasted so sharply with the administrative process that progressives had formerly preferred.[85]

The Court had exercised deference to the new agencies since the crisis of 1937.[86] By the 1970s, the courts were goading the agencies to do more, and made it easier for citizens and interest groups to sue them. Congress also increased access to the courts and enacted attorney fee laws to incentivize suits. The Civil Rights Act of 1964, for example, permitted individual suits, turning plaintiffs into "private attorneys general."[87] The American legal system's permitting of contingency fee counseling and its lack of a "loser pays" allocation of court costs also spurred litigation. Older tax-and-spend liberalism had become mandate-and-sue liberalism, as one scholar notes.[88]

Conservatives saw these suits as collusive, a way of getting courts to give the agencies powers that they could not obtain by legislation.[89] This obtained especially in the District of Columbia court of appeals, which oversees federal regulatory agencies and has become something of a "junior Supreme Court."

Judge David Bazelon, Burger's liberal antagonist on that court, said in 1971, "We stand on the threshold of a new era in the long and fruitful collaboration of administrative agencies and reviewing courts."[90] When the "fourth branch" of administrative agencies arose in the late nineteenth century, the courts had looked upon them as rivals and tried to contain them. After 1937, however, the courts learned to live with their erstwhile rivals, and by the 1960s, the judiciary co-opted and directed them.

In 1937, James Landis, one of the architects of the administrative state, noted that the "new liberties" or entitlements of the New Deal "for their protection seek the administrative and not the judicial process."[91] By adopting many administrative methods, especially the substitution of equity for law, the courts could direct the administrative state. In 1907, Charles Evans Hughes had said, "We live under a Constitution, but the Constitution is what the judges say it is."[92] A century later he might have said "the Constitution is what the judges let the administrators say it is." One could say that the Court's administrative law did more to undermine the separation of powers than did its own direct usurpation of the legislative function.

Federal courts, especially the DC circuit court of appeals, frustrated the Reagan administration's attempt to reduce federal regulation.[93] Much as the courts had preferred the Department of Health, Education, and Welfare over the Justice Department in desegregation, they sided with old National Highway Traffic Safety Administration rules over new administration efforts to weaken auto safety standards.[94] Conservative justice Antonin Scalia, more than anyone a Frankfurter–Bickelite opponent of judicial supremacy, at first thought that judicial deference to the fourth branch might spur the first branch to do its constitutional duty—to legislate. This case heralded what we call "Chevron deference": the Court would treat unclear laws as a congressional *intention* to delegate lawmaking power to the agencies and would accept their interpretations unless deemed "arbitrary and capricious."[95] Scalia saw that Congress did not respond, and moved toward the judicial duty of enforcing a "nondelegation" doctrine, but that still remains largely potential and speculative.

The federal courts began to take over the administration of public schools, prisons, hospitals, and other institutions. They compelled the Department of Health, Education, and Welfare to enforce the Civil Rights Act, with no deference to the Nixon Justice Department's effort to delay school integration. They made the new Department of Housing and Urban Development remove lead paint from public housing. They ordered the Department of the Interior to protect Indians on trading posts, the Federal Housing Administration to comply with local building codes, and the Treasury to protect domestic milk producers from competition. "Judges thus began to assume the ultimate protection of the collective social interests which administrative schemes were designed to serve," one scholar observed.[96] For instance, Alabama district judge Frank Johnson provided a code for a state hospital: no excessive medication, the right to physical exercise, no more than six patients per room, no room smaller than one hundred square feet, ten square feet per inmate in the dining room, one toilet for every eight and one shower for every fifteen inmates, and a room temperature between 68 and 83 degrees Fahrenheit.[97] The judge explained his extraordinary intervention as an extension of the *Brown* imperative.[98]

Courts had gone beyond judicial lawmaking into judicial administration. This added something new to the old fear that judges would usurp the legislative function. Their grasp of the executive role meant that the courts had combined all three powers of government, which Publius had called "the very definition of tyranny."[99] One law professor called the new system "public law litigation."[100] Lawsuits no longer settled disputes between private parties or defended individual rights versus government. Now they constructed public policy for interest groups. The old common law and writ system, and legal ethics, had tried to discourage litigation by channeling, narrowing, and focusing it.[101] The new system tried to expand and encourage it. It particularly adopted the more flexible, open-ended, ad hoc methods of equity. It aimed not at a judgment settling past disputes but at decrees that entailed ongoing supervision of future conduct. Judges saw it as part of their job to call attention to social problems, to "raise consciousness," and to nudge legislators to act. As we have seen at the national level, local politicians often gladly shifted controversial political issues onto the judges.[102]

America had become a "litigious society."[103] The United States had about thirteen lawyers per 100,000 people into the twentieth century; that number rose to more than four hundred by 2018.[104] It also had twice as many lawsuits and three times as many judges per capita as most other industrial countries. The number of federal lawsuits rose from thirty thousand a year in 1950 to 175,000 by 1990. Thus we see again the long-run impact of the *Brown* case.[105] The unorthodox nature of that decision, and especially its enforcement, became accepted and spawned the new "public law litigation" model and its application to a host of new settings.[106]

Progressives and New Dealers had wanted to use civil lawsuits to achieve economic redistribution and social reform. The adoption of the Federal Rules of Civil Procedure in 1938 and the *Erie* case's abandonment of a federal common law displayed this. In the progressive view, nineteenth-century courts had shifted the costs of industrialization from entrepreneurs onto farmers, consumers, and workers. The twentieth-century project was to redress that, and they devised a theory of "enterprise liability."[107] As the number of lawyers in America exploded, professional legal ethics were altered. One legal ethicist declared a professional obligation to "chase ambulances."[108] Plaintiff lawyers fancied themselves crusaders for social justice.

ORIGINALISM

While judicial liberals after 1937 argued over the process restraint (or procedural liberal) and activist (or substantive liberal) approaches, conservatives took a while to offer a jurisprudential alternative. It came to center on "originalism," a term coined in 1980 by constitutional scholar Paul Brest.[109] Originalists opined that judges should interpret the Constitution according to the original intent or the original understanding of its framers and ratifiers. Notably, nobody seemed to stress that legislators or executives should do the same, as judicial supremacism had read them out of the constitution-interpreting picture.[110] Originalism did not necessarily challenge modern judicial supremacism (for one could make an originalist case for judicial supremacy), but it usually did.

Until "living constitutionalism" arose, politicians and lawyers had taken originalism for granted. Lincoln and Douglas, and Taney and Curtis, on the *Dred Scott* case, all made originalist claims about the Founders and slavery.[111] Even in their triumph, the progressives and New Dealers affirmed originalism. They claimed that the laissez-faire jurists had departed from the Founders' view of the commerce power or due process. Scholar Howard Gillman called this their "failure of nerve," an unwillingness to own up to their radicalism.[112] Warren Court activism made this untenable, and its untethered judicial policymaking prompted a conservative alternative.[113]

Robert Bork's 1971 article "Neutral Principles and Some First Amendment Problems" launched the originalist movement, and law professor Raoul Berger based his 1977 account of *Government by Judiciary* upon it. Notably, Berger took his title from Louis Boudin, a socialist who decried laissez-faire jurisprudence in the early twentieth century. Reagan's attorney general, Edwin Meese, raised the profile of the issue in a 1985 American Bar Association address. He mostly reiterated Alexander Hamilton's and John Marshall's fundamental point that the United States had a written constitution, adopted by "reflection and choice," coming not from a "dark and mythical realm." "The presumption of a written document is that it conveys meaning," Meese argued.

Only in the twentieth century did theories of a "living constitution" arise. Meese disingenuously but necessarily presented the *Brown* decision as a piece of originalism (what he called "a jurisprudence of original intention"). *Brown* provided the trump card of liberal living constitutionalism; any theory that did not produce *Brown* sank. Meese claimed that originalism sought to "depoliticize the law," but he seemed to make it result-oriented when it entered the *Brown* empyrean.[114] The attorney general similarly reaffirmed the old theory of "departmentalism," denying the judicial monopoly theory of constitutional interpretation, but the Reagan administration would ultimately focus on judicial personnel rather than judicial power.

Justice Brennan responded to Meese, who had indirectly chided him as interpreting the Constitution according to his own "concept of human dignity." No Supreme Court justice had so prominently defended himself since John Marshall in 1819. Brennan called the Constitution an often obscure, ambiguous document that required interpretation. He took judicial supremacy for granted, paraphrasing Robert Jackson, that "We Justices are certainly aware that we are not final because we are infallible; we know that we are infallible only because we are final." Judges should not try to divine the Founding generation's intent but should express the current generation's take on general constitutional terms. The justices "speak for their community," and could only go as far as the people would accept. The originalist claim to speak for "a world that is dead and gone" he called "arrogance cloaked as humility." We cannot and should not try to recover origins. We could not, as Warren had put it in *Brown*, "turn back the clock."[115]

Brennan called the Constitution "a sublime oration on the dignity of man, a bold commitment by a people to an ideal of libertarian dignity protected through law," and he stated that "the demands of human dignity would never cease to evolve." This expressed the substantive agenda of post–New Deal judicial liberalism. It hardly reflected the view of the Founders on human nature. *The Federalist* usually describes man as wicked and depraved, with constitutional forms designed to make him free but governable. "It may be a reflection [that is, a sober recognition] on human nature that such devices should be necessary to control the abuses of government," Publius wrote in *Federalist* 51. "But what is government itself but the greatest of all reflections on human nature? If men were angels, no government would be necessary."

The debate over originalism and liberal jurisprudence reflected the cultural revolution that accompanied the Warren Court. By the late twentieth century, all could see the "dignity" at issue in racial segregation and the benefit of judicial activism in *Brown*. But when that power purportedly released murderers and rapists, or protected what many saw as infanticides and sodomites, the population split severely. And religious conservatives and radical feminists alike, and many in between, struggled to see how unfettered pornography advanced human dignity. Warren and his successors' Court became a siege point in the late twentieth-century "culture war."

Given the apparently shared assumption of judicial supremacy on both sides of the debate, Reagan and Meese focused on putting originalists on the bench. This challenge to liberal constitutionalism came to a head when President Reagan nominated Robert Bork to the Court in 1987. Reagan had his first Court vacancy when the idiosyncratic, occasionally moderately conservative Justice Potter Stewart retired in 1981. Reagan had pledged to appoint a woman to the Court, but his staff could find few women to excite the right, especially pro-life, social conservatives.[116] His choice, Sandra Day O'Connor, would become just as idiosyncratic, but somewhat more conservative, than Stewart. In 1986, Chief Justice Burger retired. Reagan elevated William Rehnquist to the center chair and nominated Antonin Scalia for the associate spot. The Republicans still had a Senate majority and confirmed both. Senate Democrats again made some noise about Rehnquist but approved Scalia unanimously.[117] Later that year, the Republicans lost control of the Senate.

Lewis Powell stepped down in June 1987 and President Reagan nominated Bork in July. This set in motion an unprecedented campaign by hundreds of interest groups to defeat him. In what one scholar called "a patent fit of gross hyperbole," Massachusetts senator Ted Kennedy set the tone by saying, upon the announcement:

> Robert Bork's America is a land in which women would be forced into back-alley abortions, Blacks would sit at segregated lunch counters, rogue police could break down citizens' doors in midnight raids, schoolchildren could not be taught about evolution, writers and artists could be censored at the whim of the government, and the doors of the federal courts would be shut on the fingers of millions of citizens for whom the judiciary is—and is often the only—protector of the individual rights that are the heart of our democracy.

Reagan, he said, "should not be able to reach out from the muck of Irangate, reach into the muck of Watergate, and impose his reactionary vision of the Constitution on the Supreme Court and on the next generation of

Americans."[118] Kennedy's tirade gave a substantive expression of Justice Brennan's defense of liberal judicial activism. After a long campaign and extensive televised hearings, the Senate rejected Bork by an unusually wide margin of 58–42.[119]

How did Scalia sail through while Bork ran aground? Most obviously, the Republicans had lost their Senate majority in the 1986 midterm elections. (While Republican presidents filled ten vacancies from 1969 to 1993, only two—O'Connor and Scalia—won confirmation by Republican Senates.) The Iran–Contra affair ("Irangate," as Kennedy called it) had weakened President Reagan. Many considered impeachment not unlikely.[120] Scalia had replaced Burger, a relative conservative and becoming more so on abortion, while Powell represented a crucial swing vote.

Washington had never seen such a well-organized campaign against a nominee, with some three hundred interest groups decrying Bork and recruiting celebrities like Gregory Peck to broadcast advertisements against him. The verb "to bork," to organize a blitzkrieg of character assassination, entered the American political lexicon. The media blitz caught the administration flat-footed. While Bork differed little ideologically from Scalia, the administration could not decide whether to accentuate or minimize Bork's conservatism. Nor did the candidate help himself much. Scalia benefited from the Democrats' focus on Rehnquist's elevation, and by his identity as the first-ever Italian American nominee. Bork represented no minority group. Nobody would call him telegenic. He lacked charm and especially "empathy," and he did not suffer Judiciary Committee fools gladly.[121]

With Bork defeated, Reagan turned first to Douglas Ginsburg, a libertarian law professor and DC circuit court judge. But questions of financial improprieties and, at the apex of the "war on drugs," allegations of marijuana use led him to withdraw within a week, before the president had formally nominated him. Reagan at last succeeded with Anthony Kennedy, who along with O'Connor would become the decisive swing vote on the Court for the next three decades. Kennedy, like Harry Blackmun, could call himself "old number three."

But the Bork debacle did not discredit originalism. Instead, liberal activists learned to love originalism and turn it to their own ends. They spoke of "living originalism" and claimed that "we're all originalists now."[122] This came into high relief when avowed originalist Neal Gorsuch made the manifestly ridiculous claim that the framers of the Civil Rights Act of 1964 meant to prohibit discrimination based on sexual orientation, gender identity, or transgender status—as if those terms would have meant anything to the members of the

Eighty-Eighth Congress. Justice Alito called this decision "a pirate ship flying an originalist flag."[123]

A FAILED CONSTITUTIONAL MOMENT

Nothing happened with regard to the two key judicially fabricated policies that conservatives hoped new personnel would undo, affirmative action and abortion. The Court did tighten the standards by which states and the federal government could set aside public funds for minority contractors, but twenty years later the US Commission on Civil Rights reported that government agencies largely ignored the strict scrutiny standard.[124] Inertia explained a lot: once the Court had accepted racial preferences in government programs, interest groups and politicians got used to them and they became hard to dislodge except by individual lawsuits.

One scholar has described opposition to affirmative action as broad but shallow, and support for it as narrow but deep.[125] This reflected the classic minority-benefit phenomenon that economist Mancur Olson described in *The Logic of Collective Action* (1965): with diffuse costs and concentrated benefits, minority interest groups can prevail in majority rule systems. Olson's insight belied the assumption of *Carolene Products* about the weakness of minority groups, as well as Publius's belief that "if a faction consists of less than a majority, relief is supplied by the republican principle, which enables the majority to defeat its sinister views by regular vote."[126]

Similarly, big business lobbied Reagan not to end the Labor Department's affirmative action contracting program, which he could abolish by executive order. "Diversity management" had become part of corporate culture. If anything, Wall Street wanted affirmative action regulatory costs more forcefully imposed on their Main Street competitors.[127] The Court also tried to tighten up the disparate impact standard in Title VII cases in 1989.[128] Congress responded by adopting the old standard in the Civil Rights Act of 1991.

With regard to school integration, the Court also made it harder to justify "magnet" programs to attract white students to Black schools, but it did not insist on a color-blind standard. It also reaffirmed the *Bakke* diversity rationale, but not hard-and-fast quotas, in a pair of University of Michigan cases in 2003. One sees the legislative compromise nature of the principle in Justice O'Connor's disclaimer about affirmative action as a temporary step and her prediction that "we expect, twenty-five years from now, the use of racial preferences will no longer be necessary."[129] Justice Ginsburg more forthrightly called outright quotas "preferable to achieving similar numbers through winks, nods, and disguises."[130]

The Court had fashioned affirmative action in conjunction with federal bureaucrats, but it unleashed abortion entirely on its own. In 1989, with three Reagan appointees, it looked like it might undertake a major reconsideration of *Roe,* upholding some Missouri abortion restrictions—declaring that life began at conception, for example, and prohibiting abortions in public hospitals. (It dismissed the "life" declaration as merely hortatory.)[131] But nobody knew exactly how many justices wanted to overturn *Roe* altogether; Justice Kennedy's position, in particular, was unknown. The prospect became acute when two of the *Roe* stalwarts, Brennan and Marshall, left the Court in 1990–91. Their replacements, David Souter and Clarence Thomas, both assiduously avoided making commitments about *Roe* during their confirmation hearings. George H. W. Bush chose Souter precisely because he lacked any "paper trail." Most regarded Thomas as the more likely conservative. The last-minute accusations of sexual harassment that dramatized his confirmation hearings provided transparent cover for liberals' ideological fears.

The Court heard an appeal of a Pennsylvania abortion law, in 1992, that required parental and paternal notification, data reporting from abortion providers, an expression of informed consent, and a twenty-four-hour waiting period before abortion. The Court upheld all of these except the paternal notification. Two old liberals, Blackmun and Stevens, objected to these restrictions. Four conservatives (Rehnquist, Scalia, Thomas, and White) would overturn *Roe* altogether. The center (O'Connor, Souter, and Kennedy) issued a joint opinion that preserved the "central holding" of *Roe* but refounded it. The Court finally jettisoned the right to privacy; abortion became a "liberty," protected by the due process clause of the Fourteenth Amendment. Substantive due process came out of the closet. The Court abandoned the ridiculously distorted history that went into *Roe* (though a group of historians did again traduce their profession by making a similar historical appeal). It was the history since, rather than before, 1973 that mattered.[132]

The joint opinion declared, "At the heart of liberty is the right to define one's own concept of existence, of meaning, of the universe, and of the mystery of human life. Beliefs about these matters could not define the attributes of personhood were they formed under the compulsion of the State."[133] This extravagant statement of anarchical liberty made Douglas's "penumbras and emanations" sound buttoned-down. Justice Scalia would mock this eruption of *Gefühlsjurisprudenz* as the "mystery passage." They riffed on Brennan's view of the Constitution as a "sublime oration on the dignity of man" and of "libertarian dignity."[134] It reflected the emotive, therapeutic culture of "the sovereign self" in postwar America, adumbrated in *Brown's* sociopsychological discussion of the "hearts and minds" of segregated schoolchildren.[135] The Court shelved the "trimester" scheme, since the conjunction of viability with the third trimester had long succumbed to ever-greater medical ability to keep neonates alive. States could protect the unborn after viability, but only if they did not impose an "undue burden" on the abortion option. *Roe's* provision of abortion on demand remained.

Whatever its philosophical premises, the Court really said that the time to overturn *Roe* had passed. "Reliance interests" had set in after twenty years.[136] They could not "refuse to face the fact that for two decades of economic and social developments" women had arranged their lives with the expectation that they could abort unwanted pregnancies. "The ability of women to participate equally in the economic and social life of the nation has been facilitated by their ability to control their reproductive lives," the Court held. "An entire generation has come of age free to assume *Roe's* concept of liberty in defining the capacity of women to act in society."[137] Abortionists after *Roe*, unlike Black children after *Brown*, got results immediately. Unlike *Brown*, *Roe* did not need the cooperation of the political branches. The Court *made* policy less than it dismantled existing policy; its power always negated better than it constructed. Courts could permit the dismembering of children more effectively than they could have them sent to integrated schools.

The Court's statement about itself and about judicial supremacy leaped off the page. The Court had overruled *Lochner* in 1937 and *Plessy* in 1954, due to new understandings of economics and sociology.[138] "In the present case, however . . . the terrible price would be paid for overruling." It would "seriously weaken the Court's capacity to exercise judicial power and function as the Supreme Court of a nation dedicated to the rule of law." In *Roe*, the Court had "called the contending sides of a national controversy to end their national division by accepting a common mandate rooted in the Constitution." It did not do this very often. So when it did, its decisions acquired a "rare precedential value." (The Court did not mention *Dred Scott* as an example of judicial controversy settling.)

This statement cluelessly admitted that *Roe* had legislated rather than adjudicated. The Constitution does not give the Court the power to settle "national controversies" between "sides" on issues like abortion, much less to turn such political interventions into "superprecedents." Even *Roe's* defenders blushed to call it "rooted in the Constitution." The Court went on to say, in effect, that their *failure* to settle the controversy provided the reason to preserve it—the *wronger* the decision, the more sacred it became. Otherwise, the Court might have to admit its fallibility. "So to retreat under fire . . . would subvert the Court's legitimacy," they candidly said.

In an astonishing assertion of sovereign power, they also announced that the people had an obligation to stand by erroneous Court decisions out of respect for its supremacy. They called on the people "to be tested by following" the Court. They concluded that constitutional government or the rule of law depended on judicial supremacy. Americans' "belief in themselves as a people who aspire to live according to the rule of law is not readily separable from their understanding of the Court invested with the authority to decide their constitutional cases and speak before all others for their constitutional ideals."[139]

Justice Scalia upbraided the Court for clinging to the original error of *Roe.* He recognized that the undue burden standard did not alter the abortion-on-demand license of the case.[140] *Casey* rested on reliance interests that the Court had itself established. "*Roe* created a vast new class of abortion consumers and abortion providers by eliminating the moral opprobrium that had attached to the act." The inertia that had saved affirmative action now saved abortion. "The imperial judiciary lives," he concluded.[141]

Justice Blackmun, the author of *Roe,* recognized that the Court had salvaged the substance of his 1973 abortion ruling. He had feared that the Court would "cast into darkness the hopes and visions" of *Roe,* if not the hopes of 30 million abortees. "But now, just when so many expected the darkness to fall, the flame has grown bright." But, he cautioned, "I am 83 years old. I cannot remain on this Court forever, and when I do step down, the confirmation process for my successor well may focus on the issue before us today."[142]

After Bill Clinton became president the following year, Blackmun and White retired and Clinton replaced them with proabortion justices Ruth Bader Ginsburg and Stephen Breyer. Kennedy had agreed to preserve *Roe* with the expectation that the Court would uphold reasonable limits. He, too, may have misunderstood that the central holding of the case meant abortion on demand. In the 1990s, several states prohibited "partial-birth abortion" (intact dilation and extraction), a late-term procedure in which the abortionist delivers all but the head of the child, then punctures the skull and suctions out the brain.[143] The Court struck down a Nebraska prohibition in 2000, because the law did not contain a health exception and because the ban on this particular method might inhibit physicians from using others.[144]

The two Clinton justices produced a proabortion majority that no longer needed Kennedy. In his dissent, he rather pathetically expressed his sense of betrayal with his long and detailed description of the gruesome procedure.[145] The conservatives had some symbolic payback when Congress prohibited partial-birth abortion. But constitutional conservatives had to swallow the irony that they upheld it on commerce clause grounds—the act prohibited the procedure "in or affecting interstate commerce."[146]

Court conservatives, on the other hand, decided some federalism cases that liberals decried as "revolutionary" evidence of conservative judicial activism. The federalism revival dated from 1976, when the Court held that Congress could not apply the Fair Labor Standards Act to state employment.[147] The Court had not placed any limits on the commerce power since the New Deal. They overruled this decision in 1985, but seemed to restore it in 1992. Along with several decisions beefing up sovereign immunity under the Eleventh Amendment, it concerned the sovereign attributes of the states more than the commerce power.

In 1995, the Court struck down the Gun-Free School Zones Act, which had made it a crime to possess a firearm around schools.[148] In this instance, Congress had clearly exercised a police power that had nothing to do with the regulation of interstate commerce. Indeed, Congress did not even bother to pretend that it did; no language in the statute referred to commerce, unlike the Civil Rights Act or the Partial-Birth Abortion Act, which similarly dressed up police regulations in commerce garb. Five years later, the Court struck down the Violence Against Women Act.[149]

But this federalism revival proved very shallow. In 2005, the Court upheld Congress's power to prohibit marijuana trafficking over a California law that legalized it for medicinal use.[150] Justice Scalia joined the majority. Even this most prominent advocate of originalism confessed the theory's limits. Scalia called himself "a faint-hearted originalist" and said, "I'm an originalist and a textualist. I'm not a nut."[151] As Justice Thomas said in the Gun-Free School Zones case, "Although I might be willing to return to the original understanding, I recognize that many believe that it is too late in the day to undertake a fundamental reexamination of the past sixty years. Considerations of *stare decisis* and reliance interests may convince us that we cannot wipe the slate clean."[152] Federalism cases did not provoke much public reaction and may have reflected the conservatives' desire to avoid more controversial social issues like abortion.[153]

The 2000 *Dickerson* case illustrated the inertia of judicial supremacy. In 1968, Congress had responded to the *Miranda* decision by allowing federal courts to admit confessions made without *Miranda* warnings if suspects volunteered them. Federal prosecutors ignored the law until the 1990s. Chief Justice Rehnquist held that Congress could not amend the *Miranda* rules; per *Cooper v. Aaron*, the Court's interpretations of the Constitution equaled the Constitution. Rehnquist admitted that the Court had itself altered the *Miranda* rules. "No Court laying down a general rule can possibly foresee the various circumstances in which counsel will seek to apply it."[154]

John Marshall, in *McCulloch*, had said that a constitution could not provide for every particular means that the government might need to carry out its enumerated ends. Such a constitution "would partake of the prolixity of a legal code, and could scarcely be embraced by the human mind. It would probably never be understood by the public." A constitution articulated certain great ends and objects, but left the means to achieve those objects open. "We must never forget that it is *a constitution* that we are expounding," said the great chief justice. Rehnquist might have put it, "We must never forget that it is *Court-made constitutional law* that we are expounding" (emphasis mine). Reliance interests again pitched in, as he noted that "the warnings have become part of our national culture"; every fan of popular TV police dramas would concur. If Justice Scalia's heart became faint when the Court confronted Congress's commerce power pretentions, here his antipathy to judicial supremacy led him to dissent in favor of Congress and against the Court as "some sort of nine-headed Caesar, giving thumbs-up or thumbs-down to whatever outcome, case by case, suits or offends its collective fancy."[155]

Even Scalia abetted the muscular assertion of judicial supremacy that over-turned the Religious Freedom Restoration Act of 1993. This act was intended to correct Scalia's decision in *Employment Division v. Smith*, which held that states could impose general criminal laws over particular religious objections—in this case, penalizing the use of peyote, a hallucinogenic drug, in Native American religious rites. The Court held that Congress had power under section 5 of the Fourteenth Amendment only to enforce rights that *the Court* defined, and no power to define rights itself. The majority had to distinguish a 1966 voting rights case in which it had allowed Congress to do exactly that. (The Court had held that literacy tests did not violate the Fifteenth Amendment; Congress outlawed them in the Voting Rights Act.) It explained this away by saying that Congress had responded to clear evidence of racial discrimination then, but to no such record of religious discrimination now.

One could accuse the Court of picking and choosing among non-economic rights (involving race and religion), inserting a sort of epicycle within the

Carolene orbit. This resembled its invention of "intermediate scrutiny" for sex classifications, a new standard of review between rational basis and strict scrutiny. What's more, the dissenters in this case did not defend *Congress's* power but rather favored an earlier judicial determination that *Smith* had over-ruled.[156] As one scholar observed, "Conservative justices . . . proved as intent as liberals on proclaiming judicial supremacy."[157]

Liberals concerned about Republican dominance of the Court after Warren could console themselves with the Bork defeat and the fact that so many Republican justices "grew" to the left after confirmation. Republican presidents had ten unanswered appointments from 1969 to 1991 and had moved the Court only moderately (see Fig. 3). This largely resulted from the progressive hege-mony in the legal academy since early in the century; law schools produced very few conservatives. The rise of the postwar American "meritocracy" also had its impact on the Court. The justices, though more diverse in terms of ethnicity and sex, came increasingly from a small number of Ivy League universities, law schools, and federal appellate court backgrounds. After pass-ing through the bubble of elite educational institutions, the liberal culture of the capital city also had an iaiotropic effect. Economist Thomas Sowell called this "the greenhouse effect"—judges wanted Linda Greenhouse, who covered the Court for the *New York Times,* to write flattering articles about them and produce invitations to smart Georgetown cocktail parties.

The preservation of abortion and affirmative action, the two liberal poli-cies most dependent on judicial support, turned the "Reagan revolution" into what law professor Bruce Ackerman called a "failed constitutional moment," an unsuccessful effort to roll back the informal constitutional amendments of the Great Society and New Deal.[158] In 1996, the conservative journal *First Things* caused quite a stir with a symposium entitled "The End of Democracy? The Judicial Usurpation of Politics," which mused about whether the Court had produced a regime that had become "destructive of the ends for which governments are established." Some of its most prominent editors resigned in the face of this expression of quasi-revolutionary despair.[159] A decade later, conservatives remained the principal critics of the federal courts.[160]

But the Court's intervention in the 2000 presidential election provoked opposition to judicial supremacy from the Left. *Bush v. Gore* arose from the bold assertion of judicial power by the Florida supreme court. The elec-toral vote of that state would determine the winner of the closest election in American history. It began when the Court countermanded a decision by the Republican secretary of state to certify the election results which put Republican George W. Bush about three hundred votes ahead out of nearly 6 million votes cast in the state. The Florida Court ordered a re-recount that was tailor-made for the Democratic candidate to continue.[161] As two political scientists observed, "That a court could feel confident enough to take this step, knowing that its orders would be followed, speaks volumes about the power of courts in America today."[162]

The US Supreme Court intervened, insisting that the Florida court explain its decision in light of the fact that the US Constitution, not Florida law, controlled the presidential election process, and that it left that process to the state legislatures, not the courts. Article II says, "Each state shall appoint, in such manner as the legislature thereof may direct, a number of electors." The Republican Florida legislature might at any point have chosen its own slate of electors—a scenario that Stanford law professor Pamela Karlan inevitably likened to the "massive resistance" that had followed the *Brown* decision.

The Florida high court remained defiant, and in December it ordered its re-recount to continue. The US Supreme Court overturned that order a few days later. Seven of the justices agreed that the Florida court scheme violated the equal protection clause, but only the five "Republican" justices held that Florida could not conduct a fair recount before the deadline that Congress had established for the electors to be accepted.[163] The loser, Senator Al Gore, accepted the decision, along with everyone else.[164] One scholar noted that the case "indicated how completely America conceded ultimate authority over constitutional issues to the justices."[165]

Liberals went into paroxysms of denunciation of the Court. New York University law professor Larry Kramer entitled his 170-page "foreword" to the *Harvard Law Review* "We the Court." He and others promoted what they called "popular constitutionalism" in opposition to judicial supremacy. His book *The People Themselves* echoed the *First Things* call to revolution or mobocracy, and many liberals believed that he had gone overboard.[166]

But liberals had needlessly scared themselves. Notwithstanding those who called the Rehnquist Court "the most activist in history," it produced no genuinely conservative activism.[167] Truly conservative activism would mean declaring a color-blind constitutional rule to outlaw racial preferences, declaring the unborn to be Fourteenth Amendment persons, or holding that a progressive income tax violated the uniformity clause of Article I or the equal protection clause. More acute observers called it "judicial reactivism."[168]

Conservatives did extend some liberal principles, especially the incorporation of the Bill of Rights, for conservative ends. The courts revived the takings clause of the Fifth Amendment, just about the only Bill of Rights provision that had to do with property rights. Led by the "law and economics" movement and academics like Richard Epstein, courts began to limit government regulations as amounting to uncompensated takings. But like the neo-federalism cases, this did not amount to much, especially after the Court adopted a permissive definition of "public use" in the 2005 *Kelo* case.[169]

In 2008 and 2010, the Court denominated the Second Amendment right to bear arms an individual right and "incorporated" or applied it to the states.[170] Nobody expected the liberal Warren Court to include the right to bear arms in its wave of incorporations. Liberals showed no concern for this right (at least for the law-abiding).[171] "If I were writing the Bill of Rights now," Chief Justice Burger said in retirement, "there wouldn't be any such thing as the Second Amendment."[172] Justice Scalia drew upon a bevy of recent historical revisionism on the Second Amendment and held for the right on originalist grounds. This represented a conservative incorporation turnabout. A more old-fashioned originalist might have held that the Bill of Rights did not apply to the states and that the Second Amendment, like the rest of the Bill of Rights, principally concerned the preservation of state control over its own institutions, like the militia, and not individual rights. One commentator noted that gun ownership had *become* a part of American culture, whatever its status had been in that culture in 1791.[173]

Some observers pointed out that these cases did not really change much; they declared an abstract right but left most existing gun control laws alone. In this way, conservatives may have followed the camel's-nose approach of liberal activists, planting the seeds for further expansions of the right, as when *Griswold*'s right to contraception became the right to abortion a decade later.[174] Liberals also groused loudly when the Court struck down the McCain–Feingold campaign finance law in *Citizens United,* but even the harshest critics of the Roberts Court admit the complexity of the issue.[175] One could call the act itself something of a monument to judicial supremacy. When President George W. Bush signed it, he said that he had doubts about its constitutionality but would rely on the Court to relieve him of his duty to interpret the Constitution for himself.

Most of the judicial activism of the new century continued to advance liberal causes, even though Republicans continued to compose the Court majority. After several decades of an overwhelmingly liberal-dominated supply line to the bench, the rise of a conservative counternetwork, centered on the Federalist Society, made little impact. While the liberals on the Court stood as one, the Republicans were split between older, traditional (or "country club") Republicans and younger, movement conservatives.[176]

Conservatives also had their own fissures, similar to those of liberals after 1937. Positivists like Bork and Scalia counseled judicial restraint; natural law–oriented and libertarian academics felt more comfortable with conservative activism. The libertarians called for "judicial engagement" in the protection of property rights.[177] Chief Justice John Roberts chiefly wanted to preserve the Court's power and prestige.

The Court's liberal bias appeared most evidently in the cases concerning homosexual rights. The Warren Court had shown scant regard for this group's rights claims. In 1967, it permitted the Immigration and Naturalization Service to deport an immigrant because the INS considered homosexual conduct inherently "psychopathic."[178] In 1986, the Court upheld a Texas criminal sodomy law over a right-to-privacy challenge. Justice White dryly observed that to call homosexual conduct "deeply rooted in this nation's history and traditions . . . is, at best, facetious."[179]

In 2003, however, Justice Kennedy extended the "mystery passage" to sodomy and held that homosexuals were "entitled to respect for their private lives."[180] His reiteration of that extravagant passage testified to his widely seen pomposity and self-importance.[181] It further elaborated the psychotherapeutic ethos of emotivism that had been rising in the twentieth century and found its first expression in the "hearts and minds" analysis of *Brown*.[182] This provoked Justice Scalia to object that the Court had "signed on to the homosexual agenda" and "taken sides in the culture war." He and other critics noted that the decision must lead to striking down laws that limited marriage to heterosexuals and toward the abolition of all morals-based exercises of the police power.[183] This finally came about in the 2015 *Obergefell* case, which reflected the astonishingly rapid change in public opinion about homosexuality in the new century.[184]

The *Carolene Products* standard of strict judicial review for "personal" rights like sexual behavior and relaxed review for "economic" rights came out in the other major decision of the 2014 term, on the Affordable Care Act. Here the Court showed its willingness to abet the new administrative state, engaging in some of the most impressive interpretive contortions in its history. Chief Justice John Roberts concocted a true tour de force in the first significant challenge to the ACA, the *Sebelius* case in 2012.

The ACA depended on the "universal mandate," the requirement that everyone purchase health insurance. It also assumed that the states would expand their Medicaid programs because the federal government offered generous matching funds and severe penalties—the cutoff of all Medicaid matching funds—if they did not. The Court held that the requirement to purchase health insurance did not constitute a valid exercise of the commerce power but that it could pass as a legitimate exercise of the taxing power—despite the fact that the act referred to the mandate's enforcement not as a tax but as a regulatory penalty and that its sponsors repeatedly hid from calling it a tax, even as they made the Internal Revenue Service the enforcer of the mandate. Then, for the first time, the Court imposed limits on Congress's spending power: Congress could not tell the states that they must establish insurance exchanges or lose all of their federal matching funds.[185]

Consequently, thirty-six states did not establish state insurance exchanges. The Internal Revenue Service decided that people who enrolled in exchanges established by the states could get federal subsidies through federal exchanges in those states that did not play ball.[186] The Court sustained the IRS interpretation and again rescued the ACA. It effectively rewrote a law that now-minority congressional Democrats were no longer in a position to fix. Exchanges established "by the states" now included exchanges *not* established by the states.

Many thought Chief Justice Roberts had saved the ACA in order to save his Court's power; he wanted to prevent critics from labeling it a "Republican" court.[187] In this case, the Court continued its postwar double standard or preferred freedoms jurisprudence, acting vigorously when non-economic or minority rights presented themselves (as in the same term's homosexual marriage decision) while letting Congress regulate economic matters, like the health care industry—not only permitting it, but helping it to do so. The old constitutional system, which should have *prevented* the establishment of an unconstitutional fourth branch, instead threw its weight behind the new bureaucratic system. But the Court retained the final say as to how far the bureaucrats could go, acting as the "high commission" of the administrative state.[188]

Some important restraints on judicial power remained. In 1983, the Court declared the legislative veto unconstitutional.[189] This device arose in the twentieth century and abetted the administrative state—Congress delegated legislative power to the executive or to independent agencies but reserved the prerogative to overrule their decisions, essentially reversing the order of Articles I and II. But Congress largely ignored the Court and continued the practice of legislative veto. Because of the difficulty to getting cases before the Court (due to the lack of adverse parties), the adjudication of this apparently political question had no effect.

Foreign policy represented another area where the Court traditionally restrained itself. The Burger Court overturned a rogue federal district court that tried to enjoin President Nixon's Cambodian bombing (over the dissent of the ever-roguish Justice Douglas).[190] Many have disputed the constitutionality of the War Powers Act since its 1973 enactment. It presented another kind of legislative veto, in which Congress essentially gave the president the power to initiate a war but required congressional approval within sixty days. The Court never ruled on it, leaving it to the political branches to work out. During the post-9/11 "war on terror," the Court did say that detainees, even irregular combatants, had a constitutional right to have a court consider their status. But the Court did not render these decisions until some years after the 9/11 attacks, akin to its *post*war defenses of civil liberties in the Civil War, World War II, and the Cold War.

The Court remained responsible mostly to itself. In 1997, for example, it declined to read a right to assisted suicide into the Constitution. In a tone that one can only call haughty, Justice Souter said, "The Court should stay its hand and allow reasonable legislative consideration. While I do not decide for all time that respondents' claim should not be recognized, I acknowledge the legislative institutional competence as the better one to deal with this claim at this time."[191]

JURISTOCRACY IN THE STATES AND ABROAD

The US Supreme Court's power attracted emulators in the state courts and around the world. In 1977, afraid that the Nixon justices would take the Supreme Court in a conservative direction, Justice William Brennan called on state courts to pick up the slack.[192] Ten years later he counted some 250 cases in which state courts held that their own constitutions had more capacious guarantees than the US Constitution. He exhorted the state courts to act as what he fancied the old Warren Court had, "the keeper of the nation's conscience."[193] Liberals had reason to favor the states, whose constitutions often contained grants of "positive rights" or entitlements, unlike the "negative rights" protection of the US Constitution.[194] In 2001, future president Barack Obama lamented that America had not broken free from the "essential constraints that were placed by the Founding Fathers in the Constitution . . . that generally the Constitution is a charter of negative liberty."

Many state courts followed Brennan's advice, especially his own, the New Jersey supreme court, which was notoriously hidebound until a 1947 constitutional revision energized it. State judiciaries had become more democratic during the nineteenth century; progressives who saw the potential for judicial power wanted to reverse this trend, to insulate courts from public influence.[195] New Jersey adopted a judicial system that moved back toward, rather than away from, the insulated federal judicial model of Article III. The governor appointed the justices with the advice and consent of the Senate, for a seven-year term. If reappointed, they served until age seventy.

The Jersey justices turned cheeky from the outset. Arthur Vanderbilt, a prominent New Jersey jurist and law school dean, advised the constitution makers that the Court, not the legislature, should set the Court's procedural rules. Though the legislators did not heed his advice, Vanderbilt became chief justice in 1947 and imposed his preferred position anyway.[196] Vanderbilt forthrightly denounced "so-called judicial deference," saying that "we will do well to avoid falling into the same error in this state," though at least one dissenter warned about "judicial supremacy in rule making."[197]

Much like the adoption of the Federal Rules of Civil Procedure in 1938, the power over procedural questions (standing, mootness, ripeness, class actions, and especially equitable procedures and remedies) had a great impact on substantive law. Above all, it allowed the Court to expand its jurisdiction and remedies. When the US Supreme Court held that the Constitution did not require equal education spending, the New Jersey court held that the state constitution's guarantee of a "thorough and efficient" education did require this.[198] Governor Richard Hughes could not compel the legislature to enact an income tax to fund the schools. Then he became chief justice and ordered the schools closed until Trenton provided the money for them. "They didn't want an income tax then?" he said. "They'll want one now."[199] The state court similarly promoted low-cost housing and made significant changes in criminal procedure and tort law. It pioneered the development of a "right to die" in the Karen Ann Quinlan case. Republican governor Chris Christie took on the Court in the 2010s, not very successfully, and his opponents likened his resistance to judicial supremacy to the white South's resistance to *Brown*.[200]

Many other state judges caught the supremacist bug. California under Roger Traynor resembled New Jersey in the 1940s. Michigan became liberally active in the 1950s. North Carolina picked up in the 1970s.[201] Conservatives in the states of the mountain West chafed at liberal courts.[202] A 1988 study indicated that once a court became activist, it stayed that way, though California's liberals suffered a setback in 1986 when voters opposed to its anti–death penalty decisions ousted three incumbents in an election.[203]

The New Jersey example suggested that insulation from democratic accountability fed rather than checked judicial power, but elected judges more often took their popular mandate as a license to overawe the people's representatives.[204] As a result, judicial elections became more contentious and expensive.[205] Several state courts paved the way for the US Supreme Court's homosexual marriage decision in 2015. Notably, when Hawaii's high court struck down a heterosexual-only marriage law, the people of that state amended their constitution to overturn the decision. But then the US Supreme Court required all states to recognize homosexual marriage.[206]

The volatile 1960–70s produced the "litigious society" that opened the courts to all sorts of new victim groups and their grievances. The new millennium looked to produce a "therapeutic judiciary," hinting at in the "hearts and minds" social psychology of *Brown* and the general *Gefühlzjuriprudenz* of the Warren era. One political scientist found, in a federal district court, "a judge with microphone in hand, roaming the floor of the courtroom rather than sitting behind her bench. Like a therapist or social worker, she asks personal questions of the offenders turned 'clients' before her and encourages them in their battles against drug dependency and other criminal behaviors."[207]

In 2007, Tennessee judge Frank V. Williams described the transformation of state courts into planning bodies and social engineering boards. The expansion of tort liability widened the opportunity for judges to redress new grievances: "Every person is becoming a guarantor of the health and happiness of every other person." The new system was marked by new kinds of courts that oversaw ongoing "treatment"—drug courts, family courts, and the like.[208]

Judges in the new century had begun to implement the ideas of the countercultural revolution of the 1960s. Congress created the State Justice Institute in 1984 to improve state courts. Its conferences of state judges produced "utopian political manifestos, advancing sweeping proposals for the eventual creation of a judicial system radically different." Political scientist James A. Dator regarded judges as "more likely to be aware of cutting-edge matters— new technologies, now social movements—well ahead of the average legislator or voter . . . no one else in society has the ability or the will to make socially significant decisions from the perspective of general morality and philosophy that our judges have."[209] This accorded with the thinking of law professors like Michael Perry, who believed that judges in America occupied the role of prophets in Old Testament Israel.[210] (Not for nothing did Franklin Roosevelt refer to Louis Brandeis as "Old Isaiah.") Brennan sounded like this when he likened the Court to "the conscience of the nation," and the joint opinion in *Casey* similarly exhorted the American public to test itself by following the Court's lead "to speak for them before all others."

In a fittingly ironic conclusion to this history, the United States exported judicial supremacy, the most undemocratic and dysfunctional part of its constitutional system, to the wider world.[211] Before World War II, only the United States and (for whatever reason) Norway had judicial review.[212] After the war, the Norwegian supreme court followed the "preferred freedoms" model of the Warren Court and became more activist.[213] Judicial power became a part of some postwar constitutions that the United States and the Allies imposed or helped to contrive. African and Asian countries also adopted it when they won independence from European colonial powers. European nations established new transnational tribunals to enforce declarations of rights modeled on, but much more extensive than, the American Bill of Rights. Many included "positive rights" to education, housing, or health care, like those in American state constitutions. More bills of rights and rights guarantees came with the post–Cold War constitutions of former communist states.

The European Court of Justice made itself the most powerful institution on the continent. Originally intended to deal with interstate disputes, it expanded its reach to overturn law within the member states. Left-wing intellectual Perry Anderson recently noted that the European court's "proceedings are hidden from public scrutiny; its decisions permit no admission of dissent; its archives grant minimal access to researchers." Its judges (originally including many fascists and Nazis) face no public accountability and enjoy generous salaries. The aptly named Robert Lecourt, who became president (chief justice) in 1967, made John Marshall look like an amateur. He undertook "a systematic 'campaign of seduction'" of European officials, including champagne brunches, "aimed at disarming resistance to the supremacy it claimed." Only unanimous agreement of the member states can overrule its decisions by treaty revision. Thus, they "are set not in stone, but in granite." They represent the social and cultural values of the global elite, highly political decisions written in obfuscatory legalese that also helps to avert scrutiny. One commissioner declared that "no sane and sensible person" could read them. The court presents "enormous cryptograms beyond the patience or grasp of any democratic public." Anderson concluded, "It would be difficult to conceive of a judicial institution in the West that, from its tenebrous origins onward, was purer of any trace of democratic accountability."[214]

Judicial supremacism finally came even to Great Britain, which had long provided the model of complete parliamentary sovereignty. In 2010, it established a supreme court (to take the place held by the House of Lords), which quickly began to throw its weight around regarding the Brexit controversy.[215]

All of this amounts to what Israeli political scientist Ran Hirschl called "juristocracy," the globalization of American-style judicial supremacy.[216] Postwar global elites assumed that democracy required an independent judiciary to prevent majority tyranny. For them, the term "constitutionalism" became synonymous with juristocracy. They believed, as the US Supreme Court put it in *Casey*, that "the rule of law is not readily separable from [a people's] understanding of the Court invested with the authority to decide their constitutional cases and speak before all others for their constitutional ideals." Courts must take the place of traditional institutions that modernity had undermined, to make "value" choices for deracinated and disoriented mass man.[217] These elites believed that Nazism and fascism had arisen from populist nationalism, as many American intellectuals would distrust a democracy that produced Joseph McCarthy, Richard Nixon, and Donald Trump. This resembled the *Carolene* justification—the US Supreme Court's shift from protecting property rights to protecting minority rights took place as European totalitarianism loomed large.[218]

Hirschl traced juristocracy in Canada, New Zealand, Israel, and South Africa and found that it followed the adoption of major constitutional changes—adoptions of new written constitutions or "fundamental" or "basic" laws and bills of rights. He saw it as the device of hegemonic elites—Anglophone Canadians, whites in South Africa, and Ashkenazi Jews in Israel—who feared that rising minorities might soon overwhelm them. Robert Bork similarly saw global judicial power as an arm of a "new class" with values like those of the American legal elite.[219] They promoted women's rights (especially abortion), equality for homosexuals, and "expressive" freedom, and denigrated traditional, especially religious, and communitarian values. They thus represented a kind of international libertarian movement, promoting global economic competition and "neoliberal" economic policy, reinforced by institutions like the International Monetary Fund and the World Bank.

New Zealand, for example, rapidly dismantled its welfare state and saw increased economic inequality after it established juristocracy. High levels of income inequality marked all of these countries (and the United States as well). A New Zealand law professor suggested that juristocracy, like "woke capitalism," reflected a deliberate diversion by these elites: promoting causes like minority rights provided a cost-free mode of "virtue signaling" to conceal their promotion of economic policies that enrich themselves.[220] Hirschl essentially revived the progressive view of a century ago, in which the adoption of the US Constitution and judicial review served as masks for an oligarchical coup.

This story ends where it began, with Hebrew judges. Israel has adopted the most extreme form of judicial supremacy. It showed that a country can have "constitutional law" and juristocracy without a written constitution. Israel has instead "basic laws" that define it, for example, as Jewish and democratic but that give no guidance as to what to do when those values may conflict. The law does explicitly provide for judicial review and discretion, however. "Where a court finds that a question requiring a decision cannot be answered by reference to an enactment or a judicial precedent or by way of analogy, it shall decide the same in light of the principles of freedom, justice, equity, and peace of the heritage of Israel."[221] The American Constitution made the federal judges independent but not self-perpetuating. Israel went further, making the supreme court judges part of the judicial selection process. This court can pack itself.

Aharon Barak was Israel's John Marshall and Earl Warren combined. He turned the Knesset's basic laws into unrepealable constitutional provisions. He invented his own standard of "reasonableness" to hold government acts unconstitutional. His claim to jurisdiction went as far as Pope Boniface VIII's.[222] "Nothing falls beyond the purview of judicial review," he said. "The world is full of law; anything and everything is justiciable." As sixth circuit court of appeals judge Richard Posner put it, "Barak merely carries to its logical extreme a tendency discernible in our own courts." Robert Bork said that Barak "established a world record for judicial hubris."[223] Critics said Barak represented the economic and social interests of Ashkenazi Jews fearful of their demographic decline, and the cultural viewpoint of a secular minority over both democratic and Jewish values, consulting what he called "the views of the enlightened community in Israel" in hard cases. The original book of Judges lamented that "there was no king in Israel." In the ancient world, God replaced the judges with kings. In today's juristocracy, the judge has become the king.

APPENDIX A

"LAW AND EQUITY"

The Constitution refers to four kinds of jurisdiction or courts. Article III mentions "all cases, in law and equity," and "all cases of admiralty and maritime jurisdiction."[1] "Admiralty and maritime jurisdiction" refers to equivalent and very specialized areas of law involving war and international trade on the high seas, and this has almost never commanded wide public attention.[2] These laws concerned privateering—using merchant ships as a navy, whence the quaint power to issue "letters of marque and reprisal," and the distribution of prizes thus taken—now abolished throughout the world. It also includes things like "salvage" (the saving of distressed ships) and the labor practices, crimes, and torts peculiar to the seas.

The real tension lay between "law and equity." "Law" meant the common law, the English system of criminal and civil law that most Americans knew and still recognize. "Equity" comprised a special branch of law, often with a separate court system, that has often caused controversy.

We usually define law as a general and prospective rule by which people can and must conduct themselves. But no general law can secure justice in all particular circumstances. Hard cases always arise in which the application of a general rule or "the letter of the law" will produce substantial injustice. Equity therefore arises out of the need to make exceptions to law's inevitably fallible generality.

Aristotle's *Nicomachean Ethics* distinguished the legal from the equitable (or "decent").[3] "The equitable he calls just—not *legally* just but a correction of legal justice," because "all law is universal but about some things it is not possible to make a universal statement which shall be correct" (emphasis mine). The problem arises from the nature of the thing, the subject matter of human relations. "When the law speaks universally and a case arises which is not covered by a universal statement," the judge should say what the legislator *would have said* had he faced the situation. We might call Aristotle the original originalist. "This is the nature of the equitable, a correction of law where it is defective owing to its universality." For some matters we find it impossible to lay down a *law*; we need a *decree.* Most consider equity as a subset of law (as in the maxim "equity follows the law"), but really it rises above the law, comparable to natural law or natural justice. As the medieval philosopher Robert Grosseteste put it, equity lies "halfway between legal and natural justice."[4]

In *Rhetoric,* Aristotle called equity a law "that makes up for the defects of a community's written code of law. . . . It is, in fact, the sort of justice which goes beyond written laws." It applies to "forgivable actions" and errors of judgment. "Equity bids us be merciful to the weakness of human nature." He recognized the danger of letting equitable exceptions swallow the rule, and of judicial lawmaking. "It is of great moment that well-drawn laws should themselves define all the points they possibly can and leave as few as possible to the decision of the judges. . . . Laws are made after long consideration, whereas decisions in the courts are given at short notice. . . . The decision of the lawgiver is not particular but prospective and general. . . . In general, the judge should be allowed to decide as few things as possible."[5]

No juristocrat, Aristotle! His followers continued to recognize the potential danger in equity. Francisco Suarez, in the seventeenth century, wrote that "he whose part it is to establish the law is the one to interpret it," and warned that interpretation did not include altering the law.[6]

A classic example involves the general rule that one should return borrowed property. But what if a friend lent you his firearms and he then became insane? Should you then return them? A similar need for exceptions arises in the general rule against lying: Do you reveal Anne Frank's attic hiding spot when the Gestapo inquires?

As Alexander Hamilton put it in *Federalist* 80, "There is hardly a subject of litigation between individuals which will not involve those ingredients of *fraud, accident, trust,* or *hardship,* which would render the matter an object of equitable rather than of legal jurisdiction. It is the peculiar province, for instance, of a court of equity to relieve against what are called hard bargains: these are contracts in which, though there may have been no direct fraud or deceit sufficient to invalidate them in a court of law, yet there may have been some undue and unconscionable advantage taken of the necessities or misfortunes of one of the parties which a court of equity would not tolerate."

The English kings established courts of equity—or chancery, because chancellors rather than common-law judges presided over them. Chancellors were usually clergymen, familiar with Roman/canon law. As Blackstone noted, courts of equity "never were separated in any other country in the universe."[7] Equity represented "the king's conscience." These courts did not have to follow the elaborate rules of the common-law courts. They employed more flexible procedures, not bound by the peculiar and multifarious writs and pleadings, and especially not beholden to the juries, of the common law.[8] Their methods resembled the Roman and canon (church) law of the European continent, "inquisitorial" rather than "adversarial," more concerned with substantial justice and truth than with procedural safeguards and legalistic chicanery. But many considered them a threat to political liberty. They maximized judicial discretion and might turn arbitrary and abusive.

Equity/chancery composed one of the many "prerogative" courts established by the English kings that became associated with the Tudor and Stuart effort to establish absolute monarchy in the constitutional crisis of the seventeenth century. Equity (unlike the Star Chamber and Court of High Commission) survived that ordeal, but it never completely shed its unsavory reputation. "Equity is a roguish thing," said John Selden in the seventeenth century. "What an uncertain, random and wandering thing it is. It is all according to the chancellor's conscience. You might just as well make a rule of justice according to the length of the chancellor's foot."[9]

Equity arose to deal with uncommon, extraordinary cases. It should not take the place of ordinary legal remedies if available. Ideally, it aided the weak and vulnerable—widows, orphans, the defrauded, and victims of the powerful. One should have access to equity only if one faced irreparable harm without it, only if one had "clean hands" (was not oneself engaged in pettifogging trickery), and only if one had a relatively clear-cut case and a good chance to prevail.

If available, equity courts could act in a summary fashion—without defendant testimony or witnesses, for example—and could grant extraordinary remedies such as the injunction, an order to do or to refrain from doing something. (Common-law courts could only grant monetary damages.) Chancellors granted decrees (as in divorce cases, when nations considered divorce an extraordinary remedy, originally granted only by special legislative act), whereas judges and juries issued judgments.

Equitable jurisdiction became the bête noire of progressives in the early twentieth century, when courts used it, especially via the labor injunction, to break strikes and curb labor unions. Later in the century, progressives in the civil rights movement used it to integrate schools and other institutions, and feminists found it helpful in cases of domestic violence.

The American legal system has amalgamated law and equity over the years. In the nineteenth century, courts of equity adopted adversarial methods; in the twentieth century, law courts adopted equitable ones. This has contributed to an exceptionally litigious American society and has produced perhaps the worst of both worlds.[10] It certainly has abetted juristocracy.

APPENDIX B

THE INCORPORATION MYSTERY

In 1884, a Californian claimed that his state's denial of grand jury indictment violated the Fifth Amendment. The Supreme Court held that it did not. If due process in the amendment constituted just one of several (twenty-six) rights listed in the Bill of Rights, it could not include all the others. This "nonsuperfluous" argument appeared in Justice Stanley Matthews's opinion in *Hurtado v. California.*[1] But in the 1890 Minnesota Rate Case, the Court said that the due process clause of the Fourteenth Amendment included the takings prohibition of the Fifth Amendment, which meant that the Fifth Amendment contained its own superfluity.[2]

Ever since, judges and scholars have asked to what extent the Fourteenth Amendment applied to the states the same rights as the first eight amendments applied to the federal government. There had to be *some* overlap. The framers of the Fourteenth Amendment clearly had something substantive in mind, unless they had enacted a merely declaratory and redundant amendment.[3] This constituted the dispute between the two sides in the *Slaughterhouse Cases.* Many regarded the original Bill of Rights as redundant because it forbade Congress to do things it had no power to do in the absence of the Bill of Rights. But the states' "police power" did not resemble the enumerated powers of Congress—we assume state power unless it is limited by some constitutional provision like those in Article I, section 10. The Bill of Rights, limiting an inherently limited government, needed to do less work than the Fourteenth Amendment, which limited generally unlimited state governments.

On the other hand, (almost) nobody thought that the Fourteenth Amendment applied *all* of the Bill of Rights to the states, and certainly not in precisely the way that it limited the states. Several states, for example, did not guarantee grand jury indictments, and several states did away with them after ratifying the amendment.

This made some kind of "selective" incorporation virtually inevitable. Selective incorporation views the Fourteenth Amendment and Bill of Rights as similar but not identical. In *Palko v. Connecticut* (1938), Justice Cardozo said that selective incorporation applied rights "implicit in the concept of ordered liberty." The "total incorporation" view, proffered by Justice Black in his *Adamson* dissent, held that incorporation applied each and every one of them. This somewhat replicated the dispute at the Council of Nicaea on the relationship of the first and second persons of the Trinity. The Arians, like the selective incorporationists, said that they shared a similar nature (*homoiousious*) but not an identical one (*homoousious*). One might best gauge the similarities by consulting the Civil Rights Act of 1866, which the Fourteenth Amendment intended to make permanent. It might also follow Justice Holmes's argument that it protected "fundamental principles as they have been understood by the traditions of our people and our law."[4]

Selective incorporation won out; some minor provisions of the Bill of Rights still do not apply to the states (such as grand jury indictment or jury trial in civil suits of more than twenty dollars). But in the 1960s, when most of the incorporation took place, the so-called selective-plus position arose—the view that the Fourteenth Amendment applied most of the Bill of Rights plus others not listed there, such as the right to privacy, abortion, or sodomy. This hearkened back to the Marcionites: the new rights of the Fourteenth Amendment had nothing to do with the old rights of the original Bill of Rights.

The new rights could include those of Franklin Roosevelt's "second bill of rights" speeches in 1932 and 1944. In 1932, he called for "an economic declaration of rights, an economic constitutional order," meaning the provision of entitlements or a welfare state by a centralized, bureaucratic state. In 1944, he noted that "this republic had its beginning, and grew to its present strength, under the protection of certain inalienable political rights—among them the right of free speech, free press, free worship, trial by jury, freedom from unreasonable searches and seizures. These were our rights to life and liberty." But the time had come for "a second bill of rights under which a new basis of security can be established," including the right to a job, to adequate farm prices, housing and health care, and education.[5]

Though the Warren Court approached the line of judicial provision of such entitlements, it did not put it over. The new bill of rights does not concern "rights" as the Founding generation understood them at all. Advocates of the new entitlement regime recognize this. Law professor Cass Sunstein has advised, "The best response to those who believe that the second bill of rights does not protect rights at all is just this: unembarrassed evasion."[6]

APPENDIX C

DIRECT TAXES

If the government apportions a tax according to population, a state with 5 percent of the population will pay 5 percent of the tax and a state with 20 percent of the population will pay 20 percent of the tax. Most historians agree that the Founders defined direct taxes as those on persons (capitation, or "head taxes") and land.

Capitation taxes apportion themselves. The three-fifths clause complicated it, counting five slaves as three persons. This would reduce the tax liability of the slave states—as they meant it to. A tax on real estate would weigh more heavily on states with large populations and little land, or on states with a lot of not very valuable land.

A tax on slaves presented a very special case, because some states had no slaves. If, for example, South Carolina has 10 percent of the national population and 50 percent of its slaves, Virginia has 50 percent of the population and 10 percent of its slaves, and Massachusetts has 10 percent of the population and no slaves, Massachusetts would have to pay 10 percent of the tax but without having anything to tax. Likewise, the tax on slaves would fall much more heavily on Virginia than on South Carolina.

Congress enacted a direct tax to raise $2 million in 1798. It apportioned it by the "federal" population (taking the three-fifths clause into account): $345,000 for Virginia, $260,000 for Massachusetts, and so on. It taxed land and slaves. It first laid a flat tax of fifty cents on each slave. It assessed the remainder of each state's quota according the value of real estate in the state.[1]

Such a tax resembled the "requisition" upon which the Articles of Confederation relied. Article VIII said that common expenses "shall be defrayed out of a common treasury, which shall be supplied by the several states in proportion to the value of all land within each state . . . estimated according to such mode as" Congress would prescribe. It never used this system, and states did not meet their quotas.

The 1798 tax established a corps of federal tax collectors to estimate the value of property. Later direct tax legislation told the states that they could get a discount if they collected their quota themselves—essentially, the old confederation system.[2] The Founders considered direct taxes to be reserved for extraordinary occasions such as wartime. Congress adopted them in 1798, on the verge of a war with France, during the War of 1812, and in the Civil War.[3]

For more than a century, federal revenue came primarily from the tariff—an impost or duty—and from excise taxes on alcohol. Most considered these indirect in the sense that citizens could avoid them by not importing goods or purchasing liquor, and businesses could transfer their cost to the consumer.

The desire to tax incomes in the late nineteenth century came about because the tariff and excise taxes burdened the poor as much as the rich consumer (and thus was regressive taxation). Populists wanted to shift the burden of taxation onto the rich, so they taxed income, of which the rich had more, and exempted the first $4,000 of income, which excluded about 98 percent of the population. But if Congress apportioned the tax, it would fall more heavily on the poor states—or, more accurately, on the rich in the poor states.

Imagine two states with the same population, but with one state having ten times the income of the other. The tax would fall ten times as heavily on the poorer state. This would defeat the whole purpose of the income tax. While mathematically possible, Congress found it politically impossible to apportion an income tax. A $1 trillion income tax apportioned today would mean a rate of 9 percent for the richest state (Connecticut) and an 18 percent rate for the poorest (Mississippi).[4]

NOTES

INTRODUCTION

1. "Brutus" stands out here.
2. Wolfe, *The Rise of Modern Judicial Review*.
3. Ross, *A Muted Fury*.
4. Hamburger, *Law and Judicial Duty*.
5. Whittington, *The Political Foundations of Judicial Supremacy*.
6. Lincoln knew that the Court was legislating. He perhaps called the Court back to a proper standard of judicial behavior.
7. Bickel, *The Least Dangerous Branch*.

1. BEFORE THE CONSTITUTION

1. Boecker, *Law and the Administration of Justice*; Knierim, "Customs, Judges, and Legislators in Ancient Israel."
2. Moshe Weinfeld, "Judge and Officer in Ancient Israel and the Ancient Near East." Michael Perry has revived the idea of a prophetic role for judges. See Zuckert, "Book Review: *Morality, Politics and Law*, by Michael Perry," 446.
3. "Antidote for the Scorpion's Sting," in Dunn, *Tertullian*, 113.
4. John Wyclif, "Civil Lordship," chapter 27 [62d], in O'Donovan and O'Donovan, *From Irenaeus to Grotius*, 506.
5. One can interpret David's order regarding the spoils of war in 1 Samuel 30:23 as the act of a military commander in chief. See Boecker, *Law and the Administration of Justice*, 41.
6. Knierim, "Customs, Judges, and Legislators in Ancient Israel."
7. Levinson, *Deuteronomy and the Hermeneutics of Legal Innovation*, 110–38; Wilson, "Israel's Judicial System in the Preexilic Period," 229–48; McBride, "Polity of the Covenant People," 240–41.
8. Scullard, *A History of the Roman World*, 370; Kroger, "The Philosophical Foundations of Roman Law," 940.
9. Ehrenberg, *From Solon to Socrates*, 13, 288; J. M. Kelly, *A Short History of Western Legal Theory*; "Miscellany," 368.
10. Bartrum, "The People's Court," 283.
11. Forsdyke, "Ancient and Modern Conceptions of the Rule of Law," 184–212; Lanni, "Judicial

Review and the Athenian 'Constitution,'" 235–76; Goodell, "An Athenian Parallel to a Function of Our Supreme Court," 64–73; Hansen, "The Political Powers of the People's Court," 237–39.

12. Cammack, "The Popular Courts in Athenian Democracy"; Stockton, *The Classical Athenian Democracy.*

13. Berman, *Law and Revolution,* 12.

14. Liebs, *Summoned to the Roman Courts,* 1; Kunkel, *An Introduction to Roman Legal and Constitutional History,* 67, 72.

15. Bablitz, "Courts, Roman."

16. Goldsworthy, *Pax Romana,* 308.

17. Liebs, *Summoned to the Roman Courts,* 95; Wilson, *The Execution of Jesus,* 130.

18. Liebs, *Summoned to the Roman Courts,* 12.

19. Berman, *Law and Revolution.*

20. Maine, *Ancient Law,* 39.

21. Greenberg and Sechler, "Constitutionalism Ancient and Early Modern."

22. Berman and Reid, "The Transformation of English Legal Science," 444.

23. Cromartie, *The Constitutionalist Revolution.*

24. On the contrast of English common law with Dutch civil law in New York, see Nelson, *The Common Law in Colonial America,* 2:19.

25. Tamanaha, *On the Rule of Law,* 23.

26. *The True Law of Free Monarchies,* 723.

27. Butterfield, *The Englishman and His History,* 40, 53.

28. Holdsworth, *Some Makers of English Law,* 132.

29. Berman, "Origins of Historical Jurisprudence." Americans have used the titles Chief Justice of the United States and Chief Justice of the Supreme Court at different times in US history—Warren, *The Supreme Court in United States History,* 11.

30. *Prohibitions del Roy* (1607), in *The Selected Writings of Sir Edward Coke,* 1:481. See also Usher, "James I and Sir Edward Coke"; Cope, "Sir Edward Coke and Proclamations"; Jones, *Politics and the Bench,* 28.

31. Smith, *Sir Edward Coke and the Reformation of the Laws.* A similar conflict would arise in nineteenth-century America between advocates of "codification" and defenders of the common law.

32. Cromartie, *The Constitutionalist Revolution,* 216.

33. For a dissenting view on its significance, see McDowell, "Coke, Corwin, and the Constitution." For a more recent and balanced treatment, see Helmholz, "Bonham's Case, Judicial Review, and the Law of Nature"; and Spigelman, "Lions in Conflict," 24.

34. *Dr. Bohnam's Case* (1610), in Coke, *The Selected Writings of Sir Edward Coke,* 1:275.

35. *Of the High and Most Honorable Court of Parliament* (1644), in Coke, *The Selected Writings of Sir Edward Coke,* 3:1133.

36. Boyer, "'Understanding, Authority, and Will,'" 81–83; Smith, *Sir Edward Coke and the Reformation of the Laws,* 101, 264.

37. Boyer, "'Understanding, Authority, and Will,'" 86.

38. *Rowles v. Mason* (1612).

39. *Bagg's Case* (1615), in Coke, *The Selected Writings of Sir Edward Coke,* 1:413.

40. Cromartie, *Constitutionalist Revolution,* 212.

41. *Day v. Savadge* (1614).

42. *London v. Wood* (1702); Hamburger, "Revolution and Judicial Review," 2091–2153.

43. Smith, *Sir Edward Coke*, 101; Hill, *Intellectual Origins of the English Revolution*, 236.

44. Bilder, "Charter Constitutionalism" doubts this.

45. Stoner, *Common Law and Liberal Theory*, 189.

46. Shannon C. Stimson notes that the British see Coke as the father of parliamentary supremacy and Americans see him as originating judicial review. Stimson, *The American Revolution in the Law*.

47. Butterfield, *The Englishman and His History*, 53.

48. Several justices dissented in the *Ship Money* case, holding that the court could declare royal acts unconstitutional. Graber, "Ship Money."

49. Coke may have said "no saving" rather than "no sovereign," but it amounted to the same thing. Stoner, *Common Law and Liberal Theory*, 46; Hill, *Intellectual Origins of the English Revolution*, 219.

50. Jones, *Politics and the Bench*, 137–47.

51. "The Nineteen Propositions to Charles I and his Answer." Propositions 3, 11, and 12 concerned the judges. Charles did not respond to them directly. Smith, "An Independent Judiciary," 1106.

52. Nourse, "Law Reform Under the Commonwealth and Protectorate," 516; "Mr. Justice Van Devanter and the Common Law 'Writ of Ease.'"

53. Bartrum, "The People's Court."

54. Smith, "An Independent Judiciary"; Havighurst, "The Judiciary and Politics in the Reign of Charles II," 76, 233, 247; Watkins, *Judicial Monarchs*, 49.

55. Berman and Reid, "The Transformation of English Legal Science," 444; McIlwain, "The English Common Law."

56. Reid, "The Jurisprudence of Liberty," 256.

57. Hobbes, *Leviathan*, 1:15.

58. Finnis, "The Truth in Legal Positivism," 195.

59. Hobbes, "A Dialogue of the Common Law," 6:5.

60. Stevens, "The Act of Settlement and the Questionable History of Judicial Independence." Parliament has never removed a British judge by bill of address.

61. Locke, *The Second Treatise of Government*, section 91.

62. Locke, *The Second Treatise of Government*, sections 134, 136.

63. Locke, *The Second Treatise of Government*, sections 151–52.

64. Coke listed seventy-six kinds of court in the seventeenth century, plus sixteen particular London courts and twelve ecclesiastical courts. A century later Blackstone noted England's "prodigious variety of courts," which included, among the "forest courts," "The Court of Regard, or survey of dogs, to be holden every third year for the lawing or expedition of mastiffs, which is to be done by cutting off the claws of the forefeet, to prevent them from running after deer [in the King's forests]." "Franchise courts" included the "stannaries of Cornwall and Devon," a special court for tin mining. Jones, *Politics and the Bench*, 98.

65. Locke, *The Second Treatise of Government*, section 168.

66. Brian Tierney traces the revival of the Aristotelian tripartite division to the fourteenth century. Tierney, "Hierarchy, Consent, and the 'Western Tradition,'" 649.

67. Montesquieu, *The Spirit of the Laws*, 156–57.

68. Montesquieu, *The Spirit of the Laws*, 158.

69. A "slot machine" originally meant not a gambling device but a protocomputer. Wiecek, *The Lost World of Classical Legal Thought*, 192.

70. Montesquieu, The *Spirit of the Laws*, 160.

71. Manin, "Checks, Balances and Boundaries," 30.

72. Rahe, *Montesquieu and the Logic of Liberty;* Carrese, *The Cloaking of Power.*

73. This would involve the revival of the regional *parlements* (law courts, not legislative bodies), such as that of Bordeaux, in which Montesquieu held the presidency.

74. Carrese, *The Cloaking of Power.*

75. Haines, *The American Doctrine of Judicial Supremacy,* 475.

76. Dennis R. Nolan, "Sir William Blackstone and the New American Republic"; Vile, *Constitutionalism and the Separation of Powers,* 72.

77. Alschuler, "Rediscovering Blackstone."

78. Oldham, "Judicial Activism in Eighteenth-Century Common Law."

79. Or free enough so that he could not be forced to return to the plantations. The significance of the decision (which Mansfield himself tried to walk back) took on a life of its own, and has resurfaced in the controversy over the *New York Times*'s 1619 Project. Wiecek, "*Somerset*"; Silverstein, "We Respond."

80. Ehrlich, *Ehrlich's Blackstone,* 1:55.

81. Ehrlich, *Ehrlich's Blackstone,* 1:33.

82. Carrese, *Cloaking of Power,* 162, 173.

83. Orth, "Blackstone."

84. Oldham, "Judicial Activism."

85. Storing, "William Blackstone," 630.

86. Surrency, "The Courts in the American Colonies," 258.

87. Nelson, *The Common Law in Colonial America,* 2:55; Sydnor, *American Revolutionaries in the Making,* 74–85; Dargo, *Roots of the Republic,* 67–69.

88. They would serve at the pleasure of the proprietor in proprietary colonies (Pennsylvania, Delaware, and Maryland), and at the pleasure of the assembly in the corporate colonies of Connecticut and Rhode Island.

89. Shapiro, "Codification of the Laws in Seventeenth Century England."

90. Sosin, *English America and the Revolution of 1688,* 136.

91. Dumbauld, *The Declaration of Independence and What It Means Today,* 108.

92. Smith, "An Independent Judiciary," 1112.

93. Greene, "The Glorious Revolution and the British Empire," 264.

94. Pittman, "The Emancipated Judiciary in America."

95. Sydnor, *American Revolutionaries in the Making,* 76–78.

96. Gerber, *A Distinct Judicial Power,* 258; Presser, "An Introduction to the Legal History of Colonial New Jersey," 290; Buenger and De Muniz, *American Judicial Power,* 63. Judges did not routinely, or even often, publish their opinions until the nineteenth century.

97. Parmenter, "Nullifying the Jury," 418–19; Greene, "From the Perspective of Law," 58.

98. Klein, "Prelude to Revolution in New York"; Kammen, *Colonial New York,* 346; Dumbauld, *The Declaration of Independence and What It Means Today,* 113.

99. Gerber, *A Distinct Judicial Power*, 235.

100. Nelson, *The Common Law in Colonial America*, 4:142.

101. Smith, *Appeals to the Privy Council*, 523; Bilder, *The Transatlantic Constitution*.

102. Hamburger, *Law and Judicial Duty*, 265; Nelson, *The Common Law in Colonial America*, 4:47.

103. Hamburger, *Law and Judicial Duty*, 256.

104. Gerber, *A Distinct Judicial Power*, 222.

105. Treanor, "Judicial Review Before *Marbury*."

106. Hamburger, *Law and Judicial Duty*, 512.

107. Morris, "Judicial Supremacy and the Inferior Courts," 433.

108. Smith, *Appeals to the Privy Council*, 586; Nelson, *The Common Law in Colonial America*, 4:106; Steinfeld, "The Rejection of Horizontal Judicial Review."

109. Bloomfield, *American Lawyers in a Changing Society*, 39; Hall and Karsten, *The Magic Mirror*, 21.

110. Segado, "James Otis and the Writs of Assistance Case (1761)."

111. His notes are reprinted in Smith, *The Writs of Assistance Case*, 543.

112. Farrell, "The Writs of Assistance and Public Memory."

113. Corwin, "Establishment of Judicial Review. II," 102.

114. Segado, "James Otis and the Writs of Assistance Case"; McDowell, "Coke, Corwin, and the Constitution"; Kramer, *The People Themselves*, 19. Farrell, "The Writs of Assistance and Public Memory" argues that Adams particularly wanted to highlight the primacy of Massachusetts—and himself—in the independence movement.

115. Note the language of "executive courts," indicating the incomplete separation of executive and judicial power.

116. Frohnen, *The American Republic: Primary Sources*, 119.

117. *Robin v. Hardaway* (1772); Ray, "'The Indians of Every Denomination Were Free, and Independent of Us,'" 143.

118. Howard, *The Road from Runnymede*, 146; Ruppert, "How the Stamp Act Did Not Affect Virginia." Edmund Pendleton did the same in Caroline County; see Harrington, "Judicial Review Before John Marshall," 64.

119. Morgan and Morgan, *The Stamp Act Crisis*, 183, 222–29; Nelson, *The Common Law in Colonial America*, 4:115, 127.

120. Parmenter, "Nullifying the Jury"; Bond, "The Quit-Rent System in the American Colonies," 504.

121. Nelson, *The Common Law in Colonial America*, 4:103. Most remember the case for Henry's argument that the king's veto marked him as a tyrant no longer deserving of American allegiance.

122. Morgan and Morgan, *The Stamp Act Crisis*, 134.

123. Sosin, *English America and the Revolution of 1688*, 165.

124. Morgan and Morgan, *The Stamp Act Crisis*, 97, 364. On the fear of the imposition of an Anglican establishment, see Bridenbaugh, *Mitre and Sceptre*, 256.

125. Hamburger, *Law and Judicial Duty*, 513; Hall and Karsten, *The Magic Mirror*, 23; Dumbauld, *The Declaration of Independence and What It Means Today*, 115. The governor scotched the impeachment, but the citizenry then refused to serve as jurors under a servile judge.

126. Maryland judges may have declared the Stamp Act itself unconstitutional, though the details of this "Repudiation Day" tradition remain obscure. Bass, "Repudiation Day."

127. Pittman, "The Supremacy of the Judiciary," 391.

128. Dickerson, "Writs of Assistance," 74.

129. Morris, "Judicial Supremacy and the Inferior Courts in the American Colonies."

130. Harrington, "Judicial Review Before John Marshall," 64.

131. Bailyn et al., *The Great Republic*, 269; Greene, "From the Perspective of Law," 61.

132. Morgan and Morgan, *The Stamp Act Crisis*, 80.

2. THE CONSTITUTION

1. *Pennsylvania v. Connecticut*, 131 U.S. i (1888).

2. Gerber, *A Distinct Judicial Power*, 329. Salary guarantees also varied.

3. Samuelson, "The Constitutional Sanity of James Otis."

4. Vermont also adopted a council of censors when it joined the Union in 1791. It, too, had little impact, and became redundant by the acceptance of judicial review, but it existed until 1869. Haines, *The American Doctrine of Judicial Supremacy*, 82.

5. Gerber, *A Distinct Judicial Power*, 279; Joseph H. Smith, "An Independent Judiciary," 1124.

6. Scott Douglas Gerber notes that Adams reluctantly included bill-of-address removal in the 1780 Massachusetts constitution. Gerber, *A Distinct Judicial Power*, 89.

7. Douglas, "Judicial Review and the Separation of Powers," 183.

8. Morris, "Judicial Supremacy and the Inferior Courts in the American Colonies," 434.

9. Treanor, "Judicial Review Before *Marbury*," 562.

10. Michael, "The Role of Natural Law," 421–90.

11. Scott, "*Holmes v. Walton*"; Boudin, *Government by Judiciary*, 53.

12. Goebel, *Antecedents and Beginnings to 1801*, 126.

13. Goebel, *Antecedents and Beginnings to 1801*, 129; Hamburger, *Law and Judicial Duty*, 562.

14. Watkins, *Judicial Monarchs*, 92; Sherry, "The Founders' Unwritten Constitution."

15. Kramer, *The People Themselves*, 66.

16. Conley, "Rhode Island's Paper Money Issue"; Conley, "The Constitutional Significance of *Trevett v. Weeden* (1786)"; Polishook, "*Trevett v. Weeden* and the Case of the Judges."

17. Snowiss, *Judicial Review and the Law of the Constitution*, 47–59; Hamburger, *Law and Judicial Duty*, 472.

18. Kramer, *The People Themselves*, 69–71, analyzes this distinction.

19. McCarthy, "Presidential Vetoes in the Early Republic."

20. Goebel, *Antecedents and Beginnings*, 100; Harrington, "Judicial Review Before John Marshall," 65; Coleman, "Thomas McKean and the Origin of an Independent Judiciary," 128.

21. This is the theme of Wood, *The Creation of the American Republic*; and Kramer, *The People Themselves*.

22. States with councils of censors condemned legislative interference in judicial process. Hamburger, *Law and Judicial Duty*, 524; Gerber, *Distinct Judicial Power*, 283; Harrington, "Judicial Review Before John Marshall," 67.

23. "Vices of the Political System of the United States" (April 1787), in Kurland and Lerner, *The Founders' Constitution*, 1:16.

24. Letter to Timothy Pickering, December 22, 1814, in Kurland and Lerner, *The Founders' Constitution*, 4:299.

25. This view fumbles on the mention of specific executive powers in Article II, section 2, and the denial of particular legislative powers in Article I, section 9. Johnson, "Homage to Clio," 502.

26. As Representative William Branch Giles pointed out on February 18, 1802. See Ragsdale and Jones, *Debates on the Federal Judiciary,* 1:117.

27. Pfander, "Article I Tribunals," 643–776.

28. Kurland and Lerner, *The Founders' Constitution,* 4:225. For a provocative view that the Constitution allows other removal procedures, see Prakash and Smith, "How to Remove a Federal Judge."

29. One might consider judges of the "inferior courts" as "inferior officers" whose appointment Congress could vest in the president alone, in heads of departments, or in courts of law. Article II, section 2 only specifies "judges of the Supreme Court" as presidentially appointed.

30. *Federalist* 39 and 51.

31. Similarly, Article II, section 1 vests *the* executive power, as opposed to "all legislative powers *herein granted,*" in the president, which suggests plenary executive power, but then goes on to specify certain executive powers in sections 2 and 3.

32. Tucker, *Blackstone's Commentaries* (1803), in Kurland and Lerner, *The Founders' Constitution,* 4:279.

33. Article VI, the "supremacy clause," repeated this language. It declared the "laws of the United States *which shall be made in pursuance*" of the Constitution as the "supreme law of the land." This implied that Article III, section 2 jurisdiction over "the laws of the United States" included those laws *not* made in pursuance of the Constitution—i.e., unconstitutional laws, which the Court would hold void.

34. One peculiar theory is that the exceptions clause applies only to "facts." History and grammar render this reading untenable. Eidsmoe, "The Article III Exceptions Clause." See Fig. 1.

35. Shymansky, "'The Great Bulwark of . . Political Liberties,'" 1735.

36. The argument that "pursuance" meant laws enacted *after ratification* strains credulity. Though the Articles of Confederation referred to treaties, it did not refer to laws. Technically, the Continental Congress had made no laws. Sosin, *The Aristocracy of the Long Robe,* 252, 311.

37. Snowiss, *Judicial Review and the Law of the Constitution;* Nelson, *The Fourteenth Amendment.*

38. Knapp, "The New Jersey Plan and the Structure of the American Union," 615–50.

39. Farrand, *The Records of the Federal Convention of 1787,* 2:76.

40. Farrand, *The Records of the Federal Convention of 1787,* 1:97.

41. Farrand, *The Records of the Federal Convention of 1787,* 1:73–75.

42. Farrand, *The Records of the Federal Convention of 1787,* 2:73; Anderson, "Learning from the Great Council of Revision Debate."

43. Kurland and Lerner, *The Founders' Constitution,* 4:225.

44. Dissent of the Minority of the Pennsylvania Convention (December 18, 1787), in Kaminski and Leffler, *Federalists and Antifederalists,* 133.

45. Maier, *Ratification,* 290.

46. Most identified "Brutus" as Robert Yates; more likely, Melancton Smith was the writer. Treanor, "The Genius of Hamilton," 465.

47. Brutus I (October 18, 1787), in Ragsdale and Jones, *Debates on the Federal Judiciary,* 1:27.

48. Brutus XI (January 31, 1788), in Kaminsky and Leffler, *Federalists and Antifederalists*, 121; Brutus XII (February 7–14, 1788), in Kurland and Lerner, *The Founders' Constitution*, 4:236.

49. Brutus XV (March 20, 1788), Kurland and Lerner, *The Founders' Constitution*, 4:238.

50. Federal Farmer XV (January 18, 1788), in Kurland and Lerner, *The Founders' Constitution*, 4:232.

51. Farmer, Baltimore *Gazette* (1788), in Ragsdale and Jones, *Debates on the Federal Judiciary*, 1:34.

52. *Federalist* 16.

53. From the outset, a de facto geographic quota guided the choice of Supreme Court justices. Washington chose men from the New England, mid-Atlantic, and southern states.

54. Carrese, *The Cloaking of Power*.

55. *Eakin v. Raub*, 12 PA 330 (1825); Alfange, "*Marbury v. Madison*"; Faulkner, *The Jurisprudence of John Marshall*, 200–206.

56. Madison to Jefferson, October 15, 1788, and June 27, 1823, in Kurland and Lerner, *The Founders' Constitution*, 4:252, 341. Although here Madison treated federal or vertical review, the same principle applied.

57. This contrasts sharply with the praise of the civil jury in Story, *Commentaries on the Constitution of the United States*; and Tocqueville, *Democracy in America*, 258–64.

58. Langbein, "The Disappearance of Civil Trial."

59. Main, *The Antifederalists*, 155–58.

60. James Wilson, speech of December 7, 1787, and Oliver Ellsworth, speech of January 7, 1788, in Kurland and Lerner, *The Founders' Constitution*, 4:229, 232.

61. Geyh, *When Courts and Congress Collide*, 30.

62. John Marshall, speech on the judiciary (June 20, 1788), in Hobson, *Marshall: Writings*, 38; Sosin, *Aristocracy of the Long Robe*, 268. Marshall, like John Randolph, extolled the need for judicial protection against legislative bills of attainder, illustrated by the outlawing of Josiah Philips, though the legislature may not actually have attainted Philips. Turner, "A Phantom Precedent."

63. State House Yard speech (October 6, 1787), in Kaminski and Leffler, *Federalists and Antifederalists*, 167.

64. The term "manifest tenor" suggests review limited to clear, not doubtful, cases.

65. Goldwin, *From Parchment to Power*; Bowling, "'A Tub to the Whale.'"

66. Magliocca, *The Heart of the Constitution*, 35

67. Jefferson to Madison, March 15, 1789.

68. Jones, "Lessons from a Lost Constitution."

69. *Annals of Congress*, 1st Cong., 1st Sess. (1789), 439.

70. Amar, "The Bill of Rights as a Constitution"; Bordewich, *The First Congress*, 123.

71. *Barron v. Baltimore*, 7 U.S. 243 (1833); Mazzone, "The Bill of Rights in the Early State Constitutions"; Mercer, *Diminishing the Bill of Rights*; Nelson and Palmer, *Liberty and Community*, 106–17.

72. 1 Stat. 73 (1789).

73. Holt, "'To Establish Justice,'" 1484; Moore, "Trimming the Least Dangerous Branch."

74. Section 13, the subject of *Marbury v. Madison*, ranks among the murkiest.

75. Bourguignon, "The Federal Key to the Judiciary Act of 1789."

76. Nobody could appeal a state court decision in favor of a federal power or against a state law until 1914.

77. Ritz, *Rewriting the History of the Judiciary Act of 1789.*

78. Jay, "Origins of the Federal Common Law: Part Two," 1263; Collins, "'A Considerable Surgical Operation,'" 262.

79. Goebel, *Antecedents and Beginnings,* 457, 507.

80. Jay to Washington, September 15, 1790, in Kurland and Lerner, *The Founders' Constitution,* 4:161.

81. Whittington, *Constitutional Construction.*

82. *Annals of Congress,* 4th Cong., 1st Sess. (April 6, 1796), 772–73.

83. Prakash, "New Light on the Decision of 1789."

84. Currie, *The Constitution in Congress: The Federalist Period,* 149.

85. On the assertion that the Founders intended to do so, see Carrese, *Cloaking of Power;* on whether the Court has successfully done so, see Friedman, *The Will of the People.*

86. Justices to Washington, June 8, 1792, in Kurland and Lerner, *The Founders' Constitution,* 4:164; *Hayburn's Case,* 2 U.S. 409 (1792). The justices eventually complied, essentially stepping out of their robes and serving as voluntary "commissioners."

87. Many scholars see a related, but unreported, case involving the Invalid Pension Act as the first time the Court struck down an act of Congress. Marcus, "Judicial Review in the Early Republic," 41.

88. Jay to Washington, August 8, 1793, in Kurland and Lerner, *The Founders' Constitution,* 4:258.

89. Burset, "Advisory Opinions and the Founders' Crisis of Legal Authority."

90. For whatever reason, the secretary of state did not report the amendment as ratified until 1798.

91. Knapp, "The New Jersey Plan."

92. Jay to Adams, January 2, 1801, in Kurland and Lerner, *The Founders' Constitution,* 4:165.

93. Ewald, "James Wilson and the Drafting of the Constitution," 915.

94. Ellis, *The Jeffersonian Crisis,* 14.

95. *Ware v. Hylton,* 3 U.S. 199 (1796), 237. This also raised the question of whether treaties, like laws, must be made "in pursuance of" the Constitution, or could effectively amend the Constitution.

96. *Hylton v. United States,* 3 U.S. 171 (1796).

97. *Vanhorne's Lessee v. Dorrance,* 2 U.S. 304 (1795).

98. *Calder v. Bull,* 3 U.S. 386 (1798).

99. This question had arisen earlier in the decade. The United States accused Gideon Henfield of violating the law of nations, the 1778 treaty with France, and the president's neutrality proclamation, by entering the service of the French navy as a privateer. No specific congressional statute obtained. Though the circuit court justices charged the jury that they could convict Henfield of a crime not specified by statute, the jury acquitted him in what Larry Kramer calls a jury nullification. Kramer, *The People Themselves,* 3. In 1798, a jury convicted Robert Worrall of bribing a customs collector, though no statute defined this crime.

100. Preyer, "Jurisdiction to Punish," 223–65, with comments following by Robert C. Palmer and Stephen B. Presser; Warren, *The Supreme Court in United States History,* 1:164; Marshall to St. George Tucker, November 27, 1800, in Hobson, *Marshall: Writings,* 209.

101. Bird, "New Light on the Sedition Act of 1798"; *Lyon's Case* (1798), in Hall, *Major Problems in American Constitutional History,* 1:242–45; Gillies, "The Trial of Matthew Lyon."

102. In 1964, however, the Court declared that the "court of history" had held the act unconstitutional. *New York Times v. Sullivan,* 376 U.S. 254 (1964), 276.

103. They did complain about the concentration of legislative, judicial, and executive powers in the summary treatment of aliens under related acts.

104. *Annals of Congress,* 1st Cong., 1st Sess. (1789), 492, 596.

105. Counter-Resolutions, *American Heritage,* 237–44; Anderson, "Contemporary Opinion of the Virginia and Kentucky Resolutions," 45–63, 225–52.

106. Stephenson, *Campaigns and the Court,* 38.

107. Turner, "Federalist Policy and the Judiciary Act of 1801." As vice president, Jefferson had had to sign the bill passed by the Senate.

108. John Fowler to constituents, March 6, 1801, in Ragsdale and Jones, *Debates on the Federal Judiciary,* 1:106.

109. Jefferson to John Dickinson, December 19, 1801.

110. Jefferson expressed indifference about whether the Union remained intact or split into "Atlantic and Mississippi Confederations." His concern for the Union, however, caused him to violate the Constitution (as he understood it) by the Louisiana Purchase.

3. THE MARSHALL COURT

1. Clinton, "John Marshall's Federalism," 887–90.

2. Hobson, *The Great Chief Justice,* 14; Smith, *John Marshall.*

3. Turner, "The Appointment of Chief Justice Marshall."

4. Adams did not appoint Marshall as one of the new "midnight judges." He filled a regular vacancy when Chief Justice Oliver Ellsworth resigned.

5. Lash, "Minority Report."

6. John Marshall to Alexander Hamilton, January 1, 1801; and Marshall to Charles Cotesworth Pinckney, March 4, 1801, in Hobson, *Marshall: Writings,* 213, 219. Probably for dramatic effect, Albert Beveridge, Marshall's first biographer, omitted the "not" in the second quote.

7. Hobson, *Great Chief Justice,* 15.

8. Brookhiser, *John Marshall,* 64.

9. Marshall to Charles Cotesworth Pinckney, March 4, 1801, in Hobson, *Marshall: Writings,* 219.

10. Marshall to William Paterson, April 6, 1802, in Hobson, *Marshall: Writings,* 221. As late as 1817, Justice Henry Brockholst Livingston continued to regard Supreme Court circuit duty as unconstitutional. Ragsdale and Jones, *Debates on the Federal Judiciary,* 1:205.

11. *Stuart v. Laird,* 5 U.S. 299 (1803), 309.

12. Ellis, *The Jeffersonian Crisis,* 43.

13. Marshall served as both chief justice and secretary of state for several months. This did not technically violate the Constitution, as the Constitution forbids only legislators from also holding executive or judicial offices. Republicans criticized the diplomatic missions undertaken by chief justices John Jay and Oliver Ellsworth. They had a fair complaint. Jay refused to serve in a nonjudicial office under the Disabled Pension Act, but in London he drafted a treaty that he might come to adjudicate. This echoed those who objected to a council of revision and advisory opinions that judges should not review laws that they had helped to craft.

14. Clinton, Marbury v. Madison *and Judicial Review*; Douglas, "The Rhetorical Uses of Marbury v. Madison."

15. 1 Stat. 73 (1789).

16. *Marbury v. Madison*, 5 U.S. 137 (1803), in Hobson, *Marshall: Writings*, 229–52.

17. Alfange, "*Marbury v. Madison*," 366, 393. For a contrary view, see Clinton, Marbury v. Madison *and Judicial Review*, 91–100.

18. One abstruse theory held that the exceptions clause applies only to the "both as to law and fact" part, not to the "appellate jurisdiction" part. See fig. 1.

19. Marshall assumed that the president did not have the power to remove these justices of the peace, who had five-year terms of office. If they held federal judgeships, the term limit would have violated the life-tenure clause. If not, this limit on presidential removal power seemed to overturn the plenary removal power established by congressional construction in the "rule of 1789." Eventually the Court would decide that Congress could limit the terms of judges outside of the states.

20. Marcus, "Judicial Review in the Early Republic," 46–53; Faulkner, *Jurisprudence of John Marshall*, 200; Haines, *The American Doctrine of Judicial Supremacy*, 475.

21. Bloch, "The *Marbury* Mystery."

22. Clinton, Marbury v. Madison *and Judicial Review* argues that Marshall limited judicial review to "cases of a judiciary nature" only.

23. Haskins and Johnson, *Foundations of Power*, 202.

24. Nelson, *Marbury v. Madison*, 7, 33, 59.

25. O'Donovan and O'Donovan, *From Irenaeus to Grotius*, 771. See appendix A.

26. Kelly, Harbison, and Belz, *The American Constitution*, 63.

27. His predecessor in the New Hampshire district court suffered from this affliction, as did his successor.

28. Prakash and Smith, "How to Remove a Federal Judge," 125; Glickstein, "After Midnight."

29. Turner, "The Impeachment of John Pickering," 492.

30. Ellis, *Jeffersonian Crisis*, 76–107; Perlin, "The Impeachment of Samuel Chase"; Whittington, "Reconstructing the Federal Judiciary."

31. Adams, *Memoirs of John Quincy Adams*, 1:322.

32. Haskins, *Foundations of Power*, 242.

33. Marshall joked to Oliver Wolcott that if the Republicans removed him and he returned to private practice, he would enjoy real rather than nominal good-behavior tenure. Glickstein, "After Midnight."

34. Ellis, *Jeffersonian Crisis*, 87.

35. Ragsdale and Jones, Debates on the Federal Judiciary, 1:153.

36. Levy, *Jefferson and Civil Liberties*.

37. Stone, Fisher, and Spinowitz, "Thomas Jefferson," 57.

38. Warren, *The Supreme Court in United States History*, 1:315

39. Faulkner, *The Jurisprudence of John Marshall*, 269.

40. Hobson, *Marshall: Writings*, 280, 303.

41. As historian Forrest McDonald put it, this policy supposed that "a flea could stop a dogfight by threatening suicide." McDonald, *The American Presidency*, 270.

42. *United States v. The William*, 28 F. 614 (1808).

43. *Gilchrist v. Collector*, 10 F. 355 (1808).

44. Caesar Rodney to Jefferson, July 15, 1808, 357; Levy, *Jefferson and Civil Liberties*, 129.

45. James Iredell at North Carolina Ratification Convention, July 28, 1788, in Kurland and Lerner, *The Founders' Constitution*, 4:378; Story, *Commentaries*, 321.

46. Johnson letter, August 26, 1808, 10 F. 355 (1808), 359.

47. Mannix, "Gallatin, Jefferson, and the Embargo of 1808," 167.

48. Jones, "'The Caprice of Juries.'"

49. *United States v. Hoxie*, 26 F. 397 (1808).

50. The government instituted forfeiture suits against things (*in rem*) rather than people (*in personam*). Thus, cases had titles like *United States v. 1,960 Bags of Coffee*, 8 U.S. 398 (1814).

51. Warren, The *Supreme Court in United States History*, 1:355.

52. Dowd, "Justice Joseph Story and the Politics of Appointment," 265–85.

53. Jefferson to Madison, May 25, 1810.

54. Smith, *John Marshall*, 402.

55. Warren, The *Supreme Court in United States History*, 1:654.

56. Morgan, *Justice William Johnson*, 182; Haskins, *Foundations of Power*, 380.

57. Roper, "Judicial Unanimity and the Marshall Court." Political scientists would later call this the "strategic model" of judging. Maveety, *The Pioneers of Judicial Behavior*.

58. Blakeney, "The Old Court of Appeals"; Dumbauld, "The Case of the Mutinous Mariner."

59. *United States v. Peters*, 9 U.S. 115 (1809).

60. Resolutions of the Legislature of Pennsylvania, April 3, 1809, in Ragsdale and Jones, *Debates on the Federal Judiciary*, 1:177–79.

61. Haines, *The American Doctrine of Judicial Supremacy*, 292–93; Warren, The *Supreme Court in United States History*, 1:388.

62. Ely, *The Contract Clause*.

63. Other provision of Article I, section 10, like the gold and silver tender one, and arguably the ex post facto prohibition, really composed subsets of the contract clause. *Sturges v. Crowinshield*, 17 U.S. 122 (1819), 204.

64. *Fletcher v. Peck*, 10 U.S. 87 (1810).

65. Gough, *The Social Contract*; Gilmore, *The Death of Contract*; Lutz, "From Covenant to Constitution."

66. Maine, *Ancient Law*.

67. Warren, *The Supreme Court in United States History*, 2:34. Later progressives and legal realists would call such a description naively oblivious to the actual social and economic inequalities that vitiated freedom of contract and deride it as vacuous "formalism." Classic critiques are given in Pound, "Liberty of Contract"; and Hale, "Coercion and Distribution."

68. Justice Johnson in his concurring opinion suspected collusion and objected to their characterization as innocent. Haskins, *Foundations of Power*, 344.

69. This deal split Jefferson and Randolph and saved Justice Chase.

70. Leonard, "*Fletcher v. Peck*"; Hobson, *The Great Yazoo Lands Sale*, 174.

71. *New Jersey v. Wilson*, 11 U.S. 164 (1812), 167.

72. *Dartmouth College v. Woodward*, 17 U.S. 518 (1819); Ely, *The Contract Clause*, 152.

73. Thomas, "Rethinking the *Dartmouth College* Case."

74. *Green v. Biddle*, 21 U.S. 1 (1823).

75. The Federalists had enacted a national act in 1800; the Republicans quickly repealed it.

Congress repealed an 1841 act still more quickly. An act lasted about ten years after the Civil War, but a permanent federal bankruptcy law did not take hold until 1898.

76. *Sturges v. Crowninshield*, 17 U.S. 122 (1819).

77. *United States v. Hudson and Goodwin*, 11 U.S. 32 (1812).

78. *Wheaton v. Peters*, 33 U.S. 591 (1834). This case arose from a copyright suit between two Supreme Court reporters.

79. Pashman, *Building a Revolutionary State*.

80. One such case was *Ware v. Hylton*. Haskins, *Foundations of Power*, 396.

81. Marshall more likely tempered Story than egged him on. Warren, *The Supreme Court in United States History*, 1:453; Haskins, *Foundations of Power*, 394.

82. *Martin v. Hunter's Lessee*, 14 U.S. 304 (1816), 343.

83. "Opinion on the Constitutionality of the Bill for Establishing a National Bank" (February 15, 1791), in Boyd, *The Papers of Thomas Jefferson*, 19:280.

84. Veto message (January 30, 1815), in Richardson, *A Compilation of the Messages and Papers of the Presidents*, 2:540.

85. *McCulloch v. Maryland*, 17 U.S. 316 (1819), 405. Madison drew the opposite conclusion in *Federalist* 39, noting that ratification "will not be *national* but a *federal* act"—"federal" here meaning state-based. For another view, see Ciepley, "Is the United States Government a Corporation?," 426.

86. *McCulloch v. Maryland*, 407.

87. His following phrase, about a Constitution made "to be adapted to the various crises of human affairs," also led later commentators anachronistically to see Marshall as a "living Constitution" advocate. See White, "The 'Constitutional Revolution' as a Crisis in Adaptivity," 874, 880; White, "The Arrival of History," 500.

88. *McCulloch v. Maryland*, 423.

89. Gunther, *John Marshall's Defense of* McCulloch v. Maryland.

90. James Madison to Spencer Roane, September 2, 1819.

91. John Marshall to Joseph Story, July 13, 1821, in Hobson, *Marshall: Writings*, 567.

92. Schwartz, "Misreading *McCulloch v. Maryland*."

93. Jefferson again complained of this *Marbury*-like maneuver. See Haines, *American Doctrine of Judicial Supremacy*, 303; and Posner, "Enlightened Despot."

94. *Cohens v. Virginia*, 19 U.S. 264 (1821), 404.

95. Frankfurter, *The Commerce Clause*.

96. Epstein, "The Proper Scope of the Commerce Clause."

97. The chief justice had a celebrated sense of humor, but it did not enter into his entirely earnest and grave opinions, so we ought not read this phrase as tongue-in-cheek. It did produce generations of ribald commentary. As early as 1824, Henry Seawell wrote, "I . . expect to learn that our fornication laws are unconstitutional." Warren, *The Supreme Court in United States History*, 2:66.

98. Warren, The *Supreme Court in United States History*, 1:612.

99. Leonard, "*Fletcher v. Peck*." The compensation act denied judicial review of their claims.

100. See *Hawkins v. Barney's Lessee*, 30 U.S. 457 (1831). In *Green v. Biddle*, the Court "withdrew" the original 1822 opinion by Justice Story and substituted a three-justice opinion in 1823.

Critics disputed the validity of any opinion by less than a majority (four) of the seven-man court. The Court virtually conceded this when it adopted that policy. It raised the question of whether Congress might have imposed it—or the requirement of a two-thirds supermajority, or even unanimity.

101. Warren, "Legislative and Judicial Attacks on the Supreme Court," 12.

102. Peterson, "Expounding the Constitution," 70.

103. *Padelford v. Savannah*, 14 GA 438 (1854).

104. *Elkison v. Deliesseline*, 8 F. 493 (1823); Hamer, "Great Britain, the United States, and the Negro Seamen Acts." South Carolina later responded to informal overtures from the British and relaxed the law.

105. Marshall to Story, September 26, 1823, in Hobson, *Marshall: Writings*, 601.

106. Birkner, "The New York–New Jersey Boundary Controversy."

107. Marshall to Story, September 22, 1832, in Hobson, *Marshall: Writings*, 823.

108. Drew, "The Surge and Consolidation of Judicial Power."

109. Nelson, "Changing Conceptions of Judicial Review," 1182.

110. Upton, "The Independence of the Judiciary in New Hampshire"; Douglas, "Judicial Review and Separation of Powers."

111. Utter, "Judicial Review in Early Ohio"; Aumann, "The Course of Judicial Review," 367–76.

112. Ruger, "'A Question Which Convulses a Nation.'"

113. Gillman, Graber, and Whittington, *American Constitutionalism*, 2:219; Alschuler and Deiss, "A Brief History of the Criminal Jury," 867–928; Bressler, "Reconstruction," 1133–1201; Krasity, "The Role of the Judge in Jury Trials," 595–627.

114. Hall, "The Judiciary on Trial," 337–54; "Progressive Reform and the Decline of Democratic Accountability"; Nelson, "A Revolution of Scholarly Explanations." Today, only Rhode Island's judges have life tenure. Three other states provide tenure until age seventy.

115. Haines, *American Doctrine of Judicial Supremacy*, 340; Nelson, "Changing Conceptions of Judicial Review," 1184; Sherry, "Natural Law in the States," 171–222; Ely, "The Oxymoron Reconsidered," 327; Williams, "The One and Only Substantive Due Process Clause," 454–59.

116. Johannsen, *Stephen A. Douglas*, 88–97.

117. Tocqueville, *Democracy in America*, 252, 93–97, 135–42; Kraynak, "Tocqueville's Constitutionalism."

118. Tocqueville, *Democracy in America*, 257.

119. Blackard, "The Demoralization of the Legal Profession."

120. Longaker, "Andrew Jackson and the Judiciary."

121. Veto message (July 10, 1832), in Hall, *Major Problems in American Constitutional* History, 1:339. Jackson's attorney general, Roger B. Taney, claimed to have written this forceful repudiation of judicial supremacy, but probably did not. Marshall, "The Authorship of Jackson's Bank Veto Message." It certainly does not comport with the judicial supremacism he would adopt as Marshall's successor.

122. Stephenson, *Campaigns and the Court*, 75.

123. Schwartz, "Defying *McCulloch*?"

124. Longaker, "Andrew Jackson and the Judiciary," 352.

125. *Cherokee Nation v. Georgia*, 30 U.S. 1 (1831), 17.

126. *Cherokee Nation v. Georgia*, 15, 20.

127. Burke, "The Cherokee Cases." Unlike his approach in *Marbury* and *Cohens*, Marshall began with the jurisdictional question but did express doubt on the merits. *Cherokee Nation*, 20.

128. *Worcester v. Georgia*, 31 U.S. 515 (1832), 561; Burke, "The Cherokee Cases."

129. Horace Greeley later claimed that Jackson had said this. Miles, "After John Marshall's Decision," 519. Jackson did write privately, "The decision of the Supreme Court has fall [*sic*] stillborn and they find that they cannot coerce Georgia to yield to its mandate." Garrison, "The Cherokee Cases," in Urofsky, *The Public Debate over Controversial Supreme Court Decisions*, 22.

130. Magliocca, *Andrew Jackson and the Constitution*, 49. See also Ellis, *The Union at Risk*, 31.

131. The Court did not rule on the constitutionality of the protective tariff until 1928. An effort to concoct a case in 1831 failed. Currie, *The Constitution in Congress: Democrats and Whigs*, 101.

132. "Exposition and Protest" (December 19, 1828), in Lence, *Union and Liberty*, 345.

133. Daniel Webster speech (January 26–27, 1830), in Belz, *The Webster-Hayne Debate on the Nature of the Union*, 137.

134. John Clayton speech (March 4, 1830), in Belz, *The Webster-Hayne Debate on the Nature of the Union*, 363. See also speech of Edward Livingston (March 9, 1830), 463.

135. Robert Hayne speech (January 27, 1830), in Belz, *The Webster-Hayne Debate on the Nature of the Union*, 165, 169–71.

136. John Rowan speech (February 4, 1830), in Belz, *The Webster-Hayne Debate on the Nature of the Union*, 280–93.

137. Ellis, *The Union at Risk*, 178–87.

138. Calhoun's theory imposed the burden on the supporters of a nullified act to amend the Constitution and give Congress the disputed power. If they jumped this considerable hurdle, the nullifying state had the final option of secession.

139. Brogdon, "Defending the Union."

140. Jessup, *Reaction and Accommodation*, 374.

141. *Register of Debates*, 21st Cong., 2d Sess. (January 24, 1831), app. lxxvii–lxxxvi; Ragsdale and Jones, *Debates on the Federal Judiciary*, 1:186–200.

142. Graber, "James Buchanan as Savior?"

143. Paulsen, "The Most Dangerous Branch," 312–17; Schotten, "The Art of the Judge," 330.

144. Story, *Commentaries on the Constitution*.

145. The contract clause of the Northwest Ordinance applied only to contracts "previously formed."

146. *Ogden v. Saunders*, 25 U.S. 213 (1827).

147. *Willson v. Black Bird Creek Marsh Co.*, 27 U.S. 245 (1829).

148. *Providence Bank v. Billings*, 29 U.S. 514 (1830).

149. *Craig v. Missouri*, 29 U.S. 410 (1830).

150. John Marshall to Joseph Story, October 15, 1830, in Hobson, *Marshall: Writings*, 725.

151. *Briscoe v. Bank of Kentucky*, 36 U.S. 257 (1837).

152. *Barron v. Baltimore*, 32 U.S. 423 (1833).

153. Mazzone, "The Bill of Rights in the Early State Constitutions"; Utter, "Judicial Review in Early Ohio," 10; Mercer, *Diminishing the Bill of Rights*, 136.

154. Mercer, *Diminishing the Bill of Rights*, 164, 176.

155. White, *Marshall Court*, 778; Haines, *Role of the Supreme Court*, 622.

156. Franck, *Against the Imperial Judiciary*.

4. THE COURT AND THE CRISIS OF THE UNION

1. Kutler, *Judicial Power and Reconstruction Politics*, 24; Warren, *The Supreme Court in United States History*, 2:393. The bust was approved in 1873.

2. Longaker, "Andrew Jackson and the Judiciary."

3. The 1837 Judiciary Act also established five entirely slave-state circuits, making the Court more of a proslavery institution. Gillman, "How Political Parties Can Use the Courts"; Kutler, *Judicial Power and Reconstruction Politics*, 15. Ohio's Representative James Ashley accused the Democrats on the Senate Judiciary Committee of considering only proslavery nominees. *Congressional Globe*, 36th Cong., 1st Sess. (May 29, 1860), App. 367.

4. Jackson appointed William Smith on his last day in office. After Senate confirmation, Smith declined to serve. Jackson's successor, Martin Van Buren, appointed John McKinley.

5. White, *The Jeffersonians*, 318; Kahn, "The Appointment of John McLean to the Supreme Court"; Brickner, "Reassessing Long-Accepted Truths About Justice John McLean."

6. It also "expunged" the previous Senate's censure resolution from its *Journal*.

7. Fehrenbacher, *Slavery, Law, and Politics*, 113.

8. Lerner, "The Supreme Court as Republican Schoolmaster," 100.

9. Swisher, *The Taney Period*, 261.

10. John Marshall, in 1801, had made a similar gesture in the face of Jeffersonian democracy, holding court in plain black robes instead of crimson and ermine-trimmed regalia.

11. *Charles River Bridge Co. v. Warren Bridge Co.*, 36 U.S. 420 (1837); Hobson, *The Great Yazoo Lands Sale*, 196.

12. Allen, *Origins of the Dred Scott Case*, 16; Ely, *The Contract Clause*.

13. *New York v. Miln*, 36 U.S. 102 (1837); *Willson v. Black Bird Creek Marsh Co.*, 27 U.S. 245 (1829).

14. *Briscoe v. Bank of Commonwealth of Kentucky*, 36 U.S. 257 (1837).

15. The Court had already established national rules of *equity* procedure, without controversy. Funk, "The Union of Law and Equity"; Collins, "'A Considerable Surgical Operation.'"

16. Norton and Swift may have set Tyson up. Unable to repay Swift, Norton conspired with his creditor to get Tyson to pay the debt. Tyson's note to Norton matured in six months. If Norton had waited until the note matured, Tyson would not have had to pay, for lack of consideration. So Norton quickly signed the note over to Swift, who could claim ignorance of Norton's fraud. One could call it a Yazoo land fraud writ small.

17. *Swift v. Tyson*, 41 U.S. 1 (1842), 18–19.

18. Horwitz, *The Transformation of American Law*; Purcell, *Litigation and Inequality*; Soifer, "The Paradox of Paternalism and Laissez-Faire Constitutionalism."

19. Freyer, *Forums of Order*; LaPiana, "*Swift v. Tyson* and the Brooding Omnipresence in the Sky; Karsten, *Heart Versus Head*.

20. Skowronek, *Building a New American State*, 24. See also Drew, "The Surge and Consolidation of Judicial Power."

21. Swisher, *The Taney Period*, 430.

22. *Propeller Genesee Chief v. Fitzhugh*, 53 U.S. 443 (1852).

23. Currie, *The Constitution in Congress: Democrats and Whigs*, 192.

24. *Bank of the United States v. Deveaux*, 9 U.S. 61 (1809).

25. *Louisville Railroad v. Letson*, 43 U.S. 497 (1844).

26. Swisher, *The Taney Era*, 470.

27. Dennison, *The Dorr War*. See *Luther v. Borden*, 48 U.S. 1 (1849). Congress had recognized the original, charter government.

28. Luther v. Borden, 43.

29. Dennison, "The Dorr War and Political Questions"; Haines, *The American Doctrine of Judicial Supremacy*, 475.

30. Bradley, "Shall We Ratify the New Constitution?," 125.

31. Dennison, *The Dorr War*; Weinberg, *"Luther v. Borden,"* 762.

32. Warren, The *Supreme Court in United States History*, 2:207.

33. Mark Graber makes the argument that *Dred Scott* interpreted the Constitution fairly, reflecting the Founders' compromise with the evil of slavery. Graber, *Dred Scott and the Problem of Constitutional Evil*. Leonard, "Law and Politics Reconsidered" agrees. They extend the argument of Paul Finkelman on the proslavery nature of the Constitution. See Finkelman, "Slavery and the Constitutional Convention."

34. Finkelman, *Supreme Injustice*, 97.

35. Lightner, *Slavery and the Commerce Power*.

36. Finkelman, *"Prigg v. Pennsylvania* and Northern State Courts."

37. *Strader v. Graham*, 51 U.S. 82 (1851). Though it was not a section 34 diversity suit, Justice Benjamin Curtis brought up this potential in his *Dred Scott* dissent. See Leonard, "Law and Politics Reconsidered," 779; and Schwemm, *"Strader v. Graham,"* 422.

38. Whittington, *Political Foundations of Judicial Supremacy*, 250; Whittington, "The Road Not Taken," 365–91.

39. The Court clerk misspelled his name as "Sandford."

40. *Scott v. Emerson*, 15 MO 576 (1852), 586.

41. Emerson's widow had married a Massachusetts abolitionist; they arranged Scott's sale to Sanford, a New Yorker.

42. Warren, *The Supreme Court in United States History*, 2:293.

43. The justices clearly colluded. Scantier evidence suggests that the parties brought a collusive suit.

44. Reading the decision this way resembled a Court interpreting a statute so that it does not have to declare it unconstitutional. As judges should never *assume* that legislators meant to violate the Constitution, politicians might read *Dred Scott* minimally, not assuming that the Court had misread the Constitution. When disputing a Court opinion, politicians should give judges the benefit of the doubt, as judges, when they dispute a law, should give legislators the benefit of the doubt. Friedman, "The History of the Countermajoritarian Difficulty, Part One," 427.

45. *Dred Scott v. Sanford*, 60 U.S. 393 (1857), 404–05.

46. Justice Baldwin had articulated this in a concurring opinion in *Groves v. Slaughter* (1841). Many state courts had adopted it before *Dred Scott*. Sherry, "Natural Law in the States," 171–222.

47. *Dred Scott v. Sanford*, 450. For their part, the Republicans insisted that the Fifth Amendment protected the *liberty* of all, and so *prohibited* slavery in the territories.

48. *Dred Scott v. Sanford*, 452.

49. Bestor, "State Sovereignty and Slavery."

50. Hurst, *Law and the Conditions of Freedom*, 43; Graber, *Dred Scott and the Problem of Constitutional Evil* implies that Calhoun's theory fulfilled rather than repudiated the Founding.

51. In 1856, Lincoln said, "The Supreme Court . . is the tribunal to decide such a question [of

slavery in the territories], and we will submit to its decisions." Speech at Galena (July 23, 1856), in Basler, *The Collected Works of Abraham Lincoln*, 2:355. But this statement perhaps left open his later claim to abide by the particular decision but not the general rule.

52. Warren, *The Supreme Court in United States History*, 2:328.

53. Stephen Douglas speeches in Chicago (July 9, 1858), Galesburg (October 7, 1858), and Quincy (October 13, 1858), in Johannsen, *The Lincoln–Douglas Debates of 1858*, 31–32, 242, 268.

54. Douglas speeches in Jonesboro (September 15, 1858) and Quincy (October 13, 1858), in Johannsen, *The Lincoln–Douglas Debates of 1858*, 127, 268.

55. Abraham Lincoln speech at Springfield (June 26, 1857), in Basler, *Abraham Lincoln*, 355.

56. Lincoln speech at Springfield.

57. Lincoln speech at Quincy (October 13, 1858), in Basler, *Abraham Lincoln*, 255.

58. Lincoln speech at Ottawa (August 21, 1858), in Johannsen, *The Lincoln–Douglas Debates*, 65–66; Johannsen, *Stephen A. Douglas*, 88–97; Shankman, "Partisan Conflicts."

59. Resolutions of the Wisconsin Legislature (March 19, 1859), in Ragsdale and Jones, *Debates on the Federal Judiciary*, 1:201.

60. Swisher, *The Taney Period*.

61. *Ableman v. Booth*, 62 U.S. 506 (1859); Bestor, "State Sovereignty and Slavery"; Kelly, Harbison, and Belz, *The American Constitution*, 278–79.

62. *Kentucky v. Dennison*, 65 U.S. 66 (1861).

63. *Federalist* 78. Scott's owners emancipated him shortly after the litigation—another sign of a collusive suit.

64. Abraham Lincoln, First Inaugural Address (March 4, 1861), in Basler, *Abraham Lincoln: His Speeches and Writings*, 584–86.

65. Lincoln knew that the Court was legislating. He perhaps called the Court back to a proper standard of judicial behavior.

66. Schwartz, "Defying *McCulloch*?," 143.

67. Fehrenbacher, *Slavery, Law, and Politics*, 574.

68. Fairman, *Reconstruction and Reunion, 1864–88, Part One*, 141.

69. White, "The Strangely Insignificant Role of the U.S. Supreme Court," 211–38; Grove, "The Origins (and Fragility) of Judicial Independence," 481.

70. Gillman, Graber, and Whittington, *American Constitutionalism*, 1:290.

71. The Congress (mostly) elected in the fall of 1860 would not meet until December 1861, as the Constitution provides that "the Congress shall assemble at least once in every year, and such meeting shall be on the first Monday in December, unless they shall by law appoint a different day." They had not altered this. Some states did not hold congressional elections until the spring of 1861. The Senate remained in continuous session to confirm presidential appointees.

72. Abraham Lincoln message to Congress in special session (July 4, 1861), in Basler, *Abraham Lincoln*, 593.

73. A judge fined Jackson for this, though Congress, in 1844, refunded the fine with interest. Young Representative Stephen Douglas championed Jackson's cause. Johannsen, *Stephen A. Douglas*, 129.

74. Story, *Commentaries on the Constitution*, 269.

75. "*Ex parte*" meaning "on behalf of," as Merryman could not make his own case.

76. Scholars tend to agree with Taney over Lincoln.

77. *Ex parte Merryman,* 17 F. 144 (1861), 149. See also Swisher, *Taney Period,* 849; Yoo, "Lincoln and Habeas."

78. Ex parte *Merryman,* 153.

79. Tillman, "Ex Parte *Merryman*"; Tillman, "*Merryman* Redux."

80. "Suspension of the Privilege of the Writ of Habeas Corpus," 10 Op. Att'y Gen. 74 (1863).

81. Message to Congress, July 4, 1861, in Basler, *Abraham Lincoln,* 601.

82. Habeas Corpus Act of 1863, 12 Stat. 755 (1863).

83. An earlier version of the act said that the president "shall be" empowered to suspend the writ. Dueholm, "Lincoln's Suspension of the Writ of Habeas Corpus," 47–66.

84. Abraham Lincoln letter to Erastus Corning et al. (June 12, 1863), in Basler, *Abraham Lincoln,* 703.

85. White, *Law in American History,* 1:449; Yoo, "Lincoln and Habeas."

86. Ross, *Justice of Shattered Dreams* offers a measured defense of Miller.

87. Davis himself won the presidential nomination of the Labor Reform Party in 1872. Though he declined to run, he received one electoral vote.

88. Fairman, *Reconstruction and Reunion,* 23; Kutler, *Judicial Power and Reconstruction Politics,* 23.

89. Carrington, *Justice Stephen Field's Cooperative Constitution of Liberty.*

90. *The Prize Cases,* 67 U.S. 635 (1863).

91. *Ex parte Vallandigham,* 68 U.S. 243 (1864).

92. *Mississippi v. Johnson,* 71 U.S. 475 (1867); *Georgia v. Stanton,* 73 U.S. 50 (1868); Fairman, *Reconstruction and Reunion,* 382, 389; Kutler, *Judicial Power and Reconstruction Politics,* 97. To his credit, Johnson, who did not want to enforce these acts, which passed over his veto, defended them in these cases.

93. *Ex parte Garland,* 71 U.S. 333 (1867); *Cummings v. Missouri,* 72 U.S. 277 (1867); Kutler, *Judicial Power and Reconstruction Politics,* 72.

94. *Ex parte Milligan,* 71 U.S. 2 (1866), 120–21.

95. Justice Davis, in a private letter, noted that it would not apply to the rebel states. The Indiana commission had also been established by presidential order, not by congressional legislation. Kutler, *Judicial Power and Reconstruction Politics,* 67, 80.

96. Walter D. Coles later wrote, "It was boldly suggested that it should be styled 'An act to prevent the Supreme Court from deciding McCardle's case,'" but he does not identify a source. Coles, "Politics and the Supreme Court of the United States," 203.

97. *Ex parte McCardle,* 74 U.S. 506 (1869). The 1867 expansion of habeas review was meant to aid southern freedmen and Unionists, not unreconstructed rebel editors.

98. Warren, The *Supreme Court in United States History,* 2:481.

99. Warren, The *Supreme Court in United States History,* 2:492.

100. Goedcke, "Justice Field and Inherent Rights," 205; *Congressional Globe,* 40th Cong., 2d Sess. (January 30, 1868), 862–65.

101. *Ex parte Yerger,* 75 U.S. 85 (1869), 104; Van Alstyne, "A Critical Guide to *Ex Parte McCardle.*"

102. *United States v. Klein,* 80 U.S. 128 (1871).

103. Fairman, *Reconstruction and Reunion,* 513; Meltzer, "The Story of *Ex Parte McCardle.*"

104. Salmon P. Chase to William Cullen Bryant (February 4, 1862), and to William Pitt Fessenden (February 10, 1862), in Niven, *The Salmon P. Chase Papers,* 3:129, 132.

105. Boutwell, *Reminiscences of Sixty Years in Public Affairs*, 2:29; McGinty, *Lincoln and the Court*, 340. On a scale from A (almost certainly said it) to F (almost certainly did not), Don Fehrenbacher and Virginia Fehrenbacher give Boutwell's recollection a C. Fehrenbacher and Fehrenbacher, *Recollected Words of Abraham Lincoln*, 38.

106. *Hepburn v. Griswold*, 75 U.S. 603 (1869), 615, 617, 625. The Court struggled to find a case to review, because almost all state courts had upheld the act, and the Court could not review state court decisions in *favor* of federal acts until 1914. Kentucky's high court provided the adverse decision to review. Indiana's high court had held against the legal tender acts, but voters ousted the Democratic judges and reversed it. Neely, *Lincoln and the Triumph of the Nation*, 231.

107. Kutler, *Judicial Power and Reconstruction Politics*, 121.

108. After having expanded it to ten in 1863, Congress reduced it to seven, though it never fell below eight.

109. *Legal Tender Cases*, 79 U.S. 457 (1870); Fairman, *Reconstruction and Reunion*, 755.

110. Kutler, *Judicial Power and Reconstruction Politics*, 123.

111. Many have averred that Congress reduced the Court from ten to seven in order to deny President Johnson the opportunity to appoint judges. In fact, Johnson signed the reduction bill, and then he pocket vetoed the bill restoring it to nine. Congress quickly passed it again, and the new president, Grant, approved. Kutler, *Judicial Power and Reconstruction Politics*, 40, 58.

112. Kutler, *Judicial Power and Reconstruction Politics*, 114.

113. Graber, "The Jacksonian Origins of Chase Court Activism."

114. *Gordon v. United States*, 74 U.S. 188 (1868).

115. Warren, The *Supreme Court in United States History*, 2:421.

116. *United States v. Dewitt*, 76 U.S. 41 (1869).

117. Hurst, *Law and the Conditions of Freedom*, 62.

118. *Gelpke v. Dubuque*, 68 U.S. 175 (1864), 206–07.

119. Fairman, *Reconstruction and Reunion*, 919; Ross, *Justice of Shattered Dreams*, 222.

120. *People* ex rel. *Detroit & Howell R.R. Co. v. Salem*, 20 MI 452 (1870).

121. *United States v. Union Pacific Railroad Co.*, 91 U.S. 72 (1875).

122. The question arose of whether he could break a tie vote on those rules. Sometimes he did and sometimes he didn't.

123. As in the Revolutionary War pension scheme, the justices claimed to act extracurially.

124. *Texas v. White*, 74 U.S. 700 (1869), 725.

125. Abraham Lincoln, last public address (April 11, 1865), in Basler *Abraham Lincoln*, 798. The Court echoed Lincoln's first inaugural description just before it turned its own "indestructible" phrase.

126. *Texas v. White*, 733. As for "innocent" third-party purchasers, unlike those in *Fletcher v. Peck*, they had knowingly taken their chances and must take the consequences.

127. *Texas v. White*, 739–40.

128. Kutler, *Judicial Power and Reconstruction Politics*; Wiecek, "The Reconstruction of Federal Judicial Power, 1863–75."

129. Friedman, "The History of the Countermajoritarian Difficulty, Part Two," 7, 17.

130. Wiecek, "The Reconstruction of Federal Judicial Power"; Gilman, "How Political Parties Can Use the Courts to Advance Their Agenda."

5. THE COURT IN THE INDUSTRIAL AGE

1. Hyman and Wiecek, *Equal Justice Under Law,* 485.

2. The Bill of Rights added a lot of substance, but as we have argued, this meant little because it withheld power that had not been granted in the first place and did not apply to the states. The Eleventh Amendment concerned a technical judicial provision, and the Twelfth revised the complicated process of presidential election.

3. Avins, *The Reconstruction Amendments' Debates.*

4. Fairman, *Reconstruction and Reunion, 1864–88, Part One,* 131.

5. Bond, "The Original Understanding of the Fourteenth Amendment in Illinois, Ohio, and Pennsylvania."

6. Boyce, "Originalism and the Fourteenth Amendment," 973. Kurt Lash's new two-volume collection *The Reconstruction Amendments* may provide new insight.

7. Civil Rights Act of 1866, 14 Stat. 27 (1866).

8. Barnett, "The Three Narratives of the *Slaughter-House Cases.*" The act may have helped African American butchers, who were excluded from the informal monopoly on the trade held by Gascons. Brandwein, *Rethinking the Judicial Settlement of Reconstruction,* 56.

9. Ross, *Justice of Shattered Dreams,* 201.

10. *Slaughterhouse Cases,* 83 U.S. 36 (1873)

11. Kelly, Harbison, and Belz, *The American Constitution,* 356–59.

12. Kelly, Harbison, and Belz, *The American Constitution,* 350; Franklin, "The Enforcement of the Civil Rights Act of 1875," 235.

13. *Civil Rights Cases,* 109 U.S. 3 (1883), 25; Brandwein, "The *Civil Rights Cases* and the Lost Language of State Neglect."

14. Riegel, "The Persistent Career of Jim Crow"; Hyman and Wiecek, *Equal Justice Under Law,* 441.

15. Benedict, "Preserving Federalism"; Brandwein, *Rethinking the Judicial Settlement of Reconstruction.*

16. Hyman and Wiecek, *Equal Justice Under Law,* 509; Phillips, "The Central Theme of Southern History."

17. Schwartz, *Statutory History of the United States,* 1:804, 808–09, 814.

18. Adam Winkler recycles this story in "'Corporations Are People' Is Built on an Incredible 19th-Century Lie."

19. Graham, "The 'Conspiracy Theory' of the Fourteenth Amendment"; Winkler, "'Corporations Are People' Is Built on an Incredible 19th-Century Lie"; Burns, *Packing the Court,* 80, 97.

20. *Munn v. Illinois,* 94 U.S. 113 (1877), 123, 126, 132–34.

21. Gillman, "How Political Parties Can Use the Courts," 511–24.

22. Meigs, "The Relation of the Judiciary to the Constitution." Hermann E. von Holst actually denigrated "the worship of the Constitution." von Holst, *Constitutional and Political History of the United States,* 1:64–79.

23. Seymour, "The True Meaning of the Term 'Liberty.'"

24. Thayer, "The Origin and Scope of the American Doctrine of Constitutional Law."

25. Most pointed to the railroad rate regulation case of *Chicago, Milwaukee & St. Paul Railway Co. v. Minnesota,* 134 U.S. 418 (1890), and some decisions by the New York court of appeals.

26. Wilson, *Congressional Government;* Dicey, *Introduction to the Study of the Law of the Constitution.*

27. Weaver, *A Call to Action,* 69; Pestritto, *Woodrow Wilson and the Roots of Modern Liberalism,* 118.

28. Bickel, *The Least Dangerous Branch,* 35.

29. Posner, "The Rise and Fall of Judicial Self-Restraint."

30. This represented another lame-duck Republican "lock in," as the Republicans controlled both houses of Congress and the presidency from 1889 to 1891, the only time they did so between 1875 and 1897. President Benjamin Harrison also had four vacancies on the Court in one term, an unusually high number.

31. Lovell, *Legislative Deferrals.*

32. Interstate Commerce Act, 24 Stat. 379 (1887).

33. Congress imposed limits on the president's removal power first for the comptroller of the currency, created by the National Banking Act of 1863. Stiller, *Banking America,* 91.

34. Adams, "A Decade of Federal Railway Legislation."

35. The commission could only declare a rate "unreasonable." The railroad could then establish another, which the commission might again declare unreasonable, and this might go on *ad infinitum.*

36. Berk, "Adversaries by Design," 338. See also Keller, *Regulating a New Economy.*

37. Charles Evans Hughes speech before Elmira Chamber of Commerce (May 3, 1907), in Hughes, *Addresses of Charles Evans Hughes, 1906–16,* 185–87.

38. See, for example, John of Salisbury, *Policraticus* (1159), in *Western Heritage,* 457; and Merrill, "Article III, Adjudication, and the Origins of the Appellate Model of Administrative Law," 939–1003.

39. On protecting consumers, see Bork, *The Antitrust Paradox;* on protecting small producers, see Paul, "Reconsidering Judicial Supremacy in Antitrust." See also Priest, "Bork's Strategy."

40. *United States v. E. C. Knight,* 156 U.S. 1 (1895). In fact, the decision threw the issue back to the states, which chose not to break up the trusts.

41. *United States v. Trans-Missouri Freight Association,* 166 U.S. 290 (1897); *United States v. Joint Traffic Association,* 171 U.S. 505 (1898). A similar reading applied to interstate pipe manufacturers in *Addyston Pipe and Steel Co. v. United States,* 175 U.S. 211 (1899).

42. *Swift v. United States,* 196 U.S. 375 (1905).

43. *Standard Oil v. United States,* 221 U.S. 1 (1911); *United States v. American Tobacco,* 221 U.S. 106 (1911).

44. *In re Debs,* 158 U.S. 564 (1895), 582.

45. *Baltimore & Ohio Railroad v. Baugh,* 149 U.S. 368 (1893).

46. Purcell, *Litigation and Inequality,* 26.

47. Kelly, Harbison, and Belz, *The American Constitution,* 402.

48. *Springer v. United States,* 102 U.S. 586 (1883).

49. *Hylton v. United States,* 3 U.S. 171 (1796), 178.

50. Congress could apportion a real property tax, but state sovereignty prevented any taxation of state bond income, lest the federal government destroy its ability to borrow money.

51. *Pollock v. Farmers' Loan & Trust Co.,* 157 U.S. 429 (1895) [*Pollock* I].

52. *Pollock v. Farmers' Loan & Trust Co.,* 158 U.S. 601 (1895) [*Pollock* II].

53. Magliocca, *The Tragedy of William Jennings Bryan*, 80.

54. *Congressional Record* 26 (1894), 6695.

55. *Pollock* I, 532.

56. *Pollock* I, 607.

57. *Pollock* II, 665.

58. *Pollock* II, 695.

59. Thompson, "Government by Lawyers," 685.

60. Hudspeth, "The Case of the 'Vacillating Justice,'" 103–13.

61. Clinton, *Marbury v. Madison and Judicial Review*, 121, 166, 176.

62. *Pollock* I, 554.

63. Westin, "The Supreme Court, the Populist Movement, and the Campaign of 1896."

64. Schlesinger, Israel, and Hansen, *History of American Presidential Elections, 1789–1968*, 2:1829–30.

65. Beth, *The Development of the American Constitution*, 42.

66. Hohenstein, "William Jennings Bryan and the Income Tax."

67. William Jennings Bryan speech (July 8, 1896), in Schlesinger, Israel, and Hansen, *History of American Presidential Elections, 1789–1968*, 2:1847.

68. Gilbert Fite, "Election of 1896," in Schlesinger, Israel, and Hansen, *History of American Presidential Elections, 1789–1968*, 2:1824.

69. Schlesinger, Israel, and Hansen, *History of American Presidential Elections, 1789–1968*, 2:1838.

70. Richards, "The Debates over the Retrocession," 76.

71. Tamanaha, "Sociological Jurisprudence."

72. Wiecek, *The Lost World of Classical Legal Thought*.

73. Holmes, *The Common Law*, 1.

74. Strauss, *The Living Constitution*.

75. Watson, *Living Constitution, Dying Faith*, 140. In fairness to Holmes, he seems to have recognized this and often counseled judicial restraint in constitutional law. In the end he would adopt a double standard of restraint with regard to laws he liked and strict scrutiny for ones he disfavored; see his dissent in *Gitlow v. New York*, U.S. 652 (1925), 673.

76. Pringle, *The Life and Times of William Howard Taft*, 1:47.

77. Bailey, *Guardians of the Moral Order*.

78. Lewis, "The Birth of the American Bar Association," 1002.

79. Purcell, *Litigation and Inequality*, 150, 187; Johnson, "Adaptive Jurisprudence," 21; Epp, *The Rights Revolution*, 55.

80. Haines, *The Revival of Natural Law Concepts*, 169.

81. Mott, *Due Process of Law*, 277; Cooley, *Commentaries on the Constitution of the United States*, 2:688.

82. *Chicago, Milwaukee and St. Paul Railway Co. v. Minnesota*, 134 U.S. 418 (1890).

83. It did so in *Chicago, Burlington, & Quincy Railroad v. Chicago*, 166 U.S. 226 (1897).

84. Karkkainen, "The Police Power Revisited," 826–913.

85. *Frisbie v. United States*, 157 U.S. 160 (1895), 165; *Allgeyer v. Louisiana*, 168 U.S. 578 (1897); *Lochner v. New York*, 198 U.S. 45 (1905).

86. Bernstein, *Rehabilitating Lochner*.

87. Bernstein, "Class Legislation, Fundamental Rights, and the Origins of *Lochner* and Liberty of Contract."

88. Warren, "The Progressiveness of the United States Supreme Court"; Phillips, *The Lochner Court;* Urofsky, "State Courts and Protective Legislation."

89. Lochner v. New York, 75.

90. Fiss, *The Troubled Beginnings of the Modern State*, 214.

91. *First Employers' Liability Case*, 207 U.S. 463 (1908).

92. *Adair v. United States*, 208 U.S. 161 (1908).

93. *Loewe v. Lawlor*, 208 U.S. 274 (1908).

94. *Ex parte Young*, 209 U.S. 123 (1908).

95. Giocoli, "The (Rail)Road to *Lochner."*

96. *Second Employers' Liability Case*, 223 U.S. 1 (1912).

97. Bickel and Schmidt, *The Judiciary and Responsible Government*, 581. In 1938, the Court threw out the entire idea of a "federal common law."

98. "The Three-Judge Court Act of 1910."

99. Clayton Antitrust Act, 38 Stat. 717 (1914).

100. Alschuler, *Law Without Values.*

101. Garraty, "Holmes' Appointment to the United States Supreme Court," 300.

102. William Graham Sumner, the great American acolyte of Spencer, impressed William Howard Taft at Yale. Burton, *Taft, Holmes, and the 1920s Court*, 26, 38.

103. Gillman, *The Constitution Besieged*, 131.

104. Strum, *Louis D. Brandeis*, 361.

105. Lurie, *William Howard Taft*; Pringle, *The Life and Times of William Howard Taft*, 1:339.

106. Taft, *Recollections of Full Years*, 223.

107. Pringle, *The Life and Times of William Howard Taft*, 1:128.

108. Taft, "Recent Criticism of the Judiciary."

109. Schacter, "Putting the Politics of 'Judicial Activism' in Historical Perspective," 230.

110. Smemo, "Judge Charles Amidon's Influence"; Southwick, "A Judge Runs for President," 37–50.

111. "Mr. Gompers, the Courts, and Labor" (October 28, 1908), in Burton, *The Collected Works of William Howard Taft*, 2:166; Taft, "Judicial Decisions as an Issue in Politics"; "Taft Says He Is Sure of Election," *New York Times*, October 2, 1908, p. 3.

112. Some liberals came to sympathize with the Fuller Court as a way of exonerating the judicial excesses of the Warren Court and its successors. See, for example, Fiss, *The Troubled Beginnings of the Modern State, 1888–1910.*

6. THE PROGRESSIVE AND NEW DEAL PERIOD, 1910-53

1. Bickel and Schmidt, *The Judiciary and Responsible Government*, 23, 247.

2. Pringle, *The Life and Times of William Howard Taft*, 1:529.

3. Semonche, *Charting the Future*, 201. Brewer may have shared a similar determination; see Brodhead, *David J. Brewer*, 181.

4. Tucker, "Justice Horace Harmon Lurton: The Shaping of a National Progressive"; Lurton, "A Government of Law or a Government of Men?"; Steidle, "Conservative Progressives," 247; Tamanaha, "Sociological Jurisprudence Past and Present," 501.

5. Bickel and Schmidt, *The Judiciary and Responsible Government*, 49; Danelski and Tulchin, *The Autobiographical Notes of Charles Evans Hughes*, 300.

6. Ruth Ann O'Brien, *Workers' Paradox*, 27.

7. Belknap, "Mr. Justice Pitney and Progressivism."

8. Warren, "The Progressiveness of the United States Supreme Court," 294; Warren, "A Bulwark to the State Police Power," 667; Phillips, *The Lochner Court*; Urofsky, "State Courts and Protective Legislation."

9. Lowry, "The Men of the Supreme Court," 629–30.

10. Ross, *The Chief Justiceship of Charles Evans Hughes*, 7; "The Supreme Court's Power," 252.

11. Lurie, *The Chief Justiceship of William Howard Taft, 1921–30*, 70, 74.

12. Bickel and Schmidt, *The Judiciary and Responsible Government*, 5, 24, 201.

13. Roe, *Our Judicial Oligarchy*, 22, 89, 105, 220.

14. Clinton, Marbury v. Madison *and Judicial Review*, 184.

15. Clark, "Some Defects of the Constitution of the United States" (April 27, 1906), in Brooks and Lefler, *The Papers of Walter Clark*, 2:558; Clark, "Judicial Supremacy," 148.

16. Smith, *The Spirit of American Government*.

17. With some exceptions, like Learned Hand in the 1950s.

18. Beard, "The Supreme Court—Usurper or Grantee?"

19. Clinton, Marbury v. Madison *and Judicial Review*, 189.

20. Notwithstanding his aside in the preface that many of the judges selflessly defended their plutocratic patrons and themselves died in poverty.

21. In fact, Fuller held for the plaintiff and against the railroad in every case that came before him. See Reeder, "Chief Justice Fuller," 11.

22. The American Catholic hierarchy seems to have absorbed judicial supremacy by this time. The 1891 Baltimore Catechism, comparing the unity of the Catholic Church to the endless disputes among private-judgment Protestants (and right after its explanation of papal infallibility), instructed the faithful that the "wise makers of the Constitution . . appointed judges to interpret or explain the laws and give the correct meaning when disputes arose. Then in Washington there is a chief judge for the whole United States, and when he says the words of the law mean this or that, every citizen must abide by the decision, and there is no appeal from it." *Baltimore Catechism Four*. Protestant anti–judicial supremacists would recall that *Dred Scott* came from White's only Catholic predecessor. Edward S. Corwin accused White of "casuistry" and "scholastic subtlety." Corwin, "The Anti-Trust Acts and the Constitution," 367.

23. Myers, *History of the Supreme Court*, 133, 159–60, 584–87, 702, 721–31.

24. Pound, "Liberty of Contract."

25. Warren, "The Progressiveness of the United States Supreme Court"; Phillips, *The Lochner Court*; Urofsky, "State Courts and Protective Legislation During the Progressive Era"; Lindgren, "Beyond Cases," 583–639.

26. "President Taft Makes Key Speech," *New York Times*, March 9, 1912, p. 1; "Mr. Taft Speaks Out," *New York Times*, April 26, 1912, p. 10.

27. William Howard Taft acceptance speech (August 2, 1912), in Schlesinger, Israel, and Hansen, *History of American Presidential Elections, 1789–1968*, 3:2209. Taft's home state of Ohio amended its constitution in 1912 to require a six-sevenths majority of its high court to declare an act unconstitutional. Aumann, "The Course of Judicial Review in the State of Ohio," 367–76.

28. Dubofsky, "Abortive Reform," 202. James Kerney claimed that Wilson made this statement in a letter responding to an invitation to speak at an antiboycott organization (probably the American Antiboycott Association). Kerney, *The Political Education of Woodrow Wilson.* Arthur Link, for example, refers to Kerney in *Wilson: The Road to the White House,* 127. Nobody has produced a copy of this letter, though it frequently came up in political campaigns, and it featured in Samuel Gompers's testimony during the congressional investigation of the 1919 steel strike. United States Senate, Committee on Education and Labor, *Investigation of Strikes in Steel Industries,* 98.

29. Federal Trade Commission Act, 38 Stat. 717 (1914), sec. 6.

30. Dubofsky, "Abortive Reform," 206.

31. 38 Stat. 730 (1914), sec. 6, 20.

32. Ernst, "The Labor Exemption," 1167.

33. Some protopopulists objected to Stanley Matthews in 1881 as a "railroad lawyer." Weaver, *A Call to Action,* 88; Helfman, "The Contested Confirmation of Stanley Matthews."

34. Todd, *Justice on Trial.*

35. Brandeis, "The Living Law."

36. Pringle, *Life and Times of William Howard Taft,* 2:952.

37. Judah P. Benjamin had declined offers of nomination by Presidents Fillmore and Pierce.

38. Wilson to Atlee Pomerene (May 12, 1916), in Link, *Papers of Woodrow Wilson,* 27:25.

39. Cardozo, *The Nature of the Judicial Process,* 106.

40. Dawson, "Brandeis and the New Deal," in *Brandeis and America,* 54. See also Danelski, "The Propriety of Brandeis' Extrajudicial Conduct."

41. Urofsky, "The Brandeis Agenda," in Dawson, *Brandeis and America,* 145.

42. Kelly, Harbison, and Belz, *The American Constitution,* 456.

43. *Bunting v. Oregon,* 243 U.S. 426 (1917).

44. O'Brien, *Workers' Paradox,* 27; *Coppage v. Kansas,* 236 U.S. 1 (1915).

45. *Hitchman Coal & Coke Co. v. Mitchell,* 245 U.S. 229 (1917).

46. *Wilson v. New,* 243 U.S. 332 (1917).

47. As governor, Hughes had opposed the ratification of the Sixteenth Amendment because it would enable Congress to tax the interest on state bonds. As Supreme Court justice, he held that it did not. Epstein, "The Opposition of the Cities and States to Federal Taxation of Their Securities," 186–87; Martori and Bliss, "Taxation of Municipal Bond Interest," 194–95.

48. Bickel and Schmidt, *The Judiciary and Responsible Government,* 462.

49. Compton, *The Evangelical Origins of the Living Constitution.*

50. *Clark Distilling Co. v. Western Maryland Railway Co.,* 242 U.S. 311 (1917).

51. *Hammer v. Dagenhart,* 247 U.S. 251 (1918). The act allowed a manufacturer to cease using child labor and then, after thirty days, to begin out-of-state shipment of goods no longer made by child labor.

52. In fairness to Day, he quoted a precedent, *Lane County v. Oregon,* which had misquoted the amendment. In this prejuristocratic era, nobody claimed that the *Lane County* decision had effectively amended the Constitution.

53. *Bailey v. Drexel Furniture Co.,* 259 U.S. 20 (1922).

54. *Green v. Frazier,* 253 U.S. 233 (1920); Pratt, "Socialism on the Northern Plains," 19–23; J. J. P., "Fourteenth Amendment."

55. Although he had raised the same alarm in 1916, and no vacancies arose during Wilson's second term.

56. Taft, "Mr. Wilson and the Campaign," 19.

57. Kelly, Harbison, and Belz, *The American Constitution*, 449–50.

58. Urofsky, "The Brandeis–Frankfurter Conversations," 318, 322.

59. *Bailey v. Drexel Furniture Co.*, 259 U.S. 20 (1922).

60. *Wolff Packing Co. v. Kansas*, 667 U.S. 552 (1923).

61. *Massachusetts v. Mellon*, 262 U.S. 447 (1923).

62. Post, "Defending the Lifeworld," 1489–1545; Urofsky, "The Brandeis–Frankfurter Conversations," 313.

63. *Pennsylvania Coal Co. v. Mahon*, 260 U.S. 393 (1922).

64. *Euclid v. Ambler Realty*, 272 U.S. 365 (1926).

65. *Buchanan v. Warley*, 245 U.S. 60 (1917).

66. *Pierce v. Society of Sisters*, 268 U.S. 510 (1925); *Meyer v. Nebraska*, 262 U.S. 390 (1923).

67. *Moore v. Dempsey*, 261 U.S. 86 (1923); Klarman, "The Racial Origins of Modern Criminal Procedure."

68. *Nixon v. Herndon*, 273 U.S. 536 (1927).

69. Carrott, "The Supreme Court and Minority Rights"; Post, "The Incomparable Chief Justiceship," 117.

70. *Gitlow v. New York*, 268 U.S. 652 (1925).

71. *Buck v. Bell*, 274 U.S. 200 (1927); Black, *War Against the Weak*; Whitman, *Hitler's American Model*.

72. Langum, *Crossing over the Line*.

73. McDowell, *Curbing the Courts*, 2.

74. Robert La Follette speech to American Federation of Labor convention (June 14, 1922), in Ragsdale and Jones, *Debates on the Federal Judiciary*, 2:142.

75. William E. Borah, "Five to Four Decisions as Menace to Respect for Supreme Court," in Ragsdale and Jones, *Debates on the Federal Judiciary*, 2:147.

76. Ross, *A Muted Fury*, 254–84.

77. Davis, "Present Day Problems," 557; Harbaugh, *Lawyer's Lawyer*, 72, 244. Ironically, La Follette's running mate, Burton Wheeler, became the most important *defender* of the Court when Franklin Roosevelt tried to pack it, in 1937. Davis himself would argue the segregationist side in the 1954 *Brown* case, the foundation of modern judicial supremacy.

78. Coolidge's first choice for vice president, William E. Borah, dropped his own and ultimately opposed La Follette's Court-reform proposal.

79. Schacter, "Putting the Politics of 'Judicial Activism' in Historical Perspective," 238.

80. Calvin Coolidge inaugural address (March 4, 1925), in *Supplement to the Messages and Papers of the Presidents*, 9485.

81. Ross, *A Muted Fury*, 254; Stephenson, *Campaigns and the Court*, 135.

82. Lawson, "Progressives and the Supreme Court," 427, 435.

83. Brandeis, "The Living Law."

84. Beveridge, *The Life of John Marshall*. Oliver Wendell Holmes had expressed the progressives' repudiation of Marshall's jurisprudence. This nearly jeopardized his appointment to the

Court, for Theodore Roosevelt shared what would become Beveridge's view. Faulkner, *The Jurisprudence of John Marshall*, appendix; White, "Looking at Holmes Looking at Marshall," 71; Wagner, "A Falling Out," 121.

85. Post, "Incomparable Chief Justiceship."

86. Lurie, *The Chief Justiceship of William Howard Taft, 1921–30*, 88.

87. Post, "Incomparable Chief Justiceship," 85.

88. Epp, *The Rights Revolution*, 35.

89. Lurie, *The Chief Justiceship of William Howard Taft, 1921–30*, 112.

90. Pringle, The *Life and Times of William Howard Taft*, 967.

91. Parrish, "The Great Depression," 730; Cushman, *Rethinking the New Deal Court*, 225.

92. Wiener, "Justice Hughes' Appointment," 78–91; disputed by Pusey, "The Nomination of Charles Evans Hughes," 95–100.

93. Parry-Giles, *The Character of Justice*, 52.

94. Ruth Ann O'Brien, *Workers' Paradox*, 161, 260.

95. Abraham, *Justices and Presidents*, 200. He displayed less progressivism in race cases, but the interests of organized labor and Blacks hardly coincided in this period. The American Federation of Labor and the National Association for the Advancement of Colored People opposed Parker with no cooperation.

96. Benjamin Cardozo address (April 22, 1932), *New York State Bar Association Proceedings*, 262–307.

97. Cardozo, *The Nature of the Judicial Process*, 106.

98. White House statement about signing a bill to limit the use of injunctions, March 23, 1932.

99. The Court accepted it in *Senn v. Tile Layer's Protective Union*, 301 U.S. 368 (1937). Hart, "The Power of Congress to Limit the Jurisdiction of the Federal Courts."

100. Franklin D. Roosevelt speech at Baltimore (October 25, 1932).

101. Herbert Hoover speech at New York (October 31, 1932).

102. Franklin D. Roosevelt inaugural address (March 4, 1933), in Rosenman, *The Public Papers and Addresses of Franklin D. Roosevelt*, 2:11–17.

103. Oliver Wendell Holmes had his pension cut from $20,000 to $10,000, but he could afford to take the hit. In fact, he left to the federal government an estate of $250,000. Congress decided to use it to publish a multivolume history of the Supreme Court—providing some of the principal sources for the present book. The Court ultimately held the pension reduction a violation of the salary-guarantee clause of Article III, section 1. *Booth v. United States*, 291 U.S. 339 (1934).

104. Pollard, "Four New Dissenters"; Chafee, "Liberal Trends in the Supreme Court," 344; Finkelstein, "The Dilemma of the Supreme Court"; Strout, "The New Deal and the Supreme Court," 489.

105. Nobody appears to have proposed to have Congress postpone the next meeting of the Court, as the Jeffersonians had done in 1802.

106. *Nebbia v. New York*, 291 U.S 502 (1934).

107. *Home Building and Loan Association v. Blaisdell*, 290 U.S. 435 (1934), 442.

108. Edwards, *American Default*, 176; Simon, *FDR and Chief Justice Hughes*, 256; Shlaes, *The Forgotten Man*, 158.

109. Glick, "Conditional Strategic Retreat," 811.

110. *Schechter v. United States*, 295 U.S. 495 (1935).

111. O'Brien, "Bicentennial Reflections on Herbert Hoover and the Supreme Court," 407.

112. *Louisville Joint Stock Land Bank v. Radford,* 291 U.S. 555 (1935).

113. *Humphrey's Executor v. United States,* 295 U.S. 602 (1935).

114. Simon, *FDR and Chief Justice Hughes,* 259.

115. Leuchtenburg, *The Supreme Court Reborn,* 92; "When the People Spoke, What Did They Say?" 2080–85.

116. Simon, *FDR and Chief Justice Hughes,* 221; Pusey, *Charles Evans Hughes,* 733.

117. Lash, *Dealers and Dreamers,* 428; Bernstein, *Turbulent Years,* 341.

118. Murphy, "The New Deal Agricultural Program," 165.

119. Roosevelt to Samuel B. Hill (July 6, 1935), in Rosenman, *The Public Papers and Addresses of Franklin D. Roosevelt,* 4:297.

120. Ickes, *The Secret Diary of Harold L. Ickes,* 524.

121. *United States v. Butler,* 297 U.S. 1 (1936), 62–63.

122. *United States v. Butler,* 79.

123. *West Coast Hotel v. Parrish,* 300 U.S. 379 (1937), 402.

124. *Jones v. Securities & Exchange Commission,* 298 U.S. 1 (1936).

125. *Carter v. Carter Coal Co.,* 298 U.S. 238 (1936).

126. *Morehead v. New York ex rel. Tipaldo,* 298 U.S. 597 (1936).

127. Lash, *Dealers and Dreamers,* 292; Ickes, *The Secret Diary of Harold L. Ickes,* 524; Bernstein, *The New Deal Collective Bargaining Policy,* 116.

128. Roosevelt message (February 5, 1937), in Ragsdale and Jones, *Debates on the Federal Judiciary,* 2:220.

129. Patenaude, "Garner, Sumners, and Connally," 45.

130. "Purging the Supreme Court," *Nation,* February 13, 1937, p. 173.

131. Hyneman, *The Supreme Court on Trial,* 54.

132. Charles Evans Hughes letter (March 22, 1937), in Ragsdale and Jones, *Debates on the Federal Judiciary,* 2:224.

133. *West Coast Hotel v. Parrish,* 300 U.S. 379 (1937).

134. John Q. Barrett recently tracked down the provenance of this *bon mot.* See Barrett, "Attribution Time."

135. *National Labor Relations Board v. Jones & Laughlin Steel Co.,* 301 U.S. 1 (1937).

136. For the debate on whether the Court had responded to "internal" or "external" causes, see Brinkley, "The Debate Over the Constitutional Revolution of 1937."

137. Leuchtenburg, *The Supreme Court Reborn,* 146; *Reorganization of the Federal Judiciary.*

138. Watson, *Living Constitution, Dying Faith,* 152.

139. *Reorganization of the Federal Judiciary,* 23.

140. O'Brien, "Bicentennial Reflections on Herbert Hoover and the Supreme Court," 413.

141. Newman, *Hugo Black,* 103; Hamburger, *Separation of Church and State,* 426.

142. Childs, "The Supreme Court To-Day," 582; Urofsky, "The Roosevelt Court," 65.

143. Oliphant, "A Return to Stare Decisis," 71; Harrison, "The Breakup of the Roosevelt Court," 201; Lurie, *The Chief Justiceship of William Howard Taft, 1921–30,* 128.

144. Urofsky, *Division and Discord.*

145. White, *The American Judicial Tradition,* 369–420.

146. Posner, "The Anti-Hero." See also Pulliam, "Revisiting William O. Douglas."

147. Fine, *Sit-Down*, 301.

148. Potts, "Justice Frank Murphy," 57.

149. McCune, *The Nine Young Men*, 151.

150. Strum, *Louis D. Brandeis*, 361; Posner, "The Rise and Fall of Judicial Self-Restraint," 544.

151. Leuchtenburg, *Supreme Court Reborn*, 121.

152. Lurie, *Chief Justiceship of William Howard Taft, 1921–30*, 129.

153. Alsop and Catledge, *The 168 Days*, 159.

154. Harrison, "The Breakup of the Roosevelt Court," 165, 193.

155. Urofsky, *Division and Discord*, 42; Harrison, "The Breakup of the Roosevelt Court," 167, 200.

156. At times, the Court used these terms to claim the primacy of the First Amendment *among* the rights spelled out in the Bill of Rights as well as of the Bill of Rights over other rights. See Abraham and Perry, "The 'Double Standard.'"

157. Gillman, "Preferred Freedoms," 623–53.

158. White, *The American Judicial Tradition*, 322–25.

159. Carrese, *The Cloaking of Power*.

160. Gillman, "The Collapse of Constitutional Originalism," 191–247; Hulsebosch, "The New Deal Court," 2009.

161. Surbin, "How Equity Conquered Common Law"; Surbin, "Fishing Expeditions Allowed"; Janutis, "The Struggle over Tort Reform"; McDowell, *Curbing the Courts*, 192.

162. The Federal Declaratory Judgment Act of 1934 also abetted judicial power. It permitted challenges to laws before they took effect, further weakening the requirement of a real "case or controversy" to empower judges. It practically legitimated "advisory opinions."

163. *New York Times v. Sullivan*, 376 U.S. 254 (1964).

164. *Wickard v. Filburn*, 317 U.S. 111 (1942).

165. White, "The 'Constitutional Revolution' as a Crisis in Adaptivity," 905.

166. Bickel, *The Least Dangerous Branch*, 35; Daniel J. Hulsebosch, "The New Deal Court," 1985.

167. Hogan, "Important Shifts in Constitutional Doctrine," 630.

168. Kelly, Harbison, and Belz, *The American Constitution*, 467, 487.

169. Grinnell, "The New Guesspotism," 507–11.

170. *Senn v. Tile Layer's Protective Union*, 301 U.S. 368 (1937); *Lauf v. E. G. Shinner & Co.*, 303 U.S. 323 (1938); Kersch, "The New Deal Triumph as the End of History?," 171.

171. *Thornhill v. Alabama*, 310 U.S. 88 (1940).

172. *United States v. Hutcheson*, 312 U.S. 219 (1941), 245.

173. *United States v. Teamsters*, 315 U.S. 521 (1942).

174. Dodd, "The Supreme Court and Labor, 1941–45," 1067.

175. Corwin, *The Constitution and What It Means Today*, vii.

176. Schiller, "The Era of Deference"; "Supreme Court Evaluation of Administrative Determinations of Law, 1932–42."

177. McCune, *The Nine Young Men*, 79.

178. Shapiro, *Who Guards the Guardians?*, 56.

179. *Securities and Exchange Commission v. Chenery Corp.*, 318 U.S. 80 (1943); *Securities and Exchange Commission v. Chenery Corp.*, 332 U.S. 194 (1947).

180. *Securities and Exchange Commission v. Chenery Corp. (1947)*, 211–17; Fine, *Frank Murphy*, 545.

181. *Jewell Ridge Coal Corp. v. United Mine Workers*, 325 U.S. 161 (1945).

182. Harry Truman to Bess Truman, June 11 and 14, 1946, in *Dear Bess*, 525–26.

183. This had failed in the Clayton Act. See Ernst, "The Labor Exemption, 1908–14."

184. 61 Stat. 84 (1947).

185. Hart, "The Power of Congress to Limit the Jurisdiction of the Federal Courts," 1383.

186. Urofsky, *Division and Discord*, 144.

187. Morgan, "The Portal-to-Portal Pay Case," 69.

188. Simon, *The Antagonists*, 115; Peters, "*Minersville School District v. Gobitis,*" 145–52.

189. Urofsky, *Division and Discord*, 110.

190. Rowley, "Fragmenting Parchment and the Winds of War."

191. *Ex parte Quirin*, 317 U.S. 1 (1942); Fisher, *Military Tribunals*, 113.

192. Dunne, *Hugo Black and the Judicial Revolution*, 213.

193. *Korematsu v. United States*, 323 U.S. 214 (1944), 246.

194. "Issue in Jackson–Black Dispute," 40.

195. Jaffe, "The Supreme Court Today."

196. Rodell, "The Supreme Court Is Standing Pat."

197. Urofsky, *Division and Discord*, 154. Notwithstanding this appraisal, Truman and Clark maintained a friendly correspondence. Rudko, *Truman's Court*, 33.

198. Rostow, "The Democratic Character of Judicial Review," 210.

199. Karkkainen, "The Police Power Revisited."

200. *Palko v. Connecticut*. In *Adamson*, the Fifth Amendment said that no person "shall be compelled in any criminal case to be a witness against himself." But California did not compel anyone to take the stand; it only let prosecutors take note of the fact that the defendant chose not to do so.

201. Jaffe, "Was Brandeis an Activist?," 996; Paul, *Conservative Crisis and the Rule of Law*, xiv.

202. The "incorporation" trend begun in the 1920s abated in the late 1940s and picked up again under Warren in the 1960s. Gardbaum, "New Deal Constitutionalism," 509, 541.

203. Dunne, *Hugo Black and the Judicial Revolution*, 268.

204. Hamburger, *Separation of Church and State*, 462.

205. Esbeck, "The Establishment Clause."

206. *McCollum v. Board of Education*, 333 U.S. 203 (1948).

207. *Zorach v. Clausen*, 343 U.S. 306 (1952), 313–14.

208. Patric, "The Impact of a Court Decision."

209. *Buchanan v. Warley*, 245 U.S. 60 (1917).

210. *Corrigan v. Buckley*, 271 U.S. 323 (1926). The Court tried to explain away this precedent, since it arose out of the District of Columbia, to which the Fourteenth Amendment did not apply. The parties did not plead the Fifth Amendment, and thus the Court dismissed the case "for want of a substantial question." In 1954, the Court would pursue quite a different approach to school segregation in the District, effectively applying the equal protection clause to the federal government in *Bolling v. Sharpe*.

211. *Shelley v. Kraemer*, 334 U.S. 1 (1948).

212. The Court could easily have decided *Shelley v. Kraemer* on liberty of contract grounds, just as it had in *Buchanan v. Warley*, or on real-property principles that frowned on restraints on alienation. Francis A. Allen, "Remembering *Shelley v. Kraemer*"; McGovney, "Racial Residential Segregation," 7–9; Bernstein, "Philip Sober Controlling Philip Drunk," 864.

The enforcement of racial covenants by injunction much resembled the enforcement of yellow-dog employment contracts, in which a worker agreed not to join a union. The law considers a sales contract an *executed* contract, complete when executed, with no continuation of a contractual relation between buyer and seller. It regards an employment contract as *executory,* an ongoing agreement terminable at will at any time by either party. Before the New Deal, if an employer wanted a nonunion workforce, he could freely fire any workers who joined unions. But it made no sense to allow the employer to get a court injunction against labor organizers on the claim that the organizers sought to induce a breach of contract. At-will employment contracts contain their own remedy: termination by either party. Similarly, nobody can add postexecution terms to a sales contract, just as no conditions beyond termination of the contract can supplement an at-will executory contract. We cannot consider a property really "sold" if the new owner must comply with future restrictions. Such contracts resembled bequests, akin to a private law of entail, more medieval than modern. Hume, *History of England,* 458–60. Thus, judges and commentators treated them under the "equitable servitude" doctrine. Several courts refused to enforce Major League Baseball's infamous "reserve clause" on similar grounds, describing it as not a contract but a contract *to make* a contract. *Weeghman v. Killefer,* 215 F. 168 (1914); Chardavoyne, *A Lincoln Legacy,* 98; Nathanson, "The Irrelevance of Baseball's Antitrust Exemption."

As in *Brown* and other cases, the specter of *Lochner* and "substantive due process" still spooked the Court (though they would have to resort to it in the DC segregation case, *Bolling v. Sharpe*). The justices fell for the progressive mythology about the laissez-faire era. Also as in *Brown,* the chief justice, Fred Vinson, wanted a unanimous decision and so cut some doctrinal corners to get it. This made *Shelley* an idiosyncratic jurisprudential dead end.

213. Bork, *The Tempting of America,* 152.

214. Francis A. Allen, "Remembering *Shelley v. Kraemer*"; Kurland, "Foreword," 148.

215. *Smith v. Allwright,* 321 U.S. 649 (1944), 669.

216. Though he had used it "a dozen times or so" before this. Harbaugh, *Lawyer's Lawyer,* 463.

217. Rodell, *Nine Men,* 316.

218. Purcell, *The Crisis of Democratic Theory;* Messner, "Postwar Natural Law Revival."

219. Palmer, "Hobbes, Holmes, and Hitler"; Lucey, "Natural Law and American Legal Realism."

220. Cardozo, *The Nature of the Judicial Process,* 106; MacIntyre, *After Virtue,* 14–34.

221. White, "From Sociological Jurisprudence to Realism," 1016.

7. JUDICIAL SUPREMACY ARRIVES: THE WARREN COURT

1. For two biographies, see White, *Earl Warren* and Schwartz, *Super Chief.*

2. Rodell, *Nine Men,* 284, 331.

3. White, *Earl Warren,* 185, 228, 359, 367.

4. Kalman, *The Strange Career of Legal Liberalism,* 2.

5. Kidney, "Are Judges Getting Too Powerful?"

6. Driver, "Supremacies and the Southern Manifesto," 1058, 1132.

7. Epp, *The Rights Revolution.*

8. The civil rights movement again followed the labor movement here. We saw in chapter 6 how the United Mine Workers tried to win in court what it had not won in Congress in the *Jewell Ridge* litigation. Labor similarly tried to revive "liberty of contract"—the laissez-faire-era

doctrine that union men decried as reducing workers to serfdom—to trump state right-to-work laws after the Taft–Hartley Act. But the Court rebuffed them in *Lincoln Federal Labor Union v. Northwestern Iron and Metal Co.*, 335 U.S. 525 (1949). See Kersch, "The New Deal Triumph as the End of History?," 199.

9. McNeil, *Groundwork*, 133; Fairfax, "Wielding the Double-Edged Sword," 17–44.

10. Berger, *Government by Judiciary*, 117–33; Kluger, *Simple Justice*, 623.

11. Riegel, "The Persistent Career of Jim Crow."

12. Bickel, "The Original Understanding and the Segregation Decision."

13. Alfred H. Kelly, "An Inside Story."

14. Levy, "The Right Against Self-Incrimination"; Hall, "The Warren Court in Historical Perspective," 303.

15. Ulmer, "Earl Warren and the Brown Decision," 698.

16. Simon, *Eisenhower v. Warren*, 148.

17. David M. O'Brien, *Justice Robert H. Jackson's Unpublished Opinion in* Brown *v. Board*, 82, 90; Schwartz, *Super Chief*, 89.

18. Simon, *Eisenhower v. Warren*, 191.

19. Barnett and Bernick, *The Original Meaning of the Fourteenth Amendment.*

20. *Brown v. Board of Education*, 347 U.S. 483 (1954); Yudof, "School Desegregation"; Mody, "*Brown* Footnote Eleven in Historical Context."

21. *Bolling v. Sharpe*, 347 U.S. 497 (1954).

22. Scholars have made many earnest attempts to square the *Brown* decision with the original intent of the framers and ratifiers of the Fourteenth Amendment. See McConnell, "Originalism and the Desegregation Decisions"; Calabresi and Perl, "Originalism and *Brown v. Board of Education*"; and Barnett and Bernick, *The Original Meaning of the Fourteenth Amendment.* The historical evidence cannot sustain the argument. The most thorough counterargument is Klarman, "*Brown*, Originalism, and Constitutional Theory." This has compelled jurisprudes to reject "originalism" as a theory of constitutional interpretation. They cannot accept any theory that does not vindicate *Brown.* But other means existed to reach the result in *Brown* that did not suffer from the manifest and manifold defects of Warren's opinion.

The most obvious alternate approach insisted on *substantial* equality in a separate but equal system. Balkin, *What* Brown v. Board of Education *Should Have Said.* The Court had already taken steps along this line in cases since 1938 concerning state law schools. Many southern states had begun to equalize spending and other physical facilities in anticipation of such a requirement. And this position never lacked for support in the Black community, whose leaders expressed the "segregation without discrimination" or "plural but equal" idea. Many expected that substantially separate but equal facilities would prove so expensive to maintain that southern whites would abandon them. The expense of maintaining segregated facilities, for instance, had led railroads to oppose segregation laws in the late nineteenth century.

Another alternative would have taken on Justice Brown's statement in *Plessy*, that "our Constitution is color-blind." Harlan's dissent recognized the real motive for segregation, to stigmatize Blacks and assert white supremacy, in 1896. In 1912, Brown himself practically agreed with Harlan's dissent. Brown, "The Dissenting Opinions of Mr. Justice Harlan," 338. Though Warren asserted privately that nobody could justify segregation except on the assumption of Black racial inferiority, he insisted on a "non-accusatory" opinion.

The old liberty of contract/substantive due process route also could have done the job. In 1917, the Court struck down residential apartheid. The states involved claimed that separating the races promoted public peace, reducing racial friction and preventing race riots. Louisiana made the same claim in *Plessy*. In 1917, the Court observed that while public order constituted a legitimate state concern, it could not trump individual rights. So *even if* Louisiana's motive had aimed to promote public safety rather than to stigmatize Blacks, the policy violated the Constitution.

Bolling v. Sharpe did just this. To say that segregation served no valid public purpose meant that it served an *invalid* one—the stigmatization of Black people. And since the DC case involved the Fifth Amendment, which has no equal protection but does have a due process clause, the justices really did proffer a substantive due process decision after all. But the justices felt compelled to hide it because the progressives' fanciful bad-old-days history of the laissez-faire era continued to haunt them. They ruined *Brown* due to a specter of their own creation—or of one of their law professors.

23. Thus we have books with titles like *What* Brown v. Board of Education *Should Have Said*.

24. Bickel, *The Least Dangerous Branch*, 247.

25. *Brown v. Board of Education*, 349 U.S. 294 (1955).

26. Horwitz, *The Warren Court and the Pursuit of Justice*, 29.

27. Murphy, *Congress and the Court*, 79.

28. Driver, "The Consensus Constitution," 816.

29. *Congressional Record* 102, 84th Cong., 2d Sess. (March 12, 1956), 4459–61.

30. Driver, "Supremacies and the Southern Manifesto."

31. Klarman, "How *Brown* Changed Race Relations."

32. Harbaugh, *Lawyer's Lawyer*, 509. Kahn, "Shattering the Myth About President Eisenhower's Supreme Court Appointments" makes a somewhat exaggerated case for Eisenhower's commitment to Warren and *Brown*.

33. This echoed presidential responses to *Worcester v. Georgia* and *Ex parte Merryman*.

34. Blackman, "The Irrepressible Myth of *Cooper v. Aaron*."

35. Simon, *Eisenhower v. Warren*, 204; Stern, "Eisenhower and Kennedy," 577.

36. In *Brown*, for example, the opinion began, "Mr. Chief Justice Warren delivered the opinion of the Court." *Cooper* began, "Opinion of the Court by the Chief Justice, Mr. Justice Black, Mr. Justice Frankfurter . ."

37. *Cooper v. Aaron*, 358 U.S. 1 (1958), 18. The Court in *Marbury* exercised coordinate review, overturning an act of Congress, not of the states, as in *Cooper*. Moreover, the supremacy clause applies only to state judges, not governors or legislators, who did not participate in *Cooper* anyway. Blackman, "The Irrepressible Myth of *Cooper v. Aaron*."

38. In *Brown v. Allen*, 344 U.S. 443 (1953), Justice Jackson did say, "We are not final because we are infallible, but we are infallible only because we are final." Jackson presented a single, concurring opinion, and may not have meant any more than James Madison's observation that the Court would tend to have the final say because it usually spoke last in the order of time on constitutional questions. The *Cooper* dictum, on the other hand, made a unified and deliberate *statement*.

39. *Congressional Record* 102, 84th Cong., 2d Sess. (March 12, 1956), 4462.

40. *Erie Railroad v. Tompkins*, 304 U.S. 64 (1938), 77–78.

41. *Cooper v. Aaron*, 24–26.

42. White, *Earl Warren*, 183; Schwartz, *Super Chief*, 146.

43. Garrow, "Bad Behavior Makes Big Law."

44. The Court had employed a similar method in the 1937 Labor Board cases, the first of which concerned an enormous interstate steel operation, followed by much smaller concerns.

45. Some uncertainty remains as to Sherman Minton's status as a Catholic when on the Court.

46. *Pennsylvania v. Nelson* 350 U.S. 497 (1956). Historically, the First Amendment prohibited only Congress from punishing sedition. Now the Court held that *only* Congress could do so.

47. Ober, "Communism and the Court."

48. Pritchett, *Congress Versus the Supreme Court, 1957–60*, 120; Anthony Lewis, "High Court's Critics Renew an Old Fight."

49. Pritchett, *Congress Versus the Supreme Court, 1957–60*, 38, 40.

50. Murphy, *Congress and the Court*, 262.

51. Hyneman, *The Supreme Court on Trial*, 60; Rosenberg, "Judicial Independence," 387.

52. Dahl, "Decision-Making in a Democracy."

53. Jackson, *The Supreme Court in the American System of Government.*

54. "Report of the Committee on Federal–State Relationships as Affected by Judicial Decisions."

55. Ross, "Attacks on the Warren Court by State Officials," 521; Galie, "The Other Supreme Courts"; Hagan, "Patterns of Activism."

56. "What a State Chief Justice Says About the Supreme Court"; Moreno, "In re *Huff*."

57. Gunther, *Learned Hand*, 661–62.

58. Schwartz, *Super Chief*, 276. Felix Frankfurter's excessively importunate lobbying for Hand's appointment may have spoiled Hand's chances.

59. Wechsler, "Toward Neutral Principles of Constitutional Law," 20–22.

60. Miller and Howell, "The Myth of Neutral Principles"; Miller, "Notes on the Concept of the 'Living' Constitution.'"

61. *American Federation of Labor v. American Sash and Door*, 335 U.S. 538 (1949), 555–56.

62. See Friedman's five-part "History of the Countermajoritarian Difficulty."

63. Dahl, "Decision-Making in a Democracy."

64. Gunther, "The Subtle Vices of the 'Passive Virtues,'" 3; Friedman, "The History of the Countermajoritarian Difficulty, Part Five," 243–45.

65. Elias, "Red Monday and Its Aftermath."

66. "A Regrettable Decision."

67. Ross, "Attacks on the Warren Court," 600.

68. McCloskey, "Reflections on the Warren Court," 1240; Berger, "The Activist Legacy of the New Deal Court," 784.

69. *Colegrove v. Green*, 328 U.S. 549 (1946).

70. *Gray v. Sanders*, 327 U.S. 368 (1963).

71. Congress had required states to devise compact and contiguous congressional districts, with substantially the same number of inhabitants, from 1842 until 1929.

72. Silverstein and Ginsberg, "The Supreme Court and the New Politics of Judicial Power," 377.

73. Bradley, "Shall We Ratify the New Constitution?," 125.

74. *Lucas v. Colorado*, 377 U.S. 713 (1964).

75. White, *Earl Warren*, 241.

76. Powe, *The Warren Court and American Politics*, 253.

77. Rosenberg, *The Hollow Hope*, 297.

78. *Engle v. Vitale,* 370 U.S. 421 (1962).

79. *Abington v. Schempp,* 374 U.S. 203 (1963).

80. Dierenfield, *"Engle v. Vitale,"* in Urofsky, *The Public Debate over Controversial Supreme Court Decisions,* 217; Pfeffer, "The Becker Amendment"; Green, "Evangelicals and the Becker Amendment."

81. Forte, *The Supreme Court in American Politics,* 4.

82. Magliocca, *The Heart of the Constitution.*

83. Amar, "The Bill of Rights as a Constitution," 1179.

84. *Wolf v. Colorado,* 338 U.S. 25 (1949).

85. *Linkletter v. Walker,* 381 U.S. 618 (1965).

86. Kurland, "Toward a Political Supreme Court."

87. Long, *"Mapp v. Ohio,"* in Urofsky, *The Public Debate over Controversial Supreme Court Decisions,* 210.

88. *Dickerson v. United States,* 530 U.S. 428 (2000).

89. Murphy and Tanenhaus, "Public Opinion and Supreme Court."

90. Caro, *The Years of Lyndon Johnson,* 395, 445. Even more ironic was House Judiciary Committee chairman Emmanuel Celler defending the independence of the Court. In 1937, he warned that Congress would pack the Court if it did not follow the election returns. One had to say, in 1964, "Oh come, oh come now, Emmanuel." Ross, "The Role of Judicial Issues in Presidential Campaigns," 430; "Celler in Warning to Supreme Court."

91. Kalman, *The Strange Career of Legal Liberalism,* 46.

92. Atkinson, *Leaving the Bench,* 134–36.

93. When an aide suggested that Johnson appoint district judge A. Leon Higginbotham, Johnson replied, "The only two people who ever heard of Judge Higginbotham are you and his momma. When I appoint a n----- to the bench, I want everyone to know he's a n-----." Powe, *The Warren Court and American Politics,* 291.

94. Wright, "The Role of the Supreme Court," 2.

95. *New York Times v. Sullivan,* 376 U.S. 254 (1964).

96. The Alabama courts certainly had manipulated the state libel law for the political purpose of harassing the civil rights movement. Goldberg and Zipursky, "The Supreme Court's Stealth Return to the Common Law of Torts."

97. *Erie R.R. v. Tompkins,* 304 U.S. 64 (1938).

98. Ziegler, *Beyond Abortion,* 23.

99. *Griswold v. Connecticut,* 381 U.S. 479 (1965).

100. Frank Murphy had called for this in his dissent in *Adamson v. California,* 332 U.S. 46 (1947), 123.

101. *Eisenstadt v. Baird,* 405 U.S. 438 (1972). In *Griswold,* the first-ever divorced justice, Douglas, stressed the sanctity of marriage, "a coming together for better or for worse, hopefully enduring, and intimate to the degree of being sacred." Douglas had divorced three times.

102. Dunne, *Hugo Black and the Judicial Revolution,* 357.

103. Woodward and Armstrong, *The Brethren,* 198, 280–81.

104. *Katzenbach v. McClung,* 379 U.S. 294 (1964).

105. Schwartz, *Super Chief,* 599; Powe, *The Warren Court and American Politics,* 264. The Court would retract this power in *Boerne v. Flores,* 521 U.S. 507 (1997).

106. *Jones v. Mayer,* 392 U.S. 409 (1968).

107. Belz, *A New Birth of Freedom,* 168; Kennedy, "Reconstruction and the Politics of Scholarship," 537–38; Lusky, *By What Right?,* 234; Schwartz, *From Confederation to Nation,* 193.

108. Casper, *"Jones v. Mayer,"* 96–99.

109. Reich, "The New Property."

110. It had done so in its interpretation of the Fair Labor Standards Act in the *Jewell Ridge* case, until overridden by Congress.

111. *Shapiro v. Thompson,* 394 U.S. 319 (1969).

112. *Goldberg v. Kelly,* 397 U.S. 254 (1970).

113. Homosexuals had to wait. The Court upheld the federal government's definition of homosexuality as inherently psychopathic, in 1967. Stein, *"Boutilier* and the U.S. Supreme Court's Sexual Revolution."

114. The apportionment cases followed a racial gerrymandering case, *Gomillion v. Lightfoot,* 364 U.S. 339 (1960).

115. Schwartz, *Super Chief,* 591.

116. Steiker, *Courting Death,* 51; Klarman, "The Racial Origins of Modern Criminal Procedure."

117. Or transferred income. Whether this "benefited" welfare recipients remains questionable.

118. Kelly, Harbison, and Belz, *The American Constitution,* 630.

119. Dodd, "The Supreme Court and Labor, 1941–45," 1067.

120. Miller, "The True Story of *Carolene Products.*" The dairy farmers acted like the London physicians in *Dr. Bonham's Case.*

121. *Williamson v. Lee Optical,* 348 U.S. 483 (1955), 487–88. Emphasis added.

122. Grant, "The Gild Returns to America," 303–36, 458–77.

123. Stewart's dissent in *Von's Grocery,* 384 U.S. 270 (1966). The Court also showed its style in a 1953 baseball antitrust case.

124. Schwartz, *Super Chief,* 682; Ward, "An Extraconstitutional Arrangement."

125. Spector, "Legal Historian on the United States Supreme Court," 185.

126. "Battle over Supreme Court: It Goes Beyond Fortas."

127. Marshall, *Public Opinion and the Supreme Court,* 139; Hall, "The Warren Court in Historical Perspective," 306.

128. Ross, *A Muted Fury,* 332. As noted in chapter 5, these included decisions on common law tort liability, the labor injunction, income tax, Interstate Commerce Act restrictions, and antitrust law.

8. THE METASTASIZING OF JUDICIAL SUPREMACY

1. Barkow, "More Supreme than Court."

2. Graham, "Liberalism After the 60s," 294.

3. Kalman, *Abe Fortas,* 348.

4. Hickman, "Courting the Right," 297. This phrasing nicely accessorized fascism's association with the color brown.

5. The southern strategy grew into a hoary myth, akin to Nixon's alleged secret plan to end the Vietnam War. See Kotlowski, *Nixon's Civil Rights.*

6. One should credit Hruska for his use of the subjunctive in his first sentence.

7. Vatz and Windt, "The Defeats of Judges Haynsworth and Carswell," 485; Maltese, *The Selling*

of Supreme Court Nominees, 70–85. Hruska's comment struck many as anti-Semitic, and after Fortas, the Court had no Jewish justice until 1993.

8. Smillie, "Who Wants Juristocracy?," 192.

9. Kastenburg, *The Campaign to Impeach Justice William O. Douglas*; Kauffman, "The Ford Impeachment."

10. Kluger, *Simple Justice*, 615–19; David M. O'Brien, *Justice Robert H. Jackson's Unpublished Opinion in Brown v. Board*, 56–77.

11. *San Antonio v. Rodriguez*, 411 U.S. 1 (1973).

12. Maltz, *The Chief Justiceship of Warren Burger*, 151.

13. Maltz, *The Coming of the Nixon Court*, 38.

14. *Miller v. California*, 413 U.S. 15 (1973).

15. *Green v. New Kent County*, 391 U.S. 430 (1968); *Keyes v. Denver*, 413 U.S. 189 (1973); Wilkinson, *From* Brown *to* Bakke, 108–27, 195–99.

16. *Swann v. Charlotte-Mecklenburg*, 402 U.S. 1 (1971); Wilkinson, *From* Brown *to* Bakke, 131–60.

17. 78 Stat. 241 (1964), sec. 401(b).

18. *Milliken v. Bradley*, 418 U.S. 717 (1974); Wilkinson, *From* Brown *to* Bakke, 216–49.

19. *Furman v. Georgia*, 408 U.S. 238 (1972); Steiker and Steiker, *Courting Death*, 50–70.

20. *Gregg v. Georgia*, 428 U.S. 153 (1976).

21. Gillman, Graber, and Whittington, *American Constitutionalism*, 1:16.

22. *United States v. Nixon*, 418 U.S. 683 (1974).

23. McManus and Helfman, *Liberty and Union*, 525.

24. Woodward and Armstrong, *The Brethren*, 295–303.

25. Kastenburg, *The Campaign to Impeach Justice William O. Douglas*, 25, 70, 85, 104.

26. The Nixon appointees probably made no difference in the outcome of the case; three of the four concurred in the result. Nixon replaced Warren, Fortas, Harlan, and Black. Only Black might have dissented in *Roe*.

27. The Supreme Court's baseball jurisprudence provides some of the strongest arguments against judicial power. In the 1922 *Federal Baseball* case, the Court held that Major League Baseball did not constitute "commerce among the states" that Congress could regulate under the antitrust laws. (It did not stupidly deny baseball's obviously commercial nature.) This fit seamlessly into the pre–New Deal understanding of interstate commerce. Fifteen years later, however, the Court capitulated to the New Dealers' view that Congress could regulate all economic activity as interstate commerce. In the 1953 *Toolson* case, the Court declined to overturn *Federal Baseball* and claimed that Congress had given baseball an "exemption" from the antitrust laws, which Congress could lift if it wanted. This decision typified Warren Court pragmatic judicial legislation. As the *New York Times* put it, the decision showed that the law "is not what the Congress or previous opinions of the Supreme Court itself have held it to be, but what the Court now thinks it should be." Banner, *The Baseball Trust*, 131. On the subject generally, see Briley, "Danny Gardella and Baseball's Reserve Clause"; Duquette, *Regulating the National Pastime*; McDonald, "Antitrust and Baseball: Stealing Holmes"; Nathanson, "Who Exempted Baseball Anyway?; and Nathanson, "The Irrelevance of Baseball's Antitrust Exemption."

The Court applied the antitrust laws to all other professional sports (baseball had represented the only significant professional sport in 1922). The Court had another chance to correct this absurd situation in 1972. Instead, it stuck to its guns, with novice justice Harry Blackmun opening his opinion with a paean to the game so embarrassing that several of his brethren refused to join that part of it. *Flood v. Kuhn,* 407 U.S. 258 (1972). MLB continues to enjoy this anomalous "exemption" to this day.

28. Maltz, *Coming of the Nixon Court,* 183.

29. Woodward and Armstrong, *The Brethren,* 233.

30. Rubin, *Abortion, Politics, and the Courts,* 32; Silverstein and Ginsberg, "The Supreme Court and the New Politics of Judicial Power," 383; Posner, "The Rise and Fall of Judicial Self-Restraint," 533.

31. Forsythe, *Abuse of Discretion,* 93.

32. Dellapenna, *Dispelling the Myths of Abortion History,* 841, 1003; Dellapenna, "The Historical Case Against Abortion"; Ponnuru, "Aborting History"; Finnis, "'Shameless Acts' in Colorado."

33. Many feminists denounced *Roe* as being more concerned about the rights of doctors than of women. Greenhouse and Siegel, "The Unfinished Story of *Roe v. Wade.*"

34. *Roe v. Wade,* 410 U.S. 113 (1973), 116–67. The third trimester of a normal, thirty-nine-week pregnancy would begin at week twenty-six. "Viability" already varied quite a bit from this date, and would change over time, causing no end of confusion in the law.

35. *Doe v. Bolton,* 410 U.S. 179 (1973), 181–207; Miller, "The Alley Behind First Street."

36. *Roe v. Wade,* 167–71; *Doe v. Bolton,* 209–21.

37. *Roe v. Wade,* 171–78.

38. *Doe v. Bolton,* 221–23.

39. *Doe v. Bolton,* 208. Blackmun wanted to issue a press release emphasizing this point but did not. Garrow, *Liberty and Sexuality,* 587.

40. Rosenberg, *The Hollow Hope,* 189; Bazelon, "The New Abortion Providers."

41. In the following years, the Court upheld Congress's prohibition of federal funding for nontherapeutic abortions via Medicaid.

42. Noonan, *A Private Choice,* 69–79.

43. Lyndon B. Johnson's death made the day's top story.

44. One of Justice Powell's clerks had leaked the decision to *Time,* which reported it in advance of the Court's announcement with the title "Abortion on Demand." This prompted Burger's concurrence insisting that the decision did *not* mean abortion on demand.

45. Ziegler, "*Edelin*"; Homans, "*Commonwealth v. Kenneth Edelin.*"

46. *Floyd v. Anders,* 440 F. Supp. 535 (1977), 539.

47. Arkes, *First Things,* 370–71.

48. Williams, *Defenders of the Unborn,* 236.

49. *Roe v. Wade,* 220; Garrow, *Liberty and Sexuality,* 536.

50. Clark, "Religion, Morality and Abortion."

51. Lusky, *By What Right?,* 39, 343.

52. Sitman, "The Conscience of a President"; Critchlow, *Intended Consequences,* 137.

53. Greenhouse, "Justice John Paul Stevens as an Abortion-Rights Strategist"; Greenhouse and Siegel, "Unfinished Story."

54. Balkin, *What* Roe v. Wade *Should Have Said.*

55. In Ely, *Democracy and Distrust.*

56. Ely, "The Wages of Crying Wolf," 926, 937, 940, 942; Garrow, *Liberty and Sexuality,* 615.

57. Epstein, "Substantive Due Process by Any Other Name"; Rice, "The Dred Scott Case of the Twentieth Century."

58. Uslander and Weber, "Public Support for Pro-Choice Abortion Policies"; Rosenberg, *The Hollow Hope*, 245.

59. Ginsburg, "Some Thoughts on Autonomy and Equality"; Ginsburg, "Speaking in a Judicial Voice"; Greenhouse, "On Privacy and Equality"; Heagney, "Judge Ruth Bader Ginsburg Offers Critique of *Roe v. Wade.*"

60. Guttmacher, "The Shrinking Non-Psychiatric Indications for Therapeutic Abortion"; "Therapeutic Abortion"; Quay, "Justifiable Abortion," 184, 233; Humphries, "The Movement to Legalize Abortion," 212.

61. Forsythe, *Abuse of Discretion*, 78. Justice Henry Friendly of the second circuit had prepared an opinion upholding New York's abortion law, but the more liberal 1970 law made it moot. Randolph, "Before *Roe v. Wade.*"

62. Hurwitz, "Jon O. Newman and the Abortion Decisions."

63. *Steinberg v. Brown*, 321 F. Supp. 741 (1970), 746–47.

64. Williams, *Defenders of the Unborn*, 196; Maledon, "The Law and the Unborn Child"; Dellapenna, "Abortion and the Law," 148.

65. Garrow, *Liberty and Sexuality*, 616.

66. Belz, *Equality Transformed*, 29–41; Graham, *The Civil Rights Era*, 301–45.

67. *Eastern Contractors Association v. Shultz*, 311 F. Supp. 1002 (1970); 442 F. 2d 159 (1971).

68. *Griggs v. Duke Power Co.*, 401 U.S. 424 (1971).

69. Blumrosen, "Strangers in Paradise."

70. Gould, *Black Workers in White Unions*, 92.

71. Belton, *The Crusade for Equality in the Workplace*, 187.

72. Kull, *The Color-Blind Constitution*, 5.

73. *Regents v. Bakke*, 438 U.S. 265 (1978).

74. Schuck, *Diversity in America; Wood, Diversity.*

75. *United Steelworkers v. Weber*, 443 U.S. 193 (1979).

76. *Fullilove v. Klutznick*, 448 U.S. 448 (1980).

77. Dellapenna, *Dispelling the Myths*, 970.

78. Sharp, *The Sometime Connection*, 76; Le and Citrin, "Affirmative Action," 164–66.

79. The Civil Rights Act of 1991 presented an exception. This act adopted the "disparate impact" standard under Title VII.

80. *Reed v. Reed*, 404 U.S. 71 (1971).

81. Maltz, *The Chief Justiceship of Warren Burger*, 256.

82. *Craig v. Boren*, 429 U.S. 190 (1976).

83. *United States v. Virginia*, 518 U.S. 515 (1996).

84. Melnik, "The Odd Evolution of the Civil Rights State."

85. Peck, "The EEOC."

86. Schiller, "The Age of Deference."

87. The old National Labor Relations Act, in contrast, did not allow private suits. If the Labor Board thought a worker's claim lacked merit, that closed the case.

88. Melnik, "From Tax and Spend to Mandate and Sue."

89. Teles, "Transformative Bureaucracy," 64.

90. Rosenbloom, "The Judicial Response to the Administrative State."

91. Landis, "The Development of the Administrative Commission," 18.

92. Charles Evans Hughes speech at Elmira (May 3, 1907), in *Addresses and Papers of Charles Evans Hughes*, 139.

93. Stewart, "Administrative Law in the Twenty-First Century."

94. Schiller, "An Unexpected Antagonist."

95. Merrill, "The Story of *Chevron*"; Scalia, "Remarks." "Arbitrary and capricious" looked like the administrative law equivalent to "rational basis" in constitutional law.

96. Stewart, "Reformation of American Administrative Law," 1755; Rabin, "Federal Regulation in Historical Perspective," 1309.

97. Rosenbloom, "The Judicial Response," 41; Lieberman, *The Litigious Society*, 115; Glazer, "Towards an Imperial Judiciary?"

98. Glazer, "Should Judges Administer Social Services?," 68.

99. *Federalist* 47. In *Federalist* 48 (1788), Publius noted that "the legislative department is everywhere extending the sphere of its activity into its impetuous vortex."

100. Chayes, "The Role of the Judge in Public Law Litigation"; Horowitz, *The Courts and Social Policy*.

101. Oliphant, "A Return to Stare Decisis," 73–74.

102. Lieberman, *The Litigious Society*, 126, Kidney, "Are Judges Getting Too Powerful?"; Press, "When Judges Govern."

103. Glendon, *Rights Talk*.

104. The American Bar Association reported some 1.3 million lawyers in 2018.

105. Horowitz, *Courts and Social Policy*, 10.

106. Tushnet, "Public Law Litigation and the Ambiguities of *Brown*," 23–28; Teles, *Rise of the Conservative Legal Movement*, 43.

107. Priest, "The Invention of Enterprise Liability"; Priest, "The Expansion of Modern US Tort Law."

108. Olson, *The Litigation Explosion*, 18.

109. Earlier, such awkward titles as "interpretivism" had circulated.

110. Scholars would bring them back some years later in theories of "constitutional construction." Whittington, *Constitutional Construction*.

111. Currie, *The Constitution in Congress*, xiii.

112. Gillman, "The Collapse of Constitutional Originalism," 238. See also Hulsebosch, "The New Deal Court," 2009; and Horwitz, "Republicanism and Liberalism," 57–63. As an example of this position, see Sanford Levinson's preface to McCloskey, *The American Supreme Court*, ix–x.

113. O'Neill, *Originalism in American Law and Politics*.

114. Meese, "Toward a Jurisprudence of Original Intention."

115. "William J. Brennan on the Failure of the Doctrine of Original Intent," in Hall, *Major Problems in American Constitutional History*, 2:557–66; Presser, "The Battle over 'Turning Back the Clock' in Constitutional Interpretation."

116. Flowers, "'A Prolife Disaster'"; Ziegler, *Beyond Abortion*, 210.

117. Powe, *The Supreme Court and the American Elite*, 303.

118. *Congressional Record* 133 (July 1, 1987), 18518; Abraham, *Justices, Presidents, and Senators*, 298.

119. Many sources call this the widest margin of defeat in Supreme Court history, but Alexan-

der Wolcott went down by a 9–24 vote in 1811, and a greater percentage of senators voted against John Rutledge in 1795 and George W. Woodward in 1845.

120. Hence Kennedy's reference to Watergate. Bork, as acting attorney general, had fired the special prosecutor, Archibald Cox, in the "Saturday Night Massacre." Kennedy in fact led with this event in his notorious opposition speech.

121. O'Neill, *Originalism*, 161–89.

122. Balkin, *Living Originalism in American Law and Politics;* Rogers, "Originalism's Expanding Popularity"; Semeraro, "We're All Originalists Now."

123. *Bostock v. Clayton,* 590 U.S. ___ (2020).

124. United States Commission on Civil Rights, *Federal Procurement After* Adarand; Clegg, "Unfinished Business."

125. Milkis, "Odd Evolution."

126. *Federalist* 10; McGinnis, "The Original Constitution and Its Decline," 201.

127. Detlefsen, "Affirmative Action and Business Deregulation," 556–64.

128. The lead case was *Ward's Cove Packing Co. v. Atonio,* 490 U.S. 642 (1989).

129. *Gruetter v. Bollinger,* 539 U.S. 306 (2003), 310.

130. *Gratz v. Bollinger,* 539 U.S. 244 (2003), 305.

131. *Webster v. Reproductive Health Services,* 492 U.S. 490 (1989).

132. Dellapenna, *Dispelling the Myths of Abortion History,* xii, 841; "Roundtable: Historians and the *Webster* Case."

133. *Planned Parenthood v. Casey,* 505 U.S. 833 (1992), 851.

134. The joint justices offered quite literally an expression of Giovanni Pico della Mirandola's "Oration on the Dignity of Man" (1486), in which he lauds the unfettered, autonomous individual, free to fashion his own nature.

135. See the very similar language in Zilbergeld, *The Shrinking of America,* 69.

136. The Court had never before applied "reliance interests" in a noncommercial case. In 1954, white southerners pleaded that, even if the Court had wrongly decided *Plessy v. Ferguson,* the South had arranged itself for decades on the assumed legality of segregation—it had become "part of the life of the people . . confirmed in their habits, customs, traditions, and way of life." The Court in *Brown* dismissed this claim—though the virtual non-enforcement of the decision in large part resulted from it. Forsythe, "A Draft Opinion Overruling *Roe v. Wade.*"

137. *Planned Parenthood v. Casey,* 856–60.

138. The Court used *Adkins* as a stand-in for *Lochner.* The Court explicitly overruled *Adkins* in 1937 but did not overrule *Lochner* until 1963 (in *Ferguson v. Skrupa*). Technically, *Brown* did not overrule *Plessy,* which concerned public transportation, not education. *Gayle v. Browder* did so in 1956.

139. *Planned Parenthood v. Casey,* 866–68.

140. Blackmun insisted again on the delusion that it "protects a woman's right to terminate her pregnancy *in its early stages.*"

141. *Planned Parenthood v. Casey,* 992–96. On the cultural impact of *Roe,* see Caldwell, "Pro-Lifestyle."

142. *Planned Parenthood v. Casey,* 922, 943.

143. "D&X," as opposed to dilation and evacuation, or "D&E," in which the unborn child is dismembered in utero and removed in pieces.

144. *Stenberg v. Carhart,* 530 U.S. 914 (2000).

145. The majority did not flinch to describe what it justified. One might well regard D&E as more horrific than D&X.

146. *Gonzales v. Carhart,* 550 U.S. 124 (2007).

147. *National League of Cities v. Usery,* 426 U.S. 833 (1976).

148. *United States v. Lopez,* 514 U.S. 549 (1995).

149. *Morrison v. United States,* 529 U.S. 598 (2000).

150. *Gonzales v. Raich,* 545 U.S. 1 (2005). States effectively nullified this federal prohibition when the federal government chose not to enforce it. Many more states have now legalized marijuana for medicinal and then for recreational use.

151. Scalia, "Originalism: The Lesser Evil," 864; Rosen, "What Made Scalia Great."

152. *United States v. Lopez,* 601.

153. Devins, "The Majoritarian Rehnquist Court?"

154. *Dickerson v. United States,* 530 U.S. 428 (2000), 441.

155. *Dickerson v. United States,* 443, 455.

156. *Boerne v. Flores,* 521 U.S. 507 (1997). The earlier precedent was *Sherbert v. Verner,* 374 U.S. 398 (1963).

157. Benedict, *The Blessings of Liberty,* 424.

158. Ackerman, *We the People,* 84.

159. Neuhaus, *The End of Democracy?*

160. Rosenberg, "The War on Judges."

161. A machine recount had already occurred. The Gore campaign sought a hand recount in four counties most likely to produce more Democratic ballots.

162. Ceasar and Busch, *The Perfect Tie,* 185.

163. *Bush v. Gore,* 531 U.S. 98 (2000). Republican Presidents had appointed two of the four dissenters, Stevens and Souter.

164. Purcell, *Originalism, Federalism, and the American Constitutional Enterprise,* 134.

165. Benedict, *The Blessings of Liberty,* 425.

166. Kramer, *The People Themselves;* Powe, "Are 'the People' Missing in Action?"; Forbath, "Popular Constitutionalism in the Twentieth Century."

167. Keck, *The Most Activist Supreme Court in History;* Miller, "When Congress Attacks the Federal Courts," 1019.

168. Stuart Taylor, "The 'Judicial Activists' Are Always on the Other Side," *New York Times,* 3 July 1988.

169. *Kelo v. City of New London, Connecticut,* 545 U.S. 469 (2005); Taylor, "Newest Judicial Activists Come from the Right."

170. *District of Columbia v. Heller,* 554 U.S. 570 (2008); *McDonald v. Chicago,* 561 U.S. 572 (2010).

171. Powe, The *Warren Court and American Politics,* 415.

172. Berman, "Where the Gun-Control Movement Goes Silent."

173. Michael Bellesiles, *Arming America.* This grossly fraudulent attempt to prove that gun ownership was uncommon during the colonial period occasioned one of the greatest scandals in American historiography. The work resembled historians' tendentious briefs since the *Brown* case.

174. Softness, "Preserving Judicial Supremacy Come *Heller* High Water."

175. Gottlieb, *Unfit for Democracy*, 203.

176. Tushnet, "Understanding the Rehnquist Court," 197.

177. Teles, *The Rise of the Conservative Legal Movement*, 80; Taylor, "Newest Judicial Activists"; Dorn and Manne, *Economic Liberties and the Judiciary;* Pulliam, "Against 'Judicial Engagement'"; Pulliam, "The Libertarian Constitutional Fantasy."

178. Stein, "*Boutilier* and the US Supreme Court's Sexual Revolution."

179. *Bowers v. Hardwick*, 478 U.S. 186 (1986).

180. *Lawrence v. Texas*, 539 U.S. 558 (2003).

181. Tushnet, "Understanding the Rehnquist Court," 199.

182. Johnson, *Modern Times*, 167. Credit Lytton Strachey for almost exactly predicting that the recognition of homosexual equality would come a century after 1906.

183. Lund and McGinnis, "*Lawrence v. Texas* and Judicial Hubris."

184. See, for example, Wolfe, *One Nation, After All*. American attitudes about homosexuality lagged behind other Western democracies when this study was published, but quickly converged.

185. *National Federation of Independent Business v. Sebelius*, 579 U.S. 519 (2012).

186. *King v. Burwell*, 576 U.S. 473 (2015).

187. Softness, "Preserving Judicial Supremacy Come *Heller* High Water," 627.

188. Conde and Greve, "*Yakus* and the Administrative State," 816.

189. *Immigration and Naturalization Service v. Chadha*, 462 U.S. 919 (1983).

190. *Schlesinger v. Holtzman*, 414 U.S. 1321 (1973).

191. *Washington v. Glucksburg*, 521 U.S. 702 (1997), 789.

192. Brennan, "State Constitutions and the Protection of Individual Rights."

193. Brennan, "The Bill of Rights and the States," 547; Gest, "The Swing to the Left in State Courts."

194. Williams, "Juristocracy in the American States?," 73; Dippel, "Human Rights in America," 747.

195. Williams, "Juristocracy in the American States?," 79; Hall, "Progressive Reform and the Decline of Democratic Accountability," 345.

196. Wefing, "The New Jersey Supreme Court," 703.

197. *State v. Otis Elevator*, 12 NJ 1 (1953); Andora, "Judicial Self-Restraint in New Jersey," 504.

198. The California court would do the same through the state constitution's equal protection clause.

199. Malanga, "The Court that Broke Jersey."

200. Corriher and Brown, "Chris Christie's War on Judicial Independence."

201. Hagan, "Patterns of Activism"; White, *The American Judicial Tradition*, 292–316; Posner, "Rise and Fall of Judicial Self-Restraint," 540; Gailie, "The Other Supreme Courts"; Davis, *A Warren Court of Our Own*.

202. Pendley, "State Courts Create New 'Rights.'"

203. Hagan, "Patterns of Activism on State Supreme Courts"; Mulcahy, "Modeling the Garden."

204. Wenzel, "Legislating from the State Bench"; Lindquist, "Judicial Activism in State Supreme Courts."

205. Croley, "The Majoritarian Difficulty," 734.

206. *Obergefell v. Hodges,* 576 U.S. 664 (2015).

207. Nolan, *The Therapeutic State,* 1.

208. Williams, "Reinventing the Courts."

209. Williams, "Reinventing the Courts," 625, 636.

210. Zuckert, "Book Review: *Morality, Politics and Law,* by Michael Perry," 446.

211. Lustig and Weiler, "Judicial Review in the Contemporary World"; Tamanaha, *On the Rule of Law,* 110.

212. Other sources say it dates from the mid-nineteenth century, under American influence. Helgadottir, "Status Presens—Judicial Review in Iceland"; Helgadottir, *The Influence of American Theories of Judicial Review on Nordic Constitutional Law*; Holmoyvik, "Constituent Power and Constitutionalism in 19th Century Norway."

213. Smith, "Judicial Review of Parliamentary Legislation," 601.

214. Anderson, "Ever Closer Union?"

215. Grant, "The Rise of Juristocracy"; Campbell, "*Marbury v. Madison* in the UK"; Campbell, "Procedural Innovation"; Townshend, "We're Stuck with Juristocracy."

216. Hirschl, *Towards Juristocracy;* Hirschl, "Juristocracy—Political, Not Juridical"; Goldstein, "From Democracy to Juristocracy"; "Symposium."

217. Bork, *Coercing Virtue,* 13; Lieberman, *The Litigious Society;* Neely, *How Courts Govern America.*

218. Kelly, Harbison, and Belz, *The American Constitution,* 507.

219. Bork, *Coercing Virtue,* 8.

220. Smillie, "Who Wants Juristocracy?"; Douthat, "The Rise of Woke Capital"; Hirschl, *Towards Juristocracy,* 217.

221. Pardo, "Judicial Discretion in Talmudic Times."

222. In the 1302 bull *Unam sanctam,* Boniface VIII said, "It is absolutely necessary for salvation that every human creature be subject to the Roman Pontiff."

223. Posner, "Enlightened Despot"; Bork, *Coercing Virtue,* 111.

APPENDIX A. "LAW AND EQUITY"

1. Article I, section 8 also gives Congress the power to define and punish crimes against "the law of nations."

2. Story, *Commentaries on the Constitution,* 336–39.

3. Aristotle, *Nicomachean Ethics,* book 5, chapter 10 (1137b).

4. O'Donovan and O'Donovan, *From Irenaeus to Grotius,* 771.

5. Roberts and Bywater, *The Rhetoric and Poetics of Aristotle,* book 1, chapter 1, 1354a; book 1, chapter 13, 1374a.

6. Suarez, *Selections from Three Works,* 356–73.

7. Three American states (Delaware, Mississippi, and Tennessee) retain separate courts of equity.

8. Eventually, equity developed its own sclerotic technicalities, as in Charles Dickens's *Bleak House.* See Holdsworth, *Charles Dickens as Legal Historian.*

9. Hoffer, *The Law's Conscience,* 18.

10. Collins, "Our Inquisitorial Tradition."

APPENDIX B. THE INCORPORATION MYSTERY

1. *Hurtado v. California,* 110 U.S. 516 (1884).

2. *Chicago, Milwaukee & St. Paul Railway Co. v. Minnesota,* 134 U.S. 418 (1890).

3. Perhaps they had. One theory in the Thirty-Ninth Congress held that the Thirteenth Amendment made all the former slaves citizens, entitled to the privileges and immunities of Article IV, section 2. The Supreme Court more or less adopted this view in *Jones v. Mayer* in 1968.

4. *Lochner v. New York,* 198 U.S. 45 (1905).

5. "Commonwealth Club Address," September 23, 1932, and "Annual Message to Congress," January 11, 1944, in *The U.S. Constitution: A Reader* (Hillsdale, MI: Hillsdale College Press, 2012), 719, 745.

6. Sunstein, *The Second Bill of Rights,* 213.

APPENDIX C. DIRECT TAXES

1. Parillo, "A Critical Assessment."

2. Michael Greve says that the direct tax provision looks "an awful lot like requisitions in drag." Greve, *The Upside-Down Constitution,* 158. Not that there's anything wrong with that.

3. The federal government confiscated Robert E. Lee's Arlington estate for his failure to pay the tax. Part of it became Arlington National Cemetery.

4. Einhorn, *American Taxation, American Slavery,* 159–61. Similarly, if Congress had apportioned the 1794 carriage tax, it would have meant a tax of $0.73 per carriage in Delaware and $5.69 per carriage in Georgia.

BIBLIOGRAPHY

"Abortion on Demand." *Time*, January 29, 1973.

Abraham, Henry J. *Justices and Presidents*. 2nd ed. Oxford: Oxford University Press, 1985.

———. *Justices, Presidents, and Senators*. Rev. ed. Lanham, MD: Rowman & Littlefield, 1999.

Abraham, Henry J., and Barbara A. Perry. "The 'Double Standard.'" In *Freedom and the Court*. 8th ed. Lawrence: University of Kansas Press, 2003.

Ackerman, Bruce. *We the People: Foundations*. Cambridge, MA: Harvard University Press, 1991.

Adams, Charles Francis. *Memoirs of John Quincy Adams*. 12 vols. Philadelphia: Lippincott, 1874–77.

Adams, Henry C. "A Decade of Federal Railway Legislation." *Atlantic Monthly* 81 (1898).

Alfange, Dean. "*Marbury v. Madison* and Original Understandings of Judicial Review." *Supreme Court Review* (1993).

Allen, Austin. *Origins of the Dred Scott Case*. Athens: University of Georgia Press, 2006.

Allen, Francis A. "Remembering *Shelley v. Kraemer*." *Washington University Law Review* 67 (1989).

Alschuler, Albert W. *Law Without Values: The Life, Work, and Legacy of Justice Holmes*. Chicago: University of Chicago Press, 2000.

———. "Rediscovering Blackstone." *University of Pennsylvania Law Review* 145 (1996).

Alschuler, Albert W., and Andrew G. Deiss. "A Brief History of the Criminal Jury in the United States." *University of Chicago Law Review* 61 (1994).

Alsop, Joseph, and Turner Catledge. *The 168 Days*. New York: Doubleday, 1938.

Amar, Akil Reed. "The Bill of Rights as a Constitution." *Yale Law Journal* 100 (1991).

Anderson, Frank Maloy. "Contemporary Opinion of the Virginia and Kentucky Resolutions." *American Historical Review* 5 (1899).

Anderson, Jeffrey H. "Learning from the Great Council of Revision Debate." *Review of Politics* 68 (2006).

Anderson, Perry. "Ever Closer Union?" *London Review of Books* 43 (2021).

Andora, Anthony D. "Judicial Self-Restraint in New Jersey." *Rutgers Law Review* 8 (1954).

Aristotle. *Nicomachean Ethics*. Trans. Robert C. Bartlett and Susan D. Collins. Chicago: University of Chicago Press, 2011.

Arkes, Hadley. *First Things: An Inquiry into the First Principles of Morals and Justice*. Princeton, NJ: Princeton University Press, 1986.

Atkinson, David N. *Leaving the Bench: Supreme Court Justices at the End*. Lawrence: University of Kansas Press, 1999.

Aumann, F. R. "The Course of Judicial Review in the State of Ohio." *American Political Science Review* 24 (1930).

Avins, Alfred, ed. *The Reconstruction Amendments' Debates*. Richmond: Virginia Commission on Constitutional Government, 1967.

Bablitz, Leann. "Courts, Roman." In *Oxford Classical Dictionary*. Oxford: Oxford University Press, 1949.

Bailey, Mark Warren. *Guardians of the Moral Order: The Legal Philosophy of the Supreme Court, 1860–1910*. De Kalb: Northern Illinois University Press, 2004.

Bailyn, Bernard, Robert Dallek, David Brion Davis, David Herbert Donald, John L. Thomas, and Gordon S. Wood. *The Great Republic*. 3rd ed. New York: D. C. Heath, 1985.

Balkin, Jack M. *Living Originalism*. Cambridge, MA: Harvard University Press, 2011.

———, ed. *What* Brown v. Board of Education *Should Have Said*. New York: New York University Press, 2001.

———, ed. *What* Roe v. Wade *Should Have Said*. New York: New York University Press, 2005.

Baltimore Catechism Four. 1891. Charlotte, NC: Tan, 2010.

Banner, Stuart. *The Baseball Trust*. Oxford: Oxford University Press, 2013.

Barkow, Rachel E. "More Supreme than Court." *Columbia Law Review* 102 (2002).

Barnett, Randy E. "The Three Narratives of the *Slaughter-House Cases*." *Journal of Supreme Court History* (2016).

Barnett, Randy E., and Evan Bernick. *The Original Meaning of the Fourteenth Amendment: Its Letter and Spirit*. Forthcoming.

Barrett, John Q. "Attribution Time: Cal Tinney's 1937 Quip." *Oklahoma Law Review* 73 (2020).

Bartrum, Ian. "The People's Court." *Dickinson Law Review* 125 (2020).

Basler, Roy P., ed. *Abraham Lincoln: His Speeches and Writings*. New York: Da Capo, 2001.

———, ed. *The Collected Works of Abraham Lincoln*. 8 vols. New Brunswick, NJ: Rutgers University Press, 1953.

Bass, Ryan. "Repudiation Day: Frederick's Predecessor to the Boston Tea Party." *Frederick News-Post*. November 23, 2014.

"Battle over Supreme Court: It Goes Beyond Fortas." *US News & World Report*, October 14, 1968.

Beard, Charles A. "The Supreme Court—Usurper or Grantee?" *Political Science Quarterly* 27 (1912).

Belknap, Michal R. "Mr. Justice Pitney and Progressivism." *Seton Hall Law Review* 16 (1986).

Belton, Robert. *The Crusade for Equality in the Workplace.* Lawrence: University of Kansas Press, 2014.

Belz, Herman. *Equality Transformed: A Quarter-Century of Affirmative Action.* New Brunswick, NJ: Transaction, 1991.

———. *A New Birth of Freedom: The Republican Party and Freedmen's Rights, 1861–66.* Westport, CT: Greenwood, 1976.

———, ed. *The Webster–Hayne Debate on the Nature of the Union.* Indianapolis: Liberty Fund, 2000.

Benedict, Michael Les. *The Blessings of Liberty.* 3rd ed. Lanham, MD: Rowman & Littlefield, 2017.

———. "Preserving Federalism: Reconstruction and the Waite Court." *Supreme Court Review* (1979).

Berger, Raoul. "The Activist Legacy of the New Deal Court." *Washington Law Review* 59 (1984).

———. *Government by Judiciary.* Cambridge, MA: Harvard University Press, 1977.

Berk, Gerald. "Adversaries by Design." *Journal of Policy History* 5 (1993).

Berman, Harold J. *Law and Revolution.* Cambridge, MA: Harvard University Press, 1983.

Berman, Harold J., and Charles I. Reid, Jr. "Origins of Historical Jurisprudence: Coke, Selden, Hale." *Yale Law Journal* 103 (1994).

———. "The Transformation of English Legal Science." *Emory Law Journal* (1996).

Berman, Russell. "Where the Gun-Control Movement Goes Silent." *Atlantic,* March 1, 2018.

Bernstein, David E. "Class Legislation, Fundamental Rights, and the Origins of *Lochner* and Liberty of Contract." *George Mason Law Review* 26 (2019).

———. "Philip Sober Controlling Philip Drunk: *Buchanan v. Warley* in Historical Perspective." *Vanderbilt Law Review* 51 (1998).

———. *Rehabilitating Lochner.* Chicago: University of Chicago Press, 2011.

Bernstein, Irving. *The New Deal Collective Bargaining Policy.* Berkeley: University of California Press, 1950.

———. *Turbulent Years: A History of the American Worker, 1933–41.* Boston: Houghton Mifflin, 1970.

Bestor, Arthur. "State Sovereignty and Slavery." *Journal of the Illinois State Historical Society* 54 (1961).

Beth, Loren P. *The Development of the American Constitution, 1877–1917.* Harper & Row, 1971.

Beveridge, Albert J. *The Life of John Marshall*. 4 vols. Boston: Houghton Mifflin, 1916–19.

Bickel, Alexander M. *The Least Dangerous Branch*. 2nd ed. New Haven, CT: Yale University Press, 1986.

———. "The Original Understanding and the Segregation Decision." *Harvard Law Review* 69 (1955).

Bickel, Alexander M., and Benno C. Schmidt Jr. *The Judiciary and Responsible Government, 1910–21*. New York: Macmillan, 1984.

Bilder, Mary Sarah. "Charter Constitutionalism." *North Carolina Law Review* 94 (2016).

———. *The Transatlantic Constitution*. Cambridge, MA: Harvard University Press, 2004.

Bird, Wendell. "New Light on the Sedition Act of 1798." *Law and History Review* 34 (2016).

Birkner, Michael J. "The New York–New Jersey Boundary Controversy." *Journal of the Early Republic* 12 (1992).

Black, Edwin. *War Against the Weak*. Rev. ed. Washington, DC: Dialog, 2012.

Blackard, W. Raymond. "The Demoralization of the Legal Profession in Nineteenth Century America." *Tennessee Law Review* 16 (1940).

Blackman, Josh. "The Irrepressible Myth of *Cooper v. Aaron*." *Georgetown Law Journal* 107 (2019).

Blakeney, Ben. "The Old Court of Appeals." *American Bar Association Journal* 28 (1942).

Bloch, Susan Low. "The *Marbury* Mystery." *Constitutional Commentary* 18 (2001).

Bloomfield, Maxwell. *American Lawyers in a Changing Society, 1776–1876*. Cambridge, MA: Harvard University Press, 1976.

Blumrosen, Alfred W. "Strangers in Paradise: *Griggs v. Duke Power Co.*" *Michigan Law Review* 71 (1972).

Boecker, Hans Jochen. *Law and the Administration of Justice in the Old Testament and Ancient Near East*. Trans. Jeremy Moiser. Augsburg: Fortress, 1980.

Bond, Beverly, Jr. "The Quit-Rent System in the American Colonies." *American Historical Review* 17 (1912).

Bond, James E. "The Original Understanding of the Fourteenth Amendment in Illinois, Ohio, and Pennsylvania." *Akron Law Review* 18 (1985).

Bordewich, Fergus M. *The First Congress*. New York: Simon & Schuster, 2016.

Bork, Robert H. *The Antitrust Paradox*. New York: Basic, 1978.

———. *Coercing Virtue*. Washington, DC: A.E.I. Press, 2003.

———. *The Tempting of America*. New York: Free Press, 1990.

Boudin, Louis B. *Government by Judiciary*. 2 vols. New York: William Godwin, 1932.

Bourguignon, Henry J. "The Federal Key to the Judiciary Act of 1789." *South Carolina Law Review* 46 (1995).

Boutwell, George. *Reminiscences of Sixty Years in Public Affairs*. 2 vols. New York: McClure, 1902.

Bowling, Kenneth R. "'A Tub to the Whale': The Founding Fathers and Adoption of the Federal Bill of Rights." *Journal of the Early Republic* 8 (1988).

Boyce, Bret. "Originalism and the Fourteenth Amendment." *Wake Forest Law Review* 33 (1998).

Boyd, Julian P., et al., eds. *The Papers of Thomas Jefferson.* 45 vols. to date. Princeton, NJ: Princeton University Press, 1950–.

Boyer, Allen Dillard. "'Understanding, Authority, and Will': Sir Edward Coke and the Elizabethan Origins of Judicial Review." *Boston College Law Review* 39 (1997).

Bradley, Gerard V. "Shall We Ratify the New Constitution?" In *Benchmarks: Great Constitutional Controversies in the Supreme Court.* Washington, DC: Ethics & Public Policy Center, 1995.

Brandeis, Louis D. "The Living Law." *Illinois Law Review* 10 (1916).

Brandwein, Pamela. "The *Civil Rights Cases* and the Lost Language of State Neglect." In *The Supreme Court and American Political Development,* ed. Ronald Kahn and Ken I. Kersch. Lawrence: University of Kansas Press, 2006.

———. *Rethinking the Judicial Settlement of Reconstruction.* Cambridge: Cambridge University Press, 2011.

Brennan, William J., Jr. "The Bill of Rights and the States." *New York University Law Review* 61 (1986).

———. "State Constitutions and the Protection of Individual Rights." *Harvard Law Review* 90 (1977).

Bressler, Jonathan. "Reconstruction and the Transformation of Jury Nullification." *University of Chicago Law Review* 78 (2011).

Brickner, Paul. "Reassessing Long-Accepted Truths About Justice John McLean." *Ohio Northern University Law Review* 38 (2011).

Bridenbaugh, Carl. *Mitre and Sceptre.* Oxford: Oxford University Press, 1962.

Briley, Ron. "Danny Gardella and Baseball's Reserve Clause." *Nine* 19 (2010).

Brinkley, Alan. "The Debate Over the Constitutional Revolution of 1937." *American Historical Review* 110 (October 2005).

Brodhead, Michael J. *David J. Brewer.* Carbondale: Southern Illinois University Press, 1994.

Brogdon, Matthew S. "Defending the Union." *Review of Politics* 73 (2011).

Brookhiser, Richard. *John Marshall.* New York: Basic, 2018.

Brooks, Aubrey Lee, and Hugh Talmadge Lefler, eds. *The Papers of Walter Clark.* 2 vols. Chapel Hill: University of North Carolina Press, 1948–50.

Brown, Henry B. "The Dissenting Opinions of Mr. Justice Harlan." *American Law Review* 46 (1912).

Buenger, Michael L., and Paul L. De Muniz. *American Judicial Power.* Cheltenham: Elgar, 2015.

Burke, Joseph C. "The Cherokee Cases." *Stanford Law Review* 21 (1969).

Burns, James MacGregor. *Packing the Court*. New York: Penguin, 2009.

Burset, Christian R. "Advisory Opinions and the Founders' Crisis of Legal Authority." *Vanderbilt Law Review* 74 (2021).

Burton, David H., ed. *The Collected Works of William Howard Taft*. 8 vols. Columbus: Ohio State University Press, 2001.

——. *Taft, Holmes, and the 1920s Court*. Madison, NJ: Fairleigh Dickinson University Press, 1998.

Butterfield, Herbert. *The Englishman and His History*. Hamden, CT: Archon, 1970.

Calabresi, Steven G., and Michael W. Perl. "Originalism and *Brown v. Board of Education*." *Michigan State Law Review* (2014).

Caldwell, Christopher. "Pro-Lifestyle." *New Republic*, July 5, 1999.

Cammack, Daniela. "The Popular Courts in Athenian Democracy." SSRN, May 26, 2020.

Campbell, David. "*Marbury v. Madison* in the UK: Brexit and the Creation of Judicial Supremacy." *Cardozo Law Review* 39 (2018).

——. "Procedural Innovation and the Surreptitious Creation of Judicial Supremacy in the United Kingdom." *Journal of Law and Society* 46 (2019).

Cardozo, Benjamin. *The Nature of the Judicial Process*. New Haven, CT: Yale University Press, 1921.

Caro, Robert A. *The Years of Lyndon Johnson: The Path to Power*. New York: Vintage, 1983.

Carrese, Paul. *The Cloaking of Power*. Chicago: University of Chicago Press, 2003.

Carrington, Adam M. *Justice Stephen Field's Cooperative Constitution of Liberty*. Lanham, MD: Lexington, 2017.

Carrott, M. B. "The Supreme Court and Minority Rights in the 1920s." *Northwest Ohio Quarterly* 41 (1969).

Casper, Gerhard. "*Jones v. Mayer*." *Supreme Court Review* (1968).

Ceasar, James W., and Andrew E. Busch. *The Perfect Tie*. Lanham, MD: Rowman & Littlefield, 2001.

"Celler in Warning to Supreme Court." *New York Times*, January 11, 1937, p. 9.

Chafee, Zechariah, Jr. "Liberal Trends in the Supreme Court." *Current History* 35 (1931).

Chardavoyne, David Gardner. *A Lincoln Legacy*. Detroit, MI: Wayne State University Press, 2020.

Chayes, Abraham. "The Role of the Judge in Public Law Litigation." *Harvard Law Review* 89 (1976).

Ciepley, David. "Is the United States Government a Corporation?" *American Political Science Review* 111 (2017).

Clark, Tom C. "Religion, Morality, and Abortion." *Loyola University Law Review* 2 (1969).

Clark, Walter. "Judicial Supremacy." *Arena* 39 (1908).

Clegg, Roger. "Unfinished Business." *Harvard Journal of Law and Public Policy* 32 (2009).

Clinton, Robert L. "John Marshall's Federalism." *Political Research* 47 (1994).

———. *Marbury v. Madison and Judicial Review.* Lawrence: University of Kansas Press, 1989.

Coke, Edward. *The Selected Writings of Sir Edward Coke.* 3 vols. Indianapolis, IN: Liberty Fund, 2003.

Coleman, John M. "Thomas McKean and the Origin of an Independent Judiciary." *Pennsylvania History* 34 (1967).

Coles, Walter D. "Politics and the Supreme Court of the United States," *American Law Review* 27 (1893).

Collins, Kristin A. "'A Considerable Surgical Operation.'" *Duke Law Journal* 60 (2010).

———. "Our Inquisitorial Tradition." *Cornell Law Review* 90 (2005).

Compton, John W. *The Evangelical Origins of the Living Constitution.* Cambridge, MA: Harvard University Press, 2014.

Conde, James R., and Michael S. Greve. "*Yakus* and the Administrative State." *Harvard Journal of Law and Public Policy* 42 (2018).

Conley, Patrick T. "The Constitutional Significance of *Trevett v. Weeden* (1786)." *Rhode Island Bar Journal* 24 (1976).

———. "Rhode Island's Paper Money Issue and *Trevett v. Weeden* (1786)." *Rhode Island History* 30 (1971).

Cooley, Thomas McIntyre. *Commentaries on the Constitution of the United States.* 2 vols. Boston: Little, Brown, 1891.

Cope, Esther S. "Sir Edward Coke and Proclamations." *American Journal of Legal History* 15 (1971).

Corriher, Billy, and Alex Brown. "Chris Christie's War on Judicial Independence." *American Progress* (February 2014).

Corwin, Edward S. "The Anti-Trust Acts and the Constitution." *Virginia Law Review* 18 (1932).

———. *The Constitution and What It Means Today.* 7th ed. Princeton, NJ: Princeton University Press, 1941.

———. "Establishment of Judicial Review. II." *Michigan Law Review* 9 (February 1911).

Critchlow, Donald T. *Intended Consequences.* Oxford: Oxford University Press, 1999.

Croley, Steven P. "The Majoritarian Difficulty." *University of Chicago Law Review* 62 (1995).

Cromartie, Alan. *The Constitutionalist Revolution.* Cambridge: Cambridge University Press, 2006.

Currie, David P. *The Constitution in Congress: Democrats and Whigs, 1829–61.* Chicago: University of Chicago Press, 2005.

———. *The Constitution in Congress: The Federalist Period, 1789–1801.* Chicago: University of Chicago Press, 1997.

Cushman, Barry. *Rethinking the New Deal Court.* Oxford: Oxford University Press, 1998.

Dahl, Ronald. "Decision-Making in a Democracy." *Journal of Public Law* 6 (1957).

Danelski, David J., and Joseph S. Tulchin, eds. *The Autobiographical Notes of Charles Evans Hughes.* Cambridge, MA: Harvard University Press, 1973.

Dargo, George. *Roots of the Republic.* Westport, CT: Praeger, 1974.

Davis, John W. "Present Day Problems." *American Bar Association Journal* 9 (1923).

Davis, Mark A. *A Warren Court of Our Own.* Durham, NC: Carolina Academic Press, 2019.

Dawson, Nelson L., ed. *Brandeis and America.* Lexington: University of Kentucky Press, 1989.

Dellapenna, Joseph W. "Abortion and the Law." In *Abortion and the Constitution,* ed. Dennis J. Horan, Edward R. Grand, and Paige C. Cunningham. Washington, DC: Georgetown University Press, 1987.

———. *Dispelling the Myths of Abortion History.* Durham, NC: Carolina Academic Press, 2006.

———. "The Historical Case Against Abortion." *Continuity* 13 (1989).

Dennison, George M. "The Dorr War and Political Questions." *Supreme Court Historical Society Yearbook* (1979).

———. *The Dorr War: Republicanism on Trial, 1831–61.* Lexington: University of Kentucky Press, 1973.

Detlefsen, Robert R. "Affirmative Action and Business Deregulation." *Policy Studies Journal* 21 (2004).

Devins, Neal. "The Majoritarian Rehnquist Court?" *Law and Contemporary Problems* 67 (2004).

Dicey, A. V. *Introduction to the Study of the Law of the Constitution.* 1885. Indianapolis, IN: Liberty Fund, 1982.

Dickerson, O. M. "Writs of Assistance as a Cause of the Revolution." In *The Era of the American Revolution,* ed. Richard B. Morris. New York: Columbia University Press, 1939.

Dippel, Horst. "Human Rights in America, 1776–1849." *Albany Law Review* 67 (2004).

Dodd, E. Merrick. "The Supreme Court and Labor, 1941–45." *Harvard Law Review* 58 (1945).

Dorn, James A., and Henry G. Manne. *Economic Liberties and the Judiciary.* Fairfax, VA: George Mason University Press, 1987.

Douglas, Charles G., III. "Judicial Review and the Separation of Powers Under the New Hampshire Constitutions of 1776 and 1784." *Historical New Hampshire* 31 (1976).

Douglas, Davidson "The Rhetorical Uses of *Marbury v. Madison.*" *Wake Forest Law Review* 38 (2003).

Dowd, Morgan D. "Justice Joseph Story and the Politics of Appointment." *American Journal of Legal History* 9 (1965).

Drew, Richard. "The Surge and Consolidation of Judicial Power." Paper presented at the annual meeting of the American Political Science Association, Chicago, Illinois, September 2–4, 2004.

Driver, Justin. "The Consensus Constitution." *Texas Law Review* 89 (2011).

———. "Supremacies and the Southern Manifesto." *Texas Law Review* 92 (2014).

Dubofsky, Melvyn. "Abortive Reform." In *The Experience of Labor in Europe and America, 1900–25*, ed. James E. Cronin and Carmen Sirianni. Philadelphia: Temple University Press, 1993.

Dueholm, James A. "Lincoln's Suspension of the Writ of Habeas Corpus." *Journal of the Abraham Lincoln Association* 29 (2008).

Dumbauld, Edward. "The Case of the Mutinous Mariner." *Supreme Court Historical Society Yearbook* (1977).

———. *The Declaration of Independence and What It Means Today.* Norman: University of Oklahoma Press, 1950.

Dunn, Geoffrey D., ed. *Tertullian.* London: Routledge, 2004.

Dunne, Gerald T. *Hugo Black and the Judicial Revolution.* New York: Simon & Schuster, 1977.

Duquette, Jerold J. *Regulating the National Pastime.* Westport, CT: Praeger, 1999.

Edwards, Sebastian. *American Default.* Princeton, NJ: Princeton University Press, 2018.

Ehrenberg, Victor. *From Solon to Socrates.* 2nd ed. London: Metheuen, 1973.

Ehrlich, J. W. *Ehrlich's Blackstone.* 2 vols. New York: Capricorn, 1959.

Eidsmoe, John. "The Article III Exceptions Clause." *Regent University Law Review* 19 (2006).

Einhorn, Robin L. *American Taxation, American Slavery.* Chicago: University of Chicago Press, 2006.

Elias, Elizabeth J. "Red Monday and Its Aftermath." *Hofstra Law Review* 43 (2014).

Ellis, Richard E. *The Jeffersonian Crisis: Courts and Politics in the Young Republic.* New York: Norton, 1971.

———. *The Union at Risk.* Oxford: Oxford University Press, 1987.

Ely, James W., Jr. *The Contract Clause.* Lawrence: University of Kansas Press, 2016.

———. "The Oxymoron Reconsidered." *Constitutional Commentary* 16 (1999).

Ely, John Hart. *Democracy and Distrust.* Cambridge, MA: Harvard University Press, 1980.

———. "The Wages of Crying Wolf: A Comment on *Roe v. Wade.*" *Yale Law Journal* 82 (1973).

Epp, Charles R. *The Rights Revolution.* Chicago: University of Chicago Press, 1998.

Epstein, Henry. "The Opposition of the Cities and States to Federal Taxation of Their Securities." *Proceedings of the Annual Conference on Taxation Under the Auspices of the National Tax Association* 34 (1941).

Epstein, Richard A. "The Proper Scope of the Commerce Clause." *University of Virginia Law Review* 73 (1987).

———. "Substantive Due Process by Any Other Name." *Supreme Court Review* (1973).

Ernst, Daniel. "The Labor Exemption." *Iowa Law Review* 74 (1988).

Esbeck, Carl H. "The Establishment Clause." *Federalist Society Review* 26 (2021).

Ewald, William. "James Wilson and the Drafting of the Constitution." *Journal of Constitutional Law* 10 (2008).

Fairfax, Roger A., Jr. "Wielding the Double-Edged Sword." *Harvard BlackLetter Law Journal* 14 (1998).

Fairman, Charles. *Reconstruction and Reunion, 1864–88, Part One.* New York: Macmillan, 1971.

Farrand, Max, ed. *The Records of the Federal Convention of 1787.* 4 vols. New Haven, CT: Yale University Press, 1966.

Farrell, James M. "The Writs of Assistance and Public Memory." *New England Quarterly* 79 (2006).

Faulkner, Robert K. *The Jurisprudence of John Marshall.* Westport, CT: Greenwood, 1968.

Fehrenbacher, Don E. *Slavery, Law, and Politics.* Oxford: Oxford University Press, 1981.

Fehrenbacher, Don E., and Virginia Fehrenbacher. *Recollected Words of Abraham Lincoln.* Stanford, CA: Stanford University Press, 1996.

Ferrell, Robert H., ed. *Dear Bess: The Letters from Harry to Bess Truman, 1910–59.* New York: Norton, 1983.

Fine, Sidney. *Frank Murphy: The Washington Years.* Ann Arbor: University of Michigan Press, 1984.

———. *Sit-Down: The General Motors Strike of 1936–37.* Ann Arbor: University of Michigan Press, 1969.

Finkelman, Paul. "*Prigg v. Pennsylvania* and Northern State Courts." *Civil War History* 25 (1979).

———. "Slavery and the Constitutional Convention." In *Beyond Confederation,* ed. Richard Beeman, Stephen Botein, and Edward C. Carter II. Chapel Hill: University of North Carolina Press, 1987.

———. *Supreme Injustice.* Cambridge, MA: Harvard University Press, 2018.

Finnis, John. "'Shameless Acts' in Colorado." *Academic Questions* (Fall 1994).

———. "The Truth in Legal Positivism." In *The Autonomy of Law,* ed. Robert P. George. Oxford: Oxford University Press, 1996.

Fisher, Louis. *Military Tribunals and Presidential Power.* Lawrence: University of Kansas Press, 2005.

Fiss, Owen M. *The Troubled Beginnings of the Modern State, 1888–1910.* Cambridge: Cambridge University Press, 2006.

Flowers, Prudence. "'A Prolife Disaster':The Reagan Administration and the Nomination of Sandra Day O'Connor." *Journal of Contemporary History* 53 (2017).

Forbath, William E. "Popular Constitutionalism in the Twentieth Century." *Chicago-Kent Law Review* 81 (2006).

Forsdyke, Sara. "Ancient and Modern Conceptions of the Rule of Law." In *Ancient Greek History and Contemporary Social Science,* ed. Mirko Canevaro, Andrew Erskine, Benjamin Gray, and Josiah Ober. Edinburgh: Edinburgh University Press, 2018.

Forsythe, Clarke D. *Abuse of Discretion.* New York: Encounter, 2013.

———. "A Draft Opinion Overruling *Roe v. Wade.*" *Georgetown Journal of Law and Public Policy* 16 (2018).

Forte, David F., ed. *The Supreme Court in American Politics.* New York: D. C. Heath, 1972.

Franck, Matthew J. *Against the Imperial Judiciary: The Supreme Court vs. the Sovereignty of the People.* Lawrence: University of Kansas Press, 1996.

Frankfurter, Felix. *The Commerce Clause Under Marshall, Taney, and Waite.* Chapel Hill: University of North Carolina Press, 1937.

Franklin, John Hope. "The Enforcement of the Civil Rights Act of 1875." *Prologue* (1974).

Freyer, Tony A. *Forums of Order: The Federal Courts and Business in American History.* Arkansas, 1979.

Friedman, Barry. "The History of the Countermajoritarian Difficulty, Part One." *New York University Law Review* 73 (1998).

———. "The History of the Countermajoritarian Difficulty, Part Two." *Georgetown Law Journal* 91 (2002).

———. "The History of the Countermajoritarian Difficulty, Part Five." *Yale Law Journal* 112 (2002).

———. *The Will of the People.* New York: Farrar, Straus and Giroux, 2009.

Frohnen, Bruce, ed. *The American Republic: Primary Sources.* Indianapolis, IN: Liberty Fund, 2002.

Funk, Kellen. "The Union of Law and Equity: The United States, 1800–1938." In *Law and Equity: Fusion and Fission,* ed. John C. P. Goldberg, Henry E. Smith, and P. G. Turner. Cambridge: Cambridge University Press, 2019.

Galie, Peter. "The Other Supreme Courts." *Syracuse Law Review* 32 (1982).

Gardbaum, Stephen. "New Deal Constitutionalism and the Unshackling of the States." *University of Chicago Law Review* 64 (1997).

Garrow, David J. "Bad Behavior Makes Big Law." *St. John's Law Review* 82 (2008).

———. *Liberty and Sexuality.* New York: Macmillan, 1994.

Gerber, Scott Douglas. *A Distinct Judicial Power.* Oxford: Oxford University Press, 2011.

Gest, Ted. "The Swing to the Left in State Courts." *US News & World Report,* October 23, 1989.

Geyh, Charles G. *When Courts and Congress Collide.* Ann Arbor: University of Michigan Press, 2006.

Gillies, Paul S. "The Trial of Matthew Lyon." *Vermont Bar Journal* 37 (2011).

Gillman, Howard. "The Collapse of Constitutional Originalism and the Rise of the Notion of the 'Living Constitution.'" *Studies in American Political Development* 11 (1997).

———. *The Constitution Besieged*. Durham, NC: Duke University Press, 1993.

———. "How Political Parties Can Use the Courts to Advance Their Agenda." *American Political Science Review* 96 (2002).

———. "Preferred Freedoms." *Political Research Quarterly* 47 (1994).

Gillman, Howard, Mark A. Graber, and Keith E. Whittington. *American Constitutionalism. Vol. 1, Structures of Government*. 2nd ed. Oxford: Oxford University Press, 2017.

———. *American Constitutionalism. Vol. 2, Rights and Liberties*. 2nd ed. Oxford: Oxford University Press, 2017.

Gilmore, Grant. *The Death of Contract*. Columbus: Ohio State University Press, 1974.

Ginsburg, Ruth Bader. "Some Thoughts on Autonomy and Equality in Relation to *Roe v. Wade*." *North Carolina Law Review* 63 (1985).

———. Speaking in a Judicial Voice." *New York University Law Review* 67 (1992).

Giocoli, Nicola. "The (Rail)Road to *Lochner*." *History of Political Economy* 49 (2017).

Glazer, Nathan. "Should Judges Administer Social Services?" *Public Interest* (Winter 1978).

———. "Towards an Imperial Judiciary?" In *The American Commonwealth 1976*. New York: Basic, 1976.

Glendon, Mary Ann. *Rights Talk*. New York: Free Press, 1993.

Glick, David. "Conditional Strategic Retreat." *Journal of Politics* 71 (2009).

Glickstein, Jed. "After Midnight." *Yale Journal of Law and the Humanities* 24 (2012).

Goebel, Jules. *Antecedents and Beginnings to 1801*. New York: Macmillan, 1971.

Goedcke, Robert. "Justice Field and Inherent Rights." *Review of Politics* 27 (1965).

Goldberg, John C. P., and Benjamin C. Zipursky. "The Supreme Court's Stealth Return to the Common Law of Torts." *DePaul Law Review* 65 (2016).

Goldstein, Leslie Friedman. "From Democracy to Juristocracy." *Law and Society Review* 38 (2004).

Goldsworthy, Adrian. *Pax Romana*. New Haven, CT: Yale University Press, 2016.

Goldwin, Robert A. *From Parchment to Power*. Washington, DC: A.E.I., 1997.

Goodell, T. D. "An Athenian Parallel to a Function of Our Supreme Court." *Yale Review* 2 (1893).

Gottlieb, Stephen E. *Unfit for Democracy*. New York: New York University Press, 2016.

Gough, J. W. *The Social Contract*. 2nd ed. Westport, CT: Greenwood, 1978.

Gould, William B. *Black Workers in White Unions*. Ithaca, NY: Cornell University Press, 1977.

Graber, Mark A. *Dred Scott and the Problem of Constitutional Evil*. Cambridge: Cambridge University Press, 2006.

———. "The Jacksonian Origins of Chase Court Activism." *Journal of Supreme Court History* (2000).

———. "James Buchanan as Savior?" *Oregon Law Review* 88 (2009).

———. "Ship Money: The Case that Time and Whittington Forgot." *Constitutional Commentary* 35 (2020).

Graham, Howard Jay. "The 'Conspiracy Theory' of the Fourteenth Amendment." *Yale Law Journal* 47 (1938).

Graham, Hugh Davis. *The Civil Rights Era*. Oxford: Oxford University Press, 1990.

Graham, Otis L., Jr. "Liberalism After the 60s." In *The Achievement of American Liberalism*, ed. William H. Chafe. New York: Columbia University Press, 2003.

Grant, J. A. C. "The Gild Returns to America," *Journal of Politics* 4 (1942).

Grant, James. "The Rise of Juristocracy." *Wilson Quarterly* 34 (2010).

Green, Steven K. "Evangelicals and the Becker Amendment." *Journal of Church and State* 33 (1991).

Greenberg, Janelle, and Michael J. Sechler. "Constitutionalism Ancient and Early Modern." *Cardozo Law Review* 34 (2013).

Greene, Jack P. "From the Perspective of Law." *South Atlantic Quarterly* 85 (1986).

———. "The Glorious Revolution and the British Empire, 1688–1783." In *The Revolution of 1688–89*, ed. Lois Schwoerer. Cambridge: Cambridge University Press, 1992.

Greenhouse, Linda. "Justice John Paul Stevens as an Abortion-Rights Strategist." *University of California-Davis Law Review* 43 (2010).

Greenhouse, Linda, and Reva B. Siegel. "The Unfinished Story of *Roe v. Wade*." In *Reproductive Rights and Justice Stories,* ed. Melissa Murray, Katherine Shaw, and Reva B. Siegel. St. Paul, MN: Foundation Press, 2019.

Greve, Michael. *The Upside-Down Constitution*. Cambridge, MA: Harvard University Press, 2012.

Grinnell, Frank W. "The New Guesspotism." *American Bar Association Journal* 30 (1944).

Grove, Tara Leigh. "The Origins (and Fragility) of Judicial Independence." *Vanderbilt Law Review* 71 (2018).

Gunther, Gerald, ed. *John Marshall's Defense of* McCulloch v. Maryland. Stanford, CA: Stanford University Press, 1969.

———. *Learned Hand*. New York: Knopf, 1994.

———. "The Subtle Vices of the 'Passive Virtues.'" *Columbia Law Review* 64 (1964).

Guttmacher, Alan F. "The Shrinking Non-Psychiatric Indications for Therapeutic Abortion." In *Therapeutic Abortion*, ed. Harold Rosen. New York: Julian Press, 1954.

Hagan, John Patrick. "Patterns of Activism on State Supreme Courts." *Publius* 18 (1988).

Haines, Charles Grove. *The American Doctrine of Judicial Supremacy*. 2nd ed. Berkeley: University of California Press, 1932.

———. *The Revival of Natural Law Concepts*. New York: Russell & Russell, 1965.

Hale, Robert. "Coercion and Distribution in a Supposedly Non-Coercive State." *Political Science Quarterly* 38 (1923).

Hall, Kermit L. "The Judiciary on Trial." *Historian* 45 (1983).

———. *Major Problems in American Constitutional History*. 2 vols. Lexington, MA: D. C. Heath, 1992.

———. "Progressive Reform and the Decline of Democratic Accountability." *American Bar Foundation Research Journal* (1984).

———. "The Warren Court in Historical Perspective." In *The Warren Court: A Retrospective,* ed. Bernard Schwartz. Oxford: Oxford University Press, 1994.

Hall, Kermit L., and Peter Karsten. *The Magic Mirror.* 2nd ed. Oxford: Oxford University Press, 2009.

Hamburger, Philip A. *Law and Judicial Duty.* Cambridge, MA: Harvard University Press, 2008.

———. "Revolution and Judicial Review." *Columbia Law Review* 94 (1994).

———. *Separation of Church and State.* Cambridge, MA: Harvard University Press, 2002.

Hamer, Philip M. "Great Britain, the United States, and the Negro Seamen Acts, 1822–48." *Journal of Southern History* 1 (1935).

Hand, Learned. *The Bill of Rights.* Cambridge, MA: Harvard University Press, 1960.

Hansen, Mogens Herman. "The Political Powers of the People's Court." In *The Greek City,* ed. Oswyn Murray and Simon Price. Oxford: Oxford University Press, 1990.

Harbaugh, William H. *Lawyer's Lawyer.* Oxford: Oxford University Press, 1973.

Harrington, Matthew P. "Judicial Review Before John Marshall." *George Washington Law Review* 72 (2003).

Harrison, Robert. "The Breakup of the Roosevelt Court." *Law and History Review* 2 (1984).

Hart, Henry M., Jr. "The Power of Congress to Limit the Jurisdiction of the Federal Courts." *Harvard Law Review* 66 (1953).

Haskins, George Lee, and Herbert A. Johnson. *Foundations of Power: John Marshall, 1801–15.* New York: Macmillan, 1981.

Havighurst, Alfred F. "The Judiciary and Politics in the Reign of Charles II." *Law Quarterly Review* 66 (1950).

Heagney, Meredith. "Judge Ruth Bader Ginsburg Offers Critique of *Roe* v. *Wade* During Law School Visit." University of Chicago Law School, May 15, 2013.

Helfman, Harold M. "The Contested Confirmation of Stanley Matthews to the United States Supreme Court." *Bulletin of the Historical and Philosophical Society of Ohio* 8 (1950).

Helgadottir, Ranghildur. *The Influence of American Theories of Judicial Review on Nordic Constitutional Law.* Leiden: Brill, 2006.

———. "Status Presens—Judicial Review in Iceland." *Nordisk Tidsskrift* 27 (2009).

Helmholz, R. H. "Bonham's Case, Judicial Review, and the Law of Nature." *Journal of Legal Analysis* 1 (2009).

Hickman, Chris. "Courting the Right." *Journal of Supreme Court History* (2011).

Hill, Christopher. *Intellectual Origins of the English Revolution Revisited.* Oxford: Oxford University Press, 1965.

Hirschl, Rand. "Juristocracy—Political, Not Juridical." *Good Society* 13 (2004).

———. *Towards Juristocracy.* Cambridge, MA: Harvard University Press, 2004.

Hobbes, Thomas. "A Dialogue of the Common Law." In *The English Works of Thomas Hobbes,* ed. William Molesworth. 11 vols. London: Bohn, 1840.

Hobson, Charles F. *The Great Chief Justice*. Lawrence: University of Kansas Press, 1996.

———. *The Great Yazoo Lands Sale*. Lawrence: University of Kansas Press, 2016.

———, ed. *Marshall: Writings*. New York: Library of America, 2010.

Hoffer, Peter Charles. *The Law's Conscience*. Chapel Hill: University of North Carolina Press, 1990.

Hogan, Frank J. "Important Shifts in Constitutional Doctrine." *American Bar Association Journal* 25 (1939).

Hohenstein, Kurt. "William Jennings Bryan and the Income Tax." *Journal of Law and Politics* 16 (2000).

Holdsworth, William. *Charles Dickens as Legal Historian*. New Haven, CT: Yale University Press, 1929.

———. *Some Makers of English Law*. Cambridge: Cambridge University Press, 1938.

Holmes, Oliver Wendell, Jr. *The Common Law*. Boston: Little, Brown, 1881.

Holmoyvik, Eirik. "Constituent Power and Constitutionalism in 19th Century Norway." In *Reconsidering Constitutional Formation II*, ed. Ulrike Mübig. New York: Springer, 2018.

Holt, Wythe. "'To Establish Justice.'" *Duke Law Journal* (1989).

Homans, William P., Jr. "*Commonwealth v. Kenneth Edelin*." *Criminal Justice Journal* 1 (1977).

Horowitz, Donald L. *The Courts and Social Policy*. Washington, DC: Brookings, 1977.

Horwitz, Morton J. "Republicanism and Liberalism in American Constitutional Thought." *William and Mary Law Review* 29 (1987).

———. *The Transformation of American Law, 1780–1860*. Cambridge, MA: Harvard University Press, 1977.

———. *The Warren Court and the Pursuit of Justice*. New York: Hill and Wang, 1998.

Howard, A. E. Dick. *The Road from Runnymede*. Charlottesville: University of Virginia Press, 1968.

Hudspeth, Harvey Gresham. "The Case of the 'Vacillating Justice.'" *Essays in Economic and Business History* 21 (2003).

Hughes, Charles Evans. *Addresses of Charles Evans Hughes, 1906–16*. 2nd ed. Albany, NY: G. P. Putnam's Sons, 1916.

Hulsebosch, Daniel J. "The New Deal Court." *Columbia Law Review* 90 (1990).

Hume, David. *History of England*. 1778. 6 vols. Indianapolis, IN: Liberty Fund, 1983–85.

Humphries, Drew. "The Movement to Legalize Abortion." In *Corrections and Punishment*, ed. David F. Greenberg. Beverly Hills, CA: Sage, 1977.

Hurst, James Willard. *Law and the Conditions of Freedom in the Nineteenth-Century United States*. Madison: University of Wisconsin Press, 1956.

Hurwitz, Andrew D. "Jon O. Newman and the Abortion Decisions." *New York Law School Law Review* 46 (2002).

Hyman, Harold M., and William Wiecek. *Equal Justice Under Law*. New York: Harper & Row, 1982.

Hyneman, Charles S. *The Supreme Court on Trial.* Westport, CT: Greenwood, 1974.

Ickes, Harold LeClair. *The Secret Diary of Harold L. Ickes: The First Thousand Days, 1933–36.* New York: Simon and Schuster, 1953.

"Issue in Jackson–Black Dispute: Press Appraisal of Effect on Court." *US News & World Report,* June 21, 1946.

J. J. P. "Fourteenth Amendment: Taxation for Public Purpose." *California Law Review* 8 (1920).

Jackson, Robert. *The Supreme Court in the American System of Government.* Cambridge, MA: Harvard University Press, 1955.

Jaffe, Louis L. "The Supreme Court Today." *Atlantic Monthly* 174 (December 1944).

———. "Was Brandeis an Activist?" *Harvard Law Review* 80 (1967).

James VI and I. *The True Law of Free Monarchies* (1598). In *Western Heritage: A Reader,* ed. Hillsdale College History Faculty. Hillsdale, MI: Hillsdale College Press, 2003.

Janutis, Rachel M. "The Struggle over Tort Reform and the Overlooked Legacy of the Progressives." *Akron Law Review* 39 (2006).

Jay, Stewart. "Origins of the Federal Common Law: Part Two." *University of Pennsylvania Law Review* 133 (1985).

Jessup, Dwight. *Reaction and Accommodation.* New York: Garland, 1987.

Johannsen, Robert W., ed. *The Lincoln–Douglas Debates of 1858.* 150th anniversary ed. Oxford: Oxford University Press, 2008.

———. *Stephen A. Douglas.* Rev. ed. Urbana: University of Illinois Press, 1997.

John A. Garraty. "Holmes' Appointment to the United States Supreme Court." *New England Quarterly* 22 (1949).

John of Salisbury. *Policratus* (1159). In *Western Heritage: A Reader,* ed. Hillsdale College History Faculty. Hillsdale, MI: Hillsdale College Press, 2003.

Johnson, Calvin H. "Homage to Clio." *Constitutional Commentary* 20 (2003).

Johnson, John W. "Adaptive Jurisprudence." *Historian* 40 (1977).

Johnson, Paul. *Modern Times.* Rev. ed. New York: Harper, 1991.

Jones, Douglas L. "'The Caprice of Juries.'" *American Journal of Legal History* 24 (1980).

Jones, Robert L. "Lessons from a Lost Constitution." *Journal of Law and Politics* 27 (2012).

Jones, W. J. *Politics and the Bench.* London: Allen & Unwin, 1971.

Kahn, Michael A. "The Appointment of John McLean to the Supreme Court." *Journal of Supreme Court History* (1993).

———. "Shattering the Myth About President Eisenhower's Supreme Court Appointments." *Presidential Studies Quarterly* 22 (1992).

Kalman, Laura. *Abe Fortas.* New Haven, CT: Yale University Press, 1990.

———. *The Strange Career of Legal Liberalism.* New Haven, CT: Yale University Press, 1996.

Kaminski, John P., and Richard Leffler, eds. *Federalists and Antifederalists: The Debate over the Ratification of the Constitution.* Madison, WI: Madison House, 1989.

Kammen, Michael. *Colonial New York*. New York: Scribner's, 1975.

Karkkainen, Bradley C. "The Police Power Revisited." *Minnesota Law Review* 90 (2006).

Karsten, Peter. *Heart Versus Head: Judge-Made Law in Nineteenth-Century America*. Chapel Hill: University of North Carolina Press, 1997.

Kastenburg, Joshua E. *The Campaign to Impeach Justice William O. Douglas*. Lawrence: University of Kansas Press, 2019.

Kauffman, Bill. "The Ford Impeachment." *American Enterprise* (May/June 1999).

Keck, Thomas M. *The Most Activist Supreme Court in History*. Chicago: University of Chicago Press, 2004.

Keller, Morton. *Regulating a New Economy*. Cambridge, MA: Harvard University Press, 1990.

Kelly, Alfred H. "An Inside Story: When the Supreme Court Ordered Desegregation." *US News & World Report* (February 5, 1962): 88.

———. "Clio and the Court." *Supreme Court Review* (1965).

Kelly, Alfred H., Winfred A. Harbison, and Herman Belz. *The American Constitution*. 7th ed. New York: Norton, 1991.

Kelly, J. M. *A Short History of Western Legal Theory*. Oxford: Oxford University Press, 1992.

Kennedy, Randall. "Reconstruction and the Politics of Scholarship." *Yale Law Journal* 98 (1989).

Kerney, James. *The Political Education of Woodrow Wilson*. New York: Century, 1926.

Kersch, Ken I. "The New Deal Triumph as the End of History?" In *The Supreme Court and American Political Development,* ed. Ronald Kahn and Ken I. Kersch. Lawrence: University of Kansas Press, 2006.

Kidney, James. "Are Judges Getting Too Powerful?" *US News & World Report,* January 16, 1978.

Klarman, Michael J. "*Brown,* Originalism, and Constitutional Theory." *Virginia Law Review* 81 (1995).

———. "How *Brown* Changed Race Relations." *Journal of American History* 81 (1994).

———. "The Racial Origins of Modern Criminal Procedure." *Michigan Law Review* 99 (2000).

Klein, Milton M. "Prelude to Revolution in New York." *William and Mary Quarterly* 17 (1960).

Kluger, Richard. *Simple Justice*. New York: Vintage, 1977.

Knapp, Aaron T. "The New Jersey Plan and the Structure of the American Union." *Georgetown Journal of Law and Public Policy* 15 (2017).

Knierim, Rolf P. "Customs, Judges, and Legislators in Ancient Israel." In *Early Jewish and Christian Exegesis,* ed. Craig A. Evans and William F. Stinespring. Atlanta, GA: Scholars, 1987.

Kotlowski, Dean. *Nixon's Civil Rights*. Cambridge, MA: Harvard University Press, 2001.

Kramer, Larry D. *The People Themselves*. Oxford: Oxford University Press, 2004.

Krasity, Kenneth A. "The Role of the Judge in Jury Trials." *University of Detroit Law Review* 62 (1985).

Kraynak, Robert P. "Tocqueville's Constitutionalism." *American Political Science Review* 81 (1987).

Kroger, John R. "The Philosophical Foundations of Roman Law." *Wisconsin Law Review* (2004).

Kull, Andrew. *The Color-Blind Constitution.* Cambridge, MA: Harvard University Press, 1992.

Kunkel, Wolfgang. *An Introduction to Roman Legal and Constitutional History.* 2nd ed. Trans. J. M. Kelly. Oxford: Oxford University Press, 1972.

Kurland, Philip. "Foreword." *Harvard Law Review* 78 (1964).

———. "Toward a Political Supreme Court." *University of Chicago Law Review* 37 (1969).

Kurland, Philip B., and Ralph Lerner, eds. *The Founders' Constitution.* 5 vols. Indianapolis, IN: Liberty Fund, 2000.

Kutler, Stanley I. *Judicial Power and Reconstruction Politics.* Chicago: University of Chicago Press, 1968.

Landis, James. "The Development of the Administrative Commission." In *Administrative Law: Cases and Comments,* ed. Walter Gellhorn. New York: Foundation, 1940.

Langbein, John H. "The Disappearance of Civil Trial in the United States." *Yale Law Journal* 122 (2012).

Langum, David J. *Crossing over the Line.* Chicago: University of Chicago Press, 1994.

Lanni, Adriaan. "Judicial Review and the Athenian 'Constitution.'" In *Démocratie Athénienne—Démocratie Moderna.* Geneva: Fondation Hardt, 2009.

LaPiana, William P. "*Swift v. Tyson* and the Brooding Omnipresence in the Sky: An Investigation of the Idea of Law in Antebellum America." *Suffolk University Law Review* 20 (1986).

Lash, Joseph P. *Dealers and Dreamers.* New York: Doubleday, 1988.

Lash, Kurt T. "Minority Report." *Ohio State Law Journal* 68 (2007).

———, ed. *The Reconstruction Amendments.* 2 vols. Chicago: University of Chicago Press, 2020.

Lawson, Steven F. "Progressives and the Supreme Court." *Historian* 42 (1979–80).

Le, Loan, and Jack Citrin. "Affirmative Action." In *Public Opinion and Constitutional Controversy,* ed. Nathaniel Persily, Jack Citrin, and Patrick J. Egan. Oxford: Oxford University Press, 2008.

Lence, Ross M, ed. *Union and Liberty: The Political Theory of John C. Calhoun.* Indianapolis, IN: Liberty Fund, 1992.

Leonard, Gerald. "*Fletcher v. Peck* and Constitutional Development in the Early United States." *University of California-Davis Law Review* 47 (2014).

———. "Law and Politics Reconsidered." *Law and Social Inquiry* 34 (2009).

Lerner, Ralph. "The Supreme Court as Republican Schoolmaster." In *Is the Supreme*

Court the Guardian of the Constitution?, ed. Robert A. Licht. Washington, DC: A.E.I., 1993.

Leuchtenburg, William E. *The Supreme Court Reborn.* New York: Oxford University Press, 1995.

———. "When the People Spoke, What Did They Say?" *Yale Law Journal* 108 (1999).

Levinson, Bernard M. *Deuteronomy and the Hermeneutics of Legal Innovation.* Oxford: Oxford University Press, 1997.

Levy, Leonard W. *Jefferson and Civil Liberties.* Cambridge, MA: Harvard University Press, 1963.

———. "The Right Against Self-Incrimination: History and Judicial History." *Political Science Quarterly* 84 (1969).

Lewis, Anthony. "High Court's Critics Renew an Old Fight." *New York Times,* March 16, 1958.

Lewis, Walker. "The Birth of the American Bar Association." *American Bar Association Journal* 67 (1978).

Lieberman, Jethro K. *The Litigious Society.* New York: Basic, 1981.

Liebs, Detlef. *Summoned to the Roman Courts: Famous Trials from Antiquity.* Berkeley: University of California Press, 2012.

Lightner, David. *Slavery and the Commerce Power.* New Haven, CT: Yale University Press, 2006.

Lindgren, Janet S. "Beyond Cases." *Wisconsin Law Review* (1983).

Lindquist, Stefanie A. "Judicial Activism in State Supreme Courts." *Stanford Law and Policy Review* 28 (2007).

Link, Arthur S., ed. *Papers of Woodrow Wilson.* 69 vols. Princeton, NJ: Princeton University Press, 1966–94.

———. *Wilson: The Road to the White House.* Princeton, NJ: Princeton University Press, 1947.

Locke, John. *The Second Treatise of Government,* ed. Thomas P. Peardon. Indianapolis, IN: Bobbs-Merrill, 1952.

Longaker, Richard P. "Andrew Jackson and the Judiciary." *Political Science Quarterly* 71 (1956).

Lovell, George I. *Legislative Deferrals.* Cambridge: Cambridge University Press, 2002.

Lowry, E. G. "The Men of the Supreme Court." *World's Work,* April 1914.

Lucey, Francis E. "Natural Law and American Legal Realism." *Georgetown Law Journal* 30 (1942).

Lund, Nelson, and John O. McGinnis. "*Lawrence v. Texas* and Judicial Hubris." *Michigan Law Review* 102 (2004).

Lurie, Jonathan. *The Chief Justiceship of William Howard Taft, 1921–30.* Columbia: University of South Carolina Press, 2019.

———. *William Howard Taft.* Cambridge: Cambridge University Press, 2012.

Lurton, Horace H. "A Government of Law or a Government of Men?" *North American Review* 193 (1911).

Lusky, Louis. *By What Right?* Charlottesville, VA: Michie, 1975.

Lustig, Doreen, and J. H. H. Weiler. "Judicial Review in the Contemporary World." *International Journal of Constitutional Law* 16 (2018).

Lutz, Donald S. "From Covenant to Constitution in American Political Thought." *Publius* 10 (1980).

MacIntyre, Alasdair. *After Virtue.* 2nd ed. South Bend, IN: Notre Dame University Press, 1984.

Magliocca, Gerald N. *Andrew Jackson and the Constitution.* Lawrence: University of Kansas Press, 2007.

———. *The Heart of the Constitution.* Oxford: Oxford University Press, 2018.

———. *The Tragedy of William Jennings Bryan.* New Haven, CT: Yale, 2011.

Maier, Pauline. *Ratification.* New York: Simon & Schuster, 2010.

Main, Jackson Turner. *The Antifederalists.* Chapel Hill: University of North Carolina Press, 1961.

Maine, Henry. *Ancient Law.* London: John Murray, 1920.

Malanga, Steven. "The Court that Broke Jersey." *City Journal,* Winter 2012.

Maledon, William J. "The Law and the Unborn Child." *Notre Dame Lawyer* 46 (1971).

Maltese, John Anthony. *The Selling of Supreme Court Nominees.* Baltimore: Johns Hopkins University Press, 1995.

Maltz, Earl M. *The Chief Justiceship of Warren Burger, 1969–86.* Lawrence: University of Kansas Press, 2000.

———. *The Coming of the Nixon Court.* Lawrence: University of Kansas Press, 2016.

Manin, Bernard. "Checks, Balances and Boundaries." In *The Invention of the Modern Republic,* ed. Biancamaria Fontana. Cambridge: Cambridge University Press, 1994.

Mannix, Richard. "Gallatin, Jefferson, and the Embargo of 1808." *Diplomatic History* 3 (1979).

Marcus, Maeva. "Judicial Review in the Early Republic." In *Launching the "Extended Republic,"* ed. Ronald Hoffman and Peter Albert. Charlottesville: University of Virginia Press, 1996.

Marshall, Lynn. "The Authorship of Jackson's Bank Veto Message." *Mississippi Valley Historical Review* 50 (1963).

Marshall, Thomas R. *Public Opinion and the Supreme Court.* Boston: Unwin Hyman, 1989.

Marten, David B., J. C. A. Stagg, Mary Parke Johnson, and Anna Mandeville Colony, eds. *Papers of James Madison, Retirement Series.* Vol. 2. Charlottesville: University of Virginia Press, 2009.

Martori, Joseph P., and Harold J. Bliss. "Taxation of Municipal Bond Interest." *Notre Dame Law Review* 44 (1969).

Maveety, Nancy, ed. *The Pioneers of Judicial Behavior.* Ann Arbor: University of Michigan Press, 2003.

Mazzone, Jason. "The Bill of Rights in the Early State Constitutions." *Minnesota Law Review* 92 (2007).

McBride, S. Dean, Jr. "Polity of the Covenant People." *Interpretation* 41 (1987).

McCarthy, Nolan. "Presidential Vetoes in the Early Republic." *Journal of Politics* 71 (2009).

McCloskey, Robert G. *The American Supreme Court.* 6th ed. Chicago: University of Chicago Press, 2016.

———. "Reflections on the Warren Court." *Virginia Law Review* 51 (1965).

McConnell, Michael. "Originalism and the Desegregation Decisions." *Virginia Law Review* 81 (1995).

McCune, Wesley. *The Nine Young Men.* 1947. Westport, CT: Greenwood, 1969.

McDonald, Forrest. *The American Presidency.* Lawrence: University of Kansas Press, 1994.

McDonald, Kevin. "Antitrust and Baseball." *Journal of Supreme Court History* (1988).

McDowell, Gary L. "Coke, Corwin, and the Constitution." *Review of Politics* 55 (1993).

———. *Curbing the Courts.* Baton Rouge: Louisiana State University Press, 1988.

McGinnis, John O. "The Original Constitution and Its Decline." *Harvard Journal of Law and Public Policy* 21 (1997).

McGinty, Brian. *Lincoln and the Court.* Cambridge: Cambridge University Press, 2008.

McGovney, D. O. "Racial Residential Segregation." *California Law Review* 33 (1945).

McIlwain, Charles H. "The English Common Law." *American Historical Review* 49 (1943).

McManus, Edgar J., and Tara Helfman. *Liberty and Union.* Concise ed. New York: Routledge, 2014.

McNeil, Genna Rae. *Groundwork.* Philadelphia: University of Pennsylvania Press, 1983.

Meese, Edwin. "Toward a Jurisprudence of Original Intention." *Benchmark* 2 (1986).

Meigs, William M. "The Relation of the Judiciary to the Constitution." *American Law Review* 19 (1885).

Melnik, R. Shep. "From Tax and Spend to Mandate and Sue." In *The Great Society and the High Tide of Liberalism, ed.* Sidney M. Milkis and Jerome M. Mileur. Amherst: University of Massachusetts Press, 2005.

———. "The Odd Evolution of the Civil Rights State." *Harvard Journal of Law and Public Policy* 36 (2013).

Meltzer, Daniel J. "The Story of *Ex Parte McCardle.*" In *Federal Courts Stories, ed.* Vicki C. Jackson and Judith Resnik. St. Paul, MN: Foundation, 2010.

Mercer, William Davenport. *Diminishing the Bill of Rights.* Norman: University of Oklahoma Press, 2017.

Merrill, Thomas W. "Article III, Adjudication, and the Origins of the Appellate Model of Administrative Law." *Columbia Law Review* 111 (2011).

———. "The Story of *Chevron."* In *Administrative Law Stories,* ed. Peter L. Strauss. St. Paul, MN: Foundation, 2005.

Messner, Johannes. "Postwar Natural Law Revival and Its Outcome." *Natural Law Forum* 41 (1959).

Michael, Helen K. "The Role of Natural Law in Early American Constitutionalism." *North Carolina Law Review* 69 (1991).

Miles, Edwin A. "After John Marshall's Decision." *Journal of Southern History* 39 (1973).

Miller, Arthur S. "Notes on the Concept of the 'Living' Constitution." *George Washington Law Review* 31 (1963).

Miller, Arthur S., and Ronald F. Howell. "The Myth of Neutral Principles in Constitutional Adjudication." *University of Chicago Law Review* 27 (1960).

Miller, Douglas R. "The Alley Behind First Street." *William & Mary Journal of Women and Law* 11 (2004).

Miller, Geoffrey P. "The True Story of *Carolene Products." Supreme Court Review* (1987).

Miller, Marc C. "When Congress Attacks the Federal Courts." *Case Western Reserve Law Review* 56 (2006).

"Miscellany," *Law Journal,* November 2, 1918.

Mody, Sanjay. "*Brown* Footnote Eleven in Historical Context." *Stanford Law Review* 54 (2002).

Montesquieu, Charles. *The Spirit of the Laws.* Trans. and ed. Anne M. Cohler, Basia Carolyn Miller, and Harold Samuel Stone. Cambridge: Cambridge University Press, 1989.

Moore, Tyler S. "Trimming the Least Dangerous Branch." *Tulsa Law Review* 56 (2020).

Moreno, Paul D. "In re *Huff:* Judicial Power and Democracy (I)." *Michigan Bar Journal* 88 (2009).

Morgan, Donald G. *Justice William Johnson.* Columbia: University of South Carolina Press, 1954.

Morgan, Edmund S., and Helen M. Morgan. *The Stamp Act Crisis.* 2nd ed. New York: Collier, 1962.

Morgan, Richard E. "The Portal-to-Portal Pay Case." In *The Third Branch of Government: Eight Cases in Constitutional Politics,* ed. C. Herman Pritchett and Alan F. Westin. New York: Harcourt, 1963.

Morris, Richard B. "Judicial Supremacy and the Inferior Courts in the American Colonies." *Political Science Quarterly* 4 (1940).

Mott, Rodney L. *Due Process of Law.* New York: Da Capo, 1973.

"Mr. Justice Van Devanter and the Common Law 'Writ of Ease.'" *Massachusetts Law Quarterly* 22 (1937).

Mulcahy, Kevin M. "Modeling the Garden." *Santa Clara Law Review* 40 (2000).

Murphy, Paul L. "The New Deal Agricultural Program and the Constitution." *Agricultural History* 29 (1955).

Murphy, Walter F. *Congress and the Court.* Chicago: University of Chicago Press, 1962.

Murphy, Walter F., and Joseph Tanenhaus. "Public Opinion and Supreme Court." *Public Opinion Quarterly* 32 (1968).

Myers, Gustavus. *History of the Supreme Court of the United States*. Chicago: Kerr, 1911.

Nathanson, Mitchell. "The Irrelevance of Baseball's Antitrust Exemption." *Rutgers Law Review* 58 (2005).

———. "Who Exempted Baseball Anyway?" *Journal of Sports and Entertainment* 4 (2013).

Neely, Mark E., Jr. *Lincoln and the Triumph of the Nation*. Chapel Hill: University of North Carolina Press, 2011.

Nelson, Caleb. "A Revolution of Scholarly Explanations for the Rise of the Elective Judiciary in Antebellum America." *American Journal of Legal History* 37 (1993).

Nelson, Michael. *The Fourteenth Amendment*. Cambridge, MA: Harvard University Press, 1988.

Nelson, William E. "Changing Conceptions of Judicial Review." *University of Pennsylvania Law Review* 120 (1972).

———. *The Common Law in Colonial America*. Vol. 2, *The Middle Colonies and the Carolinas, 1660–1730*. Oxford: Oxford University Press, 2013.

———. *The Common Law in Colonial America*. Vol. 4, *Law and the Constitution on the Eve of Independence, 1735–1776*. Oxford: Oxford University Press, 2008.

———. *Marbury v. Madison*. Lawrence: University of Kansas Press, 2000.

Nelson, William E., and Robert C. Palmer. *Liberty and Community*. New York: Oceana, 1987.

Neuhaus, Richard John, ed. *The End of Democracy?* Dallas, TX: Spence, 1997.

Newman, Roger K. *Hugo Black*. New York: Pantheon, 1994.

New York State Bar Association Proceedings. Albany, NY: Argus, 1932.

Niven, John, et al., eds. *The Salmon P. Chase Papers*. 5 vols. Columbus: Ohio State University Press, 1993–98.

Nolan, Dennis R. "Sir William Blackstone and the New American Republic." *New York University Law Review* 51 (1976).

Nolan, James L., Jr. *The Therapeutic State*. New York: New York University Press, 1998.

Noonan, John T., Jr. *A Private Choice*. New York: Free Press, 1979.

Nourse, G. B. "Law Reform Under the Commonwealth and Protectorate." *Law Quarterly Review* 75 (1959).

Ober, Frank B. "Communism and the Court." *American Bar Association Journal* 44 (1958).

Oberg, Barbara B., ed. *Papers of Thomas Jefferson*. Vol. 36. Princeton, NJ: Princeton University Press, 2009.

O'Brien, David M. *Justice Robert H. Jackson's Unpublished Opinion in Brown v. Board*. Lawrence: University of Kansas Press, 2017.

O'Brien, Francis. "Bicentennial Reflections on Herbert Hoover and the Supreme Court." *Iowa Law Review* 61 (1975).

O'Brien, Ruth Ann. *Workers' Paradox.* Chapel Hill: University of North Carolina Press, 1998.

O'Donovan, Oliver, and Joan Lockwood O'Donovan, eds. *From Irenaeus to Grotius: A Sourcebook in Christian Political Thought, 100–1625.* Grand Rapids, MI: Eerdmans, 1999.

Oldham, James. "Judicial Activism in Eighteenth-Century Common Law in the Time of the Founders." *Green Bag* 2d, 8 (2005).

Oliphant, Herman. "A Return to Stare Decisis." *American Bar Association Journal* 14 (1928).

Olson, Walter K. *The Litigation Explosion.* New York: Dutton, 1991.

O'Neill, Johnathan. *Originalism in American Law and Politics.* Baltimore: Johns Hopkins University Press, 2005.

Orth, John V. "Blackstone." In *The Oxford Handbook of Legal History,* ed. Markus D. Dubber and Christopher Tomlins. Oxford: Oxford University Press, 2018.

Palmer, Ben W. "Hobbes, Holmes, and Hitler." *American Bar Association Journal* 31 (1945).

Pardo, A. David. "Judicial Discretion in Talmudic Times and the Modern Era." *Cardozo Public Law, Policy, and Ethics Journal* 7 (2009).

Parillo, Nicholas R. "A Critical Assessment of the Originalist Case Against Administrative Regulatory Power." *Yale Law Journal* 130 (2021).

Parmenter, Andrew J. "Nullifying the Jury." *Washburne Law Journal* 46 (2007).

Parrish, Michael E. "The Great Depression, the New Deal, and the American Legal Order." *Washington Law Review* 59 (1984).

Parry-Giles, Trevor. *The Character of Justice.* East Lansing: Michigan State University Press, 2006.

Pashman, Howard. *Building a Revolutionary State.* Chicago: University of Chicago Press, 2018.

Patenaude, Lionel V. "Garner, Sumners, and Connally: The Defeat of the Roosevelt Court Bill in 1937." *Southwest Historical Quarterly* 74 (1970).

Patric, Gordon. "The Impact of a Court Decision." *Journal of Public Law* 6 (1957).

Paul, Arnold. *Conservative Crisis and the Rule of Law.* New York: Harper, 1969.

Paul, Sanjukta. "Reconsidering Judicial Supremacy in Antitrust." *Yale Law Journal* 131 (2021).

Paulsen, Michael Stokes. "The Most Dangerous Branch." *Georgetown Law Review* 83 (1994).

Peck, Cornelius J. "The EEOC: Developments in the Administrative Process 1965–75." *Washington Law Review* 51 (1976).

Pendley, William Perry. "State Courts Create New 'Rights.'" *Human Events,* January 14, 2000.

Perlin, Adam A. "The Impeachment of Samuel Chase." *Rutgers Law Review* 62 (2010).

Pestritto, Ronald J. *Woodrow Wilson and the Roots of Modern Liberalism.* Lanham: Rowman & Littlefield, 2005.

Peters, Shawn Francis. "*Minersville School District v. Gobitis.*" In *The Public Debate over Controversial Supreme Court Decisions,* ed. Melvin I. Urofsky. Washington, DC: CQ Press, 2006.

Peterson, Farah. "Expounding the Constitution." *Yale Law Journal* 130 (2020).

Pfander, James E. "Article I Tribunals, Article III Courts, and the Judicial Power of the United States." *Harvard Law Review* 118 (2004).

Pfeffer, Leo. "The Becker Amendment." *Journal of Church and State* 6 (1964).

Phillips, Michael J. *The Lochner Court: Myth and Reality.* Westport, CT: Greenwood, 2001.

Phillips, U. B. "The Central Theme of Southern History." *American Historical Review* 34 (1928).

Pittman, R. Carter. "The Emancipated Judiciary in America." *American Bar Association Journal* 37 (1951).

———. "The Supremacy of the Judiciary." *American Bar Association Journal* 40 (1954).

Polishook, Irving H. "*Trevett* v. *Weeden* and the Case of the Judges." *Newport History* 38 (1965).

Pollard, Joseph Percival. "Four New Dissenters." *New Republic,* September 2, 1931.

Ponnuru, Ramesh. "Aborting History." *National Review,* October 23, 1995.

Posner, Richard A. "The Anti-Hero." *New Republic,* February 24, 2003.

———. "Enlightened Despot." *New Republic,* April 23, 2007.

———. "The Rise and Fall of Judicial Self-Restraint." *California Law Review* 100 (2012).

Post, Robert. "The Incomparable Chief Justiceship of William Howard Taft." *Michigan State Law Review* (2020).

Potts, Margaret H. "Justice Frank Murphy." *Supreme Court Historical Society Yearbook* (1982).

Pound, Roscoe. "Liberty of Contract." *Yale Law Review* 18 (1909).

Powe, Lucas A., Jr. "Are 'the People' Missing in Action (and Should Anyone Care)?" *Texas Law Review* 83 (2005).

———. *The Supreme Court and the American Elite.* Cambridge, MA: Harvard University Press, 2009.

———. *The Warren Court and American Politics.* Cambridge, MA: Harvard University Press, 2000.

Prakash, Saikrishna. "New Light on the Decision of 1789." *Cornell Law Review* 91 (2006).

Prakash, Saikrishna, and Steven D. Smith. "How to Remove a Federal Judge." *Yale Law Journal* 116 (2006).

Pratt, William C. "Socialism on the Northern Plains, 1900–24." *South Dakota History* 18 (1988).

Press, Aric. "When Judges Govern." *Newsweek,* August 13, 1979.

Presser, Stephen B. "The Battle over 'Turning Back the Clock' in Constitutional Interpretation." *Historically Speaking,* November 2002.

———. "An Introduction to the Legal History of Colonial New Jersey." *Rutgers-Camden Law Journal* 7 (1976).

Preyer, Kathryn. "Jurisdiction to Punish." *Law and History Review* 4 (1986).

Priest, George L. "Bork's Strategy and the Influence of the Chicago School on Modern Antitrust Law." *Journal of Law and Economics* 57 (2014).

———. "The Expansion of Modern US Tort Law and Its Excesses." In *The American Illness*, ed. F. H. Buckley. New Haven, CT: Yale University Press, 2013.

———. "The Invention of Enterprise Liability." *Journal of Legal Studies* 14 (1985).

Pringle, Henry F. *The Life and Times of William Howard Taft.* 2 vols. New York: Farrar-Rinehart, 1939.

Pritchett, C. Herman. *Congress Versus the Supreme Court, 1957–60.* Minneapolis: University of Minnesota Press, 1961.

Pulliam, Mark. "Against 'Judicial Engagement.'" *City Journal,* February 8, 2017.

———. "The Libertarian Constitutional Fantasy." *Modern Age,* Winter 2018.

———. "Revisiting William O. Douglas." *Law and Liberty,* June 22, 2020.

Purcell, Edward A., Jr. *The Crisis of Democratic Theory.* Lexington: University of Kentucky Press, 1973.

———. *Litigation and Inequality: Federal Diversity Jurisdiction in Industrial America, 1870–1958.* Oxford: Oxford University Press, 1992.

———. *Originalism, Federalism, and the American Constitutional Enterprise.* New Haven, CT: Yale University Press, 2007.

Pusey, Merlo J. *Charles Evans Hughes.* 2 vols. New York: Macmillan, 1951.

———. "The Nomination of Charles Evans Hughes as Chief Justice." *Supreme Court Historical Society Yearbook* (1982).

Quay, Eugene. "Justifiable Abortion." *Georgetown Law Journal* 49 (1960).

Rabin, Robert L. "Federal Regulation in Historical Perspective." *Stanford Law Review* 38 (1986).

Ragsdale, Bruce A., and Jeffrey Jones, eds. *Debates on the Federal Judiciary: A Documentary History.* 3 vols. Washington, DC: Federal Judicial Center, 2013.

Rahe, Paul. *Montesquieu and the Logic of Liberty.* New Haven, CT: Yale University Press, 2009.

Randolph, A. Raymond. "Before *Roe v. Wade.*" *Harvard Journal of Law and Public Policy* 29 (2006).

Ray, Kristopher. "'The Indians of Every Denomination Were Free, and Independent of Us.'" *American Nineteenth Century History* 17 (2016).

Reeder, Robert P. "Chief Justice Fuller." *University of Pennsylvania Law Review and Law Register* 59 (1910).

"A Regrettable Decision." *New York Times,* January 2, 1960.

Reich, Charles. "The New Property." *Yale Law Journal* 73 (1964).

Reid, John Philip. "The Jurisprudence of Liberty." In *The Roots of Liberty,* ed. Ellis Sandoz Columbia: University of Missouri Press, 1993.

Reorganization of the Federal Judiciary. U.S. Senate, 75th Cong., 1st Sess., Report no. 711. Washington, DC: Government Printing Office, 1937.

"Report of the Committee on Federal–State Relationships as Affected by Judicial Decisions." *Harvard Law Record,* October 23, 1958.

Rice, Charles E. "The Dred Scott Case of the Twentieth Century." *Houston Law Review* 10 (1973).

Richards, Mark David. "The Debates over the Retrocession of the District of Columbia, 1801–2004." *Washington History* 16 (2004).

Richardson, James D., ed. *A Compilation of the Messages and Papers of the Presidents.* 20 vols. Washington, DC: Government Printing Office, 1897–1917.

Riegel, Stephen J. "The Persistent Career of Jim Crow." *American Journal of Legal History* 28 (1984).

Ritz, Wilfred J. *Rewriting the History of the Judiciary Act of 1789,* ed. Wythe Holt and L. H. LaRue. Norman: University of Oklahoma Press, 1990.

Roberts, W. Rhys, and Ingram Bywater, trans. *The Rhetoric and Poetics of Aristotle.* New York: Modern Library, 1954.

Rodell, Fred. *Nine Men.* New York: Vintage, 1964.

———. "The Supreme Court Is Standing Pat." *New Republic,* December 19, 1949.

Roe, Gilbert E. *Our Judicial Oligarchy.* New York: B. W. Huebsch, 1912.

Rogers, James R. "Originalism's Expanding Popularity." *Law and Liberty,* October 15, 2019.

Roper, Donald M. "Judicial Unanimity and the Marshall Court." *American Journal of Legal History* 9 (1965).

Rosen, Jeffrey. "What Made Scalia Great." *Atlantic,* February 15, 2016.

Rosenberg, Debra. "The War on Judges." *Newsweek,* April 25, 2005.

Rosenberg, Gerald N. *The Hollow Hope.* 2nd ed. Chicago: University of Chicago Press, 2008.

———. "Judicial Independence and the Reality of Political Power." *Review of Politics* 54 (1992).

Rosenbloom, David H. "The Judicial Response to the Administrative State." *American Review of Public Administration* 15 (1981).

Rosenman, Samuel I., ed. *The Public Papers and Addresses of Franklin D. Roosevelt.* 13 vols. New York: Macmillan and Harper, 1938–50.

Ross, Michael. *Justice of Shattered Dreams.* Baton Rouge: Louisiana State University Press, 2003.

Ross, William G. "Attacks on the Warren Court by State Officials." *Buffalo Law Review* 50 (2020).

———. *The Chief Justiceship of Charles Evans Hughes, 1930–41.* Columbia: University of South Carolina Press, 2007.

———. *A Muted Fury.* Princeton, NJ: Princeton University Press, 1994.

———. "The Role of Judicial Issues in Presidential Campaigns." *Santa Clara Law Review* 42 (2002).

Rostow, Eugene V. "The Democratic Character of Judicial Review." *Harvard Law Review* 66 (1952).

"Roundtable: Historians and the *Webster* Case." *Public Historian* 12 (1990).

Rowley, Charles K. "Fragmenting Parchment and the Winds of War." *Public Choice* 124 (2005).

Rubin, Eva A. *Abortion, Politics, and the Courts.* Westport, CT: Greenwood, 1982.

Rudko, Frances Howell. *Truman's Court.* Westport, CT: Greenwood, 1988.

Ruger, Theodore W. "'A Question Which Convulses a Nation.'" *Harvard Law Review* 117 (2004).

Ruppert, Bob. "How the Stamp Act Did Not Affect Virginia." *Journal of the American Revolution,* March 21, 2016.

Samuelson, Richard. "The Constitutional Sanity of James Otis." *Review of Politics* 61 (1999).

Scalia, Antonin. "Originalism: The Lesser Evil." *University of Cincinnati Law Review* 57 (1989).

———. "Remarks." *Administrative Law Review* 66 (2014).

Schacter, Jane S. "Putting the Politics of 'Judicial Activism' in Historical Perspective." *Supreme Court History* (2018).

Schiller, Reuel E. "The Era of Deference." *Michigan Law Review* 106 (2007).

———. "An Unexpected Antagonist." In *Making Legal History,* ed. Daniel J. Hulsebosch and R. B. Bernstein. New York: New York University Press, 2013.

Schlesinger, Arthur M., Fred L. Israel, and William P. Hansen, eds. *History of American Presidential Elections, 1789–1968.* 4 vols. New York: Chelsea House, 1971.

Schotten, Peter. "The Art of the Judge." In *History of American Political Thought,* ed. Bryan-Paul Frost and Jeffrey Sikkenga. Lanham, MD: Lexington, 2003.

Schuck, Peter H. *Diversity in America.* Cambridge, MA: Harvard University Press, 2003.

Schwartz, Bernard. *From Confederation to Nation.* Baltimore: Johns Hopkins University Press, 1973.

———, ed. *Statutory History of the United States.* 2 vols. New York: Chelsea House, 1970.

———. *Super Chief.* New York: New York University Press, 1983.

Schwartz, David S. "Defying *McCulloch*?" *Arkansas Law Review* 72 (2019).

———. "Misreading *McCulloch v. Maryland.*" *Journal of Constitutional Law* 18 (2015).

Schwemm, Robert G. "*Strader v. Graham.*" *Kentucky Law Journal* 97 (2008).

Scott, Austin. "*Holmes v. Walton.*" *American Historical Review* 4 (1899).

Scullard, H. H. *A History of the Roman World.* 3rd ed. London: Methuen, 1961.

Segado, Francisco Fernandez. "James Otis and the Writs of Assistance Case (1761)." In *Common European Legal Thinking,* ed. H.-J. Blanke, Pedro Cruz Villalón, Tonio Klein, and Jacques Ziller. New York: Springer, 2015.

Semeraro, Steven. "We're All Originalists Now." *Hofstra Law Review* 49 (2021).

Semonche, John E. *Charting the Future.* Westport, CT: Greenwood, 1978.

Shankman, Arnold. "Partisan Conflicts, 1839–41 and the Illinois Constitution." *Journal of the Illinois State Historical Society* 63 (1970).

Shapiro, Barbara. "Codification of the Laws in Seventeenth Century England." *Wisconsin Law Review* (1974).

Shapiro, Martin. *Who Guards the Guardians?* Athens: University of Georgia Press, 1988.

Sharp, Elaine B. *The Sometime Connection*. Albany: State University of New York Press, 1999.

Sherry, Suzanna. "The Founders' Unwritten Constitution." *University of Chicago Law Review* 54 (1987).

———. "Natural Law in the States." *University of Cincinnati Law Review* 61 (1992).

Shlaes, Amity. *The Forgotten Man*. New York: HarperCollins, 2007.

Shymansky, Ryan. "'The Great Bulwark of . . . Political Liberties.'" *Georgetown Law Journal* 107 (2019).

Silverstein, Jake. "We Respond to the Historians Who Critiqued the 1619 Project." *New York Times*, December 19, 2019.

Silverstein, Mark, and Benjamin Ginsberg. "The Supreme Court and the New Politics of Judicial Power." *Political Science Quarterly* 102 (1987).

Simon, James F. *The Antagonists*. New York: Touchstone, 1989.

———. *Eisenhower v. Warren*. New York: Liveright, 2018.

———. *FDR and Chief Justice Hughes*. New York: Simon & Schuster, 2012.

Sitman, Matthew. "The Conscience of a President." In *The Reagan Presidency*, ed. Paul Kengor and Peter Schweizer. Lanham, MD: Rowman & Littlefield, 2005.

Skowronek, Stephen. *Building a New American State: The Expansion of National Administrative Capacities, 1877–1920*. Cambridge: Cambridge University Press, 1982.

Smemo, Kenneth. "Judge Charles Amidon's Influence on Theodore Roosevelt's Presidential Campaign of 1912." *North Dakota History* 37 (1970).

Smillie, John. "Who Wants Juristocracy?" *Otago Law Review* 11 (2006).

Smith, Carsten. "Judicial Review of Parliamentary Legislation." *Public Law* 4 (2000).

Smith, David Chan. *Sir Edward Coke and the Reformation of the Laws*. Cambridge: Cambridge University Press, 2014.

Smith, J. Allen. *The Spirit of American Government*. 1907. Cambridge, MA: Belknap, 1965.

Smith, James H. *Appeals to the Privy Council from the American Plantations*. New York: Octagon, 1965.

Smith, Jean Edward. *John Marshall: Definer of a Nation*. New York: Holt, 1996.

Smith, Joseph H. "An Independent Judiciary: The Colonial Background." *University of Pennsylvania Law Review* 124 (1976).

Smith, M. H. *The Writs of Assistance Case*. Berkeley: University of California Press, 1978.

Snowiss, Sylvia. *Judicial Review and the Law of the Constitution*. New Haven, CT: Yale University Press, 1990.

Softness, Benjamin. "Preserving Judicial Supremacy Come *Heller* High Water." *University of Pennsylvania Law Review* 161 (2013).

Soifer, Aviam. "The Paradox of Paternalism and Laissez-Faire Constitutionalism." *Law and History Review* 5 (1987).

Sosin, J. M. *The Aristocracy of the Long Robe.* Westport, CT: Greenwood, 1989.

———. *English America and the Revolution of 1688.* Lincoln: University of Nebraska Press, 1982.

Southwick, Leslie. "A Judge Runs for President." *Green Bag* 2d, 37 (2001).

Spector, Robert M. "Legal Historian on the United States Supreme Court." *American Journal of Legal History* 12 (1968).

Spigelman, James. "Lions in Conflict." *Australian Bar Review* 34 (2013).

Stagg, J. C. A., Jeanne Kerr Cross, and Susan Holbrook Perdue, eds. *Papers of James Madison, Presidential Series.* Vol. 2. Charlottesville: University of Virginia Press, 1992.

Steidle, Barbara. "Conservative Progressives." PhD diss., Rutgers University, 1969.

Steiker, Carol S., and Jordan Steiker. *Courting Death.* Cambridge, MA: Harvard University Press, 2016.

Stein, Marc. *"Boutilier* and the US Supreme Court's Sexual Revolution." *Law and History Review* 23 (2005).

Steinfeld, Robert J. "The Rejection of Horizontal Judicial Review During America's Colonial Period." *Critical Analysis of Law* 2 (2015).

Stephenson, Donald Grier, Jr. *Campaigns and the Court.* New York: Columbia University Press, 1999.

Stern, Mark. "Eisenhower and Kennedy." *Policy Studies Journal* 21 (1993).

Stevens, Robert. "The Act of Settlement and the Questionable History of Judicial Independence." *Oxford University Commonwealth Journal* 1 (2001).

Stewart, Richard B. "Administrative Law in the Twenty-First Century." *New York University Law Review* 78 (2003).

Stiller, Jesse, ed. *Banking America: Studies in Regulatory History.* New York: Routledge, 2017.

Stimson, Shannon C. *The American Revolution in the Law.* Princeton, NJ: Princeton University Press, 1990.

Stockton, David. *The Classical Athenian Democracy.* Oxford: Oxford University Press, 1990.

Stone, Cliff, Louis Fisher, and Moshe Spinowitz. "Thomas Jefferson." In *The Presidents and the Constitution,* ed. Ken Gormley. New York: New York University Press, 2006.

Stoner, James R., Jr. *Common Law and Liberal Theory.* Lawrence: University of Kansas Press, 1992.

Storing, Herbert J. "William Blackstone." In *History of Political Philosophy,* ed. Leo Strauss and Joseph Cropsey. 3rd ed. Chicago: University of Chicago Press, 1987.

Story, Joseph. *Commentaries on the Constitution of the United States.* New Orleans: Quid Pro, 2013.

Strauss, David. *The Living Constitution*. Oxford: Oxford University Press, 2012.

Strout, Richard Lee. "The New Deal and the Supreme Court." *North American Review* 236 (1933).

Strum, Phillipa. *Louis D. Brandeis*. Cambridge, MA: Harvard University Press, 1984.

Suarez, Francisco. *Selections from Three Works*, ed. Thomas Pink. Indianapolis, IN: Liberty Fund, 2014.

Sunstein, Cass R. *The Second Bill of Rights*. New York: Basic, 2004.

Supplement to the Messages and Papers of the Presidents. Washington, DC: Bureau of National Literature, 1929.

"Supreme Court Evaluation of Administrative Determinations of Law, 1932–42." *Harvard Law Review* 56 (1942).

"The Supreme Court's Power." *New Republic*, March 31, 1917.

Surbin, Stephen N. "Fishing Expeditions Allowed." *Boston College Law Review* 39 (1988).

———. "How Equity Conquered Common Law." *University of Pennsylvania Law Review* 135 (1987).

Surrency, Edward C. "The Courts in the American Colonies." *American Journal of Legal History* 11 (1967).

Swisher, Carl B. *The Taney Period, 1836–64*. New York: Macmillan, 1974.

Sydnor, Charles S. *American Revolutionaries in the Making*. New York: Free Press, 1965.

"Symposium." *Maryland Law Review* 65 (2006).

Taft, Helen. *Recollections of Full Years*. New York: Dodd, Mead, 1914.

Taft, William Howard. "Judicial Decisions as an Issue in Politics." *McClure's Magazine*, June 1909.

———. "Mr. Wilson and the Campaign." *Yale Review* 10 (1920).

———. "Recent Criticism of the Judiciary." *American Law Review* 43 (1895).

Tamanaha, Brian Z. *On the Rule of Law*. Cambridge: Cambridge University Press, 2004.

———. "Sociological Jurisprudence Past and Present." *Law and Social Inquiry* 45 (2020).

Taylor, Stuart. "Newest Judicial Activists Come from the Right." *New York Times*, February 8, 1987.

Teles, Steven M. "Transformative Bureaucracy." *Studies in American Political Development* 23 (2009).

Thayer, James Bradley. "The Origin and Scope of the American Doctrine of Constitutional Law." *Harvard Law Review* 7 (1893).

Thomas, George. "Rethinking the *Dartmouth College* Case." *Studies in American Political Development* 29 (2015).

Thompson, Seymour. "Government by Lawyers." *American Law Review* 30 (1896).

———. "The True Meaning of the Term 'Liberty.'" *Harvard Law Review* 4 (1890).

"The Three-Judge Court Act of 1910." *Journal of Criminal Law, Criminology, and Police Science* 62 (1971).

"Therapeutic Abortion." *Columbia Forum* 13 (1954).

Tierney, Brian. "Hierarchy, Consent, and the 'Western Tradition.'" *Political Theory* 15 (1987).

Tillman, Seth Barrett. "Ex Parte *Merryman: Myth, History, and Scholarship.*" *Military Law Review* 224 (2016).

———. "*Merryman* Redux." *Chapman Law Review* 22 (2019).

Tocqueville, Alexis de. *Democracy in America.* Trans. Harvey Mansfield and Delba Winthrop. Chicago: University of Chicago Press, 2000.

Todd, A. L. *Justice on Trial.* New York: McGraw-Hill, 1964.

Treanor, William M. "The Genius of Hamilton and the Birth of the Modern Theory of the Judiciary." In *The Cambridge Companion to* The Federalist, ed. Jack N. Rakove and Colleen Sheehan. Cambridge: Cambridge University Press, 2020.

———. "Judicial Review Before *Marbury.*" *Stanford Law Review* 58 (2005).

Tucker, David M. "Justice Horace Harmon Lurton." *American Journal of Legal History* 13 (1969).

Turner, Jesse. "A Phantom Precedent." *American Historical Review* 48 (1914).

Turner, Kathryn. "The Appointment of Chief Justice Marshall." *William and Mary Quarterly* 17 (1960).

———. "Federalist Policy and the Judiciary Act of 1801." *William and Mary Quarterly* 22 (1965).

Turner, Lynn W. "The Impeachment of John Pickering." *American Historical Review* 54 (1949).

Tushnet, Mark. "Public Law Litigation and the Ambiguities of *Brown.*" *Fordham Law Review* 61 (1992).

———. "Understanding the Rehnquist Court." *Ohio Northern University Law Review* 31 (2005).

Ulmer, S. Sidney. "Earl Warren and the Brown Decision." *Journal of Politics* 33 (1971).

United States Commission on Civil Rights. *Federal Procurement After Adarand.* Washington, DC: Government Printing Office, 2005.

The U.S. Constitution: A Reader. Hillsdale, MI: Hillsdale College Press, 2012.

United States Senate, Committee on Education and Labor. *Investigation of Strikes in Steel Industries.* Washington, DC: Government Printing Office, 1919.

Upton, Richard F. "The Independence of the Judiciary in New Hampshire." *New Hampshire Bar Journal* (1959).

Urofsky, Melvin I. "The Brandeis–Frankfurter Conversations." *Supreme Court Review* (1985).

———. *Division and Discord.* Columbia: University of South Carolina Press, 1997.

———, ed. *The Public Debate over Controversial Supreme Court Decisions.* Washington, DC: CQ Press, 2006.

———. "The Roosevelt Court." In *The Achievement of American Liberalism,* ed. William H. Chafe. New York: Columbia University Press, 2003.

———. "State Courts and Protective Legislation During the Progressive Era." *Journal of American History* 72 (1985).

Usher, Ronald G. "James I and Sir Edward Coke." *English Historical Review* 18 (1903).

Uslander, Eric M., and Ronald E. Weber. "Public Support for Pro-Choice Abortion Policies." *Michigan Law Review* 77 (1979).

Utter, William T. "Judicial Review in Early Ohio." *Mississippi Valley Historical Review* 14 (1927).

Van Alstyne, William W. "A Critical Guide to *Ex Parte McCardle*." *Arizona Law Review* 15 (1973).

Vatz, Richard E., and Theodore Otto Windt Jr. "The Defeats of Judges Haynsworth and Carswell." *Quarterly Journal of Speech* 60 (1974).

Vile, M. J. C. *Constitutionalism and the Separation of Powers*. 2nd ed. Indianapolis, IN: Liberty Fund, 1998.

von Holst, Hermann E. *Constitutional and Political History of the United States*. 8 vols. Chicago: Callaghan, 1889–92.

Wagner, Richard H. "A Falling Out." *Journal of Supreme Court History* (2002).

Ward, Artemus. "An Extraconstitutional Arrangement." *White House Studies* 2 (2002).

Warren, Charles. "A Bulwark to the State Police Power—The United States Supreme Court." *Columbia Law Review* 13 (1913).

———. "Legislative and Judicial Attacks on the Supreme Court." *American Law Review* 47 (1913).

———. "The Progressiveness of the United States Supreme Court." *Columbia Law Review* 13 (1913).

———. *The Supreme Court in United States History*. Rev. ed. 2 vols. Boston: Little, Brown, 1947.

Watkins, William J., Jr. *Judicial Monarchs*. Jefferson, NC: McFarland, 2012.

Watson, Bradley C. S. *Living Constitution, Dying Faith*. Wilmington, DE: I.S.I. Books, 2009.

Weaver, James B. *A Call to Action*. Des Moines: Iowa Printing Co., 1892.

Wechsler, Herbert. "Toward Neutral Principles of Constitutional Law." *Harvard Law Review* 73 (1959).

Wefing, John B. "The New Jersey Supreme Court, 1948–98." *Rutgers Law Journal* 29 (1998).

Weinberg, Louise. "*Luther v. Borden*." *Pace Law Review* 37 (2017).

Weinfeld, Moshe. "Judge and Officer in Ancient Israel and the Ancient Near East." *Israel Oriental Studies* 7 (1977).

Wenzel, James P., Shaun Bowler, and David J. Lanoue. "Legislating from the State Bench." *American Politics Quarterly* 25 (1997).

Westin, Alan F. "The Supreme Court, the Populist Movement, and the Campaign of 1896." *Journal of Politics* 15 (1953).

"What a State Chief Justice Says About the Supreme Court." *US News & World Report,* December 12, 1958.

White, G. Edward. *The American Judicial Tradition.* Expanded ed. New York: Oxford University Press, 1988.

———. "The Arrival of History in Constitutional Scholarship." *Virginia Law Review* 88 (2002).

———. "The 'Constitutional Revolution' as a Crisis in Adaptivity." *Hastings Law Journal* 48 (1997).

———. *Earl Warren.* Oxford: Oxford University Press, 1982.

———. "From Sociological Jurisprudence to Realism." *Virginia Law Review* 58 (1972).

———. *Law in American History.* Vol. 1, *From the Colonial Years Through the Civil War.* Oxford: Oxford University Press, 2012.

———. "Looking at Holmes Looking at Marshall." *Massachusetts Legal History* 7 (2001).

White, Jonathan W. "The Strangely Insignificant Role of the US Supreme Court in the Civil War." *Journal of the Civil War Era* 3 (2013).

White, Leonard D. *The Jeffersonians.* New York: Free Press, 1951.

Whitman, James Q. *Hitler's American Model.* Princeton, NJ: Princeton University Press, 2017.

Whittington, Keith E. *Constitutional Construction.* Cambridge, MA: Harvard University Press, 1999.

———. *The Political Foundations of Judicial Supremacy.* Princeton, NJ: Princeton University Press, 2007.

———. "Reconstructing the Federal Judiciary." *Studies in American Political Development* 9 (1995).

———. "The Road Not Taken." *Journal of Politics* 63 (2001).

Wiecek, William M. *The Lost World of Classical Legal Thought.* Oxford: Oxford University Press, 1998.

———. "The Reconstruction of Federal Judicial Power, 1863–75." *American Journal of Legal History* 13 (1969).

———. "*Somerset:* Lord Mansfield and the Legitimacy of Slavery in the Anglo-American World." *University of Chicago Law Review* 42 (1974).

Wiener, Frederick B. "Justice Hughes' Appointment." *Supreme Court Historical Society Yearbook* (1981).

Wilkinson, J. Harvie, III. *From Brown to Bakke.* Oxford: Oxford University Press, 1979.

Williams, Daniel K. *Defenders of the Unborn.* Oxford: Oxford University Press, 2016.

Williams, Frank V., III "Reinventing the Courts." *Campbell Law Review* 29 (2007).

Williams, Robert G. "Juristocracy in the American States?" *Maryland Law Review* 65 (2006).

Williams, Ryan C. "The One and Only Substantive Due Process Clause." *Yale Law Journal* 120 (2010).

Wilson, Robert R. "Israel's Judicial System in the Preexilic Period." *Jewish Quarterly Review* 74 (1983).

Wilson, William Riley. *The Execution of Jesus.* New York: Scribner's, 1970.

Wilson, Woodrow. *Congressional Government.* 1885. Gloucester, MA: Peter Smith, 1973.

Winkler, Adam. "'Corporations Are People' Is Built on an Incredible 19th-Century Lie." *Atlantic,* March 5, 2018.

Wolfe, Alan. *One Nation, After All.* New York: Penguin, 1999.

Wolfe, Christopher. *The Rise of Modern Judicial Review.* Rev. ed. Lanham, MD: Rowman & Littlefield, 1994.

Wood, Gordon S. *The Creation of the American Republic, 1776–87.* New York: Norton, 1969.

Wood, Peter. *Diversity.* New York: Encounter, 2003.

Woodward, Bob, and Scott Armstrong. *The Brethren.* New York: Simon & Schuster, 1979.

Wright, J. Skelly. "The Role of the Supreme Court in a Democratic Society." *Cornell Law Review* 54 (1968).

Yoo, John. "Lincoln and Habeas." *Chapman Law Review* 12 (2009).

Yudof, Mark G. "School Desegregation." *Law and Contemporary Problems* 42 (1978).

Ziegler, Mary. *Beyond Abortion.* Cambridge, MA: Harvard University Press, 2018.

———. "Edelin." *St. Louis University Law Journal* 55 (2011).

Zilbergeld, Bernie. *The Shrinking of America.* Boston: Little, Brown, 1983.

Zuckert, Michael. "Book Review: *Morality, Politics and Law,* by Michael Perry." *Constitutional Commentary* 6 (1989).

INDEX

Blackstone, William, 11, 24, 245; influence on eighteenth-century Americans, 22–23; on unreasonable acts of Parliament, 23
Blair, John, 55, 59, 89
Bolling v. Sharpe, 285–86n22
Bonham case, 15
Borah, William, 157
Bork, Robert, 181, 224, 225, 232, 241, 242, 294n120
Boutwell, George, 117
Bradley, Joseph, 118, 119
Brandeis, Louis, 151–52, 155, 157, 159, 161, 162–63, 166–67, 194, 239
Brennan, William, 189, 191–92, 204–5, 223, 227, 237
Brest, Paul, 222
Brewer, David Josiah, 127, 132, 146
Breyer, Stephen, 229
Briscoe v. Bank of Commonwealth of Kentucky, 99
British "commonwealth," 17–18
British Constitution, eighteenth-century, 20–23
Brown, Henry, 134
Brown v. Allen (1953), 286n38
Brown v. Board of Education of Topeka, 3–4, 195, 203, 214, 215, 228, 239, 285–86n22, 294n136; and the first Warren Court, 183–91, 193
"Brutus," 46–47
Bryan, William Jennings, 135, 144
Buchanan, James, 94, 106, 110
Bunting case (1917), 167
Burger, Warren Earl, 207
Burger Court, the, 207–9, 237; and the administrative judiciary, 219–22; affirmative action decisions of, 217–19, 227; failed constitutional moment during, 226–37; jurisprudence of on women's rights, 218–29; on school desegregation and capital punishment, 209–11, 226. See also *Roe v. Wade*
Burke, Aedanus, 52
Burr, Aaron, 63, 74–75, 75–76
Bush, George H. W., 227
Bush v. Gore, 1, 232–33

Butler, Pierce, 155, 156, 161
Butler case, 177
Butterfield, Herbert, 13
Byrnes, James F., 137, 170

Calhoun, John C., 88, 93
Callender, James, 73
Campbell, John A., 111, 123
capital punishment, 209, 210–11
Cardozo, Benjamin, 152, 160, 161, 163, 182
Carswell, G. Harrold, 208
Catron, John, 106, 111
Celler, Emmanuel, 288n90
Chancery courts, 12
Chandler, Zechariah, 108
Charles I (king of England), 17
Charles River Bridge case, 99
Chase, Salmon P., 114, 117
Chase, Samuel, 59, 60, 67, 72–73, 74, 118, 119, 120
Chenery Corporation, 174
Cherokees/Cherokee nation, 92–93, 94
Chicago, Milwaukee & St. Paul Railway Co. v. Minnesota (1890), 273–74n25
Chisholm v. Georgia, 58
Christianity, 10
Church of England, 29, 30
citizenship, US, 102, 123; denial of to Blacks, 106–7
Civil Rights Act (1866), 111, 122, 248, 248
Civil Rights Act (1875), 124
Civil Rights Act (1964), 202, 203, 217, 218, 225; enforcement of, 220
Civil Rights Act (1991), 226
Civil Rights Cases (1883), 124
Clark, Tom, 177, 186, 199
Clarke, John Hessin, 152
"class legislation," 50
Clay, Henry, 94
Clayton, John, 93
Clayton Antitrust Act, 150, 155, 160
"Clio and the Court: An Illicit Love Affair" (Kelly), 186
Cohen, Felix, 127
Cohens v. Virginia (1821), 86, 87–88, 92, 94, 180
Coke, Edward, 11, 13–17, 19, 28, 60; on the

number of courts in the seventeenth
century, 255n64
Colden, Cadwallader, 25
Cold War, 191, 192, 195, 237, 240
Commentaries (Blackstone), 22, 23
*Commentaries on the Constitution of the
United States* (Story), 94
common law, English, 10–11, 13–14; federal
common law, 132, 141; integration of
the customary "law merchant" (*lex
mercatoria*) into the common law, 22–23;
three common law courts of, 12
Common Law, The (Holmes), 137
Compromise of 1850, 104
Conference of State Chief Justices, 193
Congressional Government (W. Wilson), 127
Conkling, Roscoe, 125
Connecticut, 33, 51
Connecticut Courant, 83
Constitutional Convention, 34
constitutional crisis, in England, 11–20
constitutionalism, 4, 16, 19, 80, 198, 241;
"popular constitutionalism," 102
constitutional sovereignty, 34
Cooley, Thomas McIntyre, 119
Coolidge, Calvin, 147, 155
Cooper v. Aaron (1958), 190, 286n37
Corrigan v. Buckley (1926), 283n210
Corwin, Edwin S., 28, 148, 277n22
Court of High Commission, 12
"court packing," 90, 199, 279n77. *See also*
New Deal, the Hughes Court, and
court-packing
"courts of equity," 131
Craig v. Missouri (1830), 95–96, 99
Crime Control Act (1968), 199
Cromwell, Oliver, 17
Cummings, Homer S., 165
Curtis, Benjamin, 106, 107–8, 137, 222, 269n37
Curtiss-Wright case (1936), 182
Cushing, William, 55, 78, 79

Daniel, Peter V., 111
Daniel, Price, 190

Darwinism, 136; Social Darwinism, 140
Dator, James A., 239
David (King David), 7
Davis, David, 114, 115, 119
Davis, John W., 157
Dawes, Charles, 157
Day, William R., 143
Debates (Elliot), 121
Debs, Eugene V., 131–32
Declaration of Breda, 18
Declaration of Independence, 31–32
Declaratory Act (1766), 26
democracy, direct, 149
Democrats, 133, 143, 151–52, 165, 183; "Gold"
Democrats, 135; Jacksonian Democrats, 118
Denmark Vesey slave rebellion, 88
"departmentalism," 38
desegregation, of public schools, 209–10,
226–27
Dethmers, John, 193
"Dialogue Between a Philosopher and a
Student of the Common Law" (Hobbes),
18–19
Dicey, A. V., 127
Dickerson, O. M., 30
Dickerson v. United States (2000), 230
Dickinson, John, 34, 42
Dill, Clarence, 160
Dissenters (Baptists, Quakers, Presbyterians), 29
Doe v. Bolton (1973), 213
Dorr Rebellion, 112
Douglas, Paul, 192
Douglas, Stephen, 105, 109, 222; reaction to the
Dred Scott decision, 108
Douglas, William O., 116, 169, 171, 176, 197, 200,
202, 204–5, 213, 215, 227, 237
Dr. Bonham's Case (1610), 15–16, 19, 25–26, 27,
28, 36
Drayton, William Henry, 30
Dred Scott v. Sanford (1857), 2, 3, 97, 98–99,
103–11, 117, 120, 122, 128, 133, 139, 269n33,
269n44
Duane, James, 36
Duane, William, 98

due process, 156; substantive due process, 187. *See also* legal modernism, and due process

Duval, Gabriel, 79, 98

Eakin v. Raub (1825), 49

E. C. Knight case, 134

Economic Interpretation of the Constitution, The (Beard), 148

Edelin, Kenneth, 214

Eisenhower, Dwight D., 183, 184, 189–90, 191

Electoral College, the, 42

Elizabeth I (queen of England), 12

Ellsworth, Oliver, 53, 59, 79

Ely, John Hart, 215

Emancipation Proclamation, 111, 117

Embargo Act, 78

Employers' Liability Act (1906), 141

Employment Division v. Smith, 231

Enforcement (Ku Klux Klan) Act, 123–24

England, development of a judicial system in, 11–12

English Civil War (1640s–50s), 11

English Reformation, 12

Erdman Act (1898), 141

Erie Railroad v. Tompkins, 172

Eumenides (Aeschylus), 7–8

Evarts Act (1891), 127

Everson case, 180

Ex parte Milligan, 115–16

Fair Labor Standards Act (1938), 174–75

Federal Baseball Case (1922), 290–91n27

"Federal Farmer," 47

Federal Housing Administration, 220–21

federalism, 230; compound-republic dual federalism, 86

Federalist Papers (Madison and Hamilton), 47–48; *Federalist 9,* 49; *Federalist 10,* 39; *Federalist 37,* 55–56; *Federalist 39,* 86, 94; *Federalist 44,* 81; *Federalist 50,* 34; *Federalist 51,* 41; *Federalist 73,* 57; *Federalist 78,* 48–49, 70, 91, 136, 200; *Federalist 79,* 72; *Federalist 80,* 61, 244; *Federalist 83,* 50–51; *Federalist 84,* 51–52

Federalists, 51–52, 54, 59, 88, 93; "blue-light Federalists," 76; High Federalists, 65, 67, 74, 120

Federal Rules of Civil Procedure (1938), 171, 238

Fehrenbacher, Donald, 98–99

Field, Stephen J., 114, 116, 127, 134

Filburn, Roscoe, 172

First Things, 232, 233

Five Knights case (1627), 17

Fletcher v. Peck (1810), 82, 87, 95

Ford, Gerald, 215

formalism, 136, 137, 147, 264n67

Fortas, Abe, 205

Frankfurter, Felix, 152, 157, 164, 168–69, 171, 174, 176, 182, 190–91, 193, 194, 196

Fries, John, 73

Fugitive Slave Act (1793), 104; "nullification" strategy in regard to, 109

Fuller, Melville, 121 127, 129, 146, 149, 205, 277n21, 154; and the end of the Fuller Court, 141–44

Gallatin, Albert, 77

Garber, Mark, 269n33

Gefühlsjurisprudenz, 152, 182, 184, 188, 199, 201, 227, 239

George II (king of England), 27

George III (king of England), 82

Georgia, 24, 33, 81, 92–93, 94, 115

Gerry, Elbridge, 45–46, 63

Gibbons v. Ogden (1822), 87

Gibson, John Bannister, 49, 88

Gideon, 7

Gilbert, Cass, 158

Gilchrist case, 77

Giles, Branch, 73, 74

Gillman, Howard, 222

Ginsburg, Ruth Bader, 216, 226, 229

Gitlow v. New York, 156

Glorious Revolution (1688–89), 11, 19–20, 24, 30; pre-Glorious Revolution prerogative courts, 29

Glover, Joshua, 109

James II (king of England), 19
James VI (king of Scotland), 13
Japanese Americans, interment of during
World War II, 183
Jay, John, 55, 65
Jay Treaty (1794), 83
Jefferson, Thomas, 9, 13, 50, 53, 61, 63–64, 75,
77, 78–79, 91; attitude toward the Judiciary
Act (1801), 66–67; complaint concerning
the "caucusing" of Supreme Court
decisions, 79–80. *See also* Marshall Court,
the, Jefferson v. Marshall
Jehovah's Witnesses, 175–76
Jenner, William, 192, 193
Jesus Christ, 9–10
Jewell Ridge case, 174–75
Johnson, Andrew, 272n111
Johnson, Jack, 156–57
Johnson, Lyndon B., 199
Johnson, William, 77, 83, 84–85, 103
"Judges' Bill" (1925), 158
Judges Case, 51
judicial activism, 2–3, 16, 38, 142, 193, 195–96,
234; conservative, 230, 233; "laissez-faire,"
114, 127, 141; liberal, 182, 199, 215, 225
judicial power, 3, 41, 100, 116; and republican
governments, 33–34
"judicial reactivism," 233
judicial review, 2, 4, 8, 15, 25–26, 34, 41, 110,
240; in the 1787 Constitution, 35; after
Reconstruction, 125–27; cases of in the
eighteenth century, 26–27; establishment
of, 88–89; "federal" or "vertical" judicial
review, 26; imperial judicial review, 26;
"intermediate" phase of, 141; minimalist
judicial review, 37–38; in the New York and
Pennsylvania constitutions, 34
judicial statesmanship, 96
judicial supremacy, 1–4, 13, 15, 23, 24, 26, 36,
49, 68, 77, 94, 103, 113, 120, 121, 171, 190, 193,
208, 209, 229; and the American Catholic
hierarchy, 277n22; export of from the
United States, 240–42; in Great Britain,
240–41; modern judicial supremacy,

3, 35, 124, 141, 145, 171, 183, 184, 279n77;
opposition to, 184, 220, 233, 238, 266n121;
originalist case for, 222; origins of in the
Lochner era, 144; rise of, 151
judiciary, in the 1790s, 55–64
Judiciary Act (1789), 53–55, 101, 150
Judiciary Act (1801), 63, 66–67, 72, 88, 93, 94,
127; section 34 of, 73–74, 100
Judiciary Act (1837), 268n3
jurisprudence, sociological, 136
juristocracy, 4, 6, 7, 8, 16, 21, 96, 108, 208, 246;
in the United States and abroad, 237–42
jurists, Medieval, 10
justices, independence of, 34
Justinian, 10

Kansas–Nebraska Act (1854), 105, 107
Kelly, Alfred H., 186
Kelo case, 234
Kendall, Amos, 89
Kennedy, Anthony, 225, 229, 235
Kennedy, John F., 215
Kennedy, Robert, 205
Kennedy, Ted, 224
Kent, James, 22
Kentucky, 109. *See also* Virginia and Kentucky
Resolutions
Kerney, James, 278n28
Korematsu case (1944), 176–77
Kramer, Larry, 233, 261n99
Kurland, Philip, 181

La Follette, Robert, 147, 148, 157
Landis, James, 220
Lane County v. Oregon, 278n52
law: canon law, 30; constitutional law, 137,
231; "general commercial law," 100; law
and equity, 243–46; law of nations, 103;
law of nature (natural law), 8–9, 16, 103,
136, 138; law of obscenity, 202, 204; libel
law, 204; Roman law idea of *lex regia*, 18;
"therapeutic laws," 216. *See also* common
law
Law of the Constitution (Dicey), 127

Sanford, Edward, 155
Sanford, John, 105
Scalia, Antonin, 220, 225, 227, 231, 234
Schechter v. U.S., 162–63
Seawell, Henry, 265n97
Second Continental Congress, 31, 33
Securities and Exchange Commission, 165, 174
Sedition Act (1918), 61–63, 66, 76, 126, 154; repeal of, 189
Selden, John, 245
Seward, William, 108
Shattuck, Charles E., 126
Shelley v. Kraemer (1947), 180–81, 187, 203
Sherman Antitrust Act, 128, 129–31, 132, 141
Ship-Money case (1637), 17
Skowronek, Stephen, 101
Slaughterhouse Cases, 114, 125, 139, 247
slavery, 23, 100; abolition of, 121; and the *Dred Scott* decision, 103–11; increased hostility toward, 105; as a "judicial question," 97; and the Mann "white slave act," 156–57; New York slave rebellion, 24. *See also* Denmark Vesey slave rebellion
Smith, J. Allen, 148
Social Statics (Spencer), 140
Souter, David, 227, 237
South Carolina, 24, 34; attempt by to nullify the protective tariff, 93
South Carolina Supreme Court, 26
Southern Pacific Railroad, 125
"sovereign immunity," 43
Sowell, Thomas, 232
Spaight, Richard Dobbs, 37
Spanish *cortes*, 12
Spencer, Herbert, 140
Spirit of the Laws (Montesquieu), 21
Springer case, 135
Stamp Act (1765), 29, 257n126
Star Chamber, 12, 17
state courts, in the 1780s, 35–39
Stevens, John Paul, 215
Stewart, Potter, 201, 202, 205, 209, 213, 224
Stone, Harlan Fiske, 145, 151, 155, 159, 161, 163, 164–65, 168, 170, 175, 177, 177

Story, Joseph, 78, 79, 83, 94, 97, 100–101, 103, 104, 109, 112
Strader v. Graham (1850), 104–5, 105–6
Strong, William, 118, 125
Sturges case, 95
Suarez, Francisco, 244
Sullivan, John, 35
Sumner, Charles, 97, 99
Sutherland, George, 155, 167
Swayne, Noah, 114, 118–19
Swift v. Tyson (1842), 100, 101, 102, 105, 132, 172

Taft, William Howard, 137, 142, 143, 145, 146, 147, 149, 151, 153, 154–55, 168, 277n27
Taft Court, the (1921–30), 154–59
Taft-Hartley Act (1947), 175
Taney, Roger Brooke, 1, 97, 109–10, 266n121; as a judge in the Maryland circuit court, 112–13. *See also* Taney Court, the
Taney Court, the, 97–103; and the *Ex parte Merryman* decision, 113, 190; on the issue of "ironclad oaths," 115; and issues during the Civil War, 111–15; and Jacksonian politics, 98; and the judicial/political questions of Reconstruction, 115–20; and the Ohio railroad bridge dispute, 102; slavery and the *Dred Scott* decision, 103–11 taxes: "direct tax," 59, 60, 133, 251–52, 298n2. *See also* US Congress, adoption of an income tax by
Texas v. White, 119–20
Thayer, James Bradley, 126–27, 170–71
Thomas, Clarence, 227, 230
Thomas Jefferson ship case, 101–2
Thompson, Seymour, 134, 148
Thornberry, Homer, 205
Thoughts on Government (J. Adams), 34–35
Title VII cases, 219, 226
Tocqueville, Alexis de, 90
Townshend duties, 30
Treaty of Paris, 59
Trevett v. Weeden, 37
True Law of Free Monarchies (James I), 13
Truman, Harry S., 177, 182

Trumbull, Lyman, 97

Trump, Donald, 1, 241

Tucker, St. George, 36, 37

Tudor dynasty, 12

Tyler, John, 103

Tyson, George, 100

United Mine Workers, 174, 175, 284–85n8

United States v. Carolene Products, 3, 170–72, 177, 187, 196, 200, 204, 215, 232, 235

US Commission on Civil Rights, 226

US Congress, 41, 48, 51, 63, 70, 107, 108, 111, 114, 118, 127, 128–29, 141–42, 153–54, 171, 252, 270n71, 274n33; adoption of an income tax by, 133, 145; commerce power of, 103; counterrevolution during the Nixon era, 209–11; and the definition of equal protection, 202–3; Federalist Congress, 61; Joint Committee of on Reconstruction, 125; on marijuana trafficking, 230

US Constitution, 1–2, 5, 39–46, 67, 194–95; Article I of, 41, 76, 80–81, 96, 236; Article I, section 8 of, 104, 112, 122, 133; Article I, section 9 of, 112, 133; Article II of, 41, 71, 113, 233, 236; Article III of, 40–41, 42, 44, 45, 46, 48, 53, 54, 55, 69, 71–72, 84, 93, 100, 116, 120, 158, 238; Article III, second section of, 43; Article IV of, 138; Article IV, section 2 of (the fugitive slave law), 104, 121; Article IV, section 3, 106–7; Article IV, section 4, 102; Article V, 197; Article VI of, 44–45, 259n33; Article VIII, 251–52; exceptions clause of, 43–44, *44*, 48, 69, 116, 259n34, 263n18. *See also* ratification debate, role of the judiciary in; US Constitution, amendments to

US Constitution, amendments to: Eighteenth Amendment, 153; Eleventh Amendment, 43, 58, 135; Fifth Amendment, 9, 117, 138, 139, 179, 202, 283n200; Fifteenth Amendment, 124; First Amendment, 200; Fourteenth Amendment, 9, 111, 114, 121–23, 125, 138, 140, 155 177–78, 190, 202, 203, 213, 227, 247–48; Ninth Amendment, 201, 213; Second Amendment, 234; Seventh Amendment, 52; Sixteenth Amendment, 141; Tenth Amendment, 95, 153; Thirteenth Amendment, 111, 122, 123, 124

US Supreme Court, 41–42; and the administrative judiciary, 219–22; appellate jurisdiction of, 43–44; assertion of sovereign power by, 229; first important decision of concerning the Continental Army veterans, 57; judicial behavior and ideological makeup of from FDR to George W. Bush, *178;* liberal bias of, 234–35. *See also* US Supreme Court, in the industrial age; US Supreme Court, in the New Deal and Progressive Era

US Supreme Court, in the industrial age, 121; and the applicability of the antitrust act to labor conspiracies, 131; and the end of Reconstruction, 121–25; income tax decisions during, 132–34; and new industrial problems (primarily antitrust decisions), 127–36; and the sugar trust problem, 130–31, 132; trend of the Supreme Court's antitrust doctrine, *130; See also* legal modernism, and due process

US Supreme Court, in the New Deal and Progressive Era, 145; "guesspotic" criticism of, 181; Taft, Wilson, and the White Court (1910–21), 145–54

Vanderbilt, Arthur, 238

Van Devanter, Willis, 146, 155, 166–67

"Vices of the Political System of the United States" (Madison), 39

Vinson, Fred, 145, 168, 177, 182, 184–85, 284–85n212

Virginia, 24–25, 27, 29, 80, 82, 83, 86, 135. *See also* Virginia and Kentucky Resolutions

Virginia Company, charter of, 16

Virginia and Kentucky Resolutions, 63, 93

Virginia Military Institute, 219

Virginia Plan, 45

Virginia Supreme Court, 83–84

Virginia v. Caton (1782), 35–3

www.ingramcontent.com/pod-product-compliance
Lightning Source LLC
Chambersburg PA
CBHW030255100426
42812CB00002B/441

* 9 7 8 0 8 0 7 1 7 7 8 6 0 *